# Extreme Exposure

# Extreme Exposure

An Anthology of
**Solo Performance Texts**
from the
**Twentieth Century**

Edited by
**Jo Bonney**

**Theatre Communications Group**

This publication is made possible in part with public funds from the New York State Council on the Arts, a State Agency.

TCG books are exclusively distributed to the book trade by Consortium Book Sales and Distribution, 1045 Westgate Dr., St. Paul, MN 55114.

ISBN 0-7394-1022-9

Book design and composition by Lisa Govan
Cover design by Carin Goldberg

For Eric
and his passion for the honesty
and energy of live performance

# Contents

# Preface

**W**hen I got to New York in 1979 there was so much to see—I went out every night and still couldn't get to everything. And amid the more familiar music, dance and theatre, I saw something less familiar: a kind of idiosyncratic, boundary-breaking solo performance. Not standup comedy, not cabaret, not one-character play, not lecture or reading or poetry—although bits and pieces of all of these were in there somewhere. In Off-Off-Broadway spaces, such as The Kitchen, Franklin Furnace, Performance Space 122 [P. S. 122] and The Performing Garage; in nightclubs like Club 57, the Mudd Club and Tier 3; in storefronts such as Fashion Moda and ABC No Rio; and even in the loft apartments of artists, I, along with a small but enthusiastic audience, loved the energy and originality of this new solo work.

The performances were rarely reviewed by the mainstream press and almost never turned a profit—these were artists performing for their own communities. In fact, the prospects of wider recognition or even making a living were slim. (An unfortunate situation for me personally, given that I was living with the writer/actor Eric Bogosian, and by 1981 had taken on the role of his director.)

The background and experience of these solo performers were wonderfully diverse; even more so, the artists represented in this anthology have roots in all forms of live performance—vaudeville, theatre, cabaret, music, standup comedy, poetry, the visual arts and dance. One of the challenges in beginning this project was deciding on a term to describe this disparate group. I began to see why contemporary solo artists have been conveniently shuffled into that indefinable category of "performance art." To quote Laurie Anderson, "The best thing about the term 'performance art' is that it's so ambiguous; it includes just about everything you might want to do." I love this concept, but unfortunately, in a book of this scope the term is problematic. Many of the artists included here embrace the label "performance artist," many reject it and several worked at a time when the label didn't exist or was used very specifically.

Originally "performance art" was a testing ground, the live presentation of ideas by artists exploring concepts that might later be expressed in objects such as painting and sculpture. From the Dadaists in the twenties to the "Happenings" of the sixties and the Conceptual Artists of the seventies, "performance art" was about process, not product; it was anti-object-for-sale, and provocation, not entertainment, was more often the goal. While this attitude is still at the core of some solo artists' work, the diverse backgrounds of solo performers in general have now resulted in an expanded performance style, written text and ultimately, a broader audience.

I have chosen to use "solo performance" here as a unifying term for this eclectic group of artists because it is the basic description for the form that all of them practice. Their venues range from mainstream theatres, alternative performance spaces, clubs, galleries and museums to abandoned storefronts and street corners. A few of them have become icons of American culture, while others are just becoming familiar to us. But all, in presenting their personal observations, convictions and fears, share an intimacy with their audience, built purely from their live presence and their words.

When Theatre Communications Group suggested I edit an anthology of contemporary American solo performance texts for them, I questioned the need for one more book; a couple of excellent anthologies on the present solo scene were already available. But the discussions with TCG reiterated questions I had been pondering for years: What was the genesis of the solo form I was witnessing? Was it a new art form—a product of the expansive social climate of the sixties and seventies? My personal knowledge of the solo form covered only the 1970s to the present and the period seemed so isolated in time. Was it a renaissance of an old art form? A theatrical orphan? Who were the originators and role models?

Who had contributed a genuinely fresh voice over the decades? In the absence of the performer's presence, do his or her words disappear or can the written text function as literature or as a script for others? (An important question in terms of a guiding philosophy for this book.) And finally, I wanted to find out what these artists had in common beside their lone spotlight.

More than any other form of live performance, the solo show expects and demands the active involvement of the people in the audience. They are watched as they watch, they are directly addressed, their energy resonates with that of the lone artist, and their presence in the room can trigger not only new levels of performance but, more interestingly, new material. The presence of a single performer in front of an audience of many instantly creates conflicting roles for both performer and viewer—great power and great vulnerability. As the anonymous author of "The Nature of the Monologue" wrote in *Writing for Vaudeville* in 1917, "The word monologue means 'to speak alone'—and that is often how a monologist feels. If in facing a thousand solemn faces he is not a success, no one in all the world is more alone than he."

When directing solo work, I observe (from the back of the house) the audience as much as I do the performer, for as Ruth Draper noted, the key is, ". . . to bring the audience up onto the stage and into the scene with you. It is they who must give you even more than you give them in the way of imagination and creative power."

Solo work is a format that not only tolerates but thrives on the coexistence of the illusion and reality of improvisation. There is often a "phenomenal" quality to the live shows, seemingly infused with the infectious, raw energy of spontaneous storytelling. But usually, except in the workshop phase, the semblance of spontaneity is carefully fostered by the skillful writer/performer (often with the support of offstage collaborators such as directors, co-writers, designers, composers and technicians).

At the most basic level, despite their limitless backgrounds and performance styles, all solo performers are storytellers. And if we assume that the very first performances in human history consisted of an individual telling stories in front of other members of his society/tribe, then the form is primal. The *griot*, the traditional African oral historian, was not only the purveyor of the tribe's stories but, because of his caste position, was allowed to verbally confront his audience members with impunity to assure the truth of those stories. The Greek monologist, the French *troubadour* and the medieval English traveling minstrel were all appreciated for their inventiveness and originality in the presentation of their contemporary community tales. In America, the lecture circuits, medicine and tent shows, and the vaudeville circuit of the 1800s and early twentieth century, are part of the tradition of American solo performance.

And the tradition (and the commercial attention and success of the art form) has expanded. Now in the 1990s, the very familiar "solo performance" has become a crowded division of the performing arts, with many of its artists reaching mainstream audiences through mass media.

Why has the solo show become endemic in the late twentieth century? I could echo the oft-cited bottom-line reasons—diminishing government funding for the arts; paucity of ensemble-size venues; the obvious showcase potential for an actor as a stepping stone to larger or more commercial work. But, interestingly, these have been continually cited since the early 1900s. In a 1934 article in the *Boston Herald* titled "The Rising Tide of Monodrama in the American Theatre," the writer noted that: "It is hard to recall a season where there have been so many entertainers on Boston stages who depended on themselves alone. One might say flippantly that these [artists], who are their own playwrights, actors and scene shifters, are a logical outcome of the depression, were it not that [they] plied their trade before the recent dark years plunged the stage into gloom."

For better or worse, this century has been the era of the "self"—a hundred years of shifting from the nineteenth-century emphasis on the community to the late twentieth-century elevation and examination of the individual. Solo performance, in its naked presentation of a single person(a), is very much a product and reflection of a century that has given rise to the hedonism of the twenties, the radical individualism and activism of the sixties and the so-called "me decade" of the eighties. The nineties finally made room for the previously marginalized, diverse voices of this society, and the solo form has tracked these developments.

Perhaps the proliferation of solo work lies in the desire of an artist to maintain aesthetic control of his/her material. With solo performance having its roots in so many art forms, the potential for expression is limitless. Without the buffer of an ensemble of actors and the need to deliver lines on cue, the performer is free to follow the rhythms and dimensions of each particular audience and locale.

The language and attitude of solo artists have often paralleled that of their contemporaries in the music scene: whether it's the "hipster" rhythms of black jazz musicians, the voice distortions of techno-rock, the in-your-face rants of punk rockers or the street cadences of hip-hop. In solo work, the contemporary cultural moment is quickly assimilated and fed back to us.

An exciting discovery while putting this anthology together was that even with the absence of the performer and audience, the artists' words generated their own power. Obviously the printed text lacks the kind of potency that the artists' physical presence, body language, rhythms of speech, command of dialects and sheer charisma can deliver. But these texts contain the vibrancy of the personalities that created them. Since the words were hammered out in the forge of live performance, they reflect not only the mind and soul of the performer but that of their audience as well. Each one of the shows documented here is the product of dozens, if not hundreds, of performances, and the text reflects not only the bias of the artist but that of their peers and colleagues.

The life of a solo text has tended to end at the point when the originating artist ceased performing it. But, as with the work of choreographers and composers the ideas inherent in the text need not just be embodied in the performer; here, the text lives on indefinitely, separate from the art of its live performance. (Unfortunately, I discovered in researching this anthology that even the documented work of several well-known artists from the first half of the century is now out of print and almost impossible to find.) Although a piece may have originated with improvised ranting in a club or as a highly interactive diatribe or as a quietly autobiographical narrative, the printed words now proffer the possibility of being appreciated in a different medium. Perhaps another performer, in a new context, for a new generation, maybe in another language, will rediscover the performing life of the words.

With such a rich history and so many artists, how to choose the work included in this anthology? Each artist represented here created what they performed or worked closely with the writer, each artist performed solo and each carried a unique flavor reflecting their individual personality. I focused on artists who have added a fresh voice or who have dedicated a significant part of their life's work to the solo form in America. Though many of them are also active in other media such as film, ensemble theatre, music and television, most of the artists here have returned to the form again and again with new imagination.

I have omitted several significant performers in whose work the visual or physical elements are so essential that the work would not be well served in this context. Also not included are several wonderful pieces by actors who have briefly visited the solo genre on their way to other work, or who have stood onstage by themselves reciting the works of others. A couple of artists prefer not to be in anthologies—I'm sorry I could not include them.

I asked each of the artists to choose their own introductory writer; to suggest someone familiar with their work who might best describe and comment on it. I was delighted to find that the range of their choices mapped the contours of the diverse community that actively surrounds these artists by supporting, critiquing, collaborating with and advocating for their work. In terms of this community, it was gratifying to note that each of the introductory writers, pressed by their own overloaded work schedules, contributed with great generosity and enthusiasm. I rely on their voices to further expand and contextualize this preface.

I ordered the text excerpts chronologically rather than alphabetically in an attempt to hear the flow of voices over the decades and to give a feel for the historical progression of the work. The brief artist biographies and bibliographies at the back of this book are not exhaustive but should be helpful as a starting point to find more of the work of the artists included here and to discover that of others. I encourage readers to search out the various recordings and tapes of these texts—*hearing* Lord Buckley's hip-semantic jazz riffs is a whole other experience.

This collection is just a glimpse; it is by no means comprehensive. It is my hope that this anthology serves as a useful resource, documents a small part of our literary/stage history and preserves these texts for generations to come.

With his characteristically pragmatic statement, "I am influenced by every second of my waking hours," Lenny Bruce evokes for me the attitude and commitment that has drawn me to the many voices of solo performance for the twenty years that it has informed my life. It's an art form we've all helped create simply by bearing witness to it.

*Jo Bonney*
*New York City*
*September 1999*

# Acknowledgments

One of the pleasures of editing this anthology was getting to know better the work of many people I already admired. Thank you to all the artists (not just those included) who contributed with such generosity, and to the introductory writers for their collective insight into the work.

I am grateful to TCG for urging me to take on this ultimately rewarding and fascinating subject. Special thanks to Samantha Rabetz Healy for her enthusiasm and patience as the book slowly came together, and to Terry Nemeth and Kathy Sova for their guidance throughout.

Thanks to Amanda Burroughs, who organized the vast stacks of manuscripts and source materials while patiently guiding me through the straits of electronic mail.

And thanks to Wendy Weiner and Jill Rachel Morris who gave invaluable assistance.

A book of this breadth and scope would not be possible without the help of many, many friends and colleagues, thanks to: Steven Adams; Pam Bendich and Wolfgang Franks of Fantasy, Inc.; Brandie Kathleen Bruce; Richard Buckley, Jr.; Marcelle Clements; Paula Court; Jason Cuadrado; Blake Edwards; Roy Eichelberger; Michael Feingold; Kristin Godby and

Bob Zmuda of Comic Relief; RoseLee Goldberg; Linda Greenberg; Kristen Hickey; Danny Hoch; John Howard; Sanae Ishida and Mark Vastine at Cultural Odyssey; Stanley Kaufman; Linda Kirland of Samuel French, Inc.; Stephen Koch of the Estate of Peter Hujar; George Lane; Barbara Lyon of Serpent's Tail Ltd.; Annie Leibovitz; Dona Ann McAdams; John Moffitt of Moffitt-Lee Productions; James Morgan, III of Garland Publishing; Howell W. Perkins of the Virginia Museum of Fine Arts; Irene Pinn; Jonathan Reed and Stephen Rivers of Stephen Rivers & Associates; Ozzie Rodriguez of the La MaMa E.T.C. Archive; Steven Samuels; George Shapiro of Shapiro/West and Associates; Peter Shaughnessy; Jeffrey Smith of Contact Press Images; Judy Van Herpen and Wendy McNeny of Lily Tomlin and Jane Wagner's office; Jed Wheeler; and the Billy Rose Theatre Collection, The New York Public Library for the Performing Arts; the Harvard Theatre Collection, Houghton Library; the James Danziger Gallery; the Museum of the City of New York and the Museum of Television and Radio.

**Editors' Note:** The excerpts in this anthology appear in chronological order rather than alphabetical order to create a sense of their historical progression. Some pieces are printed here in full, but most of them have been excerpted from longer pieces. To indicate that a piece has been excerpted, the word "from" appears before the title. If a title appears without that qualifier, the piece can be assumed to be printed here in its entirety. A line "————" symbol has been used in those cases when non-sequential excerpts have been printed. If the subsequent excerpts have their own sub-titles, the line symbol does not appear. In several of the excerpts, notes to the reader are included. These are set in a different font from the text and stage directions. They are not a part of the original texts, but have been included in this anthology for purposes of clarity. Most of these notes to the reader appear at the beginning of the excerpts, but on occasion, they appear within the body of the text. The artists or their representatives were involved in the process of selecting the excerpts and approved all edits to their work. Brief biographies of the introductory writers appear at the end of each introduction, while biographies and bibliographies for the artists appear at the back of the book.

# Extreme Exposure

**Beatrice Herford**

---

**Introduction** excerpted from a dissertation by **Linda Sue Long** entitled "Beatrice Herford, Cissie Loftus and Dorothy Sands within the Tradition of the Solo Performance," University of Texas at Austin, School of Communications, 1982.

Upon seeing Beatrice Herford for the first time, one of the immediate responses of critics and audiences was the recognition of her originality. The most favored term was "inimitable." Her popularity and acclaim was so extensive that it led Alexander Woollcott, *New York Times* drama critic, to respond, "If there is a more entertaining woman extant, someone has been concealing her from us . . . [A] single Beatrice Herford monologue has more art, more life and more fun in it than three-quarters of the plays along Broadway. It is one of the few perfect institutions in an imperfect world."

As the twentieth century was getting under way, Beatrice Herford, who had begun performing her own monologues in her late twenties, had reached the height of her career in middle age. Herford received wide critical acclaim because her style of performance was a new and effective approach to comedy in this time of exaggerated presentational acting. In 1901, the *Boston Evening Transcript* described her "prepossessing presence [as] . . . devoid of artifice," and her expressions as "never overdone."

3

Herford was also dubbed a phenomenon because she succeeded in a field largely restricted to men. And though critics often spoke of her charming, refined, delicate manner as a performer, members of The Vokes Players, the theatre company Herford started in 1904, painted a somewhat more complex portrait: "She swore like a trooper . . . was risqué and very Bohemian, but . . . was also a grande dame . . ."

In making her art reflective of life, Herford strove to avoid exaggeration and the sensational. She explained, "Just as soon as you begin to ramp (sic) around the stage, just as soon as you begin to overdo you cease to be an artist. Many a time in writing, a climax occurs to me; but I will not use it, for I realize I would be sacrificing the truth to a sensation."

Herford engendered this atmosphere of truth even though her monologues only suggested the dialogue of other characters. "In my monologues, I never explain. There is no need; the monologue explains itself. You gather from the conversation of the one I am impersonating just what the other is saying." In 1896 another reviewer noted:

> You see, we have here the drama reduced to its simplest expression . . . We wish those old-school playwrights who still insist that people must say things on the stages that they never would dream of saying in real life—simply to explain the plot and situation to the audience—could see her and study the workings of her system. Although she has no scenery, properties, nor other accessories, although all the dramatic persons except herself have to be taken for granted, we could not in a single instance catch her saying anything that was merely explanatory.

The humor upon which Herford relied was primarily recognition comedy. Audiences saw her monologues as travesties of everyday activities and as satires of the foibles of friends, relatives, acquaintances and sometimes even themselves. Hers was a sort of "comedy of manners of . . . [her] time," quoted one reviewer in 1951. Her recognizable portraits were "so absurd and so authentic that . . . audience[s], [though] limp with laughing, exchanged sidelong looks."

After her 1915 vaudeville debut, Herford proved her success with a variety of audience types by drawing her society admirers to the vaudeville houses and her vaudeville fans to the concert halls, with an appealing entertainment that transcended social-class barriers. "After I entered vaudeville, some of my friends remarked, 'Isn't it wonderful how *they* enjoy it?' I can't understand the classification of *they* . . . Vaudeville is cosmopolitan. It is not bound by tradition. In fact, it is at this moment the most progressive part of our theatre."

As the *New York Times* reported in 1916, Beatrice Herford ". . . graduated successfully from the gloved applause of select recitals to the thunderous approval of vaudeville . . ." because she made no changes in her expectations for audience intelligence and involvement.

# In the Art Museum

Oh, must I check my umbrella? . . . It's not wet . . . I only brought it because my niece was so sure it would rain . . . she would have come with me but her little boy has chicken pox . . . I didn't think it looked like it, but she said she was certain . . . it looked so black and now the sun is out . . . she's so positive. I think I'd better put the umbrella check in my glove . . . I have so many little things in my bag I should never find it . . . What shall I do if I come out at another door? . . . Oh, I have to come out this way? . . . It isn't my umbrella . . . it's my niece's . . . not *my* niece . . . my husband's . . . I've lost three this year, so I've given up having one . . . I forget where I leave them. I want to see the new Rembrandt . . . I forget the name of it . . . which way do I go? . . . Oh, it isn't here now? . . . It's gone out West . . . It's in California, is it? . . . Why, my niece saw it here I'm sure . . . Well, I expect to go to California some-day . . . I want to see those big trees . . . my son is out there . . . he wrote me all about one tree he saw . . . he writes very good letters . . . this one he wrote me was three hundred feet in diameter . . . Well, I'll go up to the galleries . . . there are some other pictures I want to see. I go up these stairs you say? . . . and through the Egyptian rooms? . . . Thank you.

I wish I had a catalog . . . perhaps I can borrow one . . . that lady has one . . . Would you let me look at your catalog? . . . there's a picture I rather wanted to see, it's called *Saturday Night* . . . a friend told me I must be sure and see it . . . *Saturday Night* . . . it might be those men drinking, but I hope not, I think it's a pity to depict such things . . . They number the pictures so queerly . . . now there is *Cows Resting in the Shade* and right beside it *Nuns Combing Their Hair* . . . Let me see . . . *Saturday Night* . . . there's a girl taking a bath . . . no, she's fifty-two . . . *A Modern Venus* . . . Well, I don't know what it could be, unless it is work-men or someone in a bath . . . Thank you very much. I think I'll look 'round those next rooms . . . Oh, here's something on the floor . . . a brass plate . . . twenty-five on it . . . it must be off one of the pictures . . . let me see . . . twenty-five . . . perhaps I can find the picture it fell off. There don't seem to be any without numbers . . . Oh, there's one without a number . . . that must be it . . . I'll stick it in the corner . . . I'm glad I found it. There seem to be a great many pictures of animals and fruit in this room . . . that reminds me it must be near lunchtime . . . I think I'll go along . . . Let me see, that's the staircase . . . It is raining after all . . . that reminds me I must get my umbrella . . . Will you give me my umbrella, please, or rather my niece's? . . . It has an ivory handle . . . or bone I expect . . . with a gold band . . . or brass I suppose . . . Oh, can't I get it without a check? I don't think you gave me a check, did you? . . .

Let me see now, where did I put it? . . . I didn't put it in my bag . . . Oh, do you remember? . . . In my glove? . . . Oh, now I remember . . . Oh dear! I shall lose my head next . . . Oh *mercy*! . . . of course! . . . it's raining so hard, I think I'll have another look at the pictures . . . I shall probably find the check . . . in my bag . . . I expect . . . I'll just go up . . . If the attendant sees me he'll wonder what I'm doing . . . How ridiculous of me not to know that was my umbrella check! . . . and putting it on that picture! . . . Oh dear! . . . I hope I can find the picture . . . I must have the umbrella . . . it was in this room I'm sure . . . it had animals in it I know . . . a farmyard or something . . . Oh, now that attendant is watching me . . . No, thank you . . . I'm just looking for something . . . twenty-five . . . twenty-five . . . the trouble is it belongs to my niece . . . my husband's niece . . . so I must find it . . . even if it wasn't raining . . . No, I'm not looking for a picture exactly . . . it's my umbrella . . . or rather my niece's . . . I know there were sheep in it . . . but that's all I remember . . . Oh, there are some sheep! . . . No, that isn't it . . . that's twenty-seven . . . But I do want a picture . . . it's the check for my umbrella you see . . . or rather my niece's . . . I found it on the floor and I thought it came off a picture . . . it dropped out of my glove I suppose . . . and I put it on one that had none . . . Do you know where there are any more sheep? . . . Or perhaps they were goats . . . That's it! . . . over there . . . I remember now . . . they were goats . . . that's what made me say sheep . . . this is it . . . twenty-five . . . That is an umbrella check, isn't it? . . . Well, I must hurry . . . I shall be late for lunch . . . Thank you, I'll hold it right in my hand . . . you must have thought me crazy . . . but you can't always tell the sheep from the goats.

## In the Flower Shop

I want a few flowers to take to a friend . . . just a few . . . it's only a mild attack of flu, I think. I ought to have taken her some before, I'm afraid she's almost well . . . Yes, roses are always nice, how much are those roses? . . . How much? . . . Six dollars a dozen! Oh, mercy, that's too much . . . What do you call them? . . . General Pershing? No . . . I don't want anything so expensive . . . I don't believe it's anything really more than a bad cold . . . I wonder why they always name them after Generals . . . I don't believe in coddling them . . . How much are those buds? . . . Three dollars a dozen? Well, let me see, three of those would be . . . ? Seventy-five cents you say? . . . Why, three times seventy-five cents would be only two something, wouldn't it? . . . Never mind, I expect you're right . . . you must know . . . you're doing it all the time. But I'm afraid they don't look quite enough . . . Oh, no I don't want any ferns with them . . . no . . . I don't like ferns, I mean in the house, it's different in the woods. But I have a friend who's crazy about ferns, if she has guests she always puts them in the fireplace . . . No, I don't think I want a plant . . . Hydrangeas? I didn't know they grew indoors, I don't like them anyway, they sound so like plumbing . . . I was wondering about carnations . . . they keep so long, don't they? . . . I'm having a few friends to tea this afternoon, if I used them on the tea table this afternoon they'd still be fresh to take to anyone tomorrow, wouldn't they? . . . Oh, they wouldn't be in a warm room, I don't keep my rooms hot at all, now my sister is just the opposite, I tell her she keeps hers too hot, but she has neuritis very badly, and very little sun in her rooms . . . it's mostly in her arms and they are very dark and gloomy . . . Some people don't like that odor of cloves in carnations but I always like it, my sister, not the one with the neuritis . . . she can't bear the smell of cloves in carnations or the taste of them . . . but she has a very peculiar sense of smell, she's always thinking there's a dead rat in the wall, or even in cake, I mean the taste of cloves . . . Well, I think I'll take eight of those rosebuds, that will be? . . . Two dollars? . . . Oh, will it? Well, I can use some of them for my tea. I ought to have taken her some flowers before. It will be just my luck to find she's all well again.

---

# Radio Pudding

I guess it's 'most time for that church service to begin, it's broadcasted 'bout eleven o'clock . . . Go wash your face, Johnny, and put them tools away, Willie, it won't do you boys no harm to listen. It's rainin' so hard you can't git out and you've got the rest of the day to play . . . Don't you want to set up nearer the radio, Pa? The rest of us can hear anywheres . . . Get out of that armchair, Willie, and let your pa have it. I told you to wash your face. I want yer pa to set in it so he'll be next to the radio . . . Seems to me to get deefer every day, Pa . . . See what time the kitchen clock says, Johnny, it's 'most time, I guess . . .

Ain't you 'most through in there, Abby? . . . Well, come just as soon as you git the puddin' in the oven . . . it was real good last Sabbath . . . I hope it's the same quartet they had last time . . . You don't want to miss that soprano, I think she had a real fine voice . . . It wouldn't hurt a mite to put it in the oven right away, hurry up, Abby, it's beginnin' now. They're singin' your favorite hymn, don't forget to shut the draught . . . it sounds real nice . . . did you put plenty of raisins in? . . . I love that hymn . . . last time it didn't have no vanilla in it and it wasn't near so good.

Set down there, Abby, you didn't miss much of anything . . . seems to be kind of a pause now. Maybe they're passin' the plate . . . guess Pa don't mind missin' *that*. There's the soprano now, I guess it's the same one as last Sabbath . . . What's she singin'? It's beginnin' to smell real good, Abby, how long you goin' to give it? I think likely you'd better take it out before the sermon . . . She's singin' "O Source of All Our Joys." I think hard sauce would be good with it . . . I'd like less of the organ with it, it keeps drowning out the voices . . . Maria Gibbs was tellin' me of a new sauce they use . . . That tenor's voice is real sweet . . . it's something between a hard and a soft . . . kind of foamy . . . Keep still, Johnny, we can't hear when you do that . . . it's the prayer now . . . I guess you better go in the kitchen during the prayer, Abby, it has a way of rising up and running over and Pa won't like you gittin' up in the middle of it . . . Take your feet off that chair, Willie, and take it out of your mouth or stop chewin'.

He certainly is a great hand to pray . . . Wouldn't you be more comfortable on the lounge, Pa? . . . It's real inspirin' . . . it lifts you right up . . . No, I'm all right here. This rocker's real comfortable since I put that new cushion in it. I just seen the Bixbys drivin' by. I guess they eat up to her folks every Sabbath . . . they do say he's as close as the bark on a tree. They was tellin' up to Ella's the other day that when they was talkin' of operatin' on his father's leg, he asked if it would be cheaper to have it cut off . . . Where you goin', Johnny? . . . Well, you don't need to, the canary has water and it won't hurt you a mite to set an' listen to this sermon . . .

Take it easy now, Abby set here on the lounge . . . is the puddin' all right? It's the sermon now . . . the one last Sunday took 'most two hours, but I guess the oven warn't so hot as 'tis today . . . Is this the same man preached last Sabbath? . . . He sounds awful loud and excited, I don't care for those rantin' preachers . . . No, there's nothin' burning, Pa, it's the sermon . . . I don't smell nothin' . . . What's that smoke in there, Abby? . . . Look! Good heavens! It's the puddin'!

## Introduction by Elsie A. Williams

**H**umor has the capacity to deal with almost any issue—no matter how controversial. Jackie "Moms" Mabley's coup d'état was the incorporation of the "Moms" persona which allowed the comedienne to deal skillfully with the issue of gender, race and class. By Mabley's account, the character "Moms" started to develop when she was in her twenties (in the 1920s) and was motivated by feelings of love and respect for her grandmother. By choosing the guise of the matriarch, Mabley honored the matriarchate, described by E. Franklin Frazier in his *The Negro Family in the United States* (1939), as "the guardian of the generation." On a more profound and ambiguous level, however, the "Moms" mask allowed Mabley to confront the ambiguities often related to the myth of the matriarchy and the stereotype of the "Mammy." To a "Klansman" who addressed her as "Mammy," Moms describes how she set him straight: "No damn 'Mammy,'—Moms—split-level in the suburbs, Baby." The jazzy "Moms" is no mere server of apple pie, nor is she one-dimensional.

Mabley appeared on stage without teeth, wearing a floppy hat, oversized floral print dress resembling a housecoat, knee-length Argyle socks, bedroom shoes—two sizes too big—and greeted her audience as "Children."

**9**

Moms delivered her stories, jokes and conversations with the tone, nuance and flavor of folk speech and engaged her audience in empathetic sharing and receiving. As Moms, she assumed the authority and respect generally rendered to the community elder while maintaining the boundary between herself and her audience. This strategy was especially important for early female vaudeville entertainers who were often looked upon as immoral or threatening: Ma Rainey (Gertrude Pridgett), Big Mama Blues (Lillie Mae Glover), Sweet Mama Stringbean (Ethel Waters), Last of the Red Hot Mamas (Sophie Tucker) and others.

The "Moms" persona dictated the rules: the audience was her children; world leaders and heads of state were boys; Mamie Eisenhower was "Mame" and to America's first lady Moms was "Mrs. Mabley." As Moms, she had license to chastise her audience for not "hipping" their children as soon as they were born, for teaching the children "a bunch of fairy tale lies" and for taking prayer out of the schools.

The "Moms" persona became even more intricate and complex when Mabley employed the aggressive stance of the woman of words, the trickster and the fool. The woman of words allowed Mabley to challenge the traditional expectations of the female gender and to exact retribution for sexism. The repeated, vicious ridicule of the old man her father made her marry represented Moms's feminist stance and skill in changing the joke. The insults Mabley leveled at the old man reflect the ritual technique of "playing the dozens," traditionally a game played by black, male adolescents and historically directed at the mother. "Moms," the mother figure, attacked the male, reversing the ritual insults and redirecting them toward the father figure and away from the mother.

The trickster stance provided "Moms" with unlimited freedom in testing and exceeding boundaries so as to venture into the risqué and taboo; the fool's stance sprung Mabley beyond dichotomies of black and white, rich and poor, male and female. Specifically, it was Moms's stance as the wise fool which often allowed for untutored outbursts of blinding truth.

From Mabley's perspective, her words were a "talent from God," and she was quick to add that "when I get up there, what comes up, comes out." One of Moms's drunk fool jokes best summarizes the kind of leveling philosophy, characteristic of the temper of Mabley's humor. In choosing to make herself the comic butt, she tells the story of a drunk who embarrasses her by drinking a bottle of whiskey next to her on the bus:

> I say, "Man, don't you know you're on your way to Hell?" He say, "Well, you might as well go ahead and have a drink, 'cause we on the same bus."

Everyone in Moms's audience became fair game.

**Elsie A. Williams**, Ph.D., currently teaches writing and African-American literature at the University of the District of Columbia; the second edition of her book *The Humor of Jackie Moms Mabley: An African Comedic Tradition* (Garland Publishing) is scheduled for a February 2000 release.

# from **Live at The Greek Theatre**

You know what Nick said to me the other day? He said to me, "Moms?" I said, "Whatcha want, Boy?" He said, "Moms, we're worried about the teenagers in school. Since school's opening we having a terrible time." I say, "It's your own fault. You ought to have 'hipped' them before you did." I say, "When would you say you should 'hip' a child?" For the benefit of you who don't dig "jive," "hip" means wise. "When should you wise up a child?" He said, "When it gets around ten or eleven." I say, "That's where you are wrong." From the minute it's born in the world—I dare science to deny this—a child is born with a brain, but not a mind. And your words, the first words you speak, it's like you putting a needle on a record. The minute you [do] that, it starts to register. That's the way a child's mind is, and it's very important . . . the first words you say to that child. Instead of you telling the baby the truth, you go put your big old hands in front of his face saying, "This little piggy went to market; this little piggy . . ." That baby don't want to know nothing 'bout no *damn* pig. You teach it about the dirtiest thing in the world—a pig. When it gets big enough to go to school, you throw it out in the street and talk about, "Go ahead to school, baby, and be careful, watch the lights." *Damn* the lights; watch the cars; the lights ain't never killed nobody. Get a little bigger, what's the first book you give it? Instead of giving the baby a book about life, you go out and buy some dem ole *Mother Goose* book. If I had my way, I would burn every one of 'em up. Ain't nothin' but a bunch of lies: Mother Hubbard ain't had no dog in her cupboard, Mother Hubbard hat her Scotch in her cupboard and didn't want them squares to drink it all up. Jack and Jill didn't go up no hill after no water; ain't no water running up hill. You know better than that! Mary ain't had no little lamb; Mary had a little sheep; she put it in her bed to sleep, and the sheep turned out to be a ram. Now Mary has a little lamb.

Tell the children the truth; I wish I could say what *I* want to. I got a lot more on that subject. I got everyone identified in that book. I tell the truth about all of 'em. All of 'em . . . Just dig how simple this sounds: wasn't nobody out in the woods but the wolf. Little Red Riding Hood . . . beautiful trees. Red Riding Hood—young. Hair hangin' down her back, and the wolf went ate up her bald head grandmother. That wolf should have went to a psychiatrist. That's what he should have done.

I cain't stand ole men . . . Some old man settin' there last night come winkin' at me. He was so old, he got his eye closed, stayed that way all night. He was too weak to open it. Come talkin' about could he see me home. I say, "*Damn*, you cain't see period." See me home for what? For me to hit you in the head with something? Ain't got nothing for them to do.

See, don't you, children, let these old people set around and tell you nothing about "the good ole days." What good ole days? When? I was here. Where were they at? You are living in the greatest days that ever was or ever will be right now, children, in this atomic age. Go where you want to go; do what you want to do; love who you want to love; marry who you want to marry.

But when Moms was coming along, it wasn't like that. You had to marry who your daddy say you had to marry. Ain't that a *damn* shame? No kidding, when you think about it. You got to spend your life with somebody 'cause your daddy liked him. Your daddy should have married him.

And this old, feeble, dried-up, thin, puny, *funky* man . . . old man, Old-old-old-OLD man. Older than water and twice as weak, and I had to marry him, and I wasn't but fifteen years old going on sixteen, just beginning to look at life, and there I was. I had to carry him piggyback home from the wedding. I say, "Come on, Romeo, you might as well pull down the shades; this is our wedding night." He say, "Ain't you gone help me?" I caught a hold of the shade; it slipped out of my hand, and he went right back up with the shade. I couldn't stand him; I went to cut his toenails and broke my *damn* lawn mower. He say, "Where you gonna find another man like me?" I say, "In the cemetery." I say, "Don't say nothing to me; you getting on my nerves." He say, "What's the matter?" I say, "I'm tired." He say, 'Tired of what?" I say, "Tired of you, for one thing." He say, "You would be surprised if I got up and kissed you." I say, "I would be surprised if you got up." And UGLY! Look like six o'clock straight up and down. Come running in the house one day, (no, I ain't gone tell that lie; he wasn't running). He come shuffling in the house one day, looked at me and say, "I just come from the dentist; I ain't got but one cavity." I say, "You ain't got but one tooth, fool, and it's all cavity." He say, "When I die, I want you to put a stone in my grave." I say, "All right; all you gone do is die, I'll do anything." He say, "I want you to put some writin' on it." He say, "What you gonna write on it?" I say, "Here lies John, dead as usual." Oh, he was a nuisance! And he had a brother older than he was. We went . . . his sister died and we went to the funeral; the minister walked over and touched him on the back and say, "How old are you, Pops?" He say, "Ninety-seven." The minister say, "Ain't no need of you going home." Had a brother older than he was—ninety-nine. He married a girl fourteen—fourteen! He didn't live but five days. Took three undertakers a week to get the smile off of his face. Oh, I couldn't stand him . . . Come telling me . . . some friends invited us up to the country. He come talking about . . . I say,

"You ever been to the country?" He say, "Sho, when I was a boy, I use to live in the country." I say, "When you were a boy, everybody lived in the country."

Well, let me see what time it is. Oh my goodness! Umm! See I got to keep with the time 'cause the boss man is a business man. He don't pay no overtime, and I don't do none!

*(Mabley brings her act to a close by singing and dancing to her own version of "Do the Funky Chicken.")*

I'm funky, funky, funky!
No bunk!
So funky!
They call me/Superfunk!
You know I never will forget my life . . .
It was high noon.
And I was face to face with a funky chicken.
The funky chicken flapped her wings and started scratching up the
    ground.
I jumped up cool and did my thing with the same dance all
    around.
The funky chicken moved on in
And she started pecking.
But that bird had to move one back
When I started loose-necking.
That chicken shook all over
Went down on one leg.
When she straightened out her feathers
She had laid a funky egg.
On that funky egg
That chicken sat.
She opened up her funky beak and said,
"Now git with that!"
I loosed up my funkmobile
In the front and in the rear.
I got my motor running and I put my legs in gear.
My beak took off in high
And when I made a turn
The spot got so hot
You could smell the rubber burn.
I singed that chicken's feathers
And she began to beg . . .
"I give up/Please stop
Before you cook my funky egg!"

I am funky, funky, funky, funky!
No bunk!
So funky!
They call me Superfunk!
Aah, funky!
So funky!
They call me Superfunky!

---

Alternate Version of the Old Man Theme:

## from **Moms Mabley On Stage**

. . . This *old*—d-e-a-d, p-u-n-y, m-o-l-d-y man. I mean, an OLD man. Santa Claus looked like his son. He was older than his mother. He was so old that his sister died, and we went to the funeral and after the funeral the minister leaned over and tapped him on the back and said, "How old are you, Pops?" He said, "Ninety-one." He said, "Ain't no use of you going home." . . . My daddy liked him so I had to marry that old man. My daddy should have married him; he the one that liked him. The nearest thing to death you ever seen in your life. His shadow weighed more than he did. He got out of breath threading a needle. And UGLY! He was so ugly he hurt my feelings . . . he was so ugly he had to tip on a glass to get a drink of water . . . I thought he never would die . . . I shouldn't talk like that about him though. He's dead. They say you shouldn't say nothing about the dead unless you can say something good. He's dead, GOOD! I know he's dead 'cause I had him cremated; I burnt him up—I was determined he was gonna get hot one time . . .

---

## from **Live at Sing Sing**

ANNOUNCER: It's star time, and now, without further ado, Mercury Records brings to you live from Sing Sing Prison, the funniest lady in the world, Jackie "Moms" Mabley.

MOMS: Hello, Darling! Oh, I've got to make an excuse for not comin' up when Moms was supposed to. Some two men brought a disease over here in this country, and I got that flu! Honey, I was so sick! Oh, the doctor come to see me. I said, "Do something for me, Honey, I'm dyin'." I said, "I can't hear nothin'." He said, "Moms, just drop your jaws."

But first, children . . . I want to thank this wonderful man that made it possible for Moms to be out up here today. And that's Warden Leeman. Warden? Come out here a minute, son!

C'mon out, baby! Thank you so much for bringing me up here; all of these *(Referring to prisoners)* are Mom's children, and I brought somethin' for ya . . . two of Mom's latest albums, one called *Abraham, Martin and John* and the other one is called *What Generation Gap?* Now you just go home and put them on your machine and laugh yourself to death, 'cause they funny!

WARDEN: My only concern is to have the men enjoy the show, that was what we started out with . . .

MOMS: If they don't stand up and laugh, they gone do some funny things settin' down, I tell ya that! Children, I feel safer than I've felt in a long time, 'cause baby, it's rough out there! You know, a little boy, ten years old, walked up to Moms and said, "Stick 'em up!" I said, "You too little, son, to be carrying on like that." He said, "Moms, I don't want that *damn* jive, just give me some money!" It's rough out there . . . and the weather? You're nice and warm in here and everything—the weather out there, baby, is terrible! Oh, it's awful! I was walkin' down Fifth Avenue—we just had a big storm walkin' down Fifth Avenue past the cathedral— and before I got there, this old woman, older than me, she slipped up right in front of the cathedral, fell—BOP! Right down to the ground! Some man coming down out of the cathedral picked her up, you know, and says to her, "Are you hurt, Mother?" She says, "No. I think I'm all right." She look up at him and says, "Is mass out?" He says, "No, but your hat's on crooked!"

And during the holiday, boy it was terrible! You couldn't go nowhere. One man downtown was running short of bartenders, you know. You know, his bartender got sick. Didn't have nobody but this lil' sissy boy. *(Pause)* Now, don't you all make like you don't know what I'm TALKING about! But, he was known to steal . . . You know, he'll steal the man's whiskey, the man's money and everything. The man say to himself, "Well, I can tell I ain't gone get nobody else, so I got to use this boy. So he called him up (the sissy), and he says, "C'mere!" He say, "I'm gone tell you right now, I'm gone give you this job for the holidays, but if I catch you stealing my whiskey, I'm gonna take a bottle of it and rack it over your head. And if I catch you stealin' my money, I'm gonna beat you 'til you can't see! Remember, I'm gonna be watchin' you, and if I catch you doin' anything wrong, remember, I'm gonna whip you 'til your head ropes like okra!" He say, "You understand that?" He (the sissy) say, "Yessir. I understand." The boss, he say, "All right, then kiss me and go to work!"

And you talk about poor people suffering out there! Honey, them apartments 'n' things so cold! Super says to a man, "You know, I've been with every woman in this building since I've been here, except one!" The man says, "That must be that old grouchy woman on the fourth floor." But, honey, that woman got mad! That woman got mad, and she read that super. Say, "Man, send me up some steam."

*(The band plays.)*

Hey, Super.

*(Moms sings:)*

> Hey, Super, send me up some steam!
> You are the laziest man I've ever seen!
> Put on that bottle, and do whatcha oughta,
> How can I take a bath when I ain't got no hot water?
> Listen, Super, or do you want me to call you Joe?
> Don't you know the weather out there is twenty below?
> I'm so mad at you, that I could scream!
> Super, send up some *damn* steam!
> . . . 'Cause yesterday you lied and said the heat was on it's way!
> But I haven't heard a hiss out of that radiator today.
> 'Cause I've been cold since yesterday . . .
> He said, "Go away—I don't want to hear a thing you got to
>     say . . ."
> I know *damn* well you ain't lookin' for no rent today!
> Not after what you called me yesterday!
> Oh, what do you care, if I cough or I sneeze?
> I wouldn't give you another *damn* dime
> If you fell on your knees!
> I've got to have heat, *Mr. Lindsey*,
> You promised me heat!
> I don't care what you say,
> but if my rent I'm going to pay,
> I've got to have heat!
> *Heat!*
> *Heat!*
> *Heat!*

These texts were transcribed by Elsie A. Williams from tapes of live performances given in 1970 and 1971.

## Introduction by David Kaplan and Patricia Norcia

**R**uth Draper died in her sleep in December 1956. She was seventy-two years old and had spent the day performing two shows on Broadway. From the 1920s until her death, Draper's warmly observed and hilarious portraits of society matrons and working-class women touched audiences around the world. In an era before easy air travel, Draper toured her work from Broadway to Bangkok, from the West End's Hippodrome (where her performance followed that of a tame seal) to the Court of St. James. Soon after her professional debut in 1920, her engagements on Broadway and in the West End became more or less annual events until the 1950s. During her career, she had been compared to Sarah Bernhardt and Eleonora Duse.

However, unlike those actresses, Draper chose to appear exclusively in one-woman plays of her own imagining. A little before the first world war, she had tea with her friend, Henry James. The young soloist found herself at a professional crossroads, wondering if she should try ensemble work and acting in other writers' plays. James—who had written Draper a monologue she never performed—advised the actress: "You have woven yourself a magic carpet—stand on it!"

The first Draper monologue was performed by a nine-year-old Ruth imitating the family's Jewish tailor; the last was *A Cocktail Party*, first performed in 1950. The average Draper monologue was twenty minutes long. She used no sets, no music, no furniture beyond a table or chair, and no costume pieces except perhaps a hat or shawl. She spoke many languages— English, Italian, Spanish, German, French and a Draper specialty of made-up languages such as ersatz Romanian. Without a written script, Draper created and held in her memory a repertory of 125 characters in over forty sketches. On stage she subtly improvised and revised the monologues. In 1954, friends convinced her to record ten monologues, and over the two-year period before her death a stenographer transcribed thirty-six texts.

Throughout her career, Draper used consistent and vivid storytelling techniques. She always set characters in an environment where they were at a disadvantage: the American tour guide in Italy; a Scottish girl, not in Scotland, but at Ellis Island; the great Romanian actress, not on stage but backstage. Her acting was mostly reacting; she maintained active, spirited relationships with unseen characters which prompted Kenneth Tynan to write in the *Evening Standard* in 1952: "As I watched [Draper] perform her thronging monologues, I could only conclude that this was the best and most modern group acting I had ever seen." Her biographer Dorothy Warren explains the intense connection Draper held with her audience:

> She sometimes was torn between trying to remember the words, and letting the character take control regardless of the words. She could shorten or lengthen a sketch in performance. With an alert, responsive audience new lines would spontaneously be spoken. These new lines, she held, came not from her but from the character's reaction to a stimulating audience.
>
> The surface on which she wrote was her audience for without an audience to respond, the characters of Ruth Draper did not, could not, exist.

In an interview, Draper herself made the following statement on the captivating nature of solo work, "Long ago a man who knew a great deal about the theatre told me that the old advice to actors: 'You must put it over,' was wrong. What is really important is not to put anything over, but to bring the audience up onto the stage and into the scene with you. It is they who must give you even more than you give them in the way of imagination and creative power."

Self-taught and self-produced, Draper was the first solo performer to develop character sketches with the structure and weight of three-act plays. She wasn't a musician, but her mother, a pianist, kept a salon at which Paderewski and other friends played. Draper wrote *The Italian Lesson* in perfect sonata allegro form—a theme that recurs in variations. Many Draper pieces have three movements: *Three Women and Mr. Clifford, Three Breakfasts* and *Three Generations in a Court of Domestic Relations*.

Ruth Draper won a number of playwriting awards and her work as a writer stands on its own, separate from her remarkable stage presence.

Director **David Kaplan** and actress **Patricia Norcia**, who own the rights to Draper's thirty-six published monologues, have collaborated for twenty years on restagings of the Draper repertory.

## from **Three Breakfasts**

Ruth Draper never wrote out her texts—all printed versions were originally dictated—so it is impossible to say what she would have done to format her work. Here, two sets of ellipses (. . . . . .) indicate the response of unseen characters.

### The First Breakfast: In a Suburb

*A young, newly married wife runs into the dining room laughing. She is apparently being pursued by her young husband and seizes a chair to ward him off. She laughs uncontrollably.*

Harry! Please—no! *Please*, Harry! *(Laughs)* Oh! I'm all out of breath—you chased me so fast I nearly fell downstairs . . . . . . *(She sits at the table)* Isn't it the most lovely day! . . . . . . Darling, how long is it going to take you to get to the station? . . . . . . Oh! Harry, that only gives us five minutes for breakfast! . . . . . . But, Darling, let's get up earlier! It's awfully bad for you to hurry so—and I love getting up early! . . . . . . No, really—I do— I love getting up early these nice, cold mornings—I can hardly wait to start the day! . . . . . . And there's so much to do . . . . . . Will you have your coffee now, Darling? . . . . . . It's nice and hot . . . . . . *(She pours coffee)*

Oh, I'm going to have such fun today! I'm going to accomplish so much with you out of the way! . . . . . . You don't want me to do too much without you? . . . . . . All right, my sweet . . . . . . *(She passes the cup)* Does that look right? . . . . . . I'll just do lots of little things that don't concern you very much, but which are very important just the same . . . . . . You know—all the kitchen things and the linen and the china and glass and groceries and everything. To put in order . . . . . . Then I'm going to unpack and put away all my things and get everything in apple-pie order . . . . . . Then I'm going to do something for you! I'm not going to tell you—it's going to be a surprise . . . . . . Would you rather know? Well, I'm going to unpack all your bags, Darling, and put everything away, so when you get back it will be just as though you'd always lived here! I'm going to fix all your cupboards and your closets and the bureau drawers and the desk and all your papers and get the bags out of the way, so that . . . . . . What? Why? Oh, Darling, let me! . . . . . . But I'll tell you where everything is! You'll love the way I fix it—I've got the most wonderful plan! I'm going to put your collars and your ties and your handkerchiefs in that nice . . . . . . You don't want me to touch anything? . . . . . . *(She pouts)* Yes, I'm disappointed. *(She drinks)* Because I thought that was one of the— *(She drinks)* Look out, my sweet, it's hot!—duties *(She drinks)* and privileges *(She drinks)* and pleasures of being a wife! In fact I thought that was why you married me—one of the reasons you married me! To take care of you! . . . . . . Don't you want to be taken care of? . . . . . . Don't you want me to keep things tidy so they'll be easy to find, and you'll know where they belong? . . . . . .

Well, will you put them away the way you want them, then let me keep them tidy that way? . . . . . . Because you see, Darling—you happen to be very untidy. I just happen to be very tidy . . . . . . But I like you the way you are because it gives me something I can do for you . . . . . . You mean you want me to leave everything in the middle of the floor, the way it is now? . . . . . . All right I won't touch your old things, and someday you'll be sorry—someday you'll come and ask me where something is, and I won't know . . . . . . and I won't care! *(She drinks)* . . . . . . *(She laughs)*

I know one thing I'm going to do for you today, and I'm not going to tell you what it is! *(She drinks)* You needn't guess—I'm not going to tell you. More coffee, my sweet? *(She pours coffee)* You might as well learn that I've got a very strong will, and I'm not going to tell you everything, anyway . . . . . . No I'm not! Well you are not going to get this out of me, so you needn't guess—I'm not going to tell you. *(She laughs)* Don't look at me like that, Darling. Don't look like that . . . . . . I can't bear it—I'll tell you . . . . . . If you really want to know—I'm going to make you a pudding! . . . . . . I certainly can cook! I can make seven things and they always turn out . . . . . . Well, I can make a few that don't! But seven always do, and this is the best pudding you've ever tasted . . . . . .

What? Go to the theatre next week? Oh! Do you mean it? Umm! . . . . . . What are we going to see? I don't care, Darling—anything amuses me as long as I'm with you . . . . . . Is that the way you feel? . . . . . . Then why do we go to the theatre? *(She drinks)* . . . . . . *(She laughs)* You know, Harry, lots of people have told me that it only lasts a little while . . . . . . feeling like that . . . . . . I think it's going to be rather exciting when it begins not to last . . . . . . Do you want me to tell you the brutal truth right away? Or do you want me to keep it a dark secret *(She drinks)* and pretend? . . . . . . What are you going to do? . . . . . . I don't believe it's going to be true about us! . . . . . . I don't know—I just have a feeling that it is always going to be more and more—and never less and less! . . . . . .

*(She suddenly breaks off in alarm)* Oh! Darling, you must go! You'll have to hurry, and you've had a wretched breakfast . . . . . . The eggs weren't cooked and the bacon was burned . . . . . . *(They rise)* And I'm sorry to tell you that you have a little egg on your tie! . . . . . . Oh, it doesn't show—it wasn't your fault—the egg was too soft . . . . . . It's very hard to get boiled eggs just the way you like them . . . . . . And you were an angel not to say anything about the lumps in the oatmeal . . . . . . Weren't they awful? One thing I cannot abide is lumps in oatmeal! . . . . . . But it will never happen again as long as we live, because that is one of the things I know how to cook—oatmeal without lumps . . . . . .

*(In great haste she helps him put on his coat)* Good-bye, my sweet . . . . . . Are you coming back on the four-thirty-two? . . . . . . Well, you might call me in the middle of the morning . . . . . . Oh, just to ask me how I'm getting on . . . . . . tell me how you're getting on . . . . . . *(They part at the door)* Good-bye, Darling, don't go too fast down the hill, it's slippery . . . . . . Good-bye! *(She waves good-bye to him)*

*(She breaks off as she sees her husband reappear in the doorway)* What, Darling? Forget something? . . . . . . No—you didn't—you didn't forget anything! . . . . . . I did? What did I forget? Something important? What are you talking about? . . . . . . What? . . . . . . Oh . . . . . . *(She rushes into his arms in the doorway)*

## The Second Breakfast: In the City

*It is about fifteen years later. The wife comes in. She pulls out her chair crossly, sits down at the breakfast table and beings to read her newspaper. Suddenly, looking over its edge, she sees her husband come in, carelessly watches him sit down, then goes on reading. Presently she speaks curtly and dryly.*

Morning . . . . . . *(She pours the coffee and hands it across)* Here . . . . . . got it? . . . . . . *(Pours coffee for herself. Chin on hand, she looks about the room. Then she helps herself from a platter handed by the maid. Eats and drinks in silence)*

. . . . . . Pamela? She's not coming down . . . . . . I told her to stay in bed—she has a bad cold . . . . . . *(Another silence)*

By the way, what happened to you yesterday afternoon? . . . . . . Do you mean to say that you forgot it was Pamela's birthday? . . . . . . Harry! How *could* you forget? You'd promised you'd take her out on her birthday afternoon—she'd been looking forward to it for days . . . . . . I did telephone your office . . . . . . I telephoned twice. You were not there— I naturally assumed you were on your way uptown . . . . . . I had to go to a meeting—I left her waiting for you . . . . . . Oh, well . . . . . . She'll get over it . . . . . . Just explain something . . . . . . It doesn't make any difference . . . . . . *(There is a long pause while they eat. The maid serves and goes)*

I had a telegram last night from Mr. Porter saying that Bobby is being sent home from school . . . . . . *(She breaks off, startled)* Harry! Will you *please* not use such language before the maid? Well of *course* she heard you—she was just at the door . . . . . . Now don't get so excited— he's not done anything wrong! Why should you immediately jump at the conclusion that he's done something wrong? . . . . . . He's been standing at the top of his class for over three months—which is more than *you* ever did . . . . . . He's got something the matter with his eyes . . . . . . No, not serious . . . . . . Well, he had measles, you know . . . . . . It has left him some inflammation in his eyes and the headmaster thinks he ought to see a specialist, so he's coming home for a few days . . . . . . I thought if you had nothing particular to do, you might take him out. It isn't going to be much fun for him . . . . . .

Harry! Please don't push your plate away like that—you nearly knocked it off the table . . . . . . *Why* isn't it fit to eat? Tell me what's the matter. I'll see what I can do. Don't behave like an angry child! . . . . . . What lumps in it? Well how do you expect me to know unless you tell me? I don't eat oatmeal—I've not eaten it for about fifteen years— horrible stuff. I never could see why you wanted it, anyways . . . . . . Well, I'll tell the cook. I'm sorry . . . . . .

You're going up to the farm? *(She laughs sarcastically)* Excuse me if I smile . . . . . . Well, the idea of you on the farm, in the middle of winter just makes me laugh, that's all . . . . . . How long do you think you're going to stay? . . . . . . Ha! I'll bet you'll be back within twenty-four hours. You could no more stand the country in the middle of winter . . . . . . You'd simply *hate* it . . . . . . I bet you I'd stand it a great deal better than you would . . . . . . Because I really love the country! *(She munches)* I sometimes think I'd like to go and live there. *(She mumbles)* I sometimes think . . . . . . *(She munches and mumbles)* anything would be better than this! . . . . . . Oh, never mind what I said . . . . . . Want some more coffee? . . . . . . Hold out your cup. . . .

You're not dining at home tonight? Oh, Harry—I think, you're awfully *mean*! But I *begged* you to save tonight . . . . . . Yes, I did, Harry— I told you at least three times that we had a box for the opera tonight . . . . . . The Andersons and the Millers are coming, and it's the chance of the winter to have a box tonight, because it's for *Tristan* . . . . . . *Tristan and Isolde* with that wonderful new singer . . . . . . Oh, *stop* talking like that! It's so silly to say such things—because it's one of the most beautiful things in the world . . . . . . Well, a great many people think so, and *always* have thought so and *always* will think so—very intelligent people, too! . . . . . . You're the person I'm sorry for! You're just so deliberately *deaf*—so deliberately *blind*—and you've never even tried to enjoy the things that I enjoy . . . . . . Oh, well, never mind—it doesn't make any difference. I can easily enough find somebody who'll be only too thankful to go . . . . . . I'm very disappointed, that's all—and I thought we would all have a very nice evening . . . . . .

Look at me a minute—look at me! . . . . . . Disgusting! You have some egg on your tie. Look out! It's all over it—here. *(She points)* . . . . . . Take your knife . . . . . . Disgusting! . . . . . . *(Another long pause. He rises. She remains sitting)*

Don't forget to go up and see Pamela . . . . . . Good-bye . . . . . . *(She does not look at him. Then she calls)* Harry! Come back a minute will you? . . . . . . Listen, would you come to the opera late, and bring me home? . . . . . . That new Isolde is singing—and there's a wonderful tune at the end. You'd probably recognize it—you've heard it before. It only lasts five minutes and it won't kill you . . . . . . I really think you'd enjoy it . . . . . . It's called the *Liebestod* . . . . . . Are you going to be at the club? Well, I'll send the car at a quarter to eleven . . . . . . But don't be late, or you'll miss it . . . . . . Right. Good-bye . . . . . .

*(She bends down as a puppy rushes in)* Hello, Raggles! Oh, you sweet puppy! . . . . . . Have you heard the news? Bobby's coming home. Come along, we'll go and tell Pamela. *(She walks out backward, waving the folded newspaper at the dog)* Come on, come on, come on! . . . . . . *(She leaves the room)*

## The Third Breakfast: On a Farm

*It is forty years after the first breakfast. The wife enters, now an old lady. Her grandchildren are already crowding around the breakfast table.*

Breakfast, Harry! Hal, darling—go and tell your grandfather that breakfast is ready . . . . . . I don't think he heard us . . . . . . Come on children— those lazy parents of yours are not coming . . . . . . They prefer breakfast in bed, which is something I don't understand . . . . . .

Wait, children—don't rush at your grandfather like that! . . . . . . You'll knock him over—six of you is a great many!

Thank you, Bobby— *(He pulls out her chair)* . . . . . . Thank you, Darling . . . . . . Hal—quickly, Dear! Pull out Grandfather's chair . . . . . .

Now, how are we all going to sit? . . . . . . Molly, it's your turn to sit next to Grandfather . . . . . . Come on . . . . . . Tommy, you can feed the goldfish after breakfast . . . . . . They can wait . . . . . . You sit there, Dear. . . . . . . Bobby, here . . . . . . No, little girls, don't quarrel . . . . . . Peggy was next to him yesterday, and it's Nancy's turn . . . . . . And Hal here next to me . . . . . . There we are! What a lovely party . . . . . . What are you all going to do this lovely, lovely day? I suppose you will be skating on the pond . . . . . . I saw the lovely ice from my . . . . . . Not skating? . . . . . . Coasting . . . . . . On the big hill? Oh, we must ask your grandfather. I am not at all sure . . . . . . But oh! That hill makes me very nervous . . . . . . Well perhaps I am foolish, but you see that is the hill where your dear father was very badly hurt when he was a little boy . . . . . . He never told you? Isn't that funny? *(Louder)* Isn't that funny, Harry, the boys never heard of Bobby's accident on the hill . . . . . . Well, you ask him—I'm sure that he'll remember. Let me see—your father was home from boarding school . . . . . . The very day he got here, that night your grandfather and I went to the opera. Now what was that opera? I've entirely forgotten. We'll ask your grandfather. He will remember, he has the most remarkable memory. You see if he doesn't know, the minute I ask him.

Harry dear, what was the opera we were so fond of, that we went to the night of the fire? *Tristan!* It was *Tristan and Isolde*. It comes back to me now—how beautiful it was! *Tristan and Isolde* is a very famous opera . . . . . . What was it about? Oh, it was just about two people—two people who loved each other . . . . . .

I remember now. Your grandfather did not go with me to the opera . . . . . . Well he was a very, very busy man, and he couldn't always go. But he came late, to bring me home . . . . . . As we drove into our street . . . . . . A little more coffee, Dearest? . . . . . . Hold out your grandfather's cup, Darling. As we drove into our street we realized something very exciting was going on, because there were crowds of people and policemen everywhere. Then we heard bells and whistles and sirens. Then a fire engine went tearing around the corner and then a hook and ladder! We realized, of course, that there was a very bad fire. And then, we found that the fire . . . . . . What Darling? . . . . . . Was in our house. Quite right, you guessed it! It was. Oh! It was a *dreadful* fire! . . . . . . Nobody was hurt . . . . . . but . . . . . . we never got into the house again . . . . . . Oh! Everything was burned—our books, our clothes, our furniture, our carpets and rugs . . . . . . All our precious things—all our wedding presents—everything was burned, burned to cinders and ashes! . . . . . .

But fortunately, you see—very fortunately we had this farm. So, we decided, though it was the middle of the winter to come here. And the next morning your father went off to coast . . . . . . and his sled struck the big oak tree—you remember at the foot of the hill—and your father was thrown against the stone wall and he was brought home to me unconscious! . . . . . . What a winter it was! One thing after another till I thought we would never get away . . . . . . I was telling the children about that dreadful winter and our series of accidents . . . . . . but we all got well in the end . . . . . . I say we all got well in the end.

Have you finished, Dear? . . . . . . Shall we go by the fire? Children—have you all had enough? . . . . . . Nancy—you've not eaten your breakfast! Why couldn't you eat it? . . . . . . What? Lumps in it? I've not noticed any. Harry—had you noticed any lumps in the oatmeal? . . . . . . Grandfather hadn't noticed any . . . . . . But even if there were, Darling, they wouldn't hurt you, because lumps—lumps are good for us *(She drinks)* Lumps make us grow . . . . . .

Now, run along, children . . . . . . Your grandfather and I are coming out to watch you coast from the top of the hill . . . . . . One moment, my Dear, you've got a little egg on your tie . . . . . . It doesn't show, Dear, it's not your fault . . . . . . the eggs were a little soft this morning . . . . . . It's very hard to get boiled eggs exactly as you like them . . . . . . *(She goes out slowly with her hand on his arm)*

**Lord Buckley**

## Introduction by Richard Buckley, Jr.

There is very little published reference material on Lord Buckley. Yet he is mentioned and quoted throughout the current entertainment industry as if he were doing a gig just around the corner. To someone hearing his work for the first time, it seems so fresh and contemporary. You might easily imagine a rapper laying down a version of *Marc Antony's Funeral Oration* to a back-beat: "Hipsters, flipsters and finger-poppin' daddies, / Knock me your lobes . . ."

Born in 1906 on an Indian reservation outside a coal-mining town on the outskirts of San Francisco, Richard Myrtle Buckley broke into show business in Chicago as an actor and standup comic. A one-time lumberjack, he became "Lord Buckley," an Englishman of gentry class, as a joke, perhaps stationed in India, complete with pith helmet and waxed mustache. Or maybe a Chicago gangster in pinstripes or a tuxedo with a carnation in his lapel.

From the late twenties, he performed on the medicine- and tent-show circuit, in Chicago speakeasies, as an emcee for depression-era dance marathons and increasingly in the Chicago jazz clubs. As a deejay in Kansas City in the late thirties, it was Lord Buckley who gave the great jazzman, William James Basie, the title of "Count." He toured in Ed Sullivan's USO shows and

25

played Broadway on a vaudeville tour. His inimitable style was perhaps best captured by Albert Goldman writing in 1969 for *Life* magazine.

> Standing before his audience in a tuxedo and pith helmet, with his lobster eyes and imperious waxed mustache giving him the look of an apoplectic English lord, he would open his thin, waspy lips and out would pour the thickest, blackest, funkiest stream of slum, ghetto, jive talk ever heard on an American stage. What made the act even more bizarre was the use to which he put his low-down gutter language. Buckley's monologues invariably concerned religious themes, like the life of Jesus (his most famous routine was *The Nazz*—or *Nazarene*) or the story of Jonah and the whale. Far from burlesquing these sacred subjects, he exalted them anew by pouring into them all the enthusiasm and ebullience of his own extravagant temperament.

> Like the old-time stump preachers and evangelists, Lord Buckley was possessed by the Spirit as soon as he spoke the Word. His eyes flashed, his muscular body rocked, his mighty voice—an organ of operatic range and power—swooped and soared like a drunken American eagle . . .

> Whether you look at the man as a master mixer of the media, a pop-eyed bard of blackness or the first great surfer on that sea of Eastern mysticism . . . Buckley checks out as beautiful and contemporary . . . you want to be with him . . .

This description still holds true today, nearly forty years after his mysterious death on November 12, 1960 ended a colorful, provocative and often tragic life. When the police found him in violation of New York City's notoriously corrupt cabaret card laws, the Lord was left unemployed and ailing. His death, a few days later, triggered intense public outcry against these graft-riddled laws, and ultimately ended the practice of enforced ID cards—complete with fingerprints and mug shots—for all cabaret employees. Various newspapers reported his death to be caused by a "heroine overdose," a "stroke," a "heart attack" and a "police beating," but the coroner's official report stated that he died of natural causes. I remember watching that night as the police officer pulled into the driveway and walked up to the front door to tell my mother that His Lordship, my father, had died. I was only ten years old.

Back in the early fifties, there was no easy classification for Lord Buckley's work. As his original producer Jim Dickson explained, "When his first album was made, there was no category it could be filed under. In a sense, he was a jazz comic. Jazz in the sense of improvisation on a theme—comic in that he certainly made people laugh. But his delight was that of dramatic storyteller, limited only by the audience's ability to stay with him."

For as Lord Buckley said, "Dig infinity and they dug it."

**Richard Buckley, Jr.** is a composer and filmmaker and the administrator of the Estate of Lord Buckley.

# God's Own Drunk

Just like I said before. I'm a non-drinkin' man.
Never drank for some reason or other. Didn't like it.
But like I said, too, I promised to take care of my brother-in-law's still
while he went in to vote.

Went up there and it was just where the map said it was.
And I'm a gonna tell you something—it was no little old five or ten cent still.
It was laid there just like a golden, mountain opal,
with a kind of a honeydew cry comin' from it.

I ain't a drinkin' man, like I 'splained to you,
but that big old yellow moon was a hangin' up there,
and God's lanterns was a hangin' in the sky,
and that curiosity got the best of me, and I took a slash.

And I got a crazy, revolutionary feelin' in my body.
That yellow whiskey went down my throat like honeydew vine water.
Humph, it tasted mighty good!

I felt a revolution goin' through my body
like there was great neon signs a goin' up an' sayin', "There's a Great Life
   a Comin'!"

Feelin' it talkin' to me, and I took another slash,
and I got another jolt, and I took another slash,
and I started to sing.

I started to sing.

And that big old yellow moon a hangin' out there
and God's sweet lanterns a hangin' in the sky,
and I's a singin'.

Never could sing a note before in my life,
but I's a singin' as fine and as pretty as you'd ever want to hear.

And I took another slash.

And then I took a big full . . .

That big old yellow moon a hangin' out there.
God's lanterns a hangin' in the sky,
and suddenly I got a tremendous revolution of emotion in my body
like I was fallin' in love with everything in God's sweet world
that moved, lived, didn't live, animate, inanimate, black, blue,
green, pink, mountains, fountains.

I was in love with life, 'cause I was drunk!!

I wasn't fallin' down, slippin', slidin' drunk.

I was GOD'S OWN DRUNK!

A fearless man!

And that's when I first saw the bear.

Big old Kodiak-lookin' fella, about sixteen foot tall.

I walked right on up to that bear, 'cause I was God's Own Drunk
and I loved everything in this world.
Walked right up tight to him about four-and-a-half feet
and I looked right up in his eyes
and I want to tell you somethin' brothers and sisters—
my eyes was redder than his was! Hung him up.

And he's a sniffin', he's a sniffin'. He's tryin' to smell some fear.
He can't do it, 'cause I'm God's Own Drunk and I'm a fearless man.

He expects me to do two things, flip or fly.
I don't do either. Hangs him up.

I told him, I said, "Mr. Bear, I'm God's Own Drunk
and I love every hair on your twenty-seven acre body.
I'm a fearless man!"

Said, "I want you to go . . . I know you got bear friends over the hill there.
Harry Bear and Tim Bear and Jelly Bear and Tony Bear and Teddy Bear
and Field Bear, Hazel Bear, John Bear, Pete Bear and Rare Bear!
Go over and tell all of them that I'm God's Own Drunk tonight
and I love everything in God's green creation.
I love them like brothers but if they give me any trouble
I'm gonna run every goddamn one of 'em off the hill!"

I moved up. Don't you know he moved back two feet.

I reached up and took the bear by the hand.
I said, "Mr. Bear, we're both beasts when it comes right down to it."

He's a lookin' down at me.

I said, "I want you to come with me. You're gonna be my buddy. Buddy Bear."

Took him right by his big old shaggy-man, island-sized hand,
led him on over, sat him down by the still.

Well, he's a sniffin'. He's a sniffin'.
He knows there's honeydew around there,

some kind of honey bear honeydew of some kind.
He's a sniffin'.

I know what he's a sniffin' at.

I took a slash or two myself to taste 'er out and I filled him a bottle.

Did you ever see them bears, the silhouette of them bears at the circus,
suckin' up that sasparilla? Ahhh, it's a fine lookin' sight!

And he downed another bottle. And he downed another bottle.
And I put two more in him and pretty soon he started to sniff and snort.
Tapped his foot.

And he got up and started to do The Bear Dance.
Two sniffs, three snorts, a half a turn and one grunt.

And I'm trying' to do it, but I couldn't do it
'cause it was just like a jitterbug dance,
it was so simple it evaded me.

But we was a dancin' and yellin'!

And God's sweet moon a hangin' in the sky,
and God's sweet lanterns out there
and there's jubilation and love on that hill.

And finally, my love, it up and got so strong it overwhelmed my soul,
and I laid back in the sweet, green hill
with that big old Buddy Bear's paw right in mine
and I went to sleep.

And I slept for four hours and dreamed me some tremulous dreams.

And when I woke up that old yellow moon was a hangin' in the sky,
and God's sweet lanterns is out there
and my buddy the bear was a missin'.

And you know something else, brothers and sisters?

So was the still!

# Willie the Shake

Now you see in Hip Talk, they call William Shakespeare, Willie the Shake!
You know why they called him Willie the Shake? Because *he shook
everybody*!! They gave this cat five cents worth of ink and a nickle's worth

of paper and he sat down and wrote up such a breeze, wham!!! Everybody got off! (Period!) He was a hard, tight, tough cat. Pen in hand, he was a Mother Superior.

Now you remember when Mark and Cleo were swingin' up a storm on that velvet-lined Nile barge, suckin' up a little Egyptian whiskey with that wild incense flyin' all over the place and that Buddha-headed moon, pale Jazzmin' colored flippin' the scene. It was Romantic City.

Caesar, meantime had split to Rome, went to that big Jam Session and they sliced that po' cat up all over the place. Naturally, Mark has got to put Cleo down, this was a tight move for him 'cause this Cleo was an early-day Elizabeth Taylor. This chick had more curves than the Santa Fe railroad making the Grand Canyon. But he had to split 'cause Caesar was his Main-Day Buddy Cat and they were putting Caesar in the hole. "And you know every Fox has got his Box."

The Roman Senate is jumpin' salty all over the place so Mark the Spark showed on the scene, faced all the studs, wild and otherwise, and shook up the whole scene! He Blew!!

## Marc Antony's Funeral Oration

Hipsters, flipsters and finger-poppin' daddies,
Knock me your lobes,
I came to lay Caesar out,
Not to hip you to him.
The bad jazz that a cat blows,
Wails long after he's cut out.
The groovy is often stashed with their frames,
So don't put Caesar down.
The swinging Brutus hath laid a story on you
That Caesar was hungry for power.
If it were so, it was a sad drag,
And sadly hath the Caesar cat answered it.
Here with a pass from Brutus and the other brass,
For Brutus is a worthy stud,
Yea, so are they all worthy studs,
I came to wail at Caesar's wake.
He was my buddy, and he leveled with me.
Yet, Brutus digs that he has eyes for power,
And Brutus is a solid cat.
It is true he hath returned with many freaks in chains
And brought them home to Rome.

Yea, the booty was looty
And hip the treasury well
Dost thou dig that this was Caesar's groove
For the push?
When the cats with the empty kicks hath copped out,
Yea, Caesar hath copped out, too,
And cried up a storm.
To be a world grabber a stiffer riff must be blown.
Without bread a stud can't even rule an anthill.
Yet, Brutus was swinging for the moon.
And, yea, Brutus is a worthy stud.
And all you cats were gassed on the Lupercal
When he came on like a king freak.
Three times I lay the kingly wig on him,
And thrice did he put it down.
Was this the move of a greedy hipster?
Yet, Brutus said he dug the lick,
And, yes, a hipper cat has never blown.
Some claim that Brutus's story was a drag.
But I dug the story was solid.
I came here to blow.
Now, stay cool while I blow.
You dug him all the way once
Because you were hipped that he was solid.
How can you now come on so square
Now that he's cut out of this world.
City Hall is flipped
And swung to a drunken zoo
And all of you cats are goofed to wig city.
Dig me hard.
My ticker is in the coffin there with Caesar,
And, yea, I must stay cool till it flippeth back to me.

---

# James Dean

I will never forget the first time I dug the great swinger, James Dean.
Conte Candoli and I were splitting a gig marquee-style
at a jumpin' joint in Hollywood called Jazz City.
A lot of professional cats used to fall into this place:
Benjamin Alexander, real great cat from Dragnet,
Sweet Peggy Lee, Stan Kenton, amongst the others made the scene.

I was pushing a new sound in humor.
They all had big eyes and ears to pick up on this lick
that consisted of translating Poe, Shakespeare, Einstein, Mahatma Gandhi,
and some of the miracles of the life of Christ
into the semantics of a modern language called "The Hip,"
which I, after much research, found to have a full vocabulary,
and one that was a seven-ply gasser if a cat really wanted to blow.

But the night was cool and crazy,
not too many cats digging the scene,
but the ones who were there were real tight to the attention.
I'd just finished blowing "Three Miracles from the Life of Christ" in hip
when the waitress sounded me that James Dean was on the scene
and had invited me to his table.
I think he was in the middle of the *Rebel*.
Now the 'vance grapevine had been swinging for quite some time
about what a great cat he was, and how strong and cool he was coming on.
I swung over to the booth just by the jukebox
where five young, quick-looking cats and two chicks were playing it cool.
A big cat with glasses and motorcycle shoulders stood up and made the
   introductions.
We all sat down.
But with the blowing crash of the jazz I couldn't dig the names,
so I was not hip to which one of the group was the star.
So, I played it cool and cased 'em
looking for that Hollywood type of cinerama-head,
but none of them made that category.
This young handsome cat with the glasses,
hot rod jacket, no tie and a one-day beard,
I finally dug was "The Dean."
and I said to myself, "Let me dig this solid cat
and see what jumps in that wig of his that's causing all the flip on the vine."

He asked me if I'd been digging Shakespeare for a long time to pick up
   on this lick.
I said, "Yes."
He then said he'd like to blow a little Shakespeare straight someday
and I said that would be a gasser.

He continued by telling me that he appreciated my sincerity and humility
in the translation of the life of our Savior
and added that he had my recording of the miracles.
Said it was one of his favorites.
I thanked him for his kindness.

He went on to say that this was solid,
as the young cats and kitties of our country
could use all the spiritual help they could get.
He said that the young cats, it seemed to him,
were looking for some kind of a cop-out in the face of the bad jazz of the
    Atomic Age.
That too many of them were taking the attitude "So what?
We may all flip out at any moment.
Why not have a ball before the blast?"
He went on to say that in his opinion the cats and chicks of the Atomic Age
were by far the brightest, strongest and most intelligent of all the generations.
He felt that the message of Christ brought to them in their own language
    of the hip,
should do a lot to swing them over to the power of love.
I said I thought it was very profound of him to dig the scene that way.
He went on to say that he was making some long speeches tonight
and he hoped he wasn't stayin' on stage too long.
I said, "Blow, man. I consider it a privilege to listen to you."

At that time I excused myself and returned to the stage
immediately dedicating my next epigram,
an incident in the life of Mahatma Gandhi translated in Hip,
called "The All-Solid Mahatma."
I blew that and four more pieces for him and returned to the table.
He thanked me for the dedication and said that he dug Gandhi the most.
He then informed me that in his humble opinion,
in some respects, the Mahatma
was like the return of The Man to the people.
That he, like Christ, had put forth all his efforts for the benefit of his people.
I said it was a solid thought and beautiful, too.
He returned by saying there were few people
one could discuss things of this nature with
and remain cool about it.

The young cat next to him
who was introduced to me as his manager
sounded him on the fact that he had an early call
and the time to cut was now.
Jimmy rose at once.
He apologized for having to split so early,
but that we'd chat again as he would return soon.

I never saw James Dean again but I'll never forget him.

## Introduction by Jon Kalish

> Brother Theodore is equal parts comedian, surrealist, visionary, existentialist, sidewalk prophet, hyper-intellectual basket case, and spiritual buncombe artist, yet none of these prepackaged concepts quite does him justice. What gives his act staying power is its core of genuine pain and moral gravity . . . It is a fine and courageous thing to look one's demons full in the face and subject them to the withering light of mockery . . . One leaves Theodore's black mass feeling strangely clean— as though redeemed through the purgative power of laughter.
>
> —A. J. Mell

**B**rother Theodore, the ninety-three-year-old actor known for his macabre, apocalyptic, one-man show bemoaning the futility of life, leaves audiences both mesmerized and howling with laughter.

Austrian by birth, Theodore grew up in Germany, the son of a wealthy, Jewish family. His parents were murdered by the Nazis, and Theodore spent a year in the Dachau concentration camp. He came to the United States penniless in 1941. But, sit with him nearly a half century later in his modest Upper West Side studio apartment and ask if his experience in Dachau and the fact that eight members of his family, including his parents and grandmother, perished in the Holocaust had an impact on his dark, nihilistic solo show and he will reply that they certainly did not.

"It is so easy to say, 'Well, sure, he was in a concentration camp, therefore he's depressed.' I was depressed when I was sixteen. I was a pessimist when I was the son of multi-multi-multi-multi-millionaires. I was pessimistic *before* the concentration camp. I was an unhappy child. I was an unhappy man, and now I'm an unhappy dying man."

After a job as a janitor and three years in a shipyard, Brother Theodore made his performing debut in San Francisco in the mid-forties but "there was only one person in the audience: it was my wife and she had a complimentary ticket." It was in New York that his career took off. He started doing his solo act at Café Society, followed by performances at a series of other small venues and by the late 1960s had already performed at Carnegie Recital Hall and sold out Town Hall six times. He performed his hour-long monologue at the 13th Street Theatre every Saturday night for sixteen years until the summer of 1997 when he suffered an accidental fall in his apartment. Since that time he has not performed.

On stage, Brother Theodore sits in a chair in front of a black wooden platform, his only props are a few plastic cups of water and a flashlight used to harass his "utterly repulsive" audience; he points it at people in their seats as he hurls insults at them. Theodore dresses entirely in black and has a full head of wild, white hair that is as much of a free spirit as the man himself. There's a demonic glint in his eye as he "explains it all" to you.

Often, his lines linger and it takes a little time for the humor to sink in, delaying the laughter. But in between the bursts of gibberish, punctuated frequently with a "Ladies and Gentlemen," the humor flows from a discourse on rats to his heavily fictionalized biographical details.

"Ladies and Gentlemen, I am what you might call a controversial figure, people either hate me or despise me." Actually, most people love him. "A genius of the sinister," declared the *Daily News*. "Held his audience spellbound," observed the *L.A. Times*. A reviewer for the *Village Voice* once called him "a rabble rouser without a cause—unless his cause is to promote the power of negative thinking and the glorification of anguish and despair." Despair is a big part of his act. "As long as there is death, there is hope," he declares in a still detectable German accent.

But with Brother Theodore, there's always a laugh at mortality's expense. His stage manager of more than fifteen years, Tom O'Connor, explains, "He's always been obsessed with death. He's always been aware of what a frail existence we lead, but that awareness, I think, was intellectual . . . as the years have progressed and he's seen his physical condition deteriorate, I think, of course, he can only become more aware of how true are the things that he says in his shows."

**Jon Kalish** is a newspaper and radio journalist in New York City.

# from **Theodore in Stereo**

Taped at Carnegie Recital Hall in 1959.

I had intended to speak tonight, Ladies and Gentlemen, I had intended to speak tonight on pea-green pimples. I felt I had some right to do so, having had so many myself. And over there in Europe it was this very subject which earned me my reputation as a top conversationalist and fiery orator. No matter when or where I spoke in those days, the crowd would storm the platform, knocking each other down, simply to get near me and tighten my suspenders. Mothers would hold up their unborn brats and shout for a blessing. Duchesses would laugh shrilly and dance like dervishes. Princesses would roll on the ground and beseech me for strictly personal treatment. Husky men would turn aside to hide their tears. And wherever I went, the sick in heart, same-day cleaners, women's clubs, horseflies would follow me in a whirlwind of ecstasy and settle down on my shoulders.

Americans are different. Not quite so emotional, not quite so pimple-conscious, and that's probably why it was suggested that I now select something which comes closer to *your* conception of sophisticated theatric garbage.

My first impulse was, of course, to start off with my pièce de résistance, Ophelia in her soliloquy, "Gee, what a noble mind is here overthrown." But then it occurred to me that today, as you probably know, commemorates the anniversary of the death of Willibalt Wërnecke, philosopher, metaphysician and podiatrist, who in 1909 died of running ears and athlete's foot. Just before kicking the bucket, Wërnecke managed to scribble a note of poetic farewell to Anna Mümmelman, no good hussy and cheap floozy, lady of his lifelong love. Little did he know that these last simple words were to become a milestone in German literature, were to sing on in the hearts of millions.

Ladies and Gentlemen, the translation you're about to hear is the only one in existence and I hope I have succeeded in capturing some of the witching and haunting mood of the original.

I'm afraid I can detect symptoms of idiocy in the audience. I think, Ladies and Gentlemen, I honestly think you better get sterilized or we are headed for a moronic future. It is obvious you haven't the vaguest idea of what I'm talking about, and that fills me with pride and satisfaction. The place is lousy again with juvenile delinquents. Juvenile delinquents, hoodlums, unfit mothers, anti-Theodorians, criminally insane nose-picker types.

*(Audience laughter.)*

You are too easily amused. Would you be kind enough, sir, to remove your arm from the lady's shoulder blade? I have nothing against necking, some of my best friends are neckerers, but your amateurish fumbling makes me sick.

An intelligent face in my audience. That's as rare as rocking horse manure. Incidentally, Honey, you're very, very, very pretty. You're exceedingly pretty. I can resist anything except temptation. Even in a pair of worn-out corduroy pants may beat a passionate heart. How would you like to become Theodora? *(Quietly)* Think it over.

Anyone here who would like to become Theodora? You, sir? Thank you very much indeed. I'm thrilled. I'm thrilled to see I'm making headway with the ladies of both sexes.

The name of the poem is entitled "To Anna." Why do you think it *is* entitled "To Anna"? . . . It's her NAME! You're on the right track. I'm squirming with delight, sir, I'm squirming with delight to meet an intellectual colossus. Too bad no refrigerators are given away on this program. But the rest of my performance is dedicated to you. The poem is entitled "To Anna" because the girl's name was Anna, and if you consider the girl's name was Anna, wouldn't it be perfectly foolish, revolting and ridiculous to have a poem entitled "To Florabelle"? We are not prisoners of logic here, but let's not get too sloppy in our thinking, please!

Will you be quiet? And you! I've been aware of your presence here for quite a while now and I've stopped feeling benevolent about you. If you misbehave once more, just once more I'll have you thrown out in the street and have the dogs pee on you. This is apparently what is called the "audience participation." I'm always afraid your next move will be community singing. May I remind you, in a voice cold with loathing, this is a one-man show, and you, young woman, are NOT the man!

Some members of my audience here seem to consider me a freak performer of no consequence, and that's all right with me. I know Charles Laughton is a better performer than I am, but I don't like him as well. Be that as it may, I should be greatly gratified indeed if you showed some consideration and a minimum of respect, if not for me, then at least for the late Willibalt's writings. Without the assistance of your good will I won't be able to do justice to his work. It's not a question of personal vanity on my part, it's simply that I should like to introduce to American audiences a piece of German literature that I, for one, consider a masterpiece. So if you'll bear with me for a couple of minutes and we will get it over with.

*(Coughing from audience.)*

People with a cough don't go to the doctor, they go to the theatre and cough into my best lines!

*(Unexpected laughter.)*

The mood is broken. A one-man performance is a harrowing experience, not only for the audience but for the performer, too. Before I get on stage my heart, my pulse, beat fast, my stomach aches, I sweat all over like a chunk of rancid pork.

*(More unexpected laughter.)*

I'm perfectly willing, in fact, I'm eager not to bring the poem. So if you keep on barking and bellowing indiscriminately at each of my sentences, if anything and everything I do or say is automatically, without rhyme or reason, greeted with idiot laughter we'll get absolutely nowhere. We'll simply waste your money and my time.

*(Pause. He waits for a response. Silence.)*

Thank you for this spontaneous outbreak of deafening applause.

"Oh, Anna, beloved one of all my senses, I yearn for you. You. Of you, to you, you, I to you, you to me, *we*. Who arest thou, mysterious maiden? Arest thou? People say thou arest! Let them talk! Thou wearest thy hat on thy feet and walkest on thy hands! On thy hands thou walkest! Black! I love you, Anna! I love black to you. You of you to you, you. I to you, you to me, we, wee-wee. Oh Anna fair, purple is the crimson of thy yellow hair! Oh Anna blue, golden is the tinkling of thy kangaroo! Thou homely maiden, in everyday dress, thou self-appointed kangaroo, I love to you. You, of you, to you, you. I to you, you to me, we, wee-wee! Do you know it, Anna dear, or did I try to hide from you? Even from behind, you can be spelled, and you most dependable, you most reliable one, from front *and* from behind. You're and stay: *Anna*! And I'm going to give it to you good and hot, smack in the entertainment center!"

---

from a 1996 performance at **The 13th Street Theatre**

Ladies and Gentlemen, half of the lies they tell about me are not true. The only truth is, my long life is about to end. And my long death, about to begin. Doctors are quacks. In the good hospitals, they let you die. In the bad hospitals, they kill you. They won't kill me. Tomorrow at 2:30 P.M. near West 76th Street I shall throw myself into the Hudson and shortly thereafter I shall reappear on the coast of New Jersey as a white swan. It will be a miracle. And there will be dancing in the streets. The establishment hushes it up, of course.

The circumstances under which I became a widower have never

been fully understood. On my wedding night I got up from my bed and cut the throat of my wife. An act which made a deep impression upon me at the time—an act which bound her to me forever, because only what we have lost forever we possess forever. Only where there are graves are there resurrections. Only when we have drunk from the river of darkness shall we truly see; only when our legs have rotted off shall we truly dance. As long as there is death there is hope. All our great spiritual leaders are dead. Moses is dead, Mohammed is dead, Buddha is dead and I'm not feeling so hot myself.

———

Ladies and Gentlemen, my tongue is not long enough to give you full account of what's really going on. Tonight you will have to unlearn all and everything you've ever learned before. We measure things by what we are. To the maggots in the cheese, the cheese is the universe. To the worms in the corpse, the corpse is the cosmos. How then can we be so cocksure about *our* world? Just because of our telescopes and microscopes and the splitting of the atom? All of your information is *mis*information and what you call science is really nothing else but an organized system of ignorance. There are more things in heaven and on earth than are dreamed of in your philosophy. What do we know about heaven? What do we know about the beyond? Do we know what's behind the beyond? I'm afraid some of us here hardly know what's beyond the behind. Creatures of twilight and delusion, we drift toward our unknown ends . . . and that's why I feel the best thing is not to be born. But who is as lucky as that? To whom does it happen? Not to one among millions and millions of people.

Ladies and Gentlemen, in these days of darkness and doubt, in this state of crisis and confusion, what the world needs is a truly great soul. I am that soul. I am a cosmo-dynamic personality walking through life in beauty and eternal youth. I'm in the prime of my senility. Here, on this stage, I probably look like a pile of mud. But that's only because stage lighting is still in its infancy!

I'm what you might call a controversial figure. People either hate me or despise me. They would rather shake the devil by the tail than shake me by the hand. But with every failure my reputation grows. One of these days you'll see my picture on every postage stamp! One of these days I'll Theodorize THE WORLD!

I come from extremely bad stock. The members of my family were mostly punks. Punks, blockheads, triplets, vegetarians, nail-biters. But I've always been happy. I was born in Upper and Lower Bavaria two years after the discovery of dirt. I grew up a child prodigy. At the age of six my second novel had been published; before I was ten I could change my own diapers; by the time I was eleven I knew how to wave "'bye-'bye." Tonight, at the age of ninety, I'm here to show you the way. I've just completed my book *Health Through Nutrition: Its Prevention and Cure*. I feel an itch for public service and I've got to scratch it! So, listen to me with your mouths wide open and try to profit from what you hear. I'm a voice for those who dare not speak, I'm a cry for hearts that suffer in silence, and I'm here tonight to tell you what needs to be told.

According to Pfizzner and Bokanowski, four distinct races preceded man on this planet: the Firemistpeople, the Potatobugpeople, the Yokelpeople and the Kissablechitterlings. They all had corporeal bodies and propagated by means of propagation and they all ate FOOD. Where are they now? Unfortunately, the desire to eat is widespread: an evil instinct, a feverish impulse to polish off nutrition, a bestial urge to fill your belly and the bellies of your loved ones with eatables and edibles, with paraphernalia and cadaverous things. A world teeming with paunches filled to the brim, or 1/2 to the brim, or 3/4 to the brim, or 2/3 to the brim, or 7/8 to the brim, or 9/10 to the brim with that vile, with that obscene, with that troubling substance called food.

The digesting that's going on right now in this lovely little theatre here *(With deep disgust)* is enough to turn my stomach. Food filthifies the saliva of your spittle. Food sends you staggering to the bathroom. The foodist's way of life is lunacy. It is filling what is empty and emptying what is full. It is berserkery and amockery, punctuated by the clatter of dishes and the flushing of water closets.

Ladies and Gentlemen, in spite of my excellent health, I have been ailing all my life. Can't you see what eating does to us? This morning, this very morning, I found a picture of myself when I was three months old. What a CHANGE! Frightening! Now you say, you say, life without eating is bunk. I say your filthy, butcherous notions—that's bunk. You say nutrition is essential for your diet, you say it gives you zest and zeal and a coat of healthy flesh. I say it gives you diarrhea, constipation; I say it gives you pipple-popples and slushey-pips. Just punch a finger—that's right, just punch your pinky into that healthy flesh you talk about. The dent will stay there till the cows come home to roost. And they WON'T come home. They can't come home! They have no legs! You tore them off and ate them remember? You are corpse-eaters, you are goulash ghouls, you are foodlums, you are belly bums! The human race, to which so many of you belong, looks to me like a bad joke. Like a boo boo of nature—like a miscarriage of the primal mother. Stop eating tonight!

It's hard to break with tradition and give up your preconceived ideas; I know that. But let me ask you a simple question . . . and then let me answer it. What has eating done for you? It has turned you into flotsam and jetsam. It has thrown you into an orgy of self-destruction. It has made chaos the law of your life and loneliness and despair and the imbibery of uppers and downers, the pattern of your existence, a shadow existence, a death in life. From womb to tomb, anguish; from cradle to crypt, tears. Your body, your mind, your soul, cry out for help! You swallow another pill and you say, "Shut up, body. Shut up, mind. Shut up, soul," but they won't shut up: Fungus, decomposed protein, scrofula, disgruntled liver bile wriggle their way into your blood, cripple your anatomy, mutilate your metabolism, causing spaghetti deficiency and crumbling of the T-bone and hysterical uncalled-for laughter.

You want love; do you have it? You yearn for peace; do you have it? Your way of life my friends, your way of life has failed you time and again. Might it not be wise to try another way? My way. The Lalalbagalanshreeoohboogabagiya way. I don't eat. I inhale the light of the sun and the beams of the moon and the breath of the wind. I live on the smell of daffodils. Won't *you* try it? I need fellow crusaders, I need you, my friends with your splendid intellects, the world needs you, your loved ones need you. Won't you help me help you help them? I can't do it alone, my friends, I'm not a reincarnated Joan of Arc or something. I'm just plain folks.

Foodism is cannibalosis. It is vampirism. It is the original sin. Remember Adam and Eve and the apple? They *ate* it, and ever since then things have gone from piller to post. You have learned to live without happiness. And if you hang on long enough . . . you *croak*!

This world of yours, this beautiful, wide, wide world of yours, you have turned it into a vomitorium! You have turned it into a slaughterhouse! You have turned it into a supermarket, a super-morgue for helpless, trusting fellow creatures. The animals and the vegetals! Carnage on the assembly line wherever man sets foot. Billions of good, fat chickens—decapitated and their embryos served sunny-side up. You crush the grape and drink her blood. You lap up the gore of the tomato, the breath of cabbage, the fumes from french fries, the ooze of kidneys sauté hangs heavily over the lands. There is doom in the air and the reek of cooked goose. You eat death; how can you hope to live? Can't you see where we're headed? Have you never considered in the quiet cesspool of your minds where you're going? Hell, my friends, is a hell of a place! It will never freeze over, and it won't be full till you are in it. You betcha, hallelujah!

Thank you for this spontaneous outbreak of deafening applause.

# Lenny Bruce

## **Introduction** by Nat Hentoff

**B**efore Lenny Bruce was well known enough to be busted in New York, San Francisco, Los Angeles, Chicago and other cities, he worked in West Coast clubs featuring strippers.

The jazz bands in those clubs used to disappear when the comic came on. But when Bruce was on the bill, they stayed. They not only enjoyed his barbed points of view, but they also recognized a fellow improviser.

Although Lenny did have scenarios that he repeated, they often changed according to who was in the audience and how he felt at that moment. When he played New York, I would often hear him night after night at the Village Vanguard, and there were always surprises. And he used the microphone as if it were an instrument. He played it, creating his own sound effects.

But his reputation was, of course, based on his serious, indeed nearly obsessive, concern with the lies that are endemic to our political and personal cultures. Thereby, he often surprised and disturbed even listeners who considered themselves hip—and he greatly disturbed district attorneys, the police and professional monitors of "indecent" language.

Although he was destroyed by the rampant censors of his time, he fundamentally changed the nature of comedy. Through the doors that he opened came George Carlin, Chris Rock, Richard Pryor (the only descendant worthy of Lenny's continually challenging stature) and many more. And it wasn't only his expansion and deepening of public language, but also his continuous illumination of what William Burroughs called, "The naked lunch at the end of the fork" that earned him this legacy.

The core of his performance art (and it surely was incandescently creative) was his attack on the Yiddish phrase, *zug gornischt* (say nothing). His perennial target was what he called, "The *zug gornischt* culture." During those years, it was a crime against decency to speak openly and explicitly about sexual pleasure, but Lenny revealed both the angst and the ecstasy of physical love.

Also pervasive in the culture were the rampant, unabashed lies told repeatedly by government officials and religious leaders. Were Lenny alive during the Clinton presidency, he would have been so grateful for such rich material. "What I want people to dig," Lenny said, "is the lie." And certain words were indeed being suppressed to keep those lies working. But, Lenny insisted, "If you *do* them, you should be able to say the words."

An example he loved to use was: "An out-of-town buyer checks into a hotel, goes up to his room, decides he wants a hundred-dollar prostitute. He makes the call. A few minutes later, there's a knock on the door and a bearded writer comes into the room."

Lenny was, to say the least, not "respectable" while he lived. "What *is* respectable?" he would ask. It meant that society continued keeping certain acts, certain fantasies, certain evasions, certain memories, under the covers. "So the crime I committed was pulling the covers off." When someone once called him a comedian, Lenny shook his head, "No, I'm Lenny Bruce. Do comedians get arrested? All the time?"

His timing, his acute sense of vocal dynamics, his facial transformations were all organic parts of his own life—past and present. "You don't know anything about anybody but you," he said. "Just you live in that thing. You always live alone. You're always there, even with your wife. That's why I can't sell out. That is, so long as I stay honest with myself. And that's why I'm somebody different each time out. I keep changing. I'm not bragging about this—but well, it exists, that's all I'm telling you."

An Episcopal minister once sent Lenny a note: "Thanks for caring so much about life."

**Nat Hentoff** is a syndicated columnist for the *Washington Post* and columnist for the *Village Voice*. He is also author of *Free Speech for Me but Not for Thee* (HarperCollins).

# from **How to Talk Dirty and Influence People: An Autobiography of Lenny Bruce**

I bought Aunt Mema a 12-cent jar of Vaseline. She ate it by the ton. She was a Vaseline addict. She would rub it on and stick it in anything and everything. To Mema, carbolated Vaseline was Jewish penicillin.

Perhaps at this point I ought to say a little something about my vocabulary. My conversation, spoken and written, is usually flavored with the jargon of the hipster, the argot of the underworld, and Yiddish.

In the literate sense—as literate as Yiddish can be since it is not a formal language—"goyish" means "gentile." But that's not the way I mean to use it.

To me, if you live in New York or any other big city, you are Jewish. It doesn't matter even if you're Catholic; if you live in New York you're Jewish. If you live in Butte, Montana, you're going to be goyish even if you're Jewish.

Evaporated milk is goyish even if the Jews invented it. Chocolate is Jewish and fudge is goyish. Spam is goyish and rye bread is Jewish.

Negroes are all Jews. Italians are all Jews. Irishmen who have rejected their religion are Jews. Mouths are very Jewish. And bosoms. Baton-twirling is very goyish. Georgie Jessel and Danny Thomas are Christians, because if you look closely on their bodies you'll find a boil somewhere.

To trap an old Jewish woman—they're crafty and they will lie— just seize one and you will find a handkerchief balled-up in one of her hands.

I can understand why we can't have a Jewish president. It would be embarrassing to hear the president's mother screaming love at the grandchildren: "Who's Grandma's baby! Who's Grandma's baby!"

". . . And this is Chet Huntley in New York. The First Lady's mother opened the Macy's Day Parade screaming, *'Oy zeishint mine lieber'* and furiously pinching young Stanley's cheeks . . ."

Actually, she bit his ass, going, "Oom, yum yum, is this a tush, whose tushy is that?" The Jews are notorious children's-ass-kissers. Gentiles neither bite their children's asses nor do they *hahhh* their soup.

Gentiles love their children as much as Jews love theirs; they just don't wear their hearts on their sleeves. On the other hand, Jewish mothers don't hang gold stars in their windows. They're not proud of their boys going into the service. They're always worried about their being killed.

Celebrate is a goyish word. Observe is a Jewish word. Mr. and Mrs. Walsh are *celebrating* Christmas with Major Thomas Moreland, USAF (Ret.), while Mr. and Mrs. Bromberg *observed* Hanukkah with Goldie and Arthur Schindler from Kiamesha, New York.

The difference between Jewish and goyish girls is that a gentile girl won't "touch it once," whereas a Jewish girl will kiss you and let you touch it—your own, that is.

The only Jewish thing about balling is Vaseline.

# Psychopathia Sexualis

Poetry and Jazz:

*(A Jazz band jams in the background, accenting each line of text.)*

Psychopathia Sexualis.
I'm in love with a horse that comes from Dallas.
Poor neurotica me.
When my family found out, they raised the roof
'cause I bought a ring to fit her hoof.
Poor brain, the size of a pea.
She looked so nice against the rail
with her pretty, long legs and her ponytail.
I guess, against convention I'll never win,
I'll probably end up in the loony bin.
But in my heart I'll always be free.
The head shrinker said my societal concept
had been warped by an Oedipus Rex
which caused me to hate the opposite sex.
But what he doesn't know
is that my second wife was a ten-pound goose named Tex.
I'm paranoid and sublimated,
in love with a horse that ain't been spayed-ed.

*(The band pauses.)*

Traumatic scene please let me be.

*(The band resumes playing.)*

I've been hypnotized, tranquilized, analyzed, rationalized;
taken every pill from Secanol to Dexamil.
Sittin' with my wife, neckin' in the dark

and knowing her ex-lovers are running at Hollywood park
can be a bug, I will admit.
But it's all made up when I see her running around the house
in the negligee, brace and bit.
Like most young couples we had our fights
deciding what's fair about her rights.
We finally got adjusted, and I was boss
when I woke one morning, and on our lawn I found a fiery cross!
The Ku Klux Klan said we had to get out that day,
move everything, lock, stock, horse and carriage.
The Klan wouldn't stand for no mixed marriage.
So I'm feeling blue.
Ain't got a penny in my pocket,
we're gonna volunteer for a satellite rocket
so me and her can sit and spoon and visit my first wife
who jumped over the moon.
Poetry, and all that jazz . . .

---

# The Tribunal

I feel some guilts of the fact that my salary exceeds twenty-fold school-teachers' in states like Oklahoma—they get thirty-two hundred dollars a year, which is a *disgrace*, schoolteachers' salaries. Education is the answer to everything. World leadership hinges on education. Take Zsa Zsa Gabor, who gets fifty thousand dollars a *week* in Las Vegas; and schoolteacher's top salary is six thousand dollars a year. This is really sick, to me. That's the kind of "sick" material that I wish *Time* would have written about. I'm not that much of a moralist. If I were, I would be donating my salary, then, to schoolteachers! I admit that.

If the man came to me and said, "Well, we're gonna levy a tax and we're gonna raise schoolteachers' salary to seven hundred and fifty dollars a week," I would approve of it and pay the tax like *that*. 'Cause I realize it's an insurance factor. If schoolteachers get that kind of money, then the education system will change immediately. I'm a hustler: as long as they give, I'll grab.

But I know that someday they're going to have a tribunal. We'll all have to answer, I'm sure of that. I'm just waiting for the day. I'm saving some money to give back: "I know I was stealing. I didn't mean to take it—they gave it to me." We'll all have to answer; they'll line us up. The guy will be in the black shrouds, all the performers.

TRIBUNAL JUDGE: All right, line 'em up, all the offenders there. State their names and their salaries. The sentences will be then meted out. The first offender, what is your name, there?

FIRST OFFENDER: Frankie Laine.

JUDGE: How much do you make a week, Mr. Laine?

FIRST OFFENDER: Ten, twelve thousand dollars a week.

JUDGE: That's remarkable! What do you do to earn from ten to twelve thousand dollars a week?

FIRST OFFENDER *(Sings)*: "To spend one . . ."

JUDGE: Burn his wig. Break his legs, thirty years in jail. Get them up here, the next one. What is your name?

SECOND OFFENDER: Sophie Tucker.

JUDGE: And how much do you make a week, Miss Tucker?

SECOND OFFENDER: Twenty to thirty thousand dollars a week.

JUDGE: What do you do to earn twenty to thirty thousand dollars a week?

SECOND OFFENDER: I'm the last of the red hot . . .

JUDGE: Burn her Jewish records and jellies, and the crepe gowns with the sweat under the arms. Get rid of her! Get them up here, the next one—the one that's worshipping the bronze god of Frank Sinatra. What is your name?

THIRD OFFENDER: Sammy Davis, Jr.

JUDGE: And how much do you make a week, Mr. Junior?

THIRD OFFENDER: Twenty, sometimes thirty thousand dollars a week.

JUDGE: What do you do to earn from twenty to thirty thousand dollars a week?

THIRD OFFENDER *(Imitating Jerry Lewis)*: Hey Dean, I gotta ba . . . *(Sings)* "That old black . . ."

JUDGE: Take away his Jewish star and stocking cap . . . and the religious statue of Elizabeth Taylor. Thirty years in Biloxi.

---

from a 1962 performance at **Off Broadway**

(a club in North Beach, San Francisco)

Are there any niggers here tonight?

"Oh my God, did you hear what he said? 'Are there any *niggers* here tonight?' Is that rank! Is that cruel! Is that a cheap way to get laughs?"

Well, I think I see a nigger at the bar talking to the two guinea owners, and next to them are a couple of wops, one kike, two grease-balls, a squarehead, three gooks, one frog, two limeys, a couple of sheenies, two jigaboos, one hunky, funky boogie—bid 'em up! Bid 'em up! Six more niggers! I pass with two dykes, four kikes and eight niggers!

Now, why have I done this? Is this only for shock value? Well, if all the niggers started calling each other "nigger," not only among themselves, which they do anyway, but among the ofays; if President Kennedy got on television and said, "I'm considering appointing two or three of the top niggers in the country into my cabinet"—if it was nothing but nigger, nigger, nigger—in six months "nigger" wouldn't mean any more than, "Good night," "God bless you" or "I promise to tell the truth, the whole truth and nothing but the truth so help me God." When that beautiful day comes, you'll never see another nigger kid come home from school crying because some ofay motherfucker called him a nigger.

---

# Religions, Inc.

BRUCE: We take you now to the headquarters of Religions Incorporated. And seated around the desk on Madison Avenue sit the religious leaders of our country. Religion, big business. We hear H. A. [Allen] addressing the tight little group on Madison Avenue.

H. A. ALLEN *(In a Southern accent)*: Good evening, Gentlemen. It's nice to see so many boys here tonight. See some religious leaders I haven't seen in many years. I just was talking to Billy [Graham] this afternoon, I said, "Billy, we come a long way, Sweetie, a long way." Who woulda thought back in '31—we were hustling baby pictures then, an' shingles an' siding. We're swinging, you know— we didn't know whatthehell we doin'. The CC camps were starting to move, yeah . . . I didn't know myself, you know? An' jus' like that! We came on it, you know? The Gideon, an BOP! And there we were. Hah!

Uh, the graph here tells the story, that's about it. For the first time in twelve years, Catholicism is up nine points. Judaism's up fifteen and the big "P," the Pentecostal, is starting to move, finally.

And ah, now, Gentlemen, we got Mr. Necktyuh from our religious novelty house in Chicago, who's got a beautiful seller: the genuine Jewish-star-lucky-cross-cigarette-lighter combined. And we got the kiss-me-in-the-dark mezuzah, the walk-me-talk-me-whip-me camel, an' these wonderful, little cocktail napkins with some helluva sayings there: ANOTHER MARTINI FOR MOTHER CABRINI . . . and some pretty far out things, may I say.

Now . . . as you know, there's a lotta religious leaders that we've seen here, boys we don't know; this is the first time we've really united like this—there's about six thousand boys out here from all over the country—and little favors, you know the commissioner promised there'd be no individual hustling, you know? I mean, let's make the scene together because, like, if we burn ourselves, where we gonna end up, ya dig?

Okay, NOW, I wanna introduce—OH, we got Mr. Acton here, a great man, our Seventh Day Adventist, who, on a leading tour of the leper colonies, took some beautiful color slides.

Here IS the greatest holy-roller in America today, a great man an' a great holy-roller, Oral!

ORAL ROBERTS (Shouting): Well, THANK YOU VERY MUCH! AH! Thank you boys; HERE, here boy, have a snake! Gentlemen! Tonight, tonight is THRILL NIGHT. Does thrill night seem to JAR you? Gentlemen, why is it thrill night? Is it thrill night for the teenagers, the Elvis Presleys? No Gentlemen, it's thrill night for me because tonight, for the first time in seven years, I'm talking to men of the industry. For the first time in seven years, Gentlemen, I'm not going to look into one [. . .], sweaty, Lockheed face.* Not one thick redneck! Gentlemen, tonight I stood for the last time in Oakland, I looked for the last time at nineteen-hundred square feet of canvas, I felt the heat of the gas burner on my neck, I looked down at the sawdust, I looked at these people, and I said, "Oral, TONIGHT you're going to be talking to the men." And I said, "What would I talk about?" And it came to me like THAT Gentlemen: the heavenly land and where it is.

Well, Gentlemen. Gentlemen, tonight, WHERE IS THE HEAVENLY LAND? Well I'll tell you one thing, my friends, the heavenly land is NOT in the cheap neighborhood bar; the heavenly land is NOT in a burlesque house; the heavenly land is NOT in dreamland; the heavenly land is NOT on Wall Street.

And you might say to me, "All right! You said it's not on Wall Street, you tell us it's NOT in the cheap neighborhood bar . . ." Gentlemen, did you wonder if tonight, I knew where the heavenly land is? I do my friends. The heavenly land is in one place, and one place only, and do you know where that is? Chevaz Ravine! And them sons of bitches are trying to take it away from us! With that million-dollar land grab and the city planning farmers.

Gentlemen, I know what some of you are thinking out

*When performing, Bruce often changed his texts to suit the time and place. An alternate version of this line is: ". . . you're not going to be facing God's Little Acre, tonight you're not going to be looking into the face of a factory worker, tonight you're not going to be looking at the sawdust."

there. I know what's going . . . I know what's going on in your mind. Some of you gentlemen, who have never seen me before, you're saying *(In a pseudo-BBC-British accent)*, "Oh, this man up there, this modern-day prophet there, look at him ranting and raving. Look at him—he's so smart, he told us where the heavenly land is, how does he know what to do with it when he gets it?"

Well, maybe, Gentlemen, I'm not that smart. Maybe I'm dumb. That's it. The big ole dumbbell up there. Ha-ha-ha. There's the dummy. Why don't you all have a laugh? That's right, laugh at him. HO-HO-HO-HO. There's the dummy. I'm dumb. HA-HA-HA-HA. Yes, I'm dumb. I GOT TWO LINCOLN CONTINENTALS, THAT'S HOW GODDAMN DUMB I AM! I'm dumber than hell. I don't know how much a whole lot of nines are. Now, maybe that's it, Gentlemen, maybe I don't, maybe I don't know everything in the world, maybe I'm stupid *(He trails off)* . . . but if I don't, I got some men on my staff who do.

Tell us now what to do with the heavenly land when we get it, Rabbi Wise!

RABBI WISE *(In a Jewish accent)*: Well thank you very much. I think we should subdivide.

ORAL: That's pretty kooky, Rab, that's ah, pretty far out . . . Now, Gentlemen . . . *(Aside to his assistant Billy)* What's that? What is it?

BILLY: Your long distance call just came in, sir.

ORAL: I'll take it in there. I'll talk to you boys later.

*(Into the phone)* Yes, Operator, this is 610. Yes, I'll take the charges . . . Yeah . . . HELLO JOHNNY! [Pope John XXIII] WHAT'S SHAKING, BABY? . . . Boy it's really been an election month, hasn't it, Sweetie. Well, listen I hate to . . . Yeah, the puff of white smoke knocked me out. We got an eight-page layout with Viceroy: "The New Pope Is a Thinking Man." Yeah. Well, if you want to go for the tattoo, but I figured . . . the hell with it. It would've been too far out. I thought so. Yeah . . . Uh-huh.

Listen, I hate to bug ya, but they're bugging us again with that dumb integration . . . NO, I DUNNO why the hell they want to go to school either . . . Yeah, that school bus scene . . . Well, we had to give them the bus, but there's two toilets on each bus. They're bugging us, they're saying, "Get the religious leaders. Make 'em talk about it . . ." I know it. But they're getting hip . . . Yes. They say . . . No, they don't want no more quotations from the Bible, they want us to come out and SAY things. They want us to say, "LET THEM GO TO SCHOOL WITH THEM . . ." No, I did "walking across the water" and "snake inna cane," too. They don't want to hear that jazz anymore.

And that "stop war" jazz, every time the bomb scare . . . Yeah. They keep saying, "Thou shalt not kill" just means that, and *not* "Amend section A." Yes. They don't want the bomb. Sure they're commies . . . No I ain't getting snotty but we gotta do something. Yeah. I got two . . . yeah, we got some people on our side. We got Scatman Crothers and Stepin Fetchit. It don't do no good.

No, but . . . yes, that's why I called you! What are we gonna do?

*(As the Pope, he starts praying in mock Latin.)*

ORAL: SURE THAT'S EASY FOR YOU TO SAY, YOU'RE OVER THERE! . . . Yeah, I know . . .

And thanks for the pepperoni. *(To Billy)* Billy, you wanna say something to him? *(Again into the phone)* Billy wants to know if you can get him a deal on one of them dago sports cars. a Ferraralouis or some dumb thing.

When you coming to the coast? The valley is hot, but we'll fix it . . . yeah. Yeah, that's cool. Yeah, I can get you the *Sullivan Show* the nineteenth. Yeah, send me some 8 x 10 glossies. Yeah. Just . . . It's a good television show. Just wave, that's all. Wear the big ring. Yeah. The ratings—we can fix that, ha-ha-ha *(He chortles)* I'm sorry . . . all right, I'm cool. *(To Billy)* Billy, Joe says, "Hello." *(Again into the phone)* Yeah. Oh, did you dig [Cardinal] Spellman on *Stars of Jazz*? Yeah, yeah, uh-huh, okay, Sweetie. Yeah, you cool it, too. No, nobody knows you're Jewish.

---

# Father Flotski's Triumph

BRUCE: . . . the prison picture. With Charles Bickford, Barton Maclane, George E. Stone, Frankie Darrow, Warren Hymer, Nat Pendleton and the woman across the bay, Anne Dvorak—and her two hooker friends, Iris Adrian and Glenda Farrell. Cut to the tower, the warden—Hume Cronyn.

PRISON WARDEN *(Harsh, heavy voice, heard over the loudspeaker)*: All right Dutch—this is the warden. You've got eighteen men down there, prison guards who have served me faithfully. Give up, Dutch, and we will meet any reasonable demands you men want—except the vibrators. Forget it, you're not getting them! Dutch! Can you hear me? This is the warden.

DUTCH: Yatta-yatta! Yatta-yatta-yatta-yatta, Warden!

WARDEN: Never mind those Louis Armstrong impressions. Give up! You're a rotten, vicious criminal, a menace to society.

BRUCE: Now the handsome, but mixed-up prison doctor: H. B. Warner.

DOCTOR: Oh, my son . . . my son . . . many years ago, when I knew your father, ehhh . . .

WARDEN: Will you come off that Billy Daniels jazz, you nitwit! Shut up, I'm the warden here—I don't want to kill anybody. Dutch, you punk, you're pushing me too far—you better give up.

DUTCH: Yatta-yatta!

WARDEN: Shut up, you goddamned nut, you! "Yatta-yatta"—I'm sorry I gave him that library card, now. I don't know what the hell to do. Maybe if we just, maybe if we kill a few for an example . . . that may do it. (Over the loudspeaker) Tower C—ya wanna put the cards down for a minute, huh, hm hm hm? That's right. Kill about seven hundred, down there. Go ahead! I said it's all right—now kill 'em! Come on, don't get snotty, you guys! You gonna kill 'em now? The ones in the gray shirts. (Pause) The bullets? Look in the back of my brown slacks. Forget it. Cockamamie prison, here. No one wants to help ya—I'll just . . . hm, I'll kill about sixty with my police special.

FATHER FLOTSKI (With a thick brogue): Wait a moment! Before there's any killing . . . I'll go down there.

WARDEN: Not you, Father Flotski!

FATHER FLOTSKI: Son, I'm going down there!

WARDEN: Will you come off the Pat O'Brien bits, now? Father, you don't understand—these guys are monsters, they're vicious criminals, they've got knives and guns.

FATHER FLOTSKI: Son, you seem to forget, don't you . . . that I've got something stronger than a gun.

WARDEN: You mean? . . .

FATHER FLOTSKI: That's right! Jujitsu. (He does karate chops)

WARDEN: Well, you're making a mistake, Father Flotski.

FATHER FLOTSKI: Son, the mistake is mine to make, and I'm going down there.

BRUCE: Cut to the worst part of the last mile—real Uncle Tom scene—Death Row. The first cell.

BLACK PRISONER (Sings in deep baritone): Hmm, wadduh-boy! Well, well. Soon I gwine up ta heben on de big riberboat. Den when I gets up dere, I gwinna gets me a lotta fried chicken an waddymelone. Fried chicken an waddeymelone, fried chicken an waddeymelone—dat's what I gwinna get when I get up to dat big riberboat in heben, goddamn! Yassuh, boss. You see, you don' min' dyin', boss, if ya got a nach'ral sense of rhythm, yock-yock-yock-yock.

BRUCE: The next cell.

ITALIAN PRISONER: Somebody's gonna get fried tonight . . . *(Sings)* "Tonight, tonight, someone get fried tonight." *(Pause)* "More people using natural gas than ever before . . . tonight . . ."

ANOTHER PRISONER: Shut 'im up! Shut that nut up!

ITALIAN PRISONER *(Sings)*: "Fry somebody tonight . . . they're gonna fry somebody . . ."

ANOTHER PRISONER: Shut 'im up! Shut that nut up!

ITALIAN PRISONER: You won't call me a nut when it's published.

BRUCE: It goes *(Sings)* ". . . fry somebody tonight." Back to the bridge. It's a wild tune. All right. Now the guy is going to the chair—the last mile.

FIFTH PRISONER: So long, Marty. Here's my playin' cards, kid. Here's my mezuzah, Wong. And there's that door! I don't wanna go in there—I don't know what to do, I don't know what to do!

BLACK PRISONER: Don' siddown, massuh!

BRUCE: Back to the yard with Father Flotski.

FATHER FLOTSKI: Hello, Dutch. Dutch, you don't remember Father Flotski, now do ya, Son? You know, Dutch, you know, there's an old story that . . . once a boy goes the bad road, the good road is hard to follow. When the good road is hard to follow, the bad road opens, when the good road closes . . . You're not a bad boy, Dutch. Killing six children doesn't make anybody bad, now. You don't remember, do ya Dutch, that this is Arthur Shields for Swiss Colony Wine?

Now Dutch, I told them up there in the tier that I'd take the gun away from ya, and I'm gonna do it, Dutch. Now come on—there he's going to give it to me. Come on, Dutch, give me that gun, now. *(Sotto voce)* Come on, Dutch! Don't be a schmuck and give me the gun . . . give me that gun there . . .

DUTCH: Yatta-yatta. Yatta-yatta, Father!

FATHER FLOTSKI *(Incredulous)*: You're right—he's a goddamn nut! Tried to give me all that Rosicrucian jazz, and all those other nonscheduled theologies, there. They're no good, the lot of them. Pour it in.

WARDEN: You men—the prison guards. I know this smacks of an insalubrious deed. I've got a job to do. The pension I'm not going to screw up. I know it's cold, guys, but what the hell, you know what this gig is—it's dog-eat-dog. You knew what the gig was when you took it. Only hope that your old ladies swung with Mutual of Omaha. Dutch, you've got three seconds—three big ones. You gonna listen to anybody?

DUTCH: I'mma lissenna nobody! I'm not listenin' to nobody in this whole stinkin' prison, Warden—nobody!

KINKY *(High, effeminate voice, over loudspeaker)*: Dutch, listen to me, *Bubby*.

DUTCH: Who is that?

KINKY: It'th Kinky, the hothpital attendant—the one who gave you the bed baths. Give up, *Bubby*, don't screw up your good time.

DUTCH: Kinky, you *nafke* [whore], you. Kinky, Baby, I'll give it all up for you.

KINKY: Did you hear that? Ooooh! He's giving it up for me. I feel just like Wally Simpson. I don't believe it—he's giving it all up for *me*! Did you hear that, you bitches in cell block eleven? Ooooh—my nerves! He's giving it up for me. Did you hear him, Warden?

WARDEN: I heard him, ya fruit.

KINKY: Watch it, Warden—don't overstep your bounds, now. Are we going to get all our demands?

WARDEN: Whaddaya want?

KINKY: A gay bar in the west wing.

WARDEN *(Yiddish inflection)*: Awright, you'll get it. What else?

KINKY: I wanna be the Avon representative of the prison.

## Introduction by Marilyn French

In the fall of 1985, something new happened in the cultural life of America, something that should hearten and encourage every person who believes this nation needs humane redirection: a show opened on Broadway starring Lily Tomlin, written by Jane Wagner, and called *The Search for Signs of Intelligent Life in the Universe*. Whoa! you say, how can a Broadway show matter that much?

Lily Tomlin first made her reputation on television. Millions of people are familiar with the characters she created on the comedy series *Laugh-In* and followed her and her longtime collaborator Jane Wagner as they expanded Tomlin's comic repertory in Emmy Award-winning television specials and an earlier Broadway show, *Appearing Nitely*, which won a Tony.

*Signs of Intelligent Life* [which also won a Tony Award] focuses on female—one might well say *human*—experience of society. It looks at a world that is pervaded by the drive to power, but it is also a hilarious critique of our society, so accurate and humane that Frank Rich of the *New York Times* called it, "The most genuinely subversive comedy to be produced on Broadway in years." One man's subversive is another's (woman or man) truth: what is most extraordinary about the Tomlin/Wagner show is the degree of truth about American society that it dares to present on a public stage to an audience educated by the artificial sunshine and artificial violence of most television and movies.

The major narrator of the performance is Trudy, a bag lady who has been "certified" mad, but whose madness is really a perception of society from the underside, the kind of seeing that Socrates called "a divine release of the soul from the yoke of custom and convention." Trudy's voice and face appear, then vanish as other characters appear—Chrissy, a young woman who lacks direction and spends hours in a health club (sometimes with a male counterpart); Kate, a wealthy woman suffering from "affluenza" ("a bored species cannot survive"); Agnus Angst, an unhappy punk adolescent who tries to use Gordon Liddy's book *Will* as a guide to life; and an entire community of friends who have been together throughout the feminist movement and who are unsure of what to do now. Tomlin moves from one role to another swiftly, unerringly, and brilliantly characterizes each of these figures. We always know who is speaking, yet she does not depend on facile mannerisms, props or costumes to distinguish them. She *moves into* them, she becomes her characters from the inside.

The point of view of the show is actually from the lowest social stratum in American society. This is intentional. Tomlin and Wagner both came from rural Southern families, although Tomlin was raised in Detroit, in a blue-collar neighborhood, among people who, she feels, did not recognize the degree to which their suffering was caused by a system rather than by each other, that "the system" was only a system, and not the very law of nature. But compassion is handled lightly in *Signs of Intelligent Life*—Wagner's script is unsentimental. Nor does it deal out blame for the social problems it addresses. Instead it focuses on our anxiety and on our dangerous tendency to harden ourselves. *Signs of Intelligent Life* is the first work I know of that simply takes it as a given that a mass audience will accept feminist attitudes, that proceeds on the assumption that these attitudes are shared and that therefore does not lecture, hector or even underline.

Underlying the gentle laughter (a Tomlin/Wagner hallmark) is the convention that we all have some power to alter the course of our world as well as our own lives. And that message is received by the audience. The atmosphere of the theatre is intense, magnetized; the roar afterward conveys the feeling that people were starving for truth in art and have finally been fed it and know it.

The show concludes with Trudy musing about mysteries—among them the catharsis that results from people who are "strangers, sitting together in the dark," watching truth enacted before them; "laughing and crying . . ." in the theatre, our small isolated lives, our quiet perceptions can be joined, can merge together in an ecstatic rush that alleviates our loneliness and helps to give direction, a moral perspective to our lives.

**Marilyn French** is a noted feminist and writer. She is author of several books including *The Women's Room* (Ballantine Books), *War Against Women* (Ballantine Books), *My Summer with George* (Knopf) and a personal memoir, *A Season in Hell* (Knopf).

# from **The Search for Signs of Intelligent Life in the Universe**

Written by Jane Wagner; performed by Lily Tomlin.

## Trudy

Here we are, standing on the corner of "Walk, Don't Walk."
You look away from me, tryin' not to catch my eye,
but you didn't turn fast enough, *did* you?
You don't like my *raspy* voice, do you?
I got this *rasp*y voice 'cause I have to yell all the time
'cause nobody around here ever LISTENS to me.
You don't like that I scratch so much; yes, and excuse me,
I scratch so much 'cause my neurons are on *fire*.
And I admit my smile is not at its Pepsodent best 'cause
I think my caps must've somehow got osteo*porosis*.
And if my eyes seem to be twirling around like fruit flies—
the better to see you with, my dears!
*Look* at me, you mammalian-brained LUNKHEADS!
I'm not just talking to myself. I'm talking to you, too.
And to you
and you
and you
and you and you and you!
I know what you're thinkin'; you're thinkin' I'm crazy.
You think I give a hoot? You people look at my shopping bags,
call me crazy 'cause I save this junk. What should we call the ones who
   *buy* it?
It's my belief we all, at one time or another, secretly ask ourselves the
   question, "Am *I* crazy?"
In my case, the answer comes back: a resounding YES!
You're thinkin': how does a person know if they're crazy or not?
Well, sometimes you don't know.
Sometimes you can go through life suspecting you *are* but never really
   knowing for sure.
Sometimes you know for sure 'cause you got so many people tellin' you
   you're crazy
that it's your word against everyone else's.
Another sign is when you see life so clear sometimes you black out.
This is your typical visionary variety who has flashes of insight
but can't get anyone to listen to 'em 'cause their insights make 'em
   sound so *crazy*!

In my case, the symptoms are subtle but unmistakable to the trained eye.
For instance, here I am, standing at the corner of "Walk, Don't Walk,"
waiting for these aliens from outer space to show up.
I call that crazy, don't you?
If I were sane, I should be waiting for the light like everybody else.
They're late as usual.
You'd think, as much as they know about time travel, they could be on
time *once* in a while.
I could kick myself.
I told 'em I'd meet 'em on the corner of "Walk, Don't Walk" 'round
lunchtime.
Do they even know what "lunch" means? I doubt it.
And "'round." Why did I say "'round"? Why wasn't I more specific?
This is so typical of what I do.
Now they're probably stuck somewhere in time,
wondering what I meant by "'round lunchtime."
And when they get here, they'll be dying to know what "lunchtime" means.
And when they find out it means going to Howard Johnson's for fried
clams, I wonder, will they be just a bit let down?
I dread having to explain tartar sauce.
This problem of time just points out how far apart we really are.
See, our ideas about time and space are different from theirs.
When we think of time, we tend to think of clock radios, coffee breaks,
afternoon naps, leisure time, halftime activities, parole time, doing
time, Minute Rice, instant tea, mid-life crises, that time of the month,
cocktail hour.
And if I should suddenly mention *space*—aha! I bet most of you thought
of your closets.
But when they think of time and space, they really think of Time and Space.
They asked me once my thoughts on infinity and I told 'em with all I had
to think about, infinity was not on my list of things to think about.
It could be time on an ego trip, for all I know.
After all, when you're pressed for time, infinity may as well not be there.
They said, to them, infinity is time-released time.
Frankly, infinity doesn't affect me personally one way or the other.
You think too long about infinity, you could go stark raving mad.
But I don't ever want to sound negative about going crazy.
I don't want to overromaticize it either, but frankly,
goin' crazy was the *best* thing ever happened to me.
I don't say it's for everybody; some people couldn't cope.
But for me it came at a time when nothing else seemed to be working.
I got the kind of madness Socrates talked about,
"A divine release of the soul from the yoke of custom and convention."

I refuse to be intimidated by reality anymore.

After all, what is reality anyway? Nothin' but a collective hunch.

My space chums think reality was once a primitive method of crowd control that got out of hand.

In my view, it's absurdity dressed up in a three-piece business suit.

I made some studies,

and reality is the leading cause of stress amongst those in touch with it.

I can take it in small doses, but as a lifestyle I found it was too confining.

It was just too needful; it expected me to be there for it *all* the time,

and with all I have to do—I had to let something go.

Now, since I put reality on a back burner, my days are jam-packed and fun-filled.

Like some days, I go hang out around Seventh Avenue; I love to do this old joke:

I wait for some music-loving tourist from one of the hotels on Central Park to go up and ask someone, "How do I get to Carnegie Hall?"

Then I run up and yell, "Practice!"

The expression on people's faces is priceless,

I never could've done stuff like that when I was in my *right* mind.

I'd be worried people would think I was *crazy*.

When I think of the fun I missed, I try not to be bitter.

See, the human mind is kind of like . . . a piñata.

When it breaks open, there's a lot of surprises inside.

Once you get the piñata perspective,

you see that losing your mind can be a peak experience.

I was not always a bag lady, you know.

I used to be a designer and a creative consultant. For big companies!

Who do you think thought up the color scheme for Howard Johnson's?

At the time, nobody was using orange and aqua in the same room together.

With fried clams.

Laugh tracks: *I* gave TV sitcoms the idea for canned laughter.

I got the idea, one day I heard voices and no one was there.

Who do you think had the idea to package panty hose in a plastic goose egg?

One thing I personally don't like about panty hose:

When you roll 'em down to the ankles the way I like 'em, you can't walk too good.

People seem amused, so what's a little loss of dignity? You got to admit: It's a look!

The only idea I'm proud of—

my umbrella hat. Protects against sunstroke, rain and muggers.

For *some* reason, muggers steer clear of people wearing umbrella hats.

So it should come as no shock . . . I am now creative consultant to these aliens from outer space. They're a kinda cosmic fact-finding committee.

Amongst other projects, they've been searching all over for Signs of Intelligent Life.

It's a lot trickier than it sounds.

We're collecting all kinds of data about life here on Earth.

We're determined to figure out, once and for all, just what the hell it all means.

I write the data on these Post-its and then we study it.

Don't worry, before I took the consulting job, I gave 'em my whole psychohistory.

I told 'em what drove *me* crazy was my *last* creative consultant job,

with the Ritz Cracker mogul, Mr. Nabisco.

It was my job to come up with snack inspirations to increase sales.

I got this idea to give Cracker Consciousness to the entire planet.

I said, "Mr. Nabisco, sir! You could be the first to sell the concept of munching to the Third World. We got an untapped market here! These countries got millions and millions of people don't even know where their next *meal* is *coming* from. So the idea of eatin' *between* meals is somethin' just never occurred to 'em!"

I heard myself sayin' *this*!

Must've been when I went off the deep end. I woke up in the nuthouse.

They were hookin' me up.

One thing they don't tell you about shock treatments,

for months afterward you got flyaway hair.

And it used to *be* my best feature.

See, those shock treatments gave me new electrical circuitry

(frankly, I think one of the doctors' hands must've been wet).

I started having these time-space continuum shifts, I guess you'd call it.

Suddenly, it was like my central nervous system had a patio addition out back.

Not only do I have a linkup to extraterrestrial channels.

I also got a hookup with humanity as a whole. Animals and plants, too.

I used to talk to plants all the time; then, one day, they started talking back.

They said, "Trudy, shut up!"

## Agnus Angst

Hello, Charlotte, listen, it is *vital* I stay over at your house tonight!

Don't ask me to explain.

You've got to make your mom let me stay over!

Can't you force her to say yes?

Look, my parents think you're a bad influence on *me, too.*

Just for that, you can't run the equipment at my gig tonight.

You are out of my life, Charlotte; you are *her*story. You are the "crumb de la crumb."

Drop off my tape at the Un-Club, or I'll sue you for all you're worth.

It is vital, Charlotte.

Don't you eyeball me, you *speck*! Can't you see I am USING this PHONE!!

And don't you *touch* that cage.

That's my parakeet in there.

Hello?

Look, it's vital I talk to the radio shrink. My name's Agnus.

I'm fifteen. My *parents* locked me out of the house today.

I want to find out if that is *legal.*

I'm in the ladies' room, House of Pancakes.

I can't wait long.

Hello? Is this Dr. Kassorla, the psychologist?

Look, Doctor, for years I've been going home after school, nobody would be there—

I'd take my key from around my neck and let myself in.

But today I go home, I put my key in the door . . .

THEY CHANGED THE LOCKS ON ME!

Yeah, maybe it *was* something I did. I didn't say I was innocent.

Whatever I do is wrong, anyway. Like, last night, my stepmom,

she accuses me of leaving dirty fingerprints on the *cheese.*

Even getting an innocent piece of cheese becomes a criminal act.

But the problem goes deeper: my real mother's not around much right now.

She's in Europe, Germany or someplace, doing her art thing.

She's a performance artist. Like me.

There was this big custody beef, see, 'cause my real mother's a lesbian.

So the *court* gave me to my dad.

He's a gene-splicer, a bio-businessman at this research lab of *mis*applied science.

Where he's working on some new bio-form he thinks he'll be able to patent.

He doesn't get that *I* am a new bio-form.

I AM USING THIS PHONE!! You IHOP speck!

So today I go by my dad's lab, to get some money for some gear for my act,

and I see this glob of bio-plasm quivering there in this petri dish.

I don't know why I did it.

Maybe it was sibling rivalry.

But I leaned over and I spit into it.

And of course, my dad had a MAD SCIENTIST ALERT!

He says I've ruined years of research.

The truth is he loves that *bio-form* more than *me*.

Yeah, I thought of calling the hot line for runaways,

but I'm worried maybe they don't take throwaways like me.

I have other family, my grandparents, but we have nothing in common,
    except that we are all carbon-based life forms.

What?

A commercial?

I can't believe you're brushing me off.

To sell some product that probably killed some poor *lab rat*.

*You've been about as helpful as an acid* FLASHBACK!

*Hey, where's my parakeet? Conway Tweety!*

THAT CREEP! STOLE MY PARAKEET!

Hey, you IHOP specks, you *must* have seen somebody leave with a cage.

You all saw me come in with one.

Don't you stare at me with those *blueberry syrup mustaches*!


## Lud and Marie

LUD: Talkin' about vibrators that way! The things you see on TV these days. What kind of crazy world do we live in?

MARIE: Lud, who was it said . . . ? That quote about, oh, you know . . . What was that quote? Do you remember, Lud?

LUD: Did you just hear what you said, Marie?

MARIE: I reckon so. I just said it . . . What?

LUD: You were about to say somethin' *some*body said—you couldn't think who said it or what it was they said.

MARIE: And that never happens to you, I suppose. That never happens to him, does it, Fluffy?

LUD: Well, if I couldn't think who it was said somethin', or what it was they said, I simply would not bring up the subject, Marie. I'd simply keep my mouth shut. Somethin' I wish *you'd* consider more often.

MARIE: I *used* to *tolerate* that kind of talk, because I told myself it was your hernia made you act so *hateful*. I have let you walk all over me. Janet used to beg me, she'd say, "*Mama*, please join a consciousness-raising group." I'd say, "Honey, what on earth would I do at a consciousness-raising group?" I missed out on it like I did everything else.

LUD: You know what your problem is, Marie?

MARIE: Yes. You!

LUD: You can't concentrate. You've got a brain like a hummingbird . . . Makes you appear dense and at the same time flighty. Did you ever see a hummingbird try to make up its mind which flower to land on? Well, picture your brain in place of that *bird* and you have a clue as to what I have to put up with. Some people have hare brains, some people have pea brains. And some people . . .

MARIE: . . . have the brains of a male chauvinist pig! Oink! Oink! Oink! Oink! Oink!

LUD: Now who's bein' hateful? Shh! What was that sound just then? Sounds like the garage door flapped up! Well, give me them damn glasses. I see somethin' glowing out there. Somethin's comin' up the driveway . . . I never seen anything like it.

AGNUS: *Granddaddy Speck* . . . LET! ME! IN!

LUD: Agnus! Turn that junk music *down*! You better learn some manners, young lady, or else . . .

AGNUS: Or else WHAT, Granddaddy Speck?

MARIE: Or else people aren't gonna *like* you, Honey. You do want to be *liked*, don't you, Honey? Everybody wants to be liked.

AGNUS: *NOT ME! I'M DIF-FER-ENT!*

LUD: Well, I can't argue with that.

MARIE: Lud, do you realize that nothing has turned out the way we planned it? Not our retirement plan. Not those Astroturf neckties. "Gonna be such a hit with sports fans, at half time." Not that cedar closet you built with *artificial* cedar. The moths just laughed. Not our patio addition out back, not our daughter, and now not our granddaughter. There's not one thing that panned out right.

LUD: You know what your problem is, Marie? Too negative. You're negative *about* ninety-two percent of the time.

MARIE: Yes, and *about* ninety-two percent of the time I am *dead* right.

LUD: Oh, hell, if you're so damn right all the time, how come we have a daughter we don't understand too good, and a pink-haired punk granddaughter got the manners of a terrorist? Leaves dirty fingerprints on the cheese? Wears somethin' makes the garage door flap up?

Old man Sanders stopped me today; says he saw somethin' odd-lookin' in the yard—says it was downright eerie! Worried we might have poltergeists. I had to say, "No, that wasn't no poltergeist, that was my granddaughter. She glows in the dark 'cause her necklace is a reflective flea collar." How do you think that makes me feel?

MARIE: Well, how do you think that makes *me* feel? Oh, Lud! Why didn't you just go and let him think it was poltergeists? Well, speak of the devil! Agnus, I demand to know where you are going at this time of night looking like that!

AGNUS: YOU! WOULDN'T! WANT TO KNOW!

LUD: Young lady, you tell me where you're going or you can march that little Day-Glo fanny back in that bedroom and stay there till the paddy wagon comes.

AGNUS: I'm going to a gig, okay? DON'T WAIT UP!!

MARIE: Lud, look! She has taken the candle out of my good centerpiece. I can't keep anything nice.

LUD: Well, come on to bed. You been stopped over that sewing, got eyes like two cherry tomatoes.

MARIE: You go on to bed. I'm gonna sit up here till she gets back. Lud . . . Remember when she was little? She'd stay over. I'd make chocolate milk, and I'd make me a little milk mustache, and pretend I didn't notice, and then you'd make one and there we'd be—the two of us with little chocolate milk mustaches. Used to just tickle her to death. You know, she's had a lot to deal with in her short lifetime.

LUD: Oh, hell. I've had *more* to deal with in my *long* lifetime. I don't take it out on the world.

MARIE: No, you take it out on *me*. I called today—her daddy says they've tried *everything* to get through to her. They've washed their hands. It's in our laps now.

LUD: Well, I bet they haven't tried little milk mustaches. I'll shut that garage door. When she comes in, we'll hear it flap up. We'll get up. Have some chocolate milk. You and me make little milk mustaches, see if she remembers.

# Andy Kaufman

**Introduction** by Steve Bodow

At the end of his legendary 1979 Carnegie Hall concert, Andy Kaufman invited his audience out for milk and cookies. It seemed like a gag. But when the crowd filed out to 57th Street, there was a fleet of school buses waiting to transport them to a school cafeteria and hundreds of chocolate chip cookies and half-pint cartons of milk. Once everyone had their snack in hand, Andy thanked them again for coming to his concert. And, he added, "The show will continue tomorrow at one o'clock on the Staten Island Ferry."

A woman asked with great sincerity, "Are you joking, Andy?" "I think he's serious . . ." muttered her bemused companion—correctly. It's a true story, and also a parable for the central paradox of Andy Kaufman's performing life: he made it virtually impossible to distinguish between his performing and his life.

Certainly there were official performances: Andy in nightclubs doing standup (declaring: "I'm not a comic, I never told a joke in my life."), on a hit sitcom, in the ring as a misogynist, semiprofessional wrestler (". . . You do understand, don't you? That guy who knocks women around comes from me, but he's not me.") A lot of Andy's appeal was that his audiences never knew what weird shit he was going to pull next. When he died in 1984 at age thirty-five, many dismissed the obit as just another gag.

Typically, Andy's Carnegie Hall show was mostly a put-on, or more precisely a performance about put-ons. He started the evening with Tony Clifton, the brusque, remarkably untalented Vegas lounge singer whom Andy always insisted was not a Kaufman character, but a real person—despite ample evidence to the contrary. Then came Foreign Man, the wide-eyed immigrant who did what might be best described as anti-standup, telling English-impaired one-liners that weren't merely unfunny, they weren't jokes. Yet, even this utterly incompetent guy could mimic standup's raw, hackneyed structure. It was a killer critique of nightclub comedy at a time when the form was starting to grow creaky. It was also, of course, hilarious.

Sometimes, Andy told how, as a TV-enraptured child, he watched the *Howdy Doody Show* live in the studio. From the "Peanut Gallery" he saw with his own eyes that the whole thing was faked—for a performer, a primal scene. When he grew up and went into show business himself, his approach mixed adoration with vengeance. He was somehow driven to expose the lie of show business—its utter artificiality—all the while showing how entertaining that artifice could be.

What was perhaps most incredible about Andy wasn't the content of his work. From reading aloud the entire text of *The Great Gatsby* to doing his laundry on stage, his stunts were often akin to the boundary-busting performances that the Duchamp-inspired art movement Fluxus had put across fifteen years earlier. But Andy was somehow able to take it mainstream. Hollywood embraced him. Paying customers lined up to see him. In the belly of the show-biz beast, he was a small triumph of conceptual art.

The ideas that Andy first explored in clubs and concerts he later brought to a much wider audience via television. Most people got to know Andy through his work on *Taxi* (his Latka Gravas character, a bumbling, immigrant car mechanic, was based directly on Foreign Man). But his edgiest TV work was almost all broadcast on NBC's *Saturday Night Live* and on ABC's *Fridays* as live performance.

Andy's material for live TV played on the audience's well-founded expectation that network entertainment would be slick and predictable. A 1981 episode of *Fridays* stands out as being anything but. In seeming protest of a lamely written sketch, Andy literally stopped the live show—much to the surprise of some of his fellow actors, who were trapped in front of a national audience with nothing to do. For those of us watching at home, it was genuinely jarring.

That was Andy's great trick: by keeping his audience guessing ceaselessly as to what about him and his act was real and what wasn't, he reinvented the enchantment that entertainment was once able to provide, back before everyone became wise to its tricks. At first glance, it may have looked like Andy was cynically trying to kill the magic of performance. In fact, he spent his life resurrecting it.

**Steve Bodow** is a writer and Co-Artistic Director of Elevator Repair Service, a New York-based theatre company.

ANNOUNCER *(Over the P.A.)*: Ladies and Gentlemen, would you please all stand for the "National Anthem" as sung to you by Mr. Tony Clifton.

*(Kaufman enters dressed as Tony Clifton—a classic lounge singer with Brooklyn accent. He wears a pink leisure jacket, ruffled tuxedo shirt, dark glasses, a slight, black mustache and a bad toupee—he smokes a cigarette throughout his act. Clifton sings the "National Anthem" in an exaggerated, slow tempo while, in the background, images of revolution-era women sewing the American flag and a swinging Liberty Bell flicker on a movie screen. As Clifton finishes the song, we see the image of a proudly unfurled American flag waving on the screen.)*

TONY CLIFTON: Thank you. You can all sit down now. You can all sit down now. Thank you very much. You can all sit. You can all sit.

> A smile in the night,
> A sigh in the night,
> A smile across a room of strangers.
> A tug of the shirt sleeves in the middle of a sad movie,
> This is a wife.
> She's the tilt of a pretty head as she passes a hallway mirror.
> She's a flounce out of a room when she's peeved about something.
> This . . . is a wife.
> She's a smile across a room of strangers.
> She's a pair of waiting arms for a weary warrior.
> She repairs frayed banners torn on daily battlefields.
> She cushions defeats and makes victories worthwhile.
> This is a wife. *(He takes a long drag on his cigarette and pauses)*
> A wife, a wife is a . . . unpredictable creature.
> She can remember a rose placed in her hand twenty-five years ago,
>     but she can't even recall if she left a note for the milkman.
> She's magic with a dish towel in her hands,
> Romance running a vacuum cleaner,
> Charm with a smudge of cake dough on her nose.
> Wives look beautiful in the oddest places,
> Like standing in a doorway,
> Or balancing on a shaky ladder painting a room,
> Or bending over a sofa rearranging a pillow,
> Or standing on her toes while reaching high on a shelf,
> Or waiting in the rain for the husband to open a car door.
> Wives are expensive luxuries and they're worth every dollar
>     and kiss they cost.

An apologetic smile when the checkbook doesn't balance.

A frown when a husband is late for dinner . . .

Contentment when a day's work is done and night falls and all, every member of the family is safe under the roof of a happy home.

This *(He pauses and nods his head)* is a wife.

Okay. Want to hear another one? Wanna hear more? *(He calls off-stage)* Okay. Is it all right? Do I have time to do more? What are you talking about? *(To the audience)* They told me I should come out here to sing the "National Anthem," but I thought I'd say a few words to you. Incidentally, ah, incidentally, *(He holds up the medallion he is wearing)* if you haven't seen this already, I'd like to just mention before I go, that ah, this is the original Tony Clifton medallion. You can buy these. There's a very limited supply so that, for t-two d-dollars and fifty cents each, they'll be selling 'em at the next intermission out in the lobby. So, ah, I suggest you buy one because you won't be able to get these in the stores. You won't be able to get these on the streets after tonight. You could say to your people, you could say, "I got this at the Carnegie Hall Concert, original Tony Clifton medallion . . ." Take it home to your sweetheart.

All right, *(He calls offstage)* how much time do I have? *(To the audience)* I want to talk to you about sumpin'. You know being a mother-in-law is, is, is not, it's, is just . . . difficult tasks in the world. *(He calls offstage)* What? *(To the audience)* The mother-in-law— *(To offstage)* All right. Okay, I'm just asked to leave. *(To the offstage stagehands)* I'm gonna, gonna get, I'm gonna get offstage. Okay, but wait a minute. All right, all right. Don't be, just don't be . . . Don't get so excited here. *(To the house-right balcony)* Ah, hey, how you doing up there? How's the, how's the weather up there? How's the weather up there? It must be, it's, ah, is it cold or hot?

*(The audience in the balcony responds: "Cold.")*

Eh, it's cold up there? Eh, it's cold. Well *(To the audience in the orchestra)*, how's the weather down there?

*(They respond: "Hot.")*

Hot. How's the weather up there?

*(They respond: "Cold.")*

Cold. Everybody say cold . . . Say cold *(He wraps his arms around himself and simulates shivering)*, brrrr, cold, brrrr, cold. *(He laughs menacingly)*

Okay, well, thank you very much. I'm, I'm very glad to be out here to, to open the show for Kaufman at Carnegie Hall. Without much further ado, I'd like to do my closing number for you right now. Ah, let's, let's take it away boys. *(The band begins to play* "Carolina in the Morning." *Clifton sings in a tinny voice)*

Nothing could be finer than to be in Carolina in the mo-o-orning.

Thank you very much, thank you.

*(He continues singing:)*

No one could be sweeter than my sweetie when I need her in the mo-o-orning.
If I had a [ . . . ] for only a day, I'd make her hear what she'd say.
Nothing could be finer than to be in Carolina in the mo-o-orning.

Okay, take it away boys.

*(The band plays while Clifton does a soft shoe.)*

Look, I'm dancing, I'm dancing. *(He continues to tap-dance and then stops)* Okay, thank you very much everybody. Good night, thank you.

*(He bows, starts off, stops and does a bit more tapping. A stagehand enters and crosses to the microphone.)*

STAGEHAND: Mr. Tony Clifton, thank you. Mr. Tony Clifton.

*(Clifton grabs the microphone from the stagehand and resumes singing. He refuses to leave the stage. The stagehand exits. The band stops playing.)*

CLIFTON: Thank you very much. Good night, thank you.

———

*Andy, in a plaid jacket, stands center stage at a microphone stand. He begins to speak in an unidentifiable "foreign" accent.*

Ladies and Gentlemen, so far everything I have done for you tonight, really I am only fooling. This is really me. And everything else was just a character I was doing for you. But, I want to say, I am very happy to be here in New York. It's a very beautiful place. But, what I don't like is too much traffic! You know, tonight I had to come in from Long Island on the Long Island Expressway . . . Thank you very much. And, I was on the highway, and it was so much traffic, it took me an hour and a half to get here. *(Long pause as Andy waits for laughter that never comes)*

But, talking about terrible things. My wife. Take my wife, please take her. Really, I am only fooling. I love my wife very much. But, she don't know how to cook. You know, one night she make steak and

Andy Kaufman

mashed potato and the night before she make spaghetti and meatballs. Her cooking is so bad . . .

*(The audience shouts: "How bad is it?" Andy steps back from the microphone, seemingly intimidated. He wipes his brow and paces back and forth. Finally, he returns to the microphone.)*

Her cooking is so bad . . .

*(Audience shouts again: "How bad is it?")*

It's terrible!

But, I would like to tell you the story of two penguins who were on a piece of ice. And one day . . . Two penguins were on a piece of ice and one day the ice broke in half. So, the two penguins, they are very crying, you know, "We will never see each other again." But, one day they see each other again. So, they get closer and closer to each other and finally, one of them say . . . something which was very funny, but I don't remember what it was.

But, right now I would like to do for you some imitations. So, first . . . Thank you very much. First, I would like to do the Archie Bunker *(Andy turns around and then turns back and grabs the microphone. Attempting a new voice, but not succeeding)* "You stupid. Everybody stupid. You, Meathead, get out of my chair! You, Dingbat, go in the kitchen and make me the food!" Thank you very much. *(Andy bows)*

Now, I would like to do, to do the Ed Sullivan.

*(Andy turns around. He turns back, hunches up his shoulders, purses his lips and wobbles his head. The audience laughs. Andy drops this pose.)*

No, no, no, wait until I give you the punch. Wait. Now I have to start all over again; I lose my place.

You know, I am very happy to be here, but one thing I don't like is too much traffic. Tonight, it was so much traffic, it took me an hour and a half to get here. But, my wife, she don't know how to cook. Her cooking is so bad . . .

*(Audience responds again: "How bad is it?" Andy steps back, wipes his brow and paces. He steps back to the microphone.)*

It's so bad, it's terrible.

But, right now, I would like to do for you the Ed Sullivan. *(Andy scrunches up his shoulders, purses his lips, wobbles his head and wipes the front of his shirt. In a new voice)* "Ladies and Gentlemum. Tonight, on the big stage . . . (Andy gestures to stage right to indicate the "big stage")* We have a rrrreally big show. So, come to see the rrrreally big show. Thank you very much." *(Andy drops the voice and pose)* Thank you very much. *(He bows)*

Now, last, but not the least, I would like to do for you the Elvis Presley.

*(Andy turns around, walks upstage and takes off his jacket. The band begins to play an Elvis tune. He places his jacket in a suitcase upstage and takes off his T-shirt revealing a black shirt underneath. Andy puts on a white and gold lamé jacket, combs back his hair and straps on a guitar. He looks over his shoulder, sneers at the audience and addresses them in his "Elvis" voice.)*

"Thank you very much."

*(Andy proceeds to play the guitar, gyrate and sing in an almost perfect Elvis impression. As Elvis, he removes his jacket and hands it to an audience member. He removes his shirt and rubs it under his arms before throwing it to someone in the audience. Andy is now in a T-shirt on which is printed "I love Grandma." He speaks again in the foreign-man voice:)*

"Thank you very much."

*(In his own voice)* Ladies and Gentlemen, right now, may I have my clothes back.

*(Andy gathers up his clothes from the audience and returns them to the upstage suitcase. He crosses back to the microphone.)*

Ladies and Gentlemen, you've been a beautiful audience. I'd like to sing you this song I . . . 'specially for you. *(He signals to the band to begin playing)* Yep, it's a friendly world. You know, we should all treat each other like brothers and sisters. So, everybody turn to the person sitting next to you and say, "Hi, Brother *(He waves)* hi, Sister." *(He waves again)* Very good. And now, everybody put your arm around the person sitting next to you and sway back and forth in rhythm to the music. Come on everybody. Come on. Come on, even if you don't like the person sitting next to you. Come on, everybody swing back and forth and sing, "The world is a wonderful place." Come on, everybody sing. It's fun, come on. *(He sings)*

"Oh, the world is such a wonderful place." *(He feeds the audience each line before they sing it)*

> Oh the world is such a wonderful place to wander through
> When you have someone to love to wander along with you.
> With the sky so full of stars and the river so full of song.
> Every heart should be so thankful.
> Thankful for this friendly, friendly world.

Okay, you want to sing it again? Okay, okay. One more time. Come on everybody, come on. "Oh . . ." come on sing. "Oh . . ." come on everybody. "Oh . . ." come on, I don't hear everybody. "Oh . . ." Okay, we can't stop till everybody sings . . . "Oh, thankful for this friendly, friendly world." Thank you very much and good night. Thank you.

## **Introduction** by Joe E. Jeffreys

"I wanted to play the great roles but who would cast me as Medea?" Ethyl Eichelberger pondered during an interview late in his life. A gangly, six-foot-two-inch, Midwestern boy, the answer to his rhetorical question was, of course, few. Undeterred, Eichelberger devoted his life and substantial talents to creating for himself the great female (and later male) roles of history and drama. His drive and talent coupled with the burgeoning East Village scene of the early 1980s assured that rarely did a night pass in New York City during that decade when Ethyl Eichelberger could not be found on a stage somewhere spinning one of his mini-epics. Through late-night performances on the tiny, clip-lit stages at bars such as the Club 57, the Pyramid Club, Club Chandelier, King Tut's Wah-Wah Hut and 8 B.C., and at more established performance venues such as Performance Space 122, Dixon Place, La MaMa E.T.C. and The Performing Garage, he paraded his constellation of grande dames on any space that might pass as a stage. During a volatile artistic moment bracketed by disco and AIDS, Eichelberger's high-octane stage presence, outrageous screwball sensibility and personal politics ignited a devoted following.

A classically trained actor, Eichelberger developed his craft through seven years of work as a character actor at the Trinity Repertory Company, where he created and performed a cut-and-paste adaptation of Robert Lowell's translation of Racine's *Phèdre*. Moving to New York City, in the early 1970s, he became a frequent performer with Charles Ludlam's Ridiculous Theatrical Company. Inspired by Ludlam, Eichelberger began to more seriously undertake writing and performing his own plays. By the time of his death in 1990, Eichelberger had created over thirty-two original plays and performed these works on stages worldwide.

Sadly, Eichelberger's printed texts only hint at the explosive talents and theatrical shtick he brought to his words in performance. For *Nefert-iti*, the first play Eichelberger wrote by himself, he played largely in profile to the audience in an attempt to suggest the two-dimensional quality of hieroglyphics. First presented at Dance Theater Workshop (DTW) in 1978, Eichelberger wore an original, black, pleated, silk, Fortuny gown. He accessorized with a large jeweled collar and papier-mâché headdress of his own construction. He played a zither for the play's songs and for its first performances at DTW was led onto the stage by a pair of saluki dogs he owned at the time. Though Eichelberger's performance magic and mania are lost on the page, in this play a reader will discover the establishment of thematic concerns and structural tactics found throughout his later works.

Meticulously researched mini-biographies, Eichelberger's solo plays from *Jocasta* (1982) to *Lola Montez* (1985) to *Medusa* (1985) pay homage to the lives of strong women who persisted against all odds. As a gay man, Eichelberger personally identified with these brave, struggling women. His take on these figures is intensely personal and deeply intertwined with his day-to-day experience. In *Nefert-iti*, for example, he writes such double-edged lines as: "Don't do that here! 'Don't be a queen,' they say!" and, "I know who I am—You know who I am—And then there is the real me who grins and hides from sight!" This play, like his later ones, spews forth its title character's life story in fantastical and ear-averting cadences and dizzying references. Songs and musical interludes are also indicated for this first play and they, too, went on to form a major part in his performance vocabulary.

A central player in New York City's downtown scene for nearly two decades, Eichelberger saw himself in a tradition of American theatre that included vaudeville stars, actors such as Joseph Jefferson and Sarah Bernhardt, and storyteller/monologists like Ruth Draper. "I'm a storyteller and a performer," he noted to an interviewer, "I'm just looking for a story to tell. And I want to do grand characters." *Nefert-iti* helped Eichelberger blaze that path and clear the way for many to follow.

**Joe E. Jeffreys** is a writer whose work has appeared in the *Village Voice*, the *Drama Review* and *Theatre History Studies*. He has introduced other Eichelberger plays in *Out of Character* (Bantam Books) and *Shattered Anatomies* (Arnolfini Live).

# Nefert-iti

*Ancient Egypt, Eighteenth Dynasty, inside the royal sunshade of Nefert-iti.*
*The Egyptian queen has barricaded herself inside the tomb built for her by*
*her husband Akhenaten. Her sisters and her lover, Bek, the artist who created*
*the queen's famed bust, pay visits, yet remain locked outside the tomb.*

Thank Aten I'm a beautiful woman!
Without that I'd have nothing, no one,
nor my self-respect!
("Impassioned hormones"
with a need to be expressed,
a professional woman,
a serious liver of life!)
Quel joie to be alone each day here in this lovely sunshade
Akhenaten built me!
Today is different, though—
All Egypt will regret!
*(Laughter like the tinkling of bells is heard from offstage.)*
It's lovely here
with no one telling me what to do!
No one turning my priceless uniqueness into worthless guilt!
Sometimes in this sunshade I have the distinct feeling I'm being watched,
but I am alone here, you can see that!
*(Knocking is heard on tomb door.)*
There is a knocking at my temple door—who could it be?
I'll ignore the eager knock!
Go away, there's no one here!
*(Listens at door.)*
I won't go back to Memphis—I won't! You can't make me!
Scarcity is valued,
so value me—
I've made myself scarce!
I'll keep right on praying to Aten, thank you.
I'm too old to change!
Time is running out!
There just aren't enough hours in the day to worship
all those other gods again!
Besides, I've sworn my Ka to Aten,
the one and only God,
the god whose golden rays come streaming down to give me life!

*(Knocking is again heard on tomb door.)*
Go 'way!
No not Osiris;
I won't let my beautiful body be shriveled into a dried-up image of Osiris—
Give me life, give me the globe, Aten;
I have no need to be preserved forever,
when I'm dead and gone they'll not forget me!
"She passed like a meteor, leaving the world astonished and amazed!"
*(Knocking on door continues.)*
Stop that pounding and send for Bek—
Have him make a bust of me, then carve my thoughts beneath it.
And for Aten's sake make sure he carves my cartouche right this time;
there is only one uraeus, not two!
My dear, if Bek paid as much attention to his work as he did to his diet,
something would get done around here!
Tell me, what good are lazy people?
Everybody has to work!
I don't mind . . .
I love to work; the busier the better! Fill my life with work!
But my father is a military genius,
I've always been moderately wealthy and relatively unhappy
—could have spoiled me rotten, but he didn't—
He cracked the whip at home and made us girls work!
"People who don't work are bums," he taught us! "Bums!"
What does he know? Who does he think he is anyway?
The father of God!
Casta diva . . .
Oh, Aten, make father Ay butt out of my life!
He doesn't give me credit for anything!
I've had to claw my way to the sanctity of this sunshade!
Isis knows it hasn't been easy!
It's a lot of hard work being a queen!
And there are factions out there who don't like what I represent!
Tough noogies!
I have a right to be here!
Don't do that here!
"Don't be a queen," they say!
The kinder ones tell me that I transcend queenery—
They let me know they'll overlook my queenly failings and benignly
be so gracious as to accept me as one of them.
It's true most people would rather queens should stay under wraps,
so to speak!
Hide!

Deny your feminine soul!
Being a queen frightens them!
But I am a queen, a beautiful one, at that!
I know who I am!
Ms. Marcia and I share the same madness—
I have seen it in a dream!
If my soul were to present itself to me within a miraculous vision,
I would have that soul emblazoned on my back for all the world to see!
*(Knocking on tomb door starts again.)*
Quit pounding on that door!
You're giving me a headache.
I don't care if the Hittites are coming I won't come out!
Oh, go on, I'm not afraid!
They wouldn't dare come in here! I am safe here!
This is a magic place!
Aten will protect me . . .
*(More knocking on tomb door is heard.)*
What light, lovely knocking now!
Mut-Nodjme, Honey, is that you, my sweet little sister?
No, Dear-heart, I shan't come out again—
I've decided to refuge myself in here forever.
Oooeee, what is that awful stench?
Mut, Honey, have you got those stinking dwarves with you again?
I don't care if the Mitannia emperor did give them to you,
do you have to take them everywhere you go?
I will not shut up! I don't *care* if I hurt their little feelings!
Let them hang around your sunshade!
Mut-Nodjme, don't go away mad!
Mut-Nodjme!
Gone!
Have a pleasant voyage back to Memphis!
I'll miss you, light of my life!
She's such a sweet girl
—ambitious—
But she's nice, my little Nodjme!
Whoever followed me about and aped my ways!
Will I never ever see happy Mut-Nodjme?
She'll remember me kindly all her days!
I'm hot!
The Aten's globe has risen to its zenith! Now is the time to pray!
*(Starts to play dulcimer and sing—stops.)*
Merytaten should be here to shake her little sistrum
while I play—ah, children!!!

What can you do with them?
All she cares for is that foolish Smenkhare and his vegetarian ways!
She'll be sorry!
Where is Meketaten now?
I miss her so! . . .
*(Pause.)*
Oh, I won't let myself get started on that; not now!
This is a joyous day! I must think positive!
If Ankhesenpaten were here, she'd tell me a joke
and tickle her little Neferneferura!
Ah, three lovely children have I now,
even though three lovely more have died
—three daughters live while three have passed over—
three out of six—not bad,
could have been worse!
Praise be to Aten . . .
*(Plays dulcimer and sings.)*
And here I sit alone—"I'm never bored!"
This must be what life is like to barren people,
disciples of Seth with never hope of having children—
actually, it's not so bad, I rather like having no one's company but my own!
*(Picks up hand mirror and looks into it.)*
I know who I am—
you know who I am—
and then there is the real me who grins and hides from sight!
Thank goodness I've brought clay tablets and senet games!
I'll summon Thoth and write 'til day is done!
Thoth—Thoth—
*(No response.)*
and here I sit alone!
Dear Aunt Tiye once told me:
"Being alone is not the worst thing in the world!"
—But, it is!!! Yes it is—
it's horrible—deplorable—
especially when the Aten begins his nightly journey beneath the Nile!
Where are my lover's arms to hold me!
Oh for pity's sake!
I hereby choose to be alone—
I renounce my children; I have no children,
I renounce my husband; I have no husband—
my belief in the Aten will sustain me—
I have my beliefs in one God to guide me!
*(Knocking on tomb door starts again.)*

Cease knocking—
I won't go back to Memphis, I won't; you can't make me!
There just aren't enough hours in the day to worship all those other gods—
I am a student of the late Amenophis-son-of-Hapu who has given me
the strength to fight for my
belief in Tiye, no, not "Inti," but "Aten!"
*(Listens at tomb door.)*
Who sighs beside my door and stirs the desert's silence?
Is it you at last?
The sound of your voice awakens flowers in my heart!
Go away!
Do not tempt me!
Let me feel nothing once again!
Yes, I long to see you, hold you, give myself up to my caged desires
like I did when you first looked into my eyes—
Do I make no sense?
I never asked you to understand me—
Joy was mine when you but listened!
No, it is too late—our lives got in the way!
No, no! Of course I love you!
You are the divine father, my lover, the sacred possessor of
Min's phallic treasures!
Call me by my rightful name again and sing to me of happiness,
make hunger fly my aching heart!
I do not choose to hear them, Bek!
For me they do not exist!
While you stand close, all I can hear are fleet gazelle and leopards
screaming when the hounds have dragged them down!
Oh bless you,
simplicity becomes you,
it is I who am pretentious—
But you will always remain in my mind
if I may use your own words: "Pretentiously unpretentious!"
All right, for Aten's sake, labels, labels, labels!
Forgive me, I've offended you again! . . .
But we don't change, do we?
. . . Good-bye! . . .
Yes, I'm telling you to go! Would you rob me of
my few remaining shreds of dignity!
Leave me, let me be! I was happy before I needed you!
No, I'm neither happy nor unhappy!
I try not to think about it anymore! I exist! . . .
Of course I have survived!

There was nothing left inside me to destroy after you had
had your way . . .
Oh, please don't leave just yet! . . .
Yes, I do remember well! It was early morning!
I was gazing out upon the azure Nile when suddenly I knew
this homely, snoring stranger lying next to me with beer upon his breath
was surely the greatest love of my life and I would live forever
needing him alone!
It made me violently depressed!
Somehow I felt short-changed, tricked, cheated.
Were you what I had lived for, hoped for, longed for all my days?
Yee-gods! "What next," I thought! . . .
Am I repeating myself again?
Yes, yes, of course I would do anything!
I won't go back to Memphis, I won't; you can't make me!
No, I can't come out,
I give myself to God.
I no longer belong to your race!
I have given myself up to the great Aten from whom I spring each morning
when the sacred lotus blooms anew!
Sometimes I truly wish with all my might that I were a human being
instead of whatever it is I am!
I can feel, I want to be like the rest!
I have a right to some sort of life like other people.
Bek, Dear-heart, it's just not that easy!
Let myself fall in love again? With whom if not with you?
Oh, a lovely thought—
the maiden returning from the tryst with a functioning looney
on her arm!
And what could I offer him, sagging flesh and swollen eyes?
Bek, Bek, you're most kind!
Yes, they'll say I was a lost woman; only my bust was found!
That splendid bust!
Do you really still have it where it was?
Bek, what must your wife think?
If only life could imitate art!
If only it were true that truth is beauty!
I can speak true!
But if truth were beauty, more girls would get their hair done at the library!
Yes, no, of course I've brought my mirror,
what queen would be without one?
All right, I'll look into it once again! Yes! Is that what you have seen?
No! Must I say?

Bek, what I see couldn't turn a trick in Boy's Town!

No, I'm not being negative!

Go then, back to your wife and leave me be!

What do you need me for?

You can create alone! You are an artist!

Bek, I didn't mean it! Bek

There is no key to let you in!

Please don't accuse me of being negative again!

I couldn't stand it! I am trying! I am trying!

I will be positive!

Oh, God, don't leave me again, Bek. I couldn't stand it to be alone, abandoned!

Bek, talk to me! Say something!

Bek, Almighty Aten, bring him back! Bek!

Don't leave me here to die alone!

All right, I'm through.

You have won.

I don't believe in you—

Is that what you want me to say?

I curse you, I curse the name of the Aten.

I believe in nothing.

Strike me dead if you will! I don't believe in you!

There is no chance of everlasting life!

When I am dead, my detractors will erase my face and name
from every building, every tablet, every wall!

Bek will leave my image here to crumble into dust when he goes back
to Memphis!

The name of Nefert-iti will be gone forever! No one will remember
who I am!

I know what will be said:

"Who is Achenchae, Nefertiti who?" "I've never heard of Akhenastae!
Who was she?"

Aten has tricked me! I believed in a calf of gold!

Hear me, Aten, I believe in you no more!

You are hateful!

You lied when in a blast of fire you told me
you were coming back to get me!

You have abandoned me! I hate you! I hate you!

Oh, why have you forsaken me?

What have I said? What does it matter?

Talk is cheap in the end

Where is the Kohl to stain my eyes?

Where is camel hair ground to bruise my lips?

There is no one left to help me! I must carry on alone?!
I have driven all away!
Once I had many friends and lovers, they are all gone now;
life goes on
*(Drinks poison. Plays dulcimer and sings "The Song of Abandon.")*
Give me a sign, kind Aten!
Send gentle spirits down to join my dance!
Is there no justice in the world? Must I accept what comes my way?
No! I am fighting back!
There must be some sort of justice, even in Egypt!
I demand it!
I won't be thrown out the door like yesterday's dinner to be eaten by
crocodiles or hippopotami!
I must be worth more than that,
I can still learn!
Hapu's son taught me to be forever a student!
To be learned is to be trained for a world already gone, he said.
Change, change and more change!
It's happening fast—too fast!
Busy, busy, busy, but I'm never too busy to count my assets!
That's rule #1 in business and I have assets,
Aten, hear me! I can work hard and long!
I can listen!
For a while, at least, I can be trusted!
I am a true friend to a few and kind to many—
I can love,
I've been burned once too often! You are looking at damaged goods!
I have been abandoned! I can't find my way!
Aten, do something! Help me! I beseech you!
I will not be ignored any longer!
Look at me!
Acknowledge me!
React or something—
Give me a sign!
Aten! Aten! Aten!
I've had it! Hapu's son was wrong! Believe in the one true God, he said
and you will have everlasting life!

*(Nefert-iti dies.)*

## **Introduction** by RoseLee Goldberg

"I have never thought of myself as a writer," says Laurie Anderson, performance artist extraordinaire, whose reams and reams of texts are the basis for almost three decades of live performances. "I think of myself as a speaker," and indeed her stage appearances include the studied pauses and rhetorical punctuation of a riveting orator. She distinguishes between words that are for reading and those that are for saying out loud, and she identifies, she says, with other writers who work verbally. Whether an ancient master of the spoken word, such as Homer, or a modern word-meister such as William Burroughs— "gravel crunching under a ten-ton truck, plastic ripping in slow motion," is how she described Burroughs's voice when she first heard it live in 1978—it is the visceral quality of the author's voice that interests her the most.

Such focus on the sound of language, on the phonic rhythms of a single vowel or the to-and-fro of ordinary conversation, has formed the basis of Anderson's work from her earliest performances in the mid-seventies. She has manipulated words and sentences in hundreds of ways; she has routed them electronically through vocoders, played them on a custom-designed violin, spoken and sung them. She has spliced and cut them and projected them onto screens behind her, giving a visual measure to their beat. And she has connected them, like so many links in a chain, to form compelling narratives. "Basically, my work is storytelling," Anderson explains, "the world's most ancient art form." These stories also end up as songs. "If they have the right rhythmic structure," Anderson explains, "stories might become songs. Some are lyrical enough without notes, others are spoken with musical backdrop."

Anderson's sensitivity to language comes as much from her acute musical ear as from her conceptually trained eye. In the seventies, words were considered an essential material of art; handwritten or printed on a page or directly on a wall, they punctuated the thoughts of a generation of artists more interested in investigating the meaning of art ideas than in the actual production of art objects. And it was in this context that Anderson's canny layering of visual and audio material took root.

Despite the cerebral atmosphere that characterized the decade, Anderson's song "O Superman" which reached the top ten on the British pop charts in 1981, was essentially a spoken text of the everyday kind: "Hello, this is your mother, are you home?" is one of its familiar lines. Quite unexpectedly, "O Superman" provided a bridge for Anderson from an obscure, downtown art scene, to the world of mass media, which triggered a discussion of high art and low and the contradictory notion of a popular avant-garde that would dominate the art of the 1980s.

Anderson's appeal across a broad spectrum—from language theorists and cultural critics to general theatre and rock-music audiences—rests as much on her ability to sashay between disciplines as on her meshing of complex subject matter in rhythmic and compelling songs. It is also the result of her determination to communicate with an audience. "It is crucial for me to cross the gap between myself and others in an immediate, sensual way," she says.

Her stories, which at first were mostly autobiographical, are personal ruminations on themes of politics, love, religion, the natural sciences. They serve a range of different functions in her performances: some stories are connective tissue (between songs), some are joints and some of her favorites are short (fifteen lines) "with questions in them," she says. "Sometimes I need to write a story to make sense of a song," at other times, stories are entirely independent of songs and have rhythms of their own.

On stage, she whispers into microphones, using electronic "audio masks" to change her voice from female to male, from natural to computerese. Their intimacy draws audiences close; drenched in the light of projected images they sit as though around a collective campfire, albeit a technological one. On these pages, readers will reflect on the texts separated from sounds and pictures, and from a pacing that moves them along at a fast clip. Reading, and rereading this material, they can more carefully absorb the subtle and often ironic pictures that she draws of her cultural and political milieu.

**RoseLee Goldberg** is the author of *Performance Art: From Futurism to the Present* (Abrams) and *Performance: Live Art Since 1960* (Abrams). Her newest book, *Laurie Anderson*, will be published by Abrams in the spring of 2000.

## from **United States**

### New York Social Life

*The performer alternates between telephone and microphone to distinguish voices. Performed very rapidly as one long, run-on sentence while the tamboura is plucked percussively to produce an extremely irritating nasal tone.*

Well, I was lying in bed one morning, trying to think of a good reason to get up, and the phone rang and it was Geri and she said, "Hey, hi! How are you? What's going on? How's your work?"

"Oh fine. You know, just waking up, but it's fine, it's going okay, how's yours?"

"Oh, a lot of work, you know, I mean, I'm trying to make some money, too. Listen, I gotta get back to it. I just thought I'd call to see how you are . . ."

And I said, "Yeah, we should really get together next week. You know, have lunch and talk."

And she says, "Yeah, I'll be in touch. Okay?"

"Okay."

"Uh, listen, take care. Okay?"

"Take it easy."

"'Bye-'bye."

"'Bye now." And I get up, and the phone rings and it's a man from Cleveland and he says, "Hey, hi! How are you? Listen, I'm doing a performance series and I'd like you to do something in it. You know, you could make a little money. I mean, I don't know how I feel about your work, you know, it's not really my style, it's kind of trite, but listen, it's just my opinion, don't take it personally. So, listen, I'll be in town next week. I gotta go now, but I'll give you a call, and we'll have lunch and we can discuss a few things."

And I hang up and it rings again and I don't answer it and I go out for a walk and I drop in at the gallery and they say, "Hey, Hi. How are you?"

"Oh, fine. You know."

"How's your work going?"

"Okay, I mean . . ."

"You know, it's not like it was in the sixties. I mean, those were the days there's just no money around now, you know. Survive! Produce! Stick it out! It's a jungle out there! Just gotta keep working."

And the phone rings and she says, "Oh, excuse me, will you? Hey hi! How are you? Uh-huh. How's your work? Good. Well, listen, stick it out, I mean, it's not the sixties, you know. Listen, I gotta go now, but uh, lunch would be great. Fine, next week? Yeah. Very busy now, but next week would be fine, okay? 'Bye-'bye. 'Bye now."

And I go over to Magoo's for a bite, and I see Frank and I go over to his table and I say, "Hey Frank. Hi, how are you? How's your work? Yeah, mine's okay, too. Listen, I'm broke you know, but uh, working . . . Listen, I gotta go now but we should really get together, you know. Why don't you drop by sometime?"

"Yeah, that would be great."

"Okay."

"Take care."

"Take it easy."

"I'll see you."

"I'll call you."

"'Bye now."

"'Bye-'bye."

And I go to a party and everyone's sitting around wearing these party hats and it's awkward and no one can think of anything to say. So we all move around—fast—and it's:

"Hi! How are you?"

"Where've you been?"

"Nice to see you."

"Listen, I'm sorry I missed your thing last week, but we should really get together, you know, maybe next week."

"I'll call you."

"I'll see you."

"'Bye-'bye."

And I go home and the phone rings and it's Alan and he says, "You know, I'm gonna have a show on cable TV and it's gonna be about loneliness, you know, people in the city who for whatever sociological, psychological, philosophical reasons just can't seem to communicate, you know. The Gap! The Gap! It'll be a talk show and people'll phone in but we will say at the beginning of each program, 'Listen, don't call in with your personal problems because we don't want to hear them.'"

And I'm going to sleep and it rings again and it's Mary and she says, "Hey, Laurie, how are you? Listen, I just called to say hi. Yeah, well don't worry. Listen, just keep working. I gotta go now. I know it's late, but we should really get together next week maybe and have lunch and talk and . . . listen, Laurie, if you want to talk before then, I'll leave my answering machine on and just give me a ring anytime."

## from **After Science, Dinner**

### On the Road

In the early seventies I went on lots of trips, field trips sort of, just to poke around, to see what was happening outside New York, back out there in America.

I had no money. No tent. No definite plans. Just a sleeping bag, a lighter, some Burroughs books, a few packs of Camels. Out on the highway, it's warm for September, and bright. A semi loaded with limestone rolls up and I climb in.

"Sexy Baby-Maker's the handle," says the scrawny, slit-eyed driver introducing himself. "Murried, rr'juh?"

"Uh, yeah. Sure, I'm married. My, uh, husband's waiting in the next town." I'm improvising.

"Well, 'juh know nine outta' tin murried wimmen go out? 'Juh know that?"

"Oh. No, gee. In-ter-interesting." The potholes are hyphenating my words.

"Yup. 'Juh one?" His hand is on my knee now. I try to aim a cigarette into my mouth. We hit another pothole and I miss. The cigarette sticks to my lower lip, bobbing up and down preposterously while I talk. "Hey, gee! I just re-re-remembered that I left a-a-a book back there." I jump out at the next corner, a flying leap.

"No point in hanging around here," I hear myself say. I have begun to talk to myself out loud.

It seems like the middle of the night. I wake up suddenly and peer out from under the rock ledge. The fire has burned down to coals and it's dark in the woods. I hear a rustle and wait for my eyes to adjust to the blackness. From my low vantage point, I can just make out the butt of a musket and a pair of cracked, spatula-shaped shoes. I crawl out of my sleeping bag and the rest of the figure looms into view: male, approximately sixty years old, a hundred and forty pounds, black hair, tight sweatshirt. Armed with what appears to be a musket. A minute or so passes. Finally, I hear a voice, "We eat critters."

I don't know what to say, so more time passes.

"We eat critters," he repeats. "Possum. Squirrel. Rabbits. That's what." Suddenly I understand. He's out hunting: night food.

The man's name is Mr. Taylor and he is twenty-two years old. He invites me back to the house ("next holler") where he lives with Mrs. Taylor, also twenty-two, and their four children: Rhonda, Jim, Jack and, oddly enough, Jim. There used to be two more Taylors, but last summer they fell down one of the holes by the Exxon's systematic strip mining.

Now that certain kinds of low-grade coal can be converted into oil, companies are reopening mines that were sealed "forever" seventy-five years ago. Holes were drilled and then left uncovered. Dense brush quickly camouflaged the holes. The holes were deep, vertical, straight down, their sides as slippery as intestines. "I could see the little 'uns out in the field and then I couldn't see them no more," explained Mrs. Taylor, recalling the incident.

Mostly we sit on the porch, Mr. Taylor, Mrs. Taylor and me, watching it rain and making small talk. Every time the rain stops for a minute, Mr. Taylor jumps up and trots around to the back of the house. We can hear intermittent hacking sounds from the tobacco patch. Then he reappears, his work done for the moment. We talk slowly. Every sentence seems to end the same way, on a kind of upswing.

"Rain's letting up. Don't you think, Rhonda?"

Twenty or thirty seconds go by.

"Yup."

"Think it's time to check the pot. Don't you think, Momma?"

"Yup."

I follow Rhonda into the cabin. Every few seconds she opens a large pot. Steam billows out. Inside there is a large piece of grayish meat, swollen and prickly, bobbing up and down in the water. "Possum," says Rhonda, stirring it. "Looks done." It is the consistency of waterlogged, shredded wood. We fish it out, then start to make the biscuits and gravy. "Red-eye gravy. Yup. That's the secret," says Rhonda. She adds a pot of yesterday's coffee, stirs in some cornmeal. We pour this over the possum and then, "because it's Sunday," we get out a rusty can of maple syrup and drizzle it over the whole thing.

"That's the secret. Maple syrup. That's the secret ingredient," Rhonda whispers. "Don't tell anyone."

---

## from **United States**

### Difficult Listening Hour

*For voice and two harmonizers.*

Good evening. Welcome to the Difficult Listening Hour. The spot on your dial for the relentless and impenetrable sound of Difficult Music.

*(The repeat mode is hit on the harmonizer and the word "Music" is caught in its memory and repeated.)*

So sit bolt upright in that straight-backed chair,
button that top button

Laurie Anderson

and get set for some
difficult music.

*(The word "Music" is canceled.)*

Ooola. Oooooola. *OOOO LA!*

*(The third "OOOO LA" is caught and repeated backward and then forward forming a kind of random audio moebius strip. It becomes the background rhythm track for the rest of the talk.)*

I came home today, and
I opened the door with my bare hands,
And I said, "Hey!
Who tore up all my wallpaper samples?
Who ate all the grapes? The ones I was saving?"
And this guy was sitting there,
And I said,
"Hey, Pal!
What's going on here?"
And he had this smile, and
When he smiled
He had these big, white teeth,
Like luxury hotels
On the Florida coastline.
And when he closed his mouth, it looked
Like a big scar. And I said to myself,
Holy Smokes!
Looks like some kind of a guest/host relationship to me.
And I said, "Hey, Pal!
What's going on here anyway?
Who are you?"
And he said,
"Now, I'm the Soul Doctor,
And you know, language is a virus from Outer Space.
And hearing your name is better
Than seeing your face."

## from **Big Science**

"Hey! pal! How do I get to town from here?"
And he said, "Well, just take a right
where they're gonna build that new

shopping mall,
go straight past where they're gonna put in the freeway,
take a left at what's gonna be the new sports center,
and keep going until you hit the place
where they're thinking of
building that drive-in bank.
You can't miss it."
And I said, "This must be the place."
Coo coo coo. Golden cities. Golden towns.
Golden cities. Golden towns.

---

## from **Talk Normal**

Around 1978, I met the comedian Andy Kaufman. He was performing his Elvis act in a club in Queens. The performance started with Andy playing the bongos and sobbing. We became friends and I acted as Andy's straight man in clubs and field trips. At the Improv in New York, Andy would begin by insulting women and saying, "I won't respect them until one of them wrestles me down!" This was my cue to jump up and fight. I sat in the front, drinking whiskies, trying to get up the nerve. Meanwhile, I was supposed to be heckling him. After three whiskies, I managed to get pretty abusive. Wrestling him down, however, was pretty hard. Andy really fought.

On our "field trips" we would go to Coney Island and stand around the "test your strength" games, the ones with the big sledgehammers and bells. Andy would make fun of all of the guys who were swinging away and I was supposed to beg him for one of the huge stuffed bunnies. "Oh Andy, Honey! Please get me a bunny! Please, please!!" Finally Andy would step up to the big thermometer and swing. The indicator would wobble up to "Try Again, Weakling." At this point, Andy would start yelling that the game was rigged and demanding to see the manager.

We also went on the Rotowhirl, the ride that plasters everyone against the walls of a spinning cylinder and stretches their bodies into dopplered blobs. Before the ride actually starts, there are a couple of awkward minutes while the attendant checks the motor, and the riders, bound head and foot, stare at each other. This was the moment that Andy seized. He would start by looking around in a panic and then he would start to cry, "I don't want to be on this ride! I've changed my mind! We're all gonna die!!!" The other riders would look around self-consciously. Should they help? He would then begin to sob uncontrollably.

I loved Andy. He would come over to my house and read from a novel he was writing. He would read all night. I don't know if any of this book was ever published. I've never been one to hope that Elvis is still hanging around somewhere hiding, but I will probably always expect to see Andy reappear someday.

## from **Stories from the Nerve Bible**

For a lot of people the sixties are still a kind of lost but ideal era, a time of intellectual rigor, sexual freedom, great music, a kind of lost utopia. For me personally, all I remember was a lot of guys doing these endless guitar feedback solos which just made the decade that much longer than it would have been anyway, not to mention all the macrame that got produced, you know macrame plant hangers, macrame place mats, tote bags. I had a nice macrame hairshirt myself, you can still find some of this stuff in the really good flea markets.

But back to the subject, the myth about the glamorous sixties. I think it can actually be traced to one particular evening, the night when Jacqueline Kennedy happened to see a Broadway musical entitled *Camelot* and it changed the face of this country from that moment on. So . . . maestro?

(Camelot *video medley plays.*)

Let's go back to that moment at the top of the decade, when Lerner and Loewe came up with their unforgettable chart-topping tale of *Camelot*. Yes back to the days of power and privilege along the Potomac, the days when Harvard intellectuals were commuting from Cambridge to D.C., when the young president himself was out writing poetry on his sail-boat. And those nights! The glittering openings as the great art patrons arrived for cultural events, sponsored by the brand-new National Endowment for the Arts.

So let's listen in to some of the greatest hits, such as: "I Wonder What the King Is Doing Tonight?" or the timeless love song "How to Handle a Woman" or one of my personal favorites, the touching "Where Are the Simple Joys of Maidenhood?" All summed up in the naive but searching question: "What Do the Simple Folk Do?"

So let's sit back and enjoy the music.

## False Documents

I went to a palm reader and the odd thing about the reading was that everything she told me was totally wrong. She said I loved airplanes, that I had been born in Seattle, that my mother's name was Hilary. But she seemed so sure of the information that I began to feel like I'd been walking around with these false documents tattooed to my hands. It was very noisy in the parlor and members of her family kept running in and out. They were speaking a high, clicking kind of language that sounded a lot like Arabic. Books and magazines in Arabic were strewn all over the floor. It suddenly occurred to me that maybe there was a translation problem, that maybe she was reading my hand from right to left instead of from left to right.

Thinking of mirrors, I gave her my other hand. Then she put her other hand out and we sat there for several minutes in what I assumed was some kind of participatory ritual. Finally I realized that her hand was out because she was waiting for money.

## Wild White Horses

In the Tibetan map of the world, the world is a circle and at the center there is an enormous mountain guarded by four gates. And when they draw a cap of the world, they draw a map in sand, and it takes months and then when the map is finished, they erase it and throw the sand into the nearest river.

Last fall the Dalai Lama came to New York city to do a two-week ceremony called the Kalachakra which is a prayer to heal the earth. And woven into these prayers were a series of vows that he asked us to take, and before I knew it I had taken a vow to be kind for the rest of my life. And I walked out of there and I thought, For the rest of my life?? What have I done? This is a disaster!

And I was really worried. Had I promised too much? Not enough? I was really in a panic. And there were all these monks walking around. They had come from Tibet for the ceremony and they were walking around midtown in their new brown shoes and I went up to one of the monks and said, "Can you come with me to have a cappuccino right now and talk?" And so we went to this little Italian place. He had never had coffee before so he kept talking faster and faster and I kept saying, "Look, I don't know whether I promised too much or too little. Can you help me, please?"

And he was really being practical. He said, "Look, don't limit yourself. Don't be so strict! Open it up!" He said, "The mind is a wild white horse and when you make a corral for it, make sure it's not too small. And another thing, 'When your house burns down, just walk away.' And another thing, 'Keep your eyes open.' And one more thing, 'Keep moving, 'cause it's a long way home.'"

# Rachel Rosenthal

## Introduction by Moira Roth

**H**ybridity, curiosity and change are at the core of Rachel Rosenthal's life and art. She is a blend of French and North American cultures (born in Paris in 1926 and based in Los Angeles since 1955), and over the last fifty years has fluidly journeyed back and forth between different mediums—theatre and performance art, dance and ceramics, writing and teaching. Early on she became inspired by Antonin Artaud (*"The Theatre and Its Double* is my theatre Bible") and Marcel Proust ("I am intoxicated with his language, and drawn to him by my aching nostalgia for the period's look, feel and smell"), and later by Ilya Prigogine (chaos theory) and Tom Regan (animals rights). After a long history of working with improvisational theatre (Instant Theatre, 1956–1966 and 1976–1977), she began to script her performances, which since 1975 formed her traveling repertoire, sometimes solo, sometimes ensemble. These spectacular, magical, haunting theatre pieces, drawing large audiences, were elegantly staged with costumes and sets, and usually with film, video and slide projections. Recently, she has returned to costumed improvisations with her Rachel Rosenthal Company, often staged in her own studio in Los Angeles for small audiences—although the Company also tours in this country and abroad with scripted works.

Rosenthal's early performance work, (created in the context of Southern California's intense feminist art scene) between 1975 and 1981, revolved around autobiographical material; from 1981 onward she became increasingly concerned with what she calls "The Big Picture." Yet as Alisa Solomon once wrote, "Knowing that her works center on ecology, the protection of animals and the preservation of the earth can hardly prepare you for the brutal way they grab at you."

I saw Rosenthal perform *filename: FUTURFAX* in San Francisco in 1995, and was dazzled by the physicality of her performance style, vitality and agility (she roamed around the stage, twisted her torso this way and that, sometimes dancing exuberantly), by the mobility of her face, gestures and body, and her bald-headed, harsh, androgynous old beauty. She was equally possessed of an incredible vocal range—by turns soft and harsh, chiding and mocking, anguished and offhand, guttural and high-pitched, enraged and debonair. She constantly engaged the members of the audience, making asides to them, joking and appealing to their sense of justice.

The time span covered by Rosenthal's performances is vast. The bleak narrative of *filename: FUTURFAX*—that of Rosenthal's meager eighty-sixth birthday celebration, the future's attempts to reach her by fax and her eventual murder by young, offstage thugs—takes place in the year 2012 after the Great Calamity. *Pangaean Dreams'* (1990) ambiance is that of the supercontinent of Pangaea of 250 million years ago. But in all her work, Rosenthal is driven by a consistent urgency: ". . . There is no time left . . . Nature is dead, or at least dying . . . The question is: are we going to get the 'prise de conscience' [literally translated as: "being grabbed by conscience"] early enough so that we can somehow manage that demise and then the transformation that will enable life to continue in a managed way on Earth."

Yet when mesmerized, watching one of Rosenthal's spectacles—be it a scene of rearing cars driven by stunt drivers in a parking lot (*KabbaLAmobile*), the multicolored Throngs surging around the frail white-clad group of the last Czar's family (*Zone*), or the huge ceremonious parade of animals, from parrot and monkey to hamster and Appaloosa mare, together with their owners (*The Others*)—audience members (myself included) are usually inspired by the vitality and imagination of Rosenthal's art, rather than oppressed by the pessimism of her underlying vision. I felt that, too, as I left the auditorium after seeing *filename: FUTURFAX*, and being surprised—given the performance's deep-seeded despair—at my reaction.

**Moira Roth** is Trefethen Professor of Art History at Mills College in Oakland, California.

Much appreciation to Daniel Quinn whose ideas inspired some of the issues and text of this piece. (The following excerpt is from the beginning half of *filename: FUTURFAX*.)

*We hear the sound of shouts, running and a door being laboriously unlocked and then rebolted. Rosenthal enters through the "door" and mimes closing it. Carrying a bag, she runs to the "window" (fourth wall downstage of coffee table) and mimes closing the blind. She peers worriedly through the "blind." Mutters under her breath as she picks up the phone and listens for a tone. There is none. She razzes it. Then she takes four carrots out of the bag and sets them carefully and triumphantly on the table and takes out a little birthday candle that has seen many birthdays—it's very small and burned—lights it with the lighter and sings to herself.*

"Happy Birthday to me . . ." (*She continues to sing the song to the end*) ". . . and please no more!"

(*Declaiming*) "Whatever became of the moment when one first knew about death? There must have been one moment in childhood when it first occurred to you that you don't go on forever. It must have been shattering. Stamped into one's memory. And yet I can't remember it. It never occurred to me at all. We must be born with an intuition of mortality for we know the word for it before we know that there are words . . . Out we come, bloodied and squalling, with knowledge of the four points of the compass. There's only one direction, and time is its only measure."

Hmmm. I wonder. Does the arrow always point East? Well, maybe here. On Earth. But there are other places . . .

Oh, by the way, that was Tom Stoppard, *Rosencrantz and Gildenstern Are Dead*. Always good to give credit. Goddess, that was a great piece of work: the play, the film . . . After all these years I still laugh when I think of it. Rosencrantz stumbling on all the great discoveries of civilization, but never realizing it! . . . (*She breaks herself up*) All the great moments: Archimedes' Eureka, Newton's Apple, the steam engine, the Wright Brothers' plane, Heisenberg's Uncertainty Principle! . . . Even the Big Mac! Rosencrantz never had a clue! Dumb, ignorant, innocent soul. Stupid too! Hee-hee! Well, perhaps not so stupid after all. Perhaps he knew all along what the really important things were, like a piece of ass—as they used to call it, or an apple in the stomach instead of hurtling down to its mangled demise to illustrate the law of gravity . . . Hell, we lived with that law since Australopithecus. Three million years of gravity. Free fall interruptus (*She falls forward and catches herself*) And we managed to do quite well, becoming Homo little by little, without ever knowing the equation. *(Picks up the metal washtub, goes to the armchair)* Still, equations are beautiful. E=MC² is pretty. Neat. Even elegant. *(She sits, takes off her shoes and socks and soaks her feet in the washtub)* God, the things one clings to! Like cleanliness. Even if it's hard. With all the rationing. I wash one thing at a time. Today, it's the feet. *(Washes her feet)* That water will have to do for feet, underwear, dishes and a plant, if I can find one.

Oh, I forgot to tell you, today's my birthday! I guess you figured, huh? Well, I made it. I'm eighty-six today: November 9, 2012! I know what you're thinking, you think I look pretty young for my age. Well that's because you see me the way I see me. I always see me twenty years younger. When I was sixty-six, I saw myself as forty-six. Saved me a lot of face-lifts . . . Nobody else did though. Always a bummer . . . *(She dries her feet and puts her socks and shoes back on)*

For a while there, people took canaries outside like they did in the old days in the mines . . . All the canaries died. Goddess, I sure miss the animals . . . *(She picks up the washtub, goes to set it down under the umbrella)*

I guess the habit of statistics lingers. I'd like to know what percentage of people remain . . . Einstein said, "Everything has changed but our way of thinking." Well, we are dying of that . . . our way of thinking. We've thought that way since the Great Revolution. No. Not the American, the French, the Russian . . . No. The *really* Great one! The planting one in 10,000 B.C. or circa . . . Agricultural Revolution! Mastery over the food supply.

Status quo. I love the Galileo story. About how he tried to show the status-quoers that Earth moved around the Sun, but when he got a whiff of where it was going—like straight to the stake, if you get my drift?—he said, "No, no, no!" He was merely presenting a clever challenge to the existing order as a way of increasing the satisfaction and certitude with which the existing order would be accepted after it triumphed over this seemingly impertinent design! Hee-hee! *(She picks up the Earth balloon and plays with it)* EARTH IS ROUND! IT ISN'T THE CENTER OF THE UNIVERSE! AND IT MOVES! *(She tosses the balloon and is doubled over with laughter)* We've been in denial ever since!

*(Wipes her eyes)* I love that story . . .

*(Wipes her face and neck)* In 1992, the New World Order declared that global warming needed further study . . . *(Gets dejected but then perks herself up)*

But. In the nineteenth century, the nineties were Gay . . . *(She goes over to the metronome on the table, and sets it ticking)* Boom box!

*(She dances over to the hanging wool carder and sitting hourglass, and sets them spinning and spilling. She begins a more energetic dance, but soon gives up, her back hurting. She stops the metronome.)*

You know, in the face of it, we never lost our faith in Eternity, in spite of the Catholic Church's invention of Purgatory. Purgatory effectively killed Eternity by infecting it with secular time. Shit. You're told that if you're bad on *this* plane you never go to Hell on *that* plane because *(She goes to sit on the chair)* there's this waiting room, this half-way house, where you stay—it's kind of warm but hey, it's not forever!—while you wait for your friends to bail you out with nice écus and liras and dollars for the pontiff! Oooo what a neat arrangement! So now, when you die, there's this deal. And Eternity is punctured like a flat tire.

So how did I end up being Eternity's champion?

*(Wipes her face and armpits)* It's so damn hot. We didn't negotiate a good deal with the Devil. Or with anyone else. We blew it.

*(Rosenthal goes to the table to scrape her carrots with the knife)* Six hours in line for these. It's worth it. All that carotene. They're mostly artificial. They don't grow in the ground, there's no ground left. Talk of dust bowls! You should have seen that cloud! It was eighteen months ago. That's when all began to fall apart. It's okay. I don't mind. I say, "Let's get it over with fast, get rid of all the people, and let the millennia try to heal the wound." What I don't like is the unraveling process. People don't all die at once. The ones who are left, after the plagues, etcetera, they're the problem. Take the lines, for instance. There's always some hooligan (or several) who gets the food at the end of a gun. All that fucking waiting for nothing. Well, no more . . . These carrots are from government hydrofarms. What's left of them. Ration #7. They taste funny, but hey . . . *(Bites off a piece)*

*(Mouth full of carrot, she uses the carrot as if it were a gun and pretends to fire it at the audience.)*

I got a gun . . . *(Munches)*

Hmmm. This business of Purgatory . . . what a great out. Time bought out of Eternity! "Time is Money." Who thought *that* one up? The Church said, "Usury is bad. Almost as bad as prostitution and acrobatics!" *(Bursts out laughing)* I like that: bankers, whores and acrobats all roasting together in Hell! Anyway. Said the Vatican, "In charging interest, the usurer sells the borrower nothing that belongs to him. He sells only Time, which belongs to God." Smart move! So the Church took over the activity, selling Eternal Time to the poor bastards. What a scam! Ushered in capitalism, materialism and monetary personal power. Nothing sacred! . . . As they used to say.

*(She goes to the metal washtub, wrings out a bunch of panties that were soaking in it and hangs them up to dry one by one with clothespins on the umbrella spokes.)*

Hope they hold. There's no more paper for toilet. All the trees were logged ten years ago. So we use a scraper *(Shows the horse scraper)* but we have to wash the panties a lot. Major water guzzler . . .

You think I ramble on a lot, don't you? Well, that's what happens when there's no more TV.

*(Looks at her hands)* I have so much Time on my hands. Like in affluent societies. Or hunter/gatherer societies . . . Waiting to die with Time on your hands. Nothing much to do . . . I can't think too much because it brings on fits.

I used to hate a lot. Francis Bacon for starters. Boy, did I hate Francis Bacon! No, no. Not the painter, the sixteenth-century guy who called Nature "this common harlot" which we had to "subdue, overwhelm, conquer and enslave." Ah, and René Descartes, the guy who said that the whole Universe was a mechanism. That animals were machines. That you could vivisect them because their screams were just the sounds of gears and springs. Boy, did I loathe him! Oh, and John Locke? The conspicuous consumption guy? The one who said, "Negation of Nature is the way to happiness!" I loathed him too. *(She goes through a frenzy of punching, stomping, kicking, gouging)* "Take that! And that! . . . " *(Now out of breath, she sits on the chair)* Oooo, I feel better. But dead as doornails as these guys were, their words were still buzzing in my ears. All around me. In the air, the airwaves, the written word, and the screams of life being extinguished everywhere. Boy, did we learn their lessons to a T! We use science like tableware, so as not to dirty our fingers with matter. "Look Ma, no hands!" Those old men, they were not innovators. They were just old ideas whose time had come. Ideas as nuclear warheads.

How did it start? Did we always think like that? Nope. The Australopithecines didn't. Homo Habilis didn't. Homo Erectus didn't. Homo Sapiens didn't. Even Homo Sapiens Sapiens didn't always think like that. It was Yogi Berra who said, "What gets us into trouble is not what we don't know, it's what we know for sure that just ain't so."

*(The phone rings.)*

*(Rosenthal looks at the phone in great amazement and picks up the receiver)* Allô! Eh! Bounzi! Quelle surprise! Oh ce que c'est gentil! Oui, oui. J'ai quatre-vingt-six ans. Et toi, quatre-vingt-un, hein? Ah, ce qu'on est vieilles! . . . Mais comment as-tu eu la communication? Ah? Ah oui, je me rappelle: la lotterie une fois par mois . . . Mais quelle chance! Un vrai coup de pot! Alors tu tiens bon? Oui, moi encore un peu.

*(The phone goes dead.)*

Allô! Allô! Ah merde, c'est coupé! *(She tries to dial)* Ça, c'est vraiment chiant!

*(She goes through a major tantrum, with screams, wails and hollers, stomping and cursing in two languages. She really loses it and falls kneeling before the table. Her demeanor and face are now animal-like. A hurt animal. She stares stupidly at the audience, not seeing.)*

That was Nicole. In Paris. She's my cousin.

*(Long pause.)*

In Paris it's tomorrow. Here, it's today.

*(Another pause.)*

If you're in Paris, it's today. Here it's yesterday.

*(She snaps out of it, stands slowly)* If you go to Paris, you arrive tomorrow, but it's still today. If you go to Tokyo, you arrive day after tomorrow but they call it yesterday. If you go to a black hole, you never arrive at all because when you get to the singularity, that's the end of Time. So you always arrive in the future. A black hole never lets you see the end of Time. There's an inherent modesty in black holes. The naked singularity is camouflaged by the event horizon. Nothing escapes the event horizon. So no one can say what goes on in there. It's a bit like the old Communist Block. Once you got caught inside the event horizon, it was good-bye, Charlie! And the rest of the world never knew the extent of it. Now they say, if you're lucky, you can escape the end of Time inside a black hole by squeezing through a worm hole somewhere in there and emerging in another universe. I guess the Soviets all crawled through a worm hole and the black hole was caught with its pants down.

Boy, I remember, way back then, the sense of triumph: capitalism won!

Then capitalism was caught with its pants down, but there were no worm holes to crawl through. So here we are.

*(She checks the phone. It's still dead. She's angry and at a loss as to what to do next. Then she remembers.)*

I've kept this especially for my birthday.

*(Filled with anticipation, she opens the crimson silk bag and takes out a teabag which she places in the cup. She tries to light the butane stove but the butane bottle is empty. She is totally dejected.)*

Time is so weird. We rotate, so if we travel at the right pace, we can catch up to the sun. Say I start at noon. I go across a time zone. It's still noon. Another time zone. Noon again. Noon, noon, noon, noonoonoonoo . . . NOON! I'm back where I started. It's still noon. BUT. I'm one day older. Now how can that be, time stood still! Ah, but not really, because of revolution.

You can beat rotation, but not revolution! So, forget it. Still, it's very arbitrary. Okay, let's say that this is a border between two time zones *(Indicates an imaginary line bisecting the audience)* "Fuseaux horaires" in French. Sounds so much better . . . Everybody on this side is 11:00 P.M. Everybody on that side is midnight. So now, kiss each other. You *(Indicating half the audience)* are kissing yesterday. You *(Indicating the other half)* are kissing tomorrow. What happens if the border between two fuseaux horaires bisects your bed? As you toss and turn during the night, you shift back and forth between one hour and the other. Must be exhausting . . .

Rotation and revolution . . . before the Great Revolution, we lived in Rotation Time. As the old bumper stickers used to say: ONE DAY AT A TIME! I imagine that for three million years you'd wake up in the morning and it was, "Gee, I wonder what's out there to gather today?" I remember gathering, when I was a child in France. In the woods. Berries, mushrooms, lilies of the valley . . . It was great. Finding something that isn't guaranteed to be there. What a rush! But then, ten thousand years ago or so, some of us wanted to be sure and started to plant. Suddenly it was Revolution Time! The weather, the seasons, the timing, the backbreaking. Slaves of fruit of our brow . . . fruit of our sweat . . . Anyway. Why? Why did we do it? We had it good, didn't we?

You know, I think I figured out why. Let me run it by you: *(She strikes a pose)* many millennia ago, a Neolithic Faust made a pact with the Devil. The Devil said, MAN IS TOP OF THE HEAP!

And Faust caught the ball and ran with it:

FOUR BILLION YEARS WENT INTO CREATING US!
WE'VE ARRIVED.
EVOLUTION IS FIRED!
GOD BREAKS THE MOLD.
WE ARE THE MASTERS.
GOD IS FIRED!
BEING THE RAISON D' ÊTRE, THE SINE QUA NON, WE ARE
    EXEMPT FROM THE LAWS OF NATURE.
THE "LAW OF LIMITED COMPETITION" DOES NOT APPLY TO
    US.
WE MAKE THE WHOLE WORLD OUR ECOLOGICAL NICHE.
NO ROOM OR RIGHTS FOR ANY OTHERS.
EVERYTHING EXCEPT OUR FOOD AND THE FOOD OF OUR
    FOOD IS OUR ENEMY AND MUST BE EXTERMINATED.
WE:
KILL OFF EVERYTHING WE CAN'T EAT.
KILL OFF EVERYTHING THAT EATS WHAT WE EAT.

KILL OFF EVERYTHING THAT DOESN'T FEED WHAT WE EAT.
AND THEN WE KILL WHAT WE EAT.
THAT'S THE WAY THINGS ARE!

And the Devil rubbed his hands together and said, "Faust, you're a good boy. I will give you Fame, Fortune and Eternal Youth!"

And he kept his word. For we exploded in a supernova flash of civilization, and we will never grow old because, at ten thousand years, we are dying in our youth!

Just before the Great Calamity, we were eight billion people who thought they were just about to master the world. Like the poor schmuck at the edge of the singularity, who thinks he's beaten the black hole!

Eight billion! What did we all think? A long time ago, Milan Kundera wrote that our way with animals was humankind's "fundamental debacle." He was right, of course, but it wasn't just animals. It was our way with EVERYTHING.

*(Voice-over)* "INTENSIFICATION OF PRODUCTION TO FEED AN INCREASE IN POPULATION LEADS TO A STILL GREATER INCREASE IN POPULATION."

*(Rosenthal plays the deluded "Man")* No, no! That's too simple! It sounds like a natural law, like gravity! It doesn't apply! To US. N/A—Not applicable! We can beat the odds! Anyway, we don't breed less, we feed more. Feed! Feed! More! More! . . . *(She stuffs her mouth with carrots until it's full to bursting. She disgorges them and is left with a gaping mouth)*

*(The lights create the effect of prison bars. Rosenthal peers out from behind the imaginary bars, and lets out a huge primal scream. The cage bars cross-fade during the following speech into the image of a galaxy.)*

I am now eighty-six, looking like sixty-six, and talking to you from the Great Calamity. And you? Where are you in all this? If you are in 1992 *(Change the year to the year FUTURFAX is performed)*, then we are all rolling around in a spiral, turning back on itself like a big doughnut, rotating and revolutionizing in this Universe, and still queasy about seeing Time as space, because, if we did, it would mean that sitting in the right chair we could see the future, just as Archimedes said that given a big lever and a place to stand, he could move the Earth. Today, yesterday and tomorrow, are just different points in space. And we can see them in every night sky. How nice to know that, where we stand, Time is an arrow, instead of that chaotic jumble out there, where every star we see this very second is another era made visible.

# Spalding Gray

## Introduction by James Leverett

As I write this introduction, Spalding Gray is working on a new monologue at New York's East Village experimental venue, P. S. 122 [Performance Space 122]. He's using a process that he's been perfecting for more than twenty years: collecting thoughts into an increasingly worn notebook; organizing those journal entries into a story; making that story tautly resonant with subplots, counterplots, themes, images. What he's doing is writing in the general sense; but, unlike most writers, a crucial step in what he does is public performance. He takes his notebook onto a stage, sits down at a barebones table, inspects the gathering before him, opens the pages and reads. Throughout the workshop stage, those readings are recorded. He takes the tapes home, listens to himself, the audience, the music. Out of that interaction among what's written, what's read and what's heard grows the piece. This one he's calling *Morning, Noon and Night*.

Ultimately, subtly, the reading becomes the performance of a reading, just as Spalding becomes the role of Spalding. It's theatre, after all, a communal ritual and illusion: the table, the notebook, the ambience (so real, so-easy-I-could-do-it-too). Spalding has become an icon of our culture, speaking out of it and back to it. Every Boy Corralled into Manhood, Every Fantasy of Boundless Sexual Adventures, Every New Home Owner, Sufferer of Symptoms, Son, Lover, Husband, Father . . .

In order to locate *Commune*, the piece of a piece selected for this anthology, we must make two strides backward: first to 1980 when Gray introduced a monologue entitled *A Personal History of the American Theatre*, then back again to 1970 when the Performance Group, of which he was a founding member, presented the eponymous collaborative work, *Commune*. 1980 was an exciting transitional time. Working with the Wooster Group, a direct descendant of the Performance Group, Gray had already created his *Rhode Island Trilogy*. The work forced its way through the most painful areas of his personal life (his mother's nervous collapse and suicide, his family's reactions) into a realm where private experience merged with general cultural history to form a provocative, utterly contemporary expression. Along with those large pieces, he invented his own pioneer form of performance art, the monologues for which he's become famous. By 1980, there had already been *Sex and Death to Age 14; Booze, Cars and College Girls*; and *India and After*.

After that extraordinarily productive period, however, there was a feeling of "what's next?" In his monologues, Gray had caught up with himself, having moved from childhood through young manhood into the present with age forty looming. How could this avatar of what, for better and worse, had become known as the "me decade" deal with personal material that wasn't so distanced and therefore so digested in the memory? And how could he continue the kind of formal experiment that made his past work so innovative and provocative?

*A Personal History of the American Theatre* provided a possible response. Gray wrote the titles of forty-seven works in which he had played some role between 1960 and 1970 on 5x8 cards. At each performance he shuffled the deck and freely associated around what he drew: *The Seagull*, rehearsed for six months in agonized homage to Stanislavski; *The Tower of Babel*, more agony, writhed in Grotowskian semidarkness; *The Reluctant Debutante*, Back Bay Community Theatre, Boston. And *Commune*.

Read today, the piece becomes an archaeological site against which an entire culture can be measured: the end of the 1960s, evoked with astonishing nuance in all of its acid-laced ecstasy; the end of the 1970s, minimalistically cool (Spalding behind the table) and self-conscious in the extreme (Spalding behind the table); the end of the 1990s with *Commune* as history.

I'll quote my review of *A Personal History of the American Theatre* published in the *Soho News* on December 17, 1980: "At [Gray's] best, like any good chronicler, he makes his experience emblematic of his time. He represents us often with uncanny accuracy: paranoid, bemused in the face of tumultuous events beyond our control, self-reflexive to the point of obsession, comforting ourselves with ironic laughter, playing hide-and-seek with the prospect of our own annihilation and the world's."

Everything has changed. Nothing has changed.

**James Leverett** is Chair of the Department of Dramaturgy and Dramatic Criticism at the Yale School of Drama.

# Commune

In 1970, I was in a play (in those days we called it "a piece") called *Commune*, directed by Richard Schechner at the Performing Garage. It was a very risky play in the sense that Richard started working with the actors' actual personalities. It was a collaborative hodgepodge soup of a work based on the alleged murder of Sharon Tate by Charles Manson. That hadn't been proved yet—it had just come out in *Life* magazine. The play was also based on the Bible, *Moby-Dick*, *Walden* and *The Tempest*.

In the middle of a rehearsal, Richard would often ask us to just begin talking about ourselves and our own feelings. It got to be a kind of $8^{1}/_{2}$ situation, where we didn't know if we were playing ourselves or characters or both. And he used a lot of typecasting. For instance, the guy who played the Charles Manson figure was an actual redneck from Oklahoma—and this created some confusion. At a party, someone would say, "Oh, I just loved that stinky old redneck you played in that play!" and he'd say, "Whut ray-ed nay-eck?" (What play?)

Then there was a white magician from Ohio, Brad Smith, who was playing the Christ figure—and in fact, he lived in a Jesus commune on Second Avenue, a loft with no heat, no one paid rent, where everyone lived in tents . . . For the Holy Eucharist, they took blotter acid, blotter LSD and then *went to God*. Brad would spend sometimes two evenings with God, then come into rehearsal the next day all aglow.

So Brad was trying gradually to convert our group to Christianity by giving us all the Holy Eucharist, then reading to us from the Bible while under the influence. But some people were rather reluctant to take the LSD. I, for one, was particularly upset about it. I didn't want to take it. I had read that if you have any schizophrenic tendencies, taking acid can be disastrous. Later on I found I was only schizoid and a Gemini—which is quite a different thing from being schizophrenic—but at the time, I was staying clear of it.

Brad's *major* plan was to convert Richard Schechner from Judaism to Christianity—he was going for broke. He thought he had a chance because Richard was searching for "symbols of possibility." *Commune* was a very dark play, and Richard was looking for a way to end it on an up note called "symbols of possibility." And none of us could figure out what "symbols of possibility" were in 1970 in New York City. But The Bees—Brad's divinely inspired music group from the Jesus commune—had an idea. At the end of the play, they would all assemble on a float with their instruments out on Wooster Street and play divinely inspired music as the garage door went up on the theatre, and they rolled in playing away. They and their music would be the "symbols of possibility."

So they were working on that, and on converting Richard. Around that time, we all went up to be in residence at SUNY New Paltz. It was summer, and we were still working on developing *Commune*. And I began to think, Hmmm. This is a good place to try that LSD. One Saturday, I was alone with Brad and I thought, why not? (In keeping with the idea of being a schizophrenic, I would start with half a tab.) So I took it, and then I said to Brad, "Now I'd like to go up to the woods, if you could drive me to Low Falls." And he said, "Uh, are you sure you don't want to stay down here?" And I thought, uh-oh. This is something we should have discussed before I took the LSD, because I think he's going to want to read to me from the Bible. And I was deeply resisting inside.

Finally, he did take me up to the woods without a problem, and when we got there I set out on my own. I walked down to this stream, waded to the middle of it and jumped onto a rock. The rushing water was pouring around the rock and I stood there, just looking straight ahead, and said, "I am."

Nothing happened, so I tried a little louder.

"I am."

The water kept rushing

"I AM!"

Then I got self-conscious and thought I might be upsetting the campers in the area. So I went back looking for Brad. The sun had just gone down, and I saw this bat fly over. Then I saw a thousand bats with peacock feathers a yard long coming from their tails. I found Brad and said, "This is incredible, fantastic, but what if—what if . . ." (I was always right in there with the what ifs) ". . . what if we were in New York on 8th Street tripping, with all the hippies?"

And just as I asked that, out of the bushes came about fifteen hippies from 8th Street. It was as if it had been rehearsed—I thought Brad had set it up. They came down and saw that we were tripping (I don't know how they knew, I guess because our faces were blue) and they took hatchets and started to attack the tree roots as they screamed and cried out, "Aaah! Argh! AAAAH! That's the fifth poisonous snake we've killed tonight!" But none of this was bothering me at all. I was so high that I saw the tree roots as tree roots.

My friend Steven Snow, he was still a little trapped in some circle of guilt so he saw the tree roots as poisonous snakes. Maybe it was because he thought that Susan Belinda Moonshine had drowned. (You see, for *Commune*, we were all asked to change our names, just like in real communes. Brad and I kept our names, but everyone else changed theirs. Ellen Shine changed hers to Susan Belinda Moonshine.) She was tripping on acid and swimming. Steven was watching her and she disappeared, and he said, "I think Susan Belinda Ellen Shine Moonshine has drowned!"

And that's when I just knew: it doesn't matter!

But Steven didn't understand what I was saying and we were lost and it was dark. These hippies had to lead us out of the woods. At last we came to the highway, and when we stepped out onto the warm road I looked up and the stars were very vivid—I couldn't believe it, it was like seeing stars for the first time in my life. No thoughts in between, no meditation. I went down on my knees and said, "Oh my God, the stars! Take me to the edge of the cliff, Brad! So I can look out."

We drove down a little way in the car and he let me out on the edge of a cliff overlooking the entire valley—and the entire valley was just *breathing*. It was breathing with my body, my body was just an outline like a Matisse drawing, and the valley was just floating through it, the whole landscape was just floating through the outline. I liked that very much. Nothing was left of me but a little pyramid at the top of my head.

As we started back down the mountain road toward New Paltz, I started in again with the "what ifs." "What if we were in *Vietnam* tripping now?" My mind became like a big ferris wheel, the little gondolas were my thoughts. I could look at them go by or stop the ferris wheel, read into them a little bit, then let it go around some more. When we got back to New Paltz, Brad said, "Now I'm going to read to you from the Bible."

But it didn't matter! The pages were blowing like the wind—though there was no wind—and Susan Belinda Moonshine had come back from the dead and she was there and everything was fine.

Now shortly after that, Brad organized a séance. It was the anniversary of the murder of Sharon Tate, and he had everyone come to his room, sit in a circle and hold hands. He asked that we empty ourselves so that the spirit of Sharon Tate could enter. I knew how to empty my body out because of the Matisse experience on the cliff. All of a sudden, my body and mind started rising out of me, just like the liquid in a thermometer.

Then the question presented itself: do I really want the spirit of Sharon Tate to enter me? Up until then, I'd considered it a privilege, but now I was not so sure. Just then, Brad said, "Well, we have a lot of resistance here tonight. I'm afraid we'll all have to stop. But anyway, I should tell you all, I was really calling Christ. I thought I'd call Him in the name of Sharon Tate because none of you guys would let Christ in but you might let Sharon Tate in disguised as Jesus." Oh, he was a trickster.

Those were the cryptic days of LSD. Our audiences thought we were tripping all the time, and they claimed they were peaking at the same time we were. But we weren't tripping—*they* were. Once, we were down at Goucher College, and at the end of the show the women came and touched our bare feet—we were barefoot during the performance—and they said, "You Know, don't you? Oh, you KNOW! You KNOW! You KNOW!"

Our beautiful production of *Commune* traveled the long and winding road of its tour, heading back to be a hit in New York City, accompanied by cryptic messages in the clouds. Joan MacIntosh, who had taken the name of Clementine, was getting dressed up one day in her Schenectady thrift shop outfit that reminded me of a Kentucky schoolgirl. Just as she put on the straw hat, someone said, "Get some music on the radio," and just as I turned the radio on, it was playing a fully orchestrated version of "Oh My Darling Clementine." Everyone went, "Ooooh! it's going to be a hit! Our show is going to be a hit!"

Just before we opened *Commune* in New York, we were asked to go to a nunnery in Darien to help revitalize the Catholic rituals. They felt their rituals were losing vitality, that they needed a theatre company to juice them up. So we broke rehearsals for *Commune* and went out to the nunnery for a long weekend workshop. Brad was ready to see Christ *organically*, because, you know, he hadn't brought any acid, and he decided that if he couldn't see Christ without the acid he was a failure.

The priest gave us a little lecture in the beginning, "In the old days, when people took the Holy Eucharist, in the good old days of Catholicism, the religion was so alive that when the wafer went in their mouths, they'd often have a vision of Christ." Brad was rolling his eyes, sitting there in his buckskin coat, having seen Jesus and gone to God many a night over the past year.

So we started in on specific rituals: the marriage ceremony, the stations of the cross. For that one, we had a drawing—everyone pulled papers out of a hat and they all had X's on them except one that said Jesus. Except we put one too many papers in, and Jesus was left over—no one chose Jesus! That was like Wow—wow—wow, because everyone wanted to be Jesus. We had to do the whole drawing over again. Finally, we got through the stations of the cross and went on to the Feast of the Immaculate Conception, which was wonderful. We all got under the table (on which a big chicken dinner with wine was waiting) and anointed each other's feet. You know, washed them. Then we could eat. The only person who didn't go under the table was Richard Schechner. He said he'd do it after dinner, but he never did.

Finally, we opened *Commune* at the Performing Garage. It was an audience-participation piece in many ways: people were asked to leave their shoes at the door and come in barefoot, and at one point in the show we used a big wave made of plywood. We asked the audience to come and sit in the middle of that wave and represent the villagers of My Lai, and we shot them with our hands. As you can imagine, some people resisted, and didn't want to come out. If anyone refused to come out, the play would not go on until they did.

Once, the play was stopped: one woman in the audience refused to come out and at last went to the phone to call her lawyer. She said she refused to leave the Garage and was going to sue for not having her ticket honored. The company started leaving and people came out of the audience to read the different roles and finish the play. At last someone volunteered to go in for the woman and the play was completed.

We toured *Commune* to Poland—they went wild in Poland. Everyone wanted to see the American spectacle. They didn't care what it was about—they just called it the American Spectacle. In Wrocław, we had five people at the gate just to control the crowd. Students would get a running start, climb right up over people like in a football game, come down the other side, shimmy up those long curtains they use to keep the cold air out—and just hang there like monkeys for the entire production. You could throw hammers at them, wrenches, screwdrivers—it wouldn't do any good. There was no knocking them down. When we played in Warsaw, a thousand people rioted in the street—the police had to be called. People began bending the bars in the men's room windows to get through and burst into the performance and we had to stop the show.

Last, we went to France and played in one of Napoleon's mistresses' chalets in Strasbourg. We had big problems with the French. Not only are they style-conscious, but they are very perverse. In a way I suppose it was our perversity against theirs. We always asked the audience to take their shoes off before they came into "the space": many of the French were wearing very stylish boots and some perverse person would steal one boot each night. One night it would be a right boot, then another night it would be a left one. We were spending two or three hundred dollars a night on new boots for the French!

**Eric Bogosian**

## Introduction by Michael Feingold

Talking about Eric Bogosian you have to proceed carefully; he's strewn the path with snares and pitfalls. He plays—no—he *embodies* characters, a dozen or so in each of his one-man shows. Solo events of his kind tend to go one of two ways: either outward, toward observation ("These are the funny people I saw on the subway."), or inward, toward confession ("This is my true story."). Looking back at Eric's work since his early days at Franklin Furnace, I realize that he takes the rare middle way: each of his embodiments is a dialectic, a figure observed from outside, but whose feelings are projected from within. They emerge from the Bogosian psyche (an early show was titled, *Men Inside*), but they arrive there from his deep, concerned survey of the panorama around him (a later piece was titled *Drinking in America*).

The passions Bogosian shares with his characters give them an extra creepy intensity that's not like the atmosphere of anyone else's solo work. He's a virtuoso, but it's not about virtuosity: seeing him embody one of his roles, you never say, "That's a stretch for him," though you may say, "What a risk that was." He restricts himself to playing men, but within that restriction, his range is so vast and his detail work so varied that he doesn't seem to have any limits at all. His people, horrible as they are, were forged in his soul—they're the losers this winner could see himself becoming, the nightmarish roads not taken, mapped by an artist's emphatic instinct.

One thing that strikes me about his people, is the extent to which they know something is horribly wrong with them, with the things they say and do, with the way they live. They have the suffering souls of artists, but without the artist's gift for expression. They aren't ruled by materialistic values—not even the lowest of them, like the wino who sang "God Bless America" joyously from his gutter in *Drinking in America*—but materialism messes up their heads; it gets confused with their love of democracy, ethics, religion, justice, morality, a good meal or even with the negative joys of revenge and destruction. That's a big blessing for people who feel uneasy in the world, but when they dive for the "big blessing," their value systems get all tangled up, each in their own tragicomic way, making their rightness come out wrong.

Eric's art gives these tangled people a voice, sometimes enthusiastically, sometimes uneasily, with a touch of guilt about the traps of condescension and manipulation. Either way, he celebrates the wonderful ways they get life wrong: they want to say the right thing, do the great thing, make the triumph, but something in the collision of our time and their nature makes them take a wrong turn.

And they get it wrong with an unholy energy. Eric is a performer who lights up on stage—off stage, he's a nice, quiet guy—on stage, I'm sometimes even a little afraid of him. But his seeming ease of performance masks a double struggle, both with his inner, artistic impulse and with the truth behind his observations.

Eric Bogosian's characters can't escape the parameters of his person— he *is* them in a way that few authors, even actor-authors, have been their own creations—but they stay in the mind, once you've seen him, as figures very distinct from Eric the writer-performer. There's a truth to them that's their own and not his—especially amazing when you think of how they lie, evade, chop logic and generally beat against the confines of the screwed-up world they live in, all concrete-block buildings and strip malls and amplified visual noise. The artist who can find the core of truth in that must be digging incredibly deep.

It makes total sense to learn that Eric's pieces have universal application: his texts have been performed all over, not just by would-be solo "Erics," but by ensembles, and not just in English. The truth at the core turns out to be visible in Poland and Italy and Argentina as well as here. For me— and for most theatregoing New Yorkers, I expect—the words will always evoke the specific physicality of Eric Bogosian. For the rest of the world they don't have to—they evoke meaning, reality and truth.

**Michael Feingold** is chief theatre critic of the *Village Voice*, a recipient of the George Jean Nathan Award, and translator of many plays, including collaborations of Bertolt Brecht and Kurt Weill.

from **Sex, Drugs, Rock & Roll**

## Dog Chameleon

*A man sits in a chair, talking into a microphone with suppressed anger. He tries to be pleasant.*

Hey, I want to be normal, just like every other guy! Don't leave me out, come on! There's got to be more to life than worrying about the price of cigarettes, getting a job, what's on TV. I know—I know about normalcy. Don't tell me about normalcy!

I want to drive a station wagon with a bunch of kids singing Christmas carols in the backseat. I want to go to the supermarket and compare prices. I want to lose weight while I sleep. I want to buy life insurance. I want to wear pajamas and a bathrobe, sneak into the kitchen in the middle of the night and steal a drumstick out of the refrigerator. Worry about my dog's nutrition. Or maybe just order something nice from the L. L. Bean catalog . . . a nice down parka maybe, a flannel shirt . . . something in corduroy!

I know all about normalcy!

I want to yell at my wife when she goes on a spending spree! I want to help my kids with the grades! I want to fertilize my lawn. I want to order my hamburger *my way*! I want to donate money to impoverished minorities!

But all that stuff costs money. Being normal is expensive, you know?

*(Short pause.)*

There was this rat scratching inside my wall the other night. After a while it sounded like it was inside my head. *And I said, "Wait a minute! Wait one minute! I'm white, I'm an American! I'm a male! I should be doing better than this!"*

Ozzie and Harriet didn't have rats in the wall. There were no roaches in the Beaver's room! Even Mister Ed had *heat*! WHAT THE FUCK IS THIS?

This rat kept scratching and I realized something: times have changed.

It's a race to the death now. Anyone waiting around for the good life to show up is a *fool*! Anyone who thinks that playing fair will get you anywhere is *blind*!

Then I said, "Calm down, calm down, you're getting all excited about nothing. Sure you're poor, you're an artist! You have an artistic sensibility! Artists are supposed to be poor."

And the rat-scratch voice inside my head said, Fuck that!

I want to be rich. And I want to be famous. These are normal desires, that should not be thwarted. If you thwart them, if you repress them, you get cancer.

Shit, I want *fame*! Look at *me*, man! Fame is what counts. Fame with money. Any jerk can go to the top of some tower with a scope rifle and start shooting at people. That's shitty fame. I want the good kind. The kind with lots and lots of money. Any slob can win the lottery, it takes *skill* and *brains* to get the fame and the money *at the same time* . . . that's success, man. So everyone looks at you, wherever you go, and they say, "That guy, he did it. He got everybody to look at him, admire him and give him money, their money, at the same time!"

I heard about this guy, he made four-hundred-million dollars. Four-hundred-million dollars! I'd be happy with fifty million. Most people would still think I was a success, even if I wasn't as successful as that guy. I don't care what they think! I wouldn't even tell them how much money I have! I'd just ride around in my stretch limousine, and when I got tired of that I'd go home and I'd have this enormous mansion with fifty rooms . . . And . . . and I'd have this room with a trench around it full of pit bulls, and I'd have a chair that tilts back and a TV set with remote control and a big bowl of potato chips!

And I'd just watch TV all day and change the channels. Maybe I'd just sit in a large bathtub with lots of bubbles. Smoke a cigar like Al Pacino in *Scarface* . . . But I wouldn't take drugs or have sex. Too dangerous. Just gimme the money, and the food and the darkroom . . . and the TV set. And a gun—so I can shoot the TV set when somebody I don't like comes on.

I hate people. They get in the way of a good time. Just when everything's getting good, they want something from you!

But I want you all to love *me*. Even though I hate all of you. Just to confirm my deep-seated feeling that you're all scum compared to my beneficence.

Just joking. Just joking. Don't get all excited. Nothing to get excited about. Just love me. Tell me I'm great. And pay me. And then we'll be even. For all the shit you've given me my whole fucking life! I know, I know what you're all thinking, "What a jerk. All he does is talk about himself." Yeah? And what do you do? LISTEN!

I was wronged when I was little. I never really got what I wanted. Now it's time to even the score. Even if I tell you my plans you can't stop me. I'm gonna be so rich and powerful, no one will touch me.

And all those rich fucks who lorded over me, all those muscular jocks who kicked sand in my face, all those big-boobed blondies who laughed at me when I asked them for a date, all those parsimonious, paternal, patronizing administrators at school and at the unemployment office and at the IRS and the police station . . . you'll all be sorry. You have no idea what I've got in store for you. Hah!

You know what it means to be really, really rich? You walk into a store and the jerk behind the counter gives you some shit like . . . like, I don't know, smirking at you because he thinks you can't afford the most expensive watch in the case . . . You know the look they give you, they humor you, "Yes sir, may I help you?"

He doesn't want to help me, he doesn't want to help anybody—he just wants to laugh at me! Won't show me the watch, won't take it out, won't even tell me the price . . .

Well, when I make it, I'm going to go back to that store and I'm not going to buy one watch, I'm not going to buy ten watches—I'm going to buy the whole store, and then I'll fire that patronizing jerk for laughing at me . . . And then, I'm going to find out where he lives and I'm going to buy his apartment building and I'm going to have him evicted . . . one more pathetic homeless person walking the streets in a state of permanent depression!

Or those big thugs that push into you when you're walking down the street and don't say they're sorry or nothing. Why? Because they think I can't fight back. They think I'm afraid of them. Well, when I make it, I'm gonna get me some bodyguards. They'll walk with me when I'm going down the street. And some fucker pushes into me and I'll just step aside and there's my boy with the sock filled with marbles. Or the straight razor. Or the .38. He won't know what's hit 'im. He'll just end up on the ground, bleeding, looking up at me with glazed eyes, and I'll just lean over and step over 'im and say, "Excuse me." *(Laughs)*

You think I should be ashamed of myself? I HAVE NO GUILT! Because I am not a man. I am a dog. *(Barks a long howl)*

You know what I find fascinating? Human nature. The nature of human beings . . . what they like, what they don't like, what turns them on, what turns them off. What incredible appetites they have. Night after night they stay glued to their TV sets watching some pinheaded newscaster going on and on about today's grisly murder or vicious rape. They munch on popcorn and suck up TV dinners as they absorb the minutiae pertaining to the day's massive mud slide or exploding chemical plant.

*(Mimicking the newscaster) "Thousands dead and dying! Hundreds blinded!"*

Munch . . . munch . . . "Carol, get some more salt while you're in the kitchen! . . . Oh wait, wait, come here, you have to see this—they're completely buried! Come on, you'll miss it, there's a commercial coming on!"

Then, these same people watch shows on educational TV about dolphins, *then* they cry . . . Then they stay up late to watch some old

Christmas movie with Jimmy Stewart standing on a bridge on Christmas Eve; *then* they go berserk!

The next morning, they jump into their sporty compact cars, drink ten cups of coffee, and race each other on the highway while they sing along with some ardent rock singer screaming and yelling about emaciated, dark-skinned, hopeless people turning to dung half a world away.

So they feel so guilty they race home and write out a check for five dollars and mail it to some post-office box in New York City and then they feel so good about themselves they go to bed with each other and they kiss and they lick and they suck each other and they hold each other really, really tight, because they really, really care . . .

*(Pause.)*

I know I'm negative. I know I'm not a nice guy. I know you all hate me. But I don't care. Because at least I realize I'm a shit, and for that tiny fragment of truth, I respect myself. That's why normalcy is so far out of my reach. Because you have to be blind to be normal. You have to like yourself, and the thought of that is so repellent to me that I'm ecstatic to be in the depressing place that I am!

---

## from **Pounding Nails in the Floor with My Forehead**

### Intro

Thank you.

*(Some people clap, if none clapped before.)*

No, no, it's too late. But thank you. I'm very happy you could all make it tonight. It really means a lot to me. Means a lot to all of us, I'm sure. Or maybe not, maybe it doesn't mean anything, I don't know.

But thanks anyway. It's great that you're all, uh, sitting out there and I'm standing up here and you're all, uh, you know, looking at me. I like to be looked at, so uh, thank you. You're doing just what I want you to do. Just sit back, relax, put on your glasses, get out your binoculars, focus your telescopes 'cause here I am.

And I want to thank you for this opportunity to reveal myself. Expose myself. Strip naked, so to speak. Take it off. Take it all off. Really show you everything I can be.

Which isn't much, I know. I mean, if you're disappointed, I understand. I've never really been a likable person. In fact I'm kind of an unlikable person. And, you know, maybe you're a *likable* person, so maybe you feel *superior* to me because you're easy to get along with and I'm not.

I don't really care what you think.

But, so, uh, is everybody ready to have a good time? Just went out and had something to eat in the neighborhood? Maybe a little nouvelle cuisine before the show? No. Something ethnic before you came by tonight? Something Third World? A little couscous, maybe, tandoori, fajita, burrito? Nothing like a nice hot ethnic dish before you go to see that semi-expensive, semi-meaningful Off-Broadway show. Nothing like a nice hot dish from a country where no one can actually *afford* to eat the very thing you're stuffing your face with.

Did you have some nice Third World beer with your burritos? Maybe some DOS EQUIS? Six pack of Dos Equis? Down front here, a couple of bottles of chardonnay. Couple of hits of acid in the back row?

I don't care what you do with your free time. You come in here and you're just so comfortable and so easygoing and likable and you're just such a nice person. And you come in here and you've got this *attitude*. No, no. I know the attitude. You don't even clap when I kill myself on the first bit. You judge me. You sit there and you *judge* me. Don't act like I can't see you, I can see you. *(He mimics an audience member whispering to her neighbor)*

I mean, you come in here, you make no effort at all. I'm supposed to jump all over the place, like some kind of puppet on a string, *entertain* you! Hey, let's get something straight, in case you don't know what you just paid thirty-five bucks to see, this is what I do. This is my work. This is my life up here. Okay? This isn't *Ace Ventura, Pet Armenian*! *(He hits the floor)* You don't like it, fine with me. Fine with fucking me. *(He moves offstage, into the wings)*

It's okay, it's okay, I'm not angry. "He's angry! He's got an angry social message. He's the cutting edge of the black hole of the American psyche! I read about it in the *Village Voice*!" *(Returning)* Fuck that shit! I'm not angry, okay? I'm happy.

Because I know that being unhappy and angry and pessimistic is a big turn-off. You didn't come here tonight to hear a lot of pessimistic, negative stuff. You came here tonight to be entertained, to be uplifted, to build up an appetite for the decaf cappuccino after the show.

And I *want* you to like me, I want to have a warm loving relationship with this audience, I don't want to have a dysfunctional relationship to this audience. I want to bond with this audience.

By the end of the night I want us to be as one, like a giant school of fish swimming shoulder to shoulder with hundreds of thousands of compadres.

And we'll move together as one to make a greater dream possible!

A world where love and harmony will rule, and everyone is happy and well fed and disease-free and PART OF.

I want to stand up here tonight and say, "I AM ONE AMONG MANY." I don't want to rock the boat, I want to help *row*!

That's what I want, and I know that's what you want, too.

You know we've all been through a lot of therapy over the past ten years, and I'm very proud of where my therapy has taken me. I learned some things. And the cornerstone of what I've learned can be said in three little words: people are special.

You know I was in my apartment last week when that big snow-storm hit and I could see the first few snowflakes falling. And I didn't get all negative. I didn't think, Oh shit another snowstorm. No. I watched those snowflakes falling, what was I watching, a hundred thousand, two hundred thousand snowflakes, and you know what I thought?

I thought, Every one of those snowflakes is different. Unique. But you know what else? They're all the same, because they're all snow.

And that's what we are. Every one of us. Every person here tonight is unique, special . . . but every person here is exactly the same. Every person here has a skull in their head, blood in their veins. Take a straight razor, run it across your wrist, every person here bleeds.

We just have our particular loves and hates, likes and dislikes. That's what makes each of us different.

*(He looks at an audience member)* You. You like Mariah Carey. Now, I, I hate Mariah Carey. So in that way, we're different. *(To another audience member)* You think Phil Collins is a genius? Phil Collins makes me puke. *(To the balcony)* Up in the balcony: you love Pearl Jam. Every time I listen to them I think, What the fuck does "Pearl Jam" mean? What does it mean???!!!

You want to know what I like? I like the sound of a jackhammer ripping concrete at six o'clock in the morning outside my bedroom window. I like the sound of a dentist's drill. I like the sound of the dial tone, real loud. I like the sound of two cats fucking. I like the sound of an eighty-year-old grandmother taking out her dentures at night.

I like the announcements they make in the subways. *(He speaks into the mike in garbled gibberish)*

What do you like? Do you like it a lot? Have you given it a lot of thought? I hope so. I really hope so. Because I'll tell you something right now, you take everybody in this room and strip all of you naked and shave your heads, stick you in a tiny little cell, feed you one watery bowl of gruel a day and you know what? IT WOULDN'T MAKE A FLYING FUCK WHAT YOU LIKE!

So thank you . . . thanks a lot for coming . . . thank you. I hope you like the show.

# Rash

*Man speaks directly to the audience, gesticulating with a large barbecue fork as he mimes grilling at a barbecue.*

So what we did, we put a chain-link fence around the whole fifteen acres. Barbed wire on top. For security, for security. 'Cause you know, Charlie, we're here all summer, the kids are running around in the yard. I sleep better at night just knowing it's out there.

Oh, yeah, we're here all summer. I go down the city maybe two, three times a month. But you know it's hot down there and we got everything we need up here. The pool. Sonia's got her tennis court, I got my griller. I just stay here all summer and grill. I put everything on this thing: steaks, chops, chicken. Last Sunday, I did some lobsters. Came out beautiful. Once they stop moving, they're a snap to cook.

Did you look at my grill, Charlie? Look at my grill. Brand new, I just got it. It's beautiful. See, right here where the steaks are, this is the grilling part. Then over here I got two stovetops, you wanna boil some peas, carrots. Underneath, oven. You can bake a cake, cookies, whatever you want.

Up here, microwave oven. Ice chest on the side, 'frigerator on the back. Three phone lines.

Very reasonable, around three grand. Got it from the Hammacher-Schlemmer catalog. I love it. I just stand here all summer and grill. Very relaxing, I just stay here by the pool, they swim, I grill. Makes me very mellow. Like meditating.

*(Shouts off)* WHAT?!! Nah, we don't want any . . . You want any goat cheese? Charlie doesn't want any either. I don't care what you did to it, we *hate* goat cheese. Listen, Honey, we're starving to death out here, send out some Doritos or something. Well, if you're too busy, Jeremy can bring 'em.

*(Calling to a different part of the stage)* Jeremy, Honey, go up to Mommy on the porch, get Daddy and Uncle Charlie some Doritos.

*(Back to Sonia)* He can do it, Sonia, just give him the Doritos. Give him the Doritos! Don't give him the goat cheese!

*(To Charlie)* Oh yeah, he loves it. He's in there all day. Like a fish. No. No. No. No. There's no chlorine in that pool, Charlie. They use chlorine in the *cheap* pools. This filter, this is the *best* you can get. Fourteen layers of charcoal, three layers of sand. Then there's a machine, you can't see it, under the tennis courts, boils the water into steam, sterilizes it drop by drop.

Comes back to the pool, completely pure. Completely pure. You can't get water like that in *nature*.

'Cause I figure we got people comin' over every weekend. Somebody's gonna come over, do a couple of laps. Guy's got herpes, next thing I know everybody in the house has herpes. What do you do with a six year old with herpes? I figure spend the money, get the filter. Why waste the aggravation?

I got a good life. I never want to leave the house. I had to go to the city last week, visit a client, it was *torture*. It was like going off to war.

I mean you go down there now, it's like the black hole of Calcutta. You been down there lately? It's depressing. They're lying on the streets, begging, on drugs. With the babies, now they're begging. I feel so bad for those poor people, 'cause it's not their fault.

But what can you say? Life isn't fair. It's the roll of the dice, they're *fucked*. I didn't make up the rules. I just say thank God he loves us. *(Fiddles with the cooking steaks)*

You like roast peppers? *(Stabs downward, then holds the fork up)* Look at this pepper, isn't it beautiful? Balducci's, five bucks each, the best you can get. I'll have one too.

See, I keep 'em on ice over here in the ice chest, anytime I want peppers, I . . . WHAT? YES! PUT THE CORN ON *NOW*. PUT THE CORN ON NOW, SONIA! THE STEAK'S GONNA BE READY IN FIVE MINUTES. YOU WANT COLD STEAK? I'M ASKING, YOU WANT COLD STEAK? THEN PUT THE CORN ON NOW!

Did I tell you about last spring when we went on vacation? No, I know you know we went on vacation, but let me tell you . . .

About three weeks before we go away, I'm working in mid-town around 48th Street. And every day, I go out to lunch, stretch my legs. And every day there's this guy in front of the building with one of those signs: WILL WORK FOR FOOD. Begging. So every day, I pass this guy, I give him a quarter, I figure, I can afford it.

The guy gets used to seeing me. Every day at lunch, sees me coming, kinda gets all perky when he sees me. Gets up on his hind legs.

So about a week before we're gonna go on vacation, I go out to lunch, I see the guy, guy sees me, I reach into my pocket, I don't have any change! He's looking at me. So I figure, what the hell, who's it gonna kill? Give the guy a buck.

I throw a buck at the guy. Turns out, it's not a buck, it's a twenty-dollar bill. Don't ask me how it happened. Guy jumps up, starts shaking my hand, blessing me, telling me God loves me, Jesus loves me. Shaking my hand in the middle of the sidewalk. And I never really looked at this guy up close before. He's got all these sores all over his face, no teeth, his breath could peel paint. And I'm thinking, you know, "I gave you the money, now go back and sit down!"

Anyway, I forget about the guy; three days later, me and Sonia go down to St. Barth's . . . Very nice hotel by the beach, they give you a brochure about the food and how there's these dolphins and you lie on the beach and watch the dolphins. Seven hundred dollars a night.

We get down there, I'm a little tense, I want to relax, so we go down the beach. I'm lying there, looking for the dolphins, no dolphins. I'm getting a strain in my neck. Turns out, there's no dolphins in the Caribbean. I'm in litigation with the hotel as we speak.

Anyway, we're lying there, Sonia says, "What's that?" She's pointing to my hand. There's this rash on the back of my hand. I say, I don't know, poison ivy from the country house. Forget about it.

Charlie, by the end of the week, this rash is halfway up my arm. We come back to the city, I go straight to my doctor's.

He says, "Good thing you came to see me. If you hadn't come to see me, that would have gone right up your arm, up your neck, into your eyes. You'd be *blind*!" Turns out . . . RIGHT! THAT'S RIGHT! The *guy*. Turns out, it's some kind of disease they give each other in the men's shelter. Some kind of bum disease.

All I'm saying, Charlie, all I'm saying is: I give the guy money, he gives me a disease!

*(Looks up)* Jeremy, what are doing?! No, Honey, don't throw Doritos in the pool. Get away from the pool, YOU'RE GONNA CLOG UP THE FILTER, IT'S GONNA COST ME FIFTY THOUSAND DOLLARS, NOW GET AWAY FROM THE POOL. JUST GO SOMEWHERE.

*(Back to Charlie)* I mean, look, I'm the world's biggest liberal. But you know I'm watching that CNN, I'm watching those riots in L.A. and I'm thinking to myself, What if they start doing that around here? What if they start running around like that around here?

I mean, look at this house, Charlie. You can't see this house from the road. We're vulnerable up here. What happens, we're up here one Sunday, we're hanging out: reading the paper, eating bagels, grinding coffee beans. I pick up the phone to call my mother, "Oh, the phone is dead!"

I look up, a couple of homies are at the back door. Breaking down the back door. They don't even have to be black, they could be anybody. Then what do I do? What do I do then? "Oh, come on in, would you like a cup of coffee? Maybe you'd like to rape my wife, kill my kids, burn my house down?"

What do I do then, Charlie? What do I do then?

That's why I have the gun. *(Fiddles with steak)* I would, I would shoot them, for the kids I would shoot. If they were from the phone company, I would still shoot them.

Anyways, these are ready. *(Calls off)* Jeremy, Honey, come out of the bushes, Daddy's not angry anymore. Come on out, we'll discuss it later. We're gonna have din-din now. No, no hot dogs, we've got fifteen-dollar-a-pound prime sirloin from Dean & DeLuca, now come out of the bush. COME ON! COME IN THE HOUSE!

## **Introduction** by Han Ong

The startling word cross-pollination and the staccato, part jazz, part rock and roll rhythms in Jessica Hagedorn's *Black: Her Story* [which later became a part of *Airport Music*] go way back to the heady ferment of the early seventies Bay Area literary scene, where Jessica did her American growing-up. So it made sense (and a kind of nice circle) that, after she and I performed the rough draft of *Airport Music*—think of unplaned wood—at The Joseph Papp Public Theater in the spring of '94, we would take the piece, revised and planed, back to the thick of the Bay Area, to Berkeley Rep. A kind of homecoming.

Jessica was part of a generation that believed that experimentation in the arts (as well as in other, more famous things such as sex, drugs and rock and roll) would pay back great dividends, that something new could be made to bloom from taking what the previous generation had laid down, and then leaping off of that, straight into the stratosphere—and what's more, that the public would be right along for the strange ride. It wasn't important that audiences understood every single thing the artist talked about, but that they knew, or sensed, an underlying architecture was behind the words, and that this architecture would help them connect those dots that had sunk in **119** and been successfully absorbed. For Jessica, that underlying architecture has been many things: a love for words, and therefore, a desire to sweep the listener up in this same love; a strong belief in intersecting the personal and the historical; a sense of *kalokohan* (Tagalog for "tomfoolery") to combat any creeping in of the highbrow; a belief, inherited from rock, and later from punk, in the power of the *sounds* of words, words as rhythm, as percussion—hence, her predilection for alliteration.

Anyway, it was a great time to grow up, and all those things we think of now as "Hagedornisms"—the art of storytelling through collage; a "multiculti" world assumed from the get-go and treated with a feathery, anything-but-sanctimonious touch; the hothouse tropics atmosphere (think Manuel Puig) crossed with the "school of cool" dialogue (think Beat)—all had their genesis in that great environment. And the best part of that legacy was this: faith. Faith in the audience, the reader, that they understood the directive as being: "Get with it, groove with it, ride it, run with it." Faith in their inherent smartness.

So. Back to Berkeley Rep. Summer of '94. There we were, myself off stage while Jessica was doing her monologue. Magellan and the spices running smack dab into Frida and her house of blue skulls doubling back on Jessica's mother and then Jessica's daughters. A riff. Connect the dots, right? Architecture, right? A woman trying to process the disparate elements of her historical legacy (Filipino), her family history (mongrel Filipino), her faith (Spanish Catholic) and the vital present tense of her children (American to the bone), while simultaneously invoking cautionary tales of a role model, Frida (Mexican). Rock and roll, it was rock and roll, spoken.

Jessica had on large, silver hoop earrings and as she talked and gesticulated they would move, making circles in the air. Her words made even more circles. As for the audience, well, we did have our share of great along-for-the-riders who whooped and hollered and hummmed, circling and circling with us, but for the most part, they were squares. Boy, were they square! They seemed to want only the straight line. (I understand this appetite for the straight line because I myself have it, but, *Airport Music*, being a refracted thing on immigrant life, well, it just couldn't get straight.) Still, Jessica would perform her dizzying word love-fest night after night, and boy, seeing that underlying faith in the audience again and again was a beautiful lesson for me. Get with it, groove with it, run with it.

That was all there was to the show, really—words, the power of words, just bodies and words circling around. And now you have this faith right before you—concretized into sturdy type—and hopefully this time an audience will cluster around and rise to the occasion. Huh? Come on guys. Get with it, groove with it, run with it. Reward the beautiful faith.

**Han Ong** has written and performed his own solo show, *Corner Store Geography*, and has recently completed his first screenplay, *Cantonese Pop Star*, which he will be directing.

# Black: Her Story
## (The Mexican Mother Meets the Oldest Living Virgin of Manila)

In 1993, Alva Rogers invited Jessica Hagedorn to share a double bill with her at Dixon Place. Both women were to perform solo pieces inspired somehow by the Mexican artist Frida Kahlo. Hagedorn created *Black: Her Story* and invited Han Ong to see the piece. *Black: Her Story* later became a part of *Airport Music*, a multimedia theatre collaboration between Hagedorn and Ong, which was presented in 1993 at the L.A. Festival and at The Joseph Papp Public Theater and Berkeley Repertory Theatre in 1994.

*Queridisimo Doctorcito: thank you for the fetus you sent me. The baby boy. Would you say I was a jazz poem, spit from the mouth of a saxophone? Or would you send me straight to hell? Pensamiento, pentimento, pimiento . . . Can you believe my mother is dead? And her twin sister? And my father, too? All within a matter of months, yet none of them liked each other. Here then, my grocery list of fickle desires. Once again, I am. Your monkey. Your Frida.*

*Reddish-purple: Aztec. Old blood of prickly pear. The most alive and oldest color.*

*Black: nothing is black. Really, nothing.*

*His story. Her story.* I lose patience with the obvious and clench my fists. Imagine. Lim Ah Hong. Big Wong. Manong. All wrong. What my Mexican mother said before she died: *the joke of a dream. The red vision. I cannot tolerate morphine.* Forty years later, my Chinese brother says to my brother: *O, you Filipinos. You love us, you hate us, you kidnap us. But you can't live without us.*

Here's another version: "O, you Filipinos. Can't stop dreaming about us. Blame us, love us, hate us, kidnap our children and kill us. Burn our houses down . . . But you can't live without us."

Here's my version: "O, you Filipinos. You so *f-ed* up."

What to do when the English no longer makes sense? *Ay, puta. Ay naku. Buwisit. Putang ina mo. Que asco. Que barbaridad. Que horror.*

Imagine. It is 1963 and I have just arrived here. You are still sitting on a mound of dirt over there, watched over by Jesuits. We curse in Tagalog, Spanish, English, Fukkienese, Mandarin. You study the faces of old immigrant men and women, terrified. You are not born yet. It is 1963. Soon, Kennedy and then Malcolm X will be assassinated. Does America live up or down to my expectations? Is it the Hollywood of our colonized imaginations? You are born. The Vietnam War is finally over. I am mistaken for a *pachuca* in high school. *You pachuco pachuca chicana greaser girl?* Yeah, I say. Sure.

*What is a Filipino? Kinda like a Mexican, I say. But not really. How about this image: we're small-time gangsters who can dance. Yo-yo champions of the world. Isn't that an easy one for you to access? O, they say, disappointed. But. You speak English so well. How did you learn so much, swimming from island to island?*

It is 1984 and you've just arrived. I don't know you yet, but we've met somewhere before—over there, I'm sure. I already know what you're going to say as the movie projector switches on in my head. Images that recur burn up the screen. *Let us begin.*

A woman nailed to a cross. Contrary to popular opinion, she is not bleeding.

A woman suspended in a red void. Her daughters float in the sky above her. She reaches out, her legs spread, the palms of her hands up in a gesture of . . . supplication? beseeching? blessing? Is she screaming or laughing? She is childless but imagines her children into existence. A profane immaculate conception.

One daughter wears a red dress, as red as the red void in which her mother is suspended. The other daughter is a baby, a naked peach, a fierce *olmec* cherub. Like her sister in the scarlet dress, like her mother has taught her from the womb, the floating baby's eyes are shut in a constant dream. Her tiny, terrifying teeth are bared in a sly jaguar grin. She is beautiful. Her sister in the bloody dress is beautiful. A poet materializes into the frame. She is the mother's twin, a woman from Alhambra shrouded in black velvet. Her glass bangles make too much noise, and the baby almost wakes up. "Look what you've done," the twins accuse each other.

The mother's legs scissor the red horizon. Her back splits open: magnolia, plumeria and calla lilies unfurl on her broken spine. Her flesh a map of scars. A map of the universe. Manong, manong. Walk the dog. Stand still. Big Wong. What went wrong?

*Dear Doctorcito. Find a soft spot, what's left of my skin, and inject. There. There.* I have learned that what is possible is often not visible. I'm a monkey. I devour bananas, crackers and cheese. I pour hot wax on my bald, bent head. I howl even when I sleep. I'm a scammer, a thief, the queen of self-pity, the Empress of Sorrow. I paint everything gold. The stove, the refrigerator, the radio, the telephone, the bed, the plates, the silver. *Midasina, Medea, Medusa.* Jump cut. My twin sister poet holds up a tube of red lipstick. My mother-sister puckers her lips. *Find a soft spot. There. There.* Mother, sister, daughter, daughter, sister, sister, niece, aunt. Twin. There are too many women in this house. A cluster of spikes, not snakes. The woman nailed to a cross grows bored with the nails embedded in her palms, embedded in her beautifully manicured feet. There is no blood. The nails are brand-new, rustproof. Dipped in hydrogen peroxide before being hammered in. I grow bored with my anguish, screech with rage and writhe for my salvation. My children howl along with me, a chorus of thorns.

*"Somebody yank this shit out."*

There is too much light in the room. The movie abruptly ends.

Imagine. The Philippine landscape lit by a pale gold moon. You've been there. We were born in a cemetery, a tropical burial ground made unholy by Christian generals, immortal tyrants and their lacquered wives. Your mother's ghost dances on a piano in a haunted house in Sarrat. Your father gasps for breath and jabs at the air with a knife. It is you he wants. Mine gasps for air and weeps like a child in that hospital in Makati. Like yours, he's been dying for years. Love him, hate him, burn his house down.

Your mother shrieks with joy: *so much gold it lights up the night!* Our mothers . . . whose pleasures were Catholic, forbidden and therefore fleeting.

*Knock knock. Who's there? Emy. Emy who? Emygrant.* A diva I once knew defined motherhood as "the ultimate censorship." On the telephone, I can't tell her voice apart from her daughter's. It's the main reason I don't call her anymore.

Imagine. Delicious obsessions. You flew here on an airplane. I sailed on a ship. Magellan went looking for spices. All those mad Europeans went looking for spices. Their lives lacked chili pepper and heat, they longed for something they could not name, what was possible was not visible, so in the name of God and the Fat, Pale Queen they went sailing in search of gold, pepper, saffron and souls. And here we are, the bastards of Discovery, quincentennial years later! You flew here on an airplane. You flew here in a rage. I sailed on a ship for an eternity of seventeen days to California, and shut my eyes to save myself and dream. *Little Richard, Chuck Berry, Fats Domino . . .*

Bad vibes back home. In my dream, the natives throw a fiesta but they smell something fishy. For once, they aren't buying into it—not the blue-eyed priest, not the startling skin, not the gold of the conquistador's hair or the gold of his cross, not the smell or shape or shine of any of it. It is 1521 on the island of Mactan. The air stinks of paranoia, Spanish sweat and death. No one's feeling hospitable. Unlike Columbus, Magellan gets dissed, ambushed and decapitated. WHACKED off by the tribal chief Lapu Lapu, Magellan's head rolls on and on and on across the bloody sand of the beach and disappears into the salty Pacific Ocean.

In the official version, the armor-suited Magellan is felled by arrows and left to die on the beach. But I like mine better.

*How we remember. What we remember. Why? Who? What? Where? When? Who? Who else? Who with? Who said? How? How much? With what? With whom? Where else? Why? Why? Why? Why is the cross of Magellan a tourist attraction in the Philippines? Why is a scavenger fish named after Lapu Lapu in the Philippines?*

O Ferdinand, O Isabella, O Cristofer, O Cortez, O Lopez de Legaspi, O Ponce, O Balboa, O Vasco de Gama, O Popes of manifest destiny. There was never enough gold to mine. This was never Peru, and all you found was cinnamon.

Wrong again. It is 1941 and I'm in my *casita azul*. I'm wearing your pants and smoking a cigarette. It's one I rolled myself, I'm terrible at rolling anything—the tobacco keeps falling out, the paper is soaked with saliva and I keep having to relight the cigarette. But I look good, don't I? A pensive pose—*kalachuchi* flower stuck in my thick black hair . . . dead center, so you can't miss it in the photograph. The one where I stand next to Trotsky. Somber yet stunning. *Just so*, how I lean against the wall of my little blue house of skulls.

Did you decide early on if you were ugly or pretty? Were you considered a barrio beauty? You have to choose—it helps you endure. Filipinos know how to endure, don't they? *Magtiis ka lang*, we say. I decided early on that I was magnificent. I smoked my cigars, I wore my rustling skirts with their layers of ostentatious ruffles and itchy lace, I was Diego's sequined monkey bride with my sunflower headdress instead of a veil. The starched rays of my *Tehuantepec* crown jutting out from the sides of my head. I was your mother, goddamnit, the leopard queen bitch of kitsch. I nag you from my grave, in my eternal agony, glorious still.

*And where are Dolores, Bessie and Perlita? La Chinita Anna May? El maldito Nelson Rockefeller? And that fucking Maria Felix . . . how dare she outlive me!*

*Dear Doctorcito: I'm wearing my motorcycle jacket. The one that's black and smells of skin. Caimito de Guayabal is perched on my shoulder. Sweet monkey. I ape the ape Caimito, I'm your monkey perched on a pew. My mustache is waxed, my silver fur brushed and gleaming with Tres Flores pomade. The airless chapel is fragrant with my fecal perfume. My dainty, black, old-lady hands are clasped in prayer. Father. Hear my confession. Mother. Bless your little monkey for I have sinned. Sin vergüenza, your Jessica.*

*Dear Doctorcito. I want a shave, please. Give me a close shave. Don't shave me too close. I am very thin-skinned.*

Everything you made up is true. My brother exists. He's a twentieth-century zealot on lithium, ranting the scriptures in Tagalog and English to anyone who listens. No one does. *Cobalt blue: electricity, pure love.*

I'm a nun on fire, I wear your baggy pants, I'm Diego in love. Rub my rotunda of a belly three times for good luck. On your knees, you hobble like a cripple from one station of the cross to the other. There are exactly fourteen. Take your time. Don't ask too many questions. Keep the faith. The church is our motherfucker, this abstract ménage à trois, a sacred passion.

Where do we live now? Here or there? Are you disappointed? Have your dreams and ways of speaking become too precise and American?

*Dear Doctorcito: some say the yo-yo was invented by a Filipino. Some say the Chinese. Why do they always say the Chinese? Some say it once was a jungle weapon. Even the French have tried claiming it as theirs. In English, "yo-yo" connotes flakiness. The back and forth motion of indecision. A toy. In Spanish, "yo-yo" means "I, I." I read somewhere that in Tagalog, "yo-yo" means "to return."*

Beware of yellow. Frida defined it as the color of madness, sickness, fear. But also as the color of the sun and joy. *Maginghat ka, ha. Maraming mga hayop duun . . . at dito rin, sa gabi . . . in the night.* While my daughters sleep, we'll laugh and steal each other's words. Reinvent geography. Recall our flight from one shifting continent to the next. Wallow in the mud of mistaken identities. Cross-dress to Calvary.

## Introduction by Michael Flanagan

In discussing the performance work of Diamanda Galás, a primary element to mention initially is the passion and intensity of the performance. In addition to her visceral commitment to her politics, the infusion of passion into her work has its theoretical basis in her study of German Expressionist theatre and cinema, particularly the work of Oskar Kokoschka, Lotte Eisner and Felix Emmel. In this school of thought, the transformation of the performer occurs through his/her linking of performance to states of consciousness, such as possession and trance, experienced by shamans and mystics.

The influence of Expressionist theatre was apparent in Galás's *Medéa Tarántula* (1979), which, through black, angular sets with multilevel platforms and mirrors, black vinyl costumes and makeup, simulating the human skull, all emphasized the representation of mental constructs (emotional states) through revealed light and shadow. Expressionist design was used in *Masque of the Red Death* (1986), with large bleachers and shadow-inducing lights; *Plague Mass* (1989), performed in the Cathedral of St. John the Divine, with red back-lighting, smoke and black robes; *Insekta* (1993), with its battlefield scenarios, cages and black harnesses; and *Schrei 27/Schrei X* (1994), performed in total darkness.

The influence of Expressionist performance can also be noted in Galás's extended vocal techniques. Though the genesis of her vocal style can be associated with the free jazz movement, it is also true that in *Geist* and *Schrei*, both Expressionist play forms, performers were instructed to speak ecstatically, repeat themselves, shout as if possessed and fade their voices hoarsely into the sounds of the orchestra. This performance style is apparent in *Vena Cava* (1991), where Galás uses her voice to capture the dissociated mental and physical properties of comatose and near-death states.

The effect of audio technology further distinguishes Galás's work. Her use of multiple microphones, mixing consoles, graphic equalizers, reverberation devices, tape decks and multiple-speaker sound systems allow Galás to inform her work with multiple voices, and to position these voices throughout her performances spaces. Unlike other performance artists, her voices do not only assume human characteristics, they also represent archetypal expressions that attack, avenge and express themselves in the context of Galás's works. Given her outstanding techniques, it would be possible to perform these works without this technology, but the work would be forced into smaller spaces, and she could not experiment with frequencies that do not exist in nature—frequencies that affect both human physicality and consciousness. This technology further facilitates her extended vocal techniques and her three-and-a-half octave range.

Diamanda Galás's work is characterized by extreme emotional and/or political content. In *Medéa Tarántula* the context is mourning and rage at Jason's betrayal, shock and anger at the choices Medéa is forced to make and self-loathing for finding herself in this condition. *Masque of the Red Death*, *Plague Mass* and *Vena Cava* respond to the abasement and abandonment met by people with AIDS, the willful neglect by individuals and governments, the posturing of religious hypocrites and the slow horror of physical and mental dissolution into death. *Insekta* is based upon covert psychological and physical torture and medical experimentation that governments, cults and "liberation movements" use on their victims and the disassociation which occurs in victims of this treatment. And *Schrei 27/Schrei X* investigates torture and abuse in more personal contexts: the torture, abuse and rape of individuals by criminals both known to them (e.g., familial battery and abuse) and unknown.

In addition to her performance work, Galás has made several recordings icluding: *Tragouthia Apo To Amia Exoun Fonos (Song for the Blood of Those Murdered)*, *Panoptikon* and *Wild Women with Steak Knives,*which all echo the emotional and political content of the performances. The virtuosity of her vocal expression has drawn directors such as Francis Ford Coppola and Derek Jarman to use her work in their films.

**Michael Flanagan** is a writer and the former president and archivist of the Documentation of AIDS Issues and Research. He has acted as Diamanda Galás's primary research assistant since 1987 and is currently working on her biography.

# Let Us Praise the Masters of Slow Death

In these worms reside the secrets of the gods
paving truth in yards of putrid flesh
weaving labyrinths of despair.

O children let us pray
*see the white and loving kindness of his grace*
*see the silken robes fall down, oh Paradise*
*oh good children pray.*

Their teeth tell tales of ages past
and while they make an angry sewage of my flesh
I know I'm not the only one.

O Angels do I see the rotting corpse
of a savage one among you?
A faceless one who comes to rob my soul
with praises of His goodness
and do I hear a laugh?

How does this body fly to us each night—
frail creatures wondering of his love,
so full of questions we,
warmed by the ceaseless voyages of worms—

It is we who see the passage of the time
in black and red:
pale strangers do not know our names.
It is not this sea of shrieking worms
that could inspire a tender look . . .

What sympathy in death discloses
we who fester here
are very *much* alive
and watch unmanned compassion flee
to safer zones.
Let us praise the Masters of Slow Death . . .

## There Are No More Tickets to the Funeral

Text by Diamanda Galás with excerpts from "Were You There When They Crucified My Lord" by Roy Acuff.

Were you a WITNESS?
Were you a WITNESS?

And on that holy day
And on that bloody day

Were you a WITNESS?
Were you a WITNESS?

And on that holy day
And on that bloody day
And on his dying bed he told me
"Tell all my friends I was fighting, too,
But to all the cowards and voyeurs:
There are no more tickets to the funeral
There are no more tickets to the funeral."

Were you a WITNESS?
Were you a WITNESS?

And on that holy day
And on that bloody day
There are no more tickets to the funeral
There are no more tickets to the funeral
The funeral crowded.

Were you a WITNESS?
Were you a WITNESS?

"Were you there when they crucified my Lord
Were you there when they nailed him to the cross
Sometimes it causes me to tremble, tremble, tremble
Were you there when they crucified my Lord?"

Were you a WITNESS?
Were you a WITNESS?

"Were you there when they dragged him to the grave"
*Were you there when they dragged him to the grave?*

"Sometimes it causes me to wonder, wonder, wonder"
*Were you there when they dragged him to the grave?*

And on that holy day
And on that bloody day
Were you a WITNESS?

"Were you there when they laid him in the tomb
Were you there when they laid him in the tomb
Sometimes it causes me to tremble, tremble, tremble
Were you there when they crucified my Lord?"

Were you a WITNESS?
Were you a WITNESS?

SWING SWING
> A band of Angels coming after me
> coming for to carry me home

SWING SWING
> A band of Devils coming after me
> coming for to drag me to the grave

SWING SWING
> But I will not go
> And I shall not go
> I will wake up
> And I shall walk from this room into the sun
> Where the dirty angel doesn't run
> Where the dirty angel cannot go
> And brothers in this time of pestilence
> > do know
> Each time that we meet we hear another sick
> > man sigh
> Each time that we meet we hear another man
> > has died

And I see angels angels angels devils
Angels angels devils
Angels angels devils
Coming for to drag me to the grave
> Angels!

Mr. Sandman makes a filthy bed for me
But I will not rest
And I shall not rest
As a man who has been blinded by the storm

and waits for angels by the road
while the devil waits for me at night
with knives and lies and smiles
and sings the "swing low sweet chariot"
of death knells
one by one
like a sentence of the damned
and one by one
of my brothers die

Unloved, unsung, unwanted
Die, and faster please,
we've got no money for extended visits
says the sandman

But we who have gone before
Do not rest in peace

*Remember me?*
*Unburied*
*I am screaming in the bloody furnaces of Hell*
*and only ask for you*
*to raise your weary eyes into the sun*
*until the sun has set*

For we who have gone before
Do not rest in peace
We who have died
Shall NEVER rest in peace
There is no rest until the fighting's done
And I see Angels Angels
Devils
Angels Angels
Devils
Angels Angels
Devils
Coming for to take me to the grave

ANGELS!

## Let's Not Chat about Despair

You who speak of crowd control,
of karma, or the punishment of God:

Do you fear the cages they are building
in Kentucky, Tennessee and Texas
while they're giving ten to forty years to find a cure?

Do you pray each evening out of horror or of fear
to the savage God whose bloody hand
commands you now to die, alone?

LET'S NOT CHAT ABOUT DESPAIR.
LET'S NOT CHAT ABOUT DESPAIR.

Do you taste the presence of the living dead
while the skeleton beneath your open window
waits with arms outstretched?

Do you spend each night in waiting
for the Devil's little angels' cries
to burn you in your sleep?

Do you wait for miracles in small hotels
with seconal and compazine
or for a ticket to the house of death in Amsterdam?

LET'S NOT CHAT ABOUT DESPAIR.
LET'S NOT CHAT ABOUT DESPAIR.

Do you wait in prison for the dreadful day
the office of the butcher comes to carry you away?

Do you wait for saviors or the paradise to come
in laundry rooms, in toilets or in Cadillacs?

Are you crucified beneath the life machines
with a shank inside your neck
and a head which blossoms like a basketball?

LET'S NOT CHAT ABOUT DESPAIR.
LET'S NOT CHAT ABOUT DESPAIR.

Do you tremble at the timid steps
of crying, smiling faces who, in mourning,
now have come to pay their last respects?

In Kentucky, Harry buys a round of beer
to celebrate the death of Billy Smith, the queer,
whose mother still must hide her face in fear.

You who mix the words of torture, suicide and death
with scotch and soda at the bar,

we're all real decent people, aren't we,
but there's no time left for talk:

LET'S NOT CHAT ABOUT DESPAIR.
LET'S NOT CHAT ABOUT DESPAIR.
LET'S NOT CHAT ABOUT DESPAIR.
LET'S NOT CHAT ABOUT DESPAIR.
PLEASE
Don't chat about Despair.


## Séance

I miss you—it's been so long—how are you—
I'm fine—been out here so long—I remember us
together—so green there—so black there—
I just wonder how long I can go on—I think of you
always—I think of mother and patepa and gordon—
is he okay—I live in dreams now and try to
remember every detail of the past—I try to make
a perfect memory of everything that has gone
before—
now so far away from life—how many in the
hole now, falling off the earth like old men with
no history—do you remember—was I ever there
or am I dreaming—you must remember for me
because I'm losing days—help me o'er that
bridge it is too far—I cannot make it—one step
two steps—three steps—am I breathing—is this
a god I see crawling to my grave on hands and
knees and falling falling falling out of light and
into darkness—hold me hold me ghosts of love
and lovely eyes can hold me in the sun when life
is done my angel are you there can you hear me
I am far away but not too far for dreams—your face
your face—grab me by the hand I will show you
where I am—darkness darkness—feel the wind
my angel are you there—hear my breathing—
I am near you waiting waiting see me smiling
smiling sun is everywhere . . . Now they take me
down the stairs . . . slowly, slowly—hold me,
hold me near . . . is that my judge? He sees me . . .

# Untitled

Last night you came back, and you said you were
feeling so much better. Your feet were torn in two,
and your bowels were hanging from your mouth.
Your face was rotting, and I was afraid of you, come
back from the dead to ask if you could rejoin us now,
and you didn't die after all, it just kept rotting you
away, and it had only appeared to us that you had
died and destruction stopped—no instead you had
been taken, you had been taken somewhere else and
no one knew, not even you, but you stood in the
room saying, "But, look! I'm so much better," and
you frightened me because I knew then that you
could never come back to the land of the living, but
that you were condemned to live in the land of the
dead forever, in the colony of lepers that would have
you, you so frightening to behold . . . Then our father
came into the room with a large black dog, said, "I've
got to take the dog for a walk now," to send you back
to the grave where you really live now, he was
surprised that you had the temerity to try and rejoin
the healthy, and then I saw you leave us through the
garden, your head bent down, crying softly, and then
I awoke to a horror much greater than ever before
because there is no peace where you are dead, not for
you and not for me, never, never anything but sadness,
and we will never never never never never never
be happy, ever again.

## Introduction by Kestutis Nakas

The first incubator of Ann Magnuson's work was Club 57, established by her in the basement of a little Polish church at 57 St. Mark's Place in New York City in 1979. It was the prototypical "East Village performance club," supporting a community of emerging young artists. They recycled, synthesized and celebrated American pop and junk cultures years before the cable and video industries' aggressive mass marketing of similar motifs. Magnuson aimed for a do-it-yourself theatrical equivalent of punk rock's "anyone-can-play" approach. 57's escapades combined costume party, talent show and environmental theatre. Performance art changed from a high-art, gallery event to a show-bizzy, low-art funfest.

During the eighties she skewered grim, Soviet political realities in *Depravnik Island* (a theme party/performance for the now-defunct club, Danceteria) and explored ideas of family in *The Manson Family Musical.* Her fascination with religion intensified, especially the fervent spirituality from the Appalachia of her native West Virginia. There were her ensembles—the sixties folk group, Bleaker Street Incident; the heavy metal band, Vulcan Death Grip; the pot-head burnout band, Bongwater; and the TV show

*Anything But Love,* in which she was a scene-stealing series regular. *Anything But Love,* brought Ann to Los Angeles where she was finally on TV—like in her earlier video *Made for TV*: trapped in a television, changing identities with every change of the channel, she displayed both a fascination and a horror for the medium. Her solo tour de force *You Could Be Home Now* debuted at Lincoln Center in 1990, was then produced in 1992 at The Joseph Papp Public Theater/New York Shakespeare Festival and was further developed for regional productions.

In person, and in character, she searches for "home" and meaning along her New York/Hollywood/West Virginia axis. An engaging, versatile and highly skilled show-woman, she subverts each show-stopping number with moments of insightful self-awareness. There is little attempt at classic unities, instead she rides the subtextual energies of rock and roll. Thematic tie-ins and recurring motifs do emerge, binding disparate elements. Class consciousness permeates the piece; the realization that no matter how frighteningly bewildering things can get for the "haves," the position of the "have-nots" is far less tenable. Her impoverished, disenfranchised characters are clearly her most beloved, especially the women. Through them her political sensibilities are revealed.

In the 1995 *The Luv Show* video, she appropriates trappings of male fantasy to become both a suave, James Bond-style, playgirl/killer and a naive, guitar-slinging waif who arrives in downtown Hollywood, eager for stardom and thrilled to audition at a flesh-peddling porn joint. Charting the territory between love and loathing of both the self and the object(s) of desire, her characters' smirking participation in their own oppression as they adopt the accoutrements of male power can be disturbing. But survival sometimes depends on inventing strategies of accommodation, while laying claim to happiness, sexual fulfillment and, especially, humor. This is strength, not surrender.

*Daughter of Horror: An Evening of Appalachian Goth Lounge* is her most recent work. A Halloween spectacular with band and back-up singers, it premiered in 1998 at West Hollywood's Luna Park. The performance juxtposes the realities of facing her beloved younger brother's death from AIDS with the story of a "Halloween Babylon" journey to a party with Marilyn Manson and friends. In her poem "Death Is Not," she spells out the difference between a real experience of death and its counterfeit: Goth/romantic death culture. The real ghosts, we learn, are the restless spirits of the wounded— family, friends and others roaming Magnuson's tortured and amused imagination. She outs her demons and, with fewer smoke and mirrors than ever, exposes her own pain. The surprising result is not despair, but hope and faith—evidence of a spiritual reserve deeper than grief. Even with its edge, *Daughter of Horror* is a hugely entertaining thrill ride. Now fully revealed, Magnuson is still true to the spirit of Club 57 and more fun than ever.

**Kestutis Nakas** is a writer, performer, director and an associate professor of theatre at the University of New Mexico. His solo shows include *Dead Man Talking: Confessions of a Zombie, Paul Through the Night* and his most recent *My Heart, My President.*

# from **You Could Be Home Now**

*We hear the sound of a dial tone which fades away as the lights change to reveal the Chanteuse examining a pair of antique earrings unearthed from a storage box in the attic.*

CHANTEUSE: Oh, I used to love these earrings. I used to wear them all the time in high school during my Stevie Nicks period. Mom wore them on their honeymoon to New York City. You can see them in the photo album over there. *(She pulls a scarf out from one of the storage boxes)*

Ooo! And this was from my mother's trousseau! It went with this little strapless number that she wore to some fancy restaurant my parents went to on 57th Street. And I remember they couldn't afford to order anything except a plate of spaghetti they shared like *Lady and the Tramp*. And Dad ordered a cup of coffee with his meal and then he overheard the waiter scoff and tell the maître d', "Coffee? With a meal? That's a farmer's drink!"

Ooo, those rude New York waiters.

*(Music up. Jazzy beat. She snaps her fingers and adopts a beat poet cadence.)*

Those rude New York waiters.

Those rude New York waiters.

They never tired of talking about those rude New York waiters.

They did everything they could to dissuade me from moving there. Your parents did too, right?

*(Sophisticated music fades in and underscores the scene. It sounds like a cross between something from the soundtrack to* Last Tango in Paris *and Bobby Short tickling the ivories at The Carlyle. She throws a handful of autumn leaves in the air, which scatter in front of her; she mimes walking the city streets.)*

## New York Stroll

But there's nothing like a crisp, autumn day in New York, is there? Just like the day we first moved here. I couldn't wait to get out of that hick town and neither could you.

Remember when we couldn't imagine living anywhere else?

We were nobodies but we managed to sneak into the VIP room of the new club. I admired your long, blond hair and you said, "Babe, let's hit every Greek diner in town and drink coffee until we're sick!"

And we laughed and laughed.

And remember when you snuck me into that bar, The Mine Shaft? And me and Lee Radziwill were the only women there? And we watched that guy put a hamster up his butt? Then he couldn't get it out. And they had to call 911 and the paramedics came and we were laughing so hard that they threw us down the stairs and into the street, but we still couldn't stop laughing and laughing.

And how about that night when we toasted AIDS research with Cristal at that uptown bash and someone gave us Ecstasy . . . but it was really Xanax? And you threw a handful of Beluga at Jay MacInerney but it missed and got stuck in Eartha Kitt's hair?

And we laughed and laughed!

And remember when we fought over that cute Norwegian model and both ended up sleeping with him? And then freaked out when he got sick and died? *(She laughs)*

Oh and what about that bakery below your apartment and that ever-present smell of fresh-baked bread . . . that you grew to hate? Or that phone-sex line advertised on Channel J? You remember "976-PEEE, the extra E is for extra pee"—oh, we used to love to laugh at that after you became bedridden and your leg had blown up to three times its size and was as black as the faces of the men who clean the windshields on Houston Street and you said the doctor "might as well just cut it off" and then you told a couple of Totie Fields jokes . . .

. . . and we laughed and laughed!

Or when your parents wouldn't let any of us visit you in the hospital because they blamed all your New York friends for your "lifestyle"? Or that time at Martin's memorial when you leaned over to me and said, "Ann, no matter what, please, please, PLEASE, don't let them sing 'Over the Rainbow' at my funeral" . . . and we laughed and laughed!

*(She sighs)* You always said you were going to make a grand exit. Go out in a "final, fucking, blaze of glory!" But you didn't. You went quiet. Just like that Podunk town you came from. *(She picks up one of the fallen leaves and caresses her face with it)*

No, there's nothing like a crisp autumn day in New York.

We couldn't imagine living anywhere else.

*(Pause.)*

*(Sadly)* Okay. So, things change. *(She tosses the leaf aside)* I mean . . . for one thing, there used to be a heck of a lot more snow around here in the

wintertime. And there were a lot more kids playing on the street—it's so deserted now. Oh well, I guess nothing stays the same, right?

I mean, look at the American auto industry. They're just a shadow of their former selves. And, God, late-night television hasn't been the same since Johnny died.

Wait a minute, he is dead, isn't he?

And then they went and discontinued the Sears catalog. The Sears catalog!

And Pan Am's history. Pan-fucking-Am! Who would've thunk? Eastern, too. All the airlines are in trouble. Even MGM Grand, the celebrity carrier, is cutting back. They only have one flight left—to the moon.

*(Lights change. Music up: Pink Floyd's* Dark Side of the Moon, *the space sounds from the track, "On the Run.")*

I'm on it.

We take off without incident. We orbit the earth once.

I look out the window as we pass over the southern tip of Africa. I can see the wandering boys of Sudan, running from hungry hyenas and Marxist rebels. They're jumping up and down, waving their spindly arms in the air like thousands of spiders yelling, "Take us with you! Take us with you! Take us with you!"

Too late. We zip through the hole in the ozone layer and speed toward the moon. I take this opportunity to acquaint myself with the other passengers. It's a very illustrious bunch—a couple of CEOs from the Fortune 500 list, Siegfried and Roy, Susan Sontag, Robert Smith from The Cure . . .

We arrive at the moon in a flash. We land without incident.

*(Music abruptly out. Silence.)*

It's so quiet. I climb into my pink, quilted jumpsuit and go exploring.

I peek over the crater . . .

*(Piano music up: Pink Floyd's "The Great Gig in the Sky.")*

. . . and see an Italian-style piazza made of pink marble stretching out to the sunny side of the moon. At the edge of the horizon is a glass-domed colony. It's a different kind of paradise. Looks a little like a college campus. Or my grandma's old neighborhood. Or . . . or . . . Mayberry! (The black-and-white episodes with Barney Fife, not the color ones with Howard Sprague.)

Everyone is sitting around sipping cappuccinos and discussing philosophy. They're all young, healthy, good-looking, stylish, happy and racially and ethnically mixed . . . just like a Benetton ad!

Wow, I think. I could start all over again on this here moon! Buy a Victorian house, fix it up, maybe adopt a little, Chinese baby girl . . .

Just then a skinny, old, junkie-hippie-girl in her forties approaches and asks for "spare change." Oh no, I think. Not up here too! I cry out in anguish over the futility of it all!

*(Music up loud: the histrionic female vocals from "The Great Gig in the Sky" kick in as the lights go to black and a strobe light flickers, illuminating the Chanteuse as she falls dramatically to her knees and lip-synchs to the wailing while indulging wildly in overblown rock-opera theatrics. After a few bars, both the singing and the strobe light stop abruptly, the lights come back up and the Chanteuse finds herself in stark silence, cringing in an embarrassed heap center stage. After a few awkward beats, she speaks.)*

You know . . . I am off on a tangent I am never going to find my way out off. *(She stands up and speaks to the lighting technician)*

Let's see . . . uh, David, can we get a special here? And something on the surround? Something kind of Garrison Keilloresque? Something that will envelop us in the warmth and security of nostalgia? You know, like that feeling you get when you watch *Nick at Night.*

*(The lights change and she pulls a chair to center stage.)*

Yeah, that's good. Now I'd like to harken us back to an earlier age. Back to a more innocent time. Back to a time when you felt all cuddly and warm in your pj's with the feet in them. Back when you used to hold onto that ratty old security blanket you called Blanky, and after *The Wonderful World of Disney* was over, Dad would carry you upstairs and tuck you into bed. And then Mom would pull out her acoustic guitar and sing you a sweet, kind-hearted lullaby. *(She pulls out an acoustic guitar from the shadows, sits on the chair and plays the intro to "Roundabout" by Yes. Then she gleefully launches into a folksy, feel-good, three-chord ditty:)*

## Folk Song

I met an anarchist in Tompkins Square Park
He was an angry man, spitting words so dark
He spoke of death to rich men, death to yuppies, too
Death to art fags, bourgeois blacks, death to landlord Jews
Kill the bankers, kill the cops, kill him, her and me
Kill them all for CBS, NBC, ABC, TBN, CNN, HBO, *Live at Five,*
"MTV Spring Break Party Weekend," *Sally Jesse Raphael,*
*Geraldo, Oprah, Arsenio, Regis and Kathy Lee*
And I said,
Hey, I admire your get-up-and-go,

Your youthful brooding and sexually charged enthusiasm
And all your other utterly naive and thoroughly endearing
    adolescent qualities
And I bet you can keep it up all night, can't you?
But I bet you don't even use a rubber,
No you don't use a rubber,
No, you never use a r-r-r-r-rubber-r-r-r-r
'Cause you think you're going to live forever.
Or you have this adorable and misguided notion
That death is something really radical and cool,
But hey, I still can't help being wildly attracted
To your fresh-faced, uncompromised, pierced and tattooed, rebel
    stance
And goddamn, I'd like to help you sing your tune . . .
But I've been making friends with this here death
And it feels a mite too soon.
So I sing,

Hello Death, good-bye Avenue A
I'm getting tired of waiting, tired of being afraid
Joseph Campbell gave me hope and now I have been saved.
So I sing,
Hello Death! Good-bye Avenue A.

*(Spoken)* Now, I'm not trying to be flippant or irreverent or exploitive or sarcastic or ironic or postmodern or hip or trendy and this is not a parody. Get it? Got it? Good.

*(She continues singing:)*

I've been thinking what he told me, that it's okay to cry
When we held the crystal Tina Chow spent twelve grand to buy,
Homeopathic mantras, fresh-squeezed wheatgrass juice
Doctors up in Bellevue, Doctors Salk and Seuss
And it's time we'll all be going home, if you can find the way.
Yes, everyone is going home, going home to stay.
And it's time to find a way to cope, a way to find some hope.
For some it's the Bible or Buddha or Muhammad
Or Krishna or cheesecake or bourbon or the Butthole Surfers
Or Giorgio Armani or Romeo Gigli
And you really can't afford it but it looks so fabulous on you
So why don't you take it on home?
And speaking of home, isn't it about time you moved out of that
    East Village hellhole,
You know the one with *The Honeymooners* view of the brick wall

Because you deserve to be around something more life affirming,

Something with a patch of grass or a tree or a flower

Or maybe you should get a cute little puppy dog

Or maybe you just want to take your boyfriend to Europe because he's never been

Or quit the job you always hated or . . . or . . .

Learn how to play the guitar—it's easy!

Or maybe you just want to get obscenely drunk at a piano bar and sing show tunes,

Show tunes

And don't be embarrassed

Because, to tell you the truth, I'd much rather see *Brigadoon* than another

Goddamned movie about another goddamned serial killer

Or maybe you're tired of dragging your saggin' butt around the nightclub scene

Where everyone is twenty years younger than you

And you're on your tenth margarita that you got from the complimentary,

Open bar at the AmFAR benefit

And you think maybe it's time to go home

Until you look around and realize, you ARE home

And you've turned into a character in an Anne Rice novel,

You know, the vampire that won't die?

So you decide it's time to get politically active

So you disrupt a presidential press conference

By shoving a five-pound, week-old stalk of broccoli between those thin, lying, lizard lips

That no one can read because half the country is illiterate

And the other half is apathetic

So then you decide maybe you should just put a bullet into Jesse Helms's pea-brain

But you know that when you start thinking like that,

When you start thinking like they do, that it's time to let go of the material world

So maybe you decide to get yourself some of that good time religion

'Cause Jesus is the way, Jesus is the way, Jesus is the way, Jesus is the way, Jesus is the way . . .

*(Spoken)* Besides, it's a hell of a lot easier to accept Jesus Christ as your personal savior when he looks like Willem Dafoe.

But maybe that stuff turns you off so you rent *Power of Myth*—it made me feel really good. Until I heard this ugly rumor that Joseph

Campbell was anti-Semitic, is that true? Oh God, there's always a catch! So, maybe you'd just rather take acid and listen to Led Zeppelin . . . *(She plays a snippet of "Stairway to Heaven" then returns to her three-chord ditty:)*

> Then again the last time I took hallucinogenic drugs was five years ago,
> I took mushrooms in Joshua Tree looking for that Carlos Castenadas kind of
> experience.
> I got off, my boyfriend didn't, he fell asleep,
> I was left alone with the TV, turned it on, tuned in to PBS and you know what was playing?
> *Berlin Alexanderplatz.*
> So I started watching it and you know what?
> I got really bummed out
> And that's when I said no to drugs, no to drugs, no, no, no, no, "Hell no!" to drugs
> And maybe you want to say no to drugs, too
> Or maybe you just want to join Atheists of America
> Or the Madonna Fan Club or watch Richard Gere follow the Dalai Llama around the world
> And then do those oh-so-Zen-like movies with those oh-so-Zen-like messages like,
> "Hey! It's fun to be a prostitute!" I can't wait to spread my legs
> Across Hollywood Boulevard because then
> Maybe some rich, handsome billionaire in a Jag will come driving up and take me shopping on Rodeo Drive and that's what a woman is all about anyway, right?
> Sucking and shopping? Sucking and shopping, sucking and shopping, sucking and shopping . . .
> Come on everybody, it's a sing-a-long!
> Sucking and shopping, sucking and shopping, sucking and shopping . . .
> But, hey! Who am I to argue? Who am I to pass judgment?
> Because it's the "feel-good movie of the summer," it's the "feel-good movie of the year,"
> It's the "feel-good movie of the millennium" and you know what?
> If it puts a smile on your face and a song in your heart and a spring in your step
> Well . . .
> Whatever makes you happy, whatever makes you happy, whatever makes you
> Happy, whatever makes you happy, whatever gives you hope . . .

*(Singing sweetly:)*

> Even if it's a truly tasteless joke
>
> So . . . fax a manifesto, pencil in a date
>
> Let me know when something gives, I hope it's not too late
>
> 'Cause I'm getting tired of waiting, tired of being afraid
>
> Joseph Campbell gave me hope and now I have been saved
>
> So I sing,
>
> Hello Death, Good-bye Avenue A
>
> Hello Death, Good-bye Avenue A
>
> Hello Death, Good-bye Avenue A.

---

## from **Pretty Songs**

### Is This Heaven?

*Monologue underscored by music: Percy Faith's theme from* A Summer Place.

I don't know if it's because I caught part two of *Doctor Zhivago* on the Superstation last night or because John just died, but I woke up the next morning feeling optimistic, unafraid of death and ready to challenge the patriarchal state.

I had seen the most beautiful place.

It was a fruited plain with green, not amber, waves of grain stretching out as far as the eye could see. The blue, blue sky was filled with incredible clouds, and bees without stingers were buzzing all around the tall grass that reached up to my pale mauve areolas.

The colors were beyond Technicolor. Was this Russia? Or South Dakota before Costner? It looked like a Chinese happy worker poster from the Cultural Revolution or . . . or . . . yes, a Vincente Minnelli film!

In the middle of the plain was an ancient oak tree with a canopy as big as a 747 wide-body jet. The Santa Ana winds blew the branches of the tree and the tall, tall grass and the big, puffy clouds and my long, naturally sun-streaked, honey-colored hair all in rhythmic unison like tasty, Hawaiian ocean waves.

Kawabunga!

I ran in slow-motion ecstasy through the grass.

I ran in slow-motion ecstasy through the grass.

I ran in slow-motion ecstasy through the grass.

I heard one of my dead friends smiling and I wondered . . . is this heaven? Or just wishful thinking?

**Introduction** by Evelyn C. White

Her hair magnificently henna-ed, Rhodessa Jones, in screaming, black velvet pants, sits center stage at the Lorraine Hansberry Theatre in San Francisco and announces to the packed house, "I'm really not interested in the kind of drama that appeals to folks who attend the Negro cotillions or high society balls. I'm here to present community art as *state of the art*. I'm talking about using art as a tool of transformation; to provide a space for people whose voices haven't been heard. Understand what I'm saying?"

Waving programs in the air and stomping their feet wildly, the crowd whoops, hollers and roars. Picture a revivalist tent exploding with that "old-time religion" and you've got a good line on the scene.

And thus begins the latest production of The Medea Project—a multimedia extravaganza that Rhodessa began in 1990 to help incarcerated women by creating original theatre pieces based on the women's personal histories. The annual production, features ex-offenders, activist artists and inmates who are released from jail a few hours each evening to perform. Under Rhodessa's direction, The Medea Project has become one of the most celebrated stage events in the region. Even the armed deputies who are posted inside the theatre to "guard" the inmates, have been known to rock out as the sisters sing, dance and shout about their trials and hard-won victories.

And you can bet that I'm in the house whenever the curtain rises on The Medea Project. I'm there because unlike most mainstream theatre, the productions are always fierce, funny, real, funky, poignant, politically charged and beautifully rendered, in short, like Rhodessa herself, who channels these voices in the solo show excerpted here, *Big Butt Girls, Hard Headed Women*.

I first saw Rhodessa perform about a decade ago in the dazzling show she crafted on the life of Tina Turner, *I Think It's Gonna Work Out Fine* (a duet with Idris Ackamoor). I swooned. A few weeks after the performance, a friend hosted a small dinner party in celebration of my birthday. When she inquired about the guest list, I shamelessly begged, "Please, please, please invite Rhodessa Jones."

Did she show? Answer: Does Tina Turner put a hurtin' on a mini-skirt?

Rhodessa came to my party bearing, like Tina's legs, her own natural gifts. They came in the exquisite form of her heart-rending stories about being a teen mother, an exploited migrant worker, a traveling circus performer, a peep-show artist and an aerobics instructor in the county jail (some of the many experiences she draws on for her solo piece, *The Blue Stories: Black Erotica on Letting Go*). She came to the gathering graceful, vulnerable, sophisticated, streetwise and free. Add to the mix the wisdom she carries as a *grandmother* (I was floored!), and you'll understand why I adore Rhodessa. In a world rife with self-aggrandizing phonies, fakes, pretenders, scam artists and deluded legends in their own lunch hours, Rhodessa stands as a performer who is not ashamed to claim, in the words of Zora Neale Hurston, that she has herself "been to sorrow's kitchen and licked all the pots."

And like Zora, Rhodessa knows that hard times can be vanquished through the transformative power of art. A production staged or performed by Rhodessa is guaranteed to be steeped in the low-down, scandalous, gritty, gut-bucket permutations of life. But you won't leave the theatre without also experiencing joy, redemption, hope, laughter and a generous dose of sensual pleasures. Feeling depressed, burned-out, blasé? See Rhodessa in action and trust me, you'll be revitalized.

Know that Rhodessa is a serious sister who has not sold out her vision of a vibrant community theatre to the folks who traffic in star names, hot properties and high-priced tickets. And in this era of dwindling support for the arts, that means she has paid a high price for her integrity—meager funds, monumental headaches and minimal attention from major media outlets. But I know that Rhodessa has reaped her reward in the quarters where it matters the most—in the hearts and minds of the marginalized masses whose lives she depicts so righteously on stage.

**Evelyn C. White** is editor of *The Black Women's Health Book* (Seal Press). Her official biography of Alice Walker is under contract with W. W. Norton.

# from **Big Butt Girls, Hard Headed Women**

*The Artist portrays a sound and movement solo,*
*juxtaposed with a sound track. She will take us from the innocence*
*of an African-American girl-child to the-all-too frequent situation/existence*
*of prostitution resulting in incarceration.*

*(In the voice of the girl-child)*

Milkshake, milkshake, cream of tartar
Tell me the name of her sweetheart-er

*(À la Aretha Franklin)*

What you want
Somebody got
What you need
You know I got it

*(She dances suggestively—hands on hips)*

I got it. I got it. I got it.

Git it, Girl! G'on Girl!

*(She freezes into a position of fatherly authority and speaks)*

Git in the house! Git yo' big butt in the house!!!

*(The girl-child whines)*

But I wasn't doin' nothin' . . . nothin', nothin'. I ain't nothin'.

*(She freezes, then speaks, assuming the attitude and posture*
*of an adolescent girl, trying to be a grown woman)*

Hey, Tony! Hey, Jerry!

*(Over her shoulder, conspiratorially)*

Girl, that looks like Tony and Jerry. Let's go to the sto'.

*(She circles downstage, ending with her back to the audience.*
*She mimes necking, petting, fondling, heavy breathing,*
*lustful panting, childish groping)*

I love you. Nobody does it like you do. Just kiss me.

*(In a masculine voice)*

Is it good? Tell me that it's good.

*(This scenario evolves from passion to labor to childbirth ending with the girl-child facing the audience holding a baby. She freezes into a position of motherly authority)*

Git in the house. Git yo' big butt in the house. Don't be so hard-headed. Haven't you done enough?!

*(She whines)*

But I wasn't doin' nothin' . . . nothin', nothin'. I ain't nothin'.

*(She moves into a frenzied dance of self defense . . . Warding off blows while holding the baby)*

You better stop, Jerry. I'ma tell my daddy. Stop!

*(She mimes being punched in the stomach, knocked to the ground and sexually assaulted, ending with her legs opened facing downstage. She rolls to her side and assumes the voice of authority)*

Git in the house. Git yo' big butt in the house. A hard head makes a soft ass.

*(She is rising from the floor. It is painful. It is a struggle)*

But I wasn't doin' nothin' . . .

*(Sound of a car horn. She beckons in a pleading voice)*

Hey, you! You wanna kiss me? Yeah, kiss me, kiss me.

*(The sound of sirens and suddenly she's handcuffed and struggling, caught)*

Motherfucker, take yo' hands off me. I wasn't doin' nothin'. Regina, call my mother. Tell her they takin' me to jail, girl. Lena they got me on a humbug. Motherfucker, take yo' hands offa me! Doris, tell my grandmama they takin' me to jail, girl, and I wasn't doin' nothin'.

*(She struggles as though she's being arrested with handcuffs, the lights change simultaneously with a musical interlude of Marvin Gaye's "What's Goin' On." In the back light we see her change into blue prison coveralls. After changing, she steps across an aerobics platform and comes center stage)*

Good morning. I am Rhodessa Jones from the California Arts Council. I will be teaching aerobics here every Wednesday morning at 9:00 A.M. My pass is newly issued. I have clearance for all the jails. You got to run a check? Look, Sergeant, why would I want to break into jail, most folks I know want to break out? Whoa—It's not that I'm trying to be a wiseass. I just have no great need to sneak into jail first thing on a Wednesday morning! Oh, this? This is my beat box. These are my tapes. Here. What does NWA stand for? "Niggas With Attitudes." They advocate what? Cop killing! Look, well, I don't know about all that. The women in my class like and requested this music. I'd love to discuss it with you, but I've got a class to teach. I beg your pardon? Read my lips: I have far better thangs to do with my time than sneaking into jail first thing in the morning. Could I have my pass please?!

*(The lights change. She is on the aerobics platform, overly enthusiastic)*

Good morning, Ladies. We're going to begin with some windmills. Now everybody smile, and one . . . two . . . three . . . four . . . C'mon Latoya, you too. All right good . . . Good. And now for all you big butt girls, it's time to get another booty for your body. That's right, we gon' do some booty building this morning! What's the use of having a big ol' butt that you can't use. You know, to express yo' self. You know, a butt that commands attention . . . One that stands alone. Let's begin by tightening up with some lunges, and press one . . . two . . . three . . . four . . .

*(She freezes. Lights change with a musical interlude. She steps down from the platform to downstage center, addressing the audience)*

In jail. A black, woman artist, working in jail. I look out at all those faces. There's my mother's face, my sister's face and my daughter's face. And I'm wondering how in the hell did they get here in the first place. And I realize that it is but for a flip of fate that it could be me in here and she out there.

*(Lights change with a musical interlude. The Falling Woman Dance: she moves as though she's catching bodies falling from the air. It is sporadic. She calls out simultaneously)*

Vanessa! Jeanita! Paula! Beverly!

*(She stops and spouts statistics)*

Eighty-five percent of all women incarcerated in U.S. penal institutions
  are women of color.
Donna! Naomi! Paulette! Jessica!
Fifty percent are African-American women.
It is a revolving door.

*(Music . . . She sings softly, lullaby-like. The Falling Women's Dance continues throughout the song)*

Can a body catch a body?
Can a body catch a body?
Can a body catch a body?

And how can I, as one woman artist, make a difference, provide a supportive environment in the face of women who know that it's so goddamn hard to live anyway. Women with no jobs, who've lost their children. How do we counter life-threatening situations such as alcoholism, drug addictions, sexual abuse? How do we discuss and explore the reality of AIDS, coming to grips with the fact that screams: "Women die far faster from it"?

*(Lights change. She returns to the aerobics platform)*

Today we're going to work with the mask—in theatre your face is the mask. Let's begin by stretching the face. Big face. Little face. Come 'on— it is an anti-aging device. Now, use the tongue. Stretch to the side . . . To the top . . . To the other side . . . All you working girls, pay attention.

*(Lights and music change)*

So many faces . . . So many masks . . . So many stories . . . So many songs.

*(Public Enemy's "Terminator" is heard. As the music plays, the Artist portrays glimpses of many different women. As the music crescendos, the Artist assumes the character of Regina Brown who is having sex with two other women. Regina is an African-American woman of about thirty. She is strong and aggressive and appears taller than she is)*

Fuck a bitch. Hit me! Bigger and better bitches than you have hit me. Just because I let you smell my pussy, don't make it your pussy. It's still my pussy. Everybody and anybody will use you so you best get to using first. I learned early, a man or a woman ain't nothin' but a plaything. I tell them all, "It's like the lotto, Baby. You got to be in it to win it." Later for all that "Ooh, Baby" this and "Ooh, Baby" that. I believe in action, so you best get on with the A team. Like Tyrone, he's in love with me, always has been, and I can understand that. But I told him, "I was born a full-grown woman, and it ain't about 'my woman this' and 'my woman that.' I'm my own woman." But, like a lot of men, he don't want to listen. Wanted to control me . . . thought he was my daddy. My daddy is dead, Baby. And my mama raised me to be strong and on my own. He got all mad, 'cause he wasn't ready for the real deal. Brought some other girl, some Lily-Lunchmeat-lookin' bitch I don't know, home! I told him, "Hey, if sister girl can hang, it's all in the family." Thought he was gonna work my nerves with that shit. And now who's crying? Tyrone. Because I'm carrying another man's baby. And that man ain't even important. The reality check has to do with me, my baby, and my baby's staying with Gerber's. I am a prostitute, straight up. I decided a long time ago, wasn't no man gonna tell me what to do. I'm a full-grown woman, straight up and down. Or my name ain't Regina Brown. WORD! Hit me bitch . . .

*(She rolls forward with a slap.*
*The Artist returns to aerobics platform and addresses her class again)*

Down on our backs . . . Okay, we're going to stretch up and down through the hands and feet. Now take the feet back over your head. Breathe and stretch. This will make you very popular. You can go home and scare him to death. He'll say, "Damn, Baby, I thought you was in the joint." Then you say, "No, Baby, I've been at a health spa." Breathe. Work the body, ladies, work the body. You can't sell chicken if it looks like Jell-O . . . Now because everyone's been working so well we're going to end with some hand dancing.

*(Addressing the audience)*

That means you've got to say what I say and do what I do. And I know you're all thinking, "She's from California, anything can happen."

*(The Artist demonstrates the American Sign Language*
*movements for the following words, as the audience mimics)*

Dancing is defined as any movement of the feet, with the feet, with the body in a standing position. Dance officials will issue a warning if two women are not dancing . . . Are not dancing.

*("As Time Goes By" is played on a saxophone.*
*The Artist addresses the character of Mama Pearl)*

Hey, Mama Pearl, I missed you in class today.

*(Artist becomes Mama Pearl, an African-American woman*
*who appears to be about seventy, though she could be younger.*
*She is a sage, a crone, and she speaks with the voice that*
*a velvet rock would have, if a rock could speak)*

Well, I can't always be coming to class now. They done made me a trustee, you know. That means I get to move around—to work.

*(Artist addressing Mama Pearl)*

You look great. I like your hair. But then, Mama Pearl, you always look spiffy, sharp.

*(As Mama Pearl)*

Baby, that's why they made me the trustee. I take pride in my appearance. They know they can send me all over this place. Yeah, I can come and go instead of sitting in that day room with all that noise and these bitches smoking. Somebody always cussin', clownin' or fightin'. But I'm glad you're here, and if you don't do nothin' else, teach them how to have enough self respect to wash they funky asses. Here my hand to God, some of them so young they don't even know how to use a tampax. I've been in and out of the joint since 1965 and I ain't never seen it as bad as it is now. The young women coming and going in this day and time don't have no sense of theyself. I got three daughters. My older daughter was born deaf and dumb. She's the reason I went to jail in the first place.

*(She pauses and looks around before continuing in a more secretive tone)*

You see, I embezzled some money from the company that I was working at so my daughter could get special training so that she could take care of herself, despite her handicap.

These girls need somebody to help them understand that you ain't got to be in and out of jail to feel important. They got to find a reason to let go of that crack and cut loose these men that pimp them for drugs, money, cars, even a leather coat. Look at them. Most of them not even twenty-five yet and have the nerve to be pregnant up in here. Like I told you, I got three daughters and I'd rather see these bitches flush these babies down the toilet than grunt them into the world and treat them the way they do. How? The way they will sell them, lease them to the dope man for some rock. They're flesh and blood, Honey. Then the dope man, he gon' get busted and then the baby is lost to child protective services. And these bitches want to cry about they babies. This ain't something I heard; I seen this with my own eyes. You know what I tell 'em? "Take that whining and complaining some place else 'coz when you was out there fucking and sucking, high out of your mind, I did not get one nut. I did not experience one thrill behind your bullshit. So take all that drama somewhere else."

*(She pauses and addresses the audience)*

Here my hand to God, please, I know that it's a hard line, but in this life I've learned you better come with something if you wanna get something.

———

Who are these women? And what are they to you and you and you?

*(The Artist points to the audience as she speaks the last line.*
*She sings a chorus from Bernice Reagon's "Joanne Little")*

She's our mama.
She's yo' lover.
That woman,
the woman who's going to carry your child.

They wear my mother's face, my sister, my daughter. And now, if I'm to believe statistics, my granddaughter? You know, working in the jails, I don't delude myself and pretend that the time I spend with these people is gonna make a whole lot of difference.

*(She mimes struggling under weight)*

Their problems are too great, too immense. Benign neglect. Alienation. Isolation. Blind rage. Living in some township just outside of Amerika.

*(Beatifically, with hands joined as in prayer)*

But I was raised in a family by a mother and a father who taught me that when you're called to something too great, too immense, you can always take it to God. Now the African in my American teaches me to take it to the Ancestors.

*(The Artist begins incantation: "Take It to the Ancestors"*
*Building a dance with a chant and a chorus)*

Take it to the Ancestors.
Build spirit catchers.
This is a spirit catcher for one
Regina Brown, age twenty-seven.

Regina: Daughter, Sister, Lover, Mama.

Regina Brown, murdered in the
winter of 1989, after her second
release from jail.

Regina: Daughter, Sister, Lover, Mama.

Regina Brown, mother of two children,
left here howling on the ground. A boy
and a girl, left to make it in this hard-luck
place called the world.

Regina: Daughter, Sister, Lover, Mama.

Regina Brown, whore with a heart of gold.

Regina: Daughter, Sister, Lover, Mama.

Regina Brown, who, with a little direction,
could have been running the world.

Regina: Daughter, Sister, Lover, Mama.

Regina Brown, one of my best drama students.

*(Dance ends with the Artist next to the altar with the spirit catcher. She picks up a brass bowl from the altar, and addresses the audience)*

I'd like to ask you here tonight to help me complete the spirit catcher with sound.

*(She reaches into the bowl and begins sprinkling water on the audience throughout the following history)*

This is a bowl of sterilized water. Because I was raised in the house of one Estella Jones, my mother, who taught me that if we kept a bowl of sterilized water in all the cupboards, and under all the beds, we could drown sorrow . . . We could read the weather . . . So, right now, I'm asking you to participate in a lullaby written by one Harriet Schiffer. It is a call and response. It goes like this.

*(The Artist and audience sing together with musical accompaniment)*

All women love babies.

All women love babies.

All women love,
All women love,
All women love babies.

All women love babies.

Regina: Daughter, Sister, Lover, Mama.

*(Again, addressing the audience)*

Thank you very much, it's a California thing.

Before I go I'd like to ask you a few questions. Please speak right up. You can talk to me. You'd be amazed at what people have said to me, so speak right up. How many people have ever been mugged? Show of hands, please. Let's keep it simple. Had your bike stolen? Apartment broken into? Car broken into? And in that car was your favorite camera with the best film you ever shot in your life? Had your credit cards misused and abused? Been raped? Know somebody, who knows somebody, who knows somebody, who knows somebody, who knows somebody who's killed somebody.

My point is, we're all involved here. My point is this ain't no time to be buying dogs and locking doors 'cause you see "them" comin'. 'Cause "they" could be "us" and you may wake up and find that you've locked yourself in and they're sitting at your breakfast table.

Let us not forget to remember that the struggle continues for all of us.

## Introduction by Ken Foster

I first encountered Tim Miller in December 1992 at a sold-out performance of *My Queer Body* at P. S. 122 in Manhattan. Unfamiliar with his performance work, but very familiar with his political activism (ACT UP; the NEA Four) I was curious to see what this remarkable man would bring forth in a performance.

In a pattern I was to learn was not atypical for Tim, he entered the stage space through the audience, touching audience members as he went, "collecting" body parts for the performance that was about to unfold. Initial titters turned, over the course of the evening, to laughter, sorrow, tears and joy. In a matter of moments he had accomplished his socio-political agenda as well as his artistic one—to create a community among the people gathered that evening.

I was struck then, as I continue to be now, by the deeply eloquent way that Tim Miller, his political activism, his performance and literary work speak to contemporary America and particularly to marginalized people. As a university presenter, I knew he would connect on multiple levels with our students, with the queer community, with anyone willing to engage him in his work. Over the next several years, observing him in university as well as community settings, I discovered that my initial perceptions were correct.

Several factors, I believe, are critical to Tim's success as a performer/ community activist/workshop leader/writer. The combination of his ineffably sweet nature and his powerfully clear language makes his work incredibly strong. His juxtaposition of a delightful movement/dance physicality with the graphic depiction and description of our physical selves creates a paradox that is alternately beguiling and stunning in its impact. Within the context of his highly interactive performance work, he uncovers the violences that are inflicted upon us, as gay men, and more poignantly, those we inflict upon ourselves. In so doing, he creates a performance experience that extends beyond narrative and beyond politics into metaphor and a profound art.

*Spilt Milk* shows us the sweetness of a young gay man coming to San Francisco for the first time and the encounters which turn into defining moments for him and for us. In this, as in all of his work, he adroitly weaves his political agenda of gay rights activism with personal stories—his and ours. In *Spilt Milk* we see a shard of that struggle; repeatedly in his work, he illuminates the seemingly endless conflict between what we know about ourselves as gay men and what the world tells us is so.

Having seen Tim perform a range of his work in a variety of settings, I am moved by how strongly he connects with audiences through the medium of the body. The body is the artistic tool with which he works and the battleground upon which he engages us and the world. His stories of love and lust; his exploration of and fascination with the times we live in and the bizarre circumstances that we encounter; the socially taboo but deeply felt physical and emotional conflicts of our lives; these are played out on the stage of the body—certainly his and often ours as well.

In keeping with his activist agenda, Tim extends this work through the workshops that he offers in the places he visits, exploring more deeply the issues raised by the performance work. In his performance workshops, participants confront the image of their body, see their life stories imprinted on their bodies and learn to use that knowledge and those understandings to guide them through the perplexities of contemporary existence. Participants explore hidden fears and pains, but also discover inner sources of strength and courage. It is those resources that he urges us to take into our personal lives and energize the political process with our own activism. Thus, every Tim Miller residency becomes a combination of performance experience, political activism and personal and communal growth. It is this unique combination of performer and activist that makes Tim's work more fully experienced by every community he touches.

Activist, storyteller, dancer, humorist, philosopher and poet; in Tim Miller, America realizes a distinctive performative style. Through his work we can honor our individuality, celebrate a sense of community and reach beyond what we know to those unexplored areas of fear, empowerment and joy.

**Ken Foster** is the Director of UApresents at the University of Arizona in Tucson.

I was hitchhiking to San Francisco. I had started out from Bakersfield first thing in the California, springtime morning, hitch-hopping with several short rides up Highway 99. My thumb, which had been in someone's ass the night before, was now out. My thumb had been out on the on-ramps of San Fernando, on the on-ramps of Delano, on the on-ramps of Fresno and a long wait on the on-ramps of dreary Merced, too.

And now my thumb was out on a postnuclear-looking stretch of Modesto. I walked backward along the freeway on-ramp, smiling in my best "I'm-not-a-serial-killer-and-I-hope-neither-are-you" manner. My thumb was out. My body was young. My heart was pure. I was emotionally completely fucked-up, and I needed a ride pronto.

I was going to San Francisco for a few days. I was nineteen. As a late seventies, Southern California, punk-rock kid, I had missed out on the hippie/antiwar/cultural revolution by about ten years, but I felt the weight of the previous generation's nostalgia as heavy as a truckload of Woodstock albums on my skinny chest.

But important things seemed to be happening up in San Francisco. There was this new mayor named Moscone, a good guy. Also, this fellow named Harvey Milk had gotten elected a few months before to citywide office. He was a fag like me. It was a revolution, a better world trying to be born. El Dorado. The Grail. The perfectible social order. So, I was on my way to check it out and offer my assistance. I had an address of a friend of a friend of a friend—and twelve dollars in my pocket. I was not nearly as smart as I thought I was, but at least I was starting to realize that.

My thumb was out. Three cars whooshed past without slowing down, not even bothering to glance in their rearview mirror.

*Maybe this '74 Vega will stop? Whoosh. Fuck!*

*Perhaps this '72 Ford Capri? Whoosh. Fucking shit!*

Finally, I heard the crackle of rubber on gravel as a canary yellow Pinto eased its way onto the shoulder. Two hours later I found myself in San Francisco at Powell and Market streets, a corner which reminded me of so many *cheap* family vacations to the Bay Area.

*I am not that kid with my family anymore.* I repeated to myself this mantra as I hoisted my backpack to my shoulders. *I am a self-motivated, young gay man who has escaped from his family. I am on a hero's journey to find immediately a cute boy or the ideal political system. I am a self-motivated, young gay man . . .*

I bought a lukewarm lemonade and watched the tourists climb onto the cable cars. Sucking noisily on the sweet drink through a straw, I noticed a clean-cut, young man and an equally young woman approaching other people under thirty who all seemed to be carrying backpacks. This couple were just a little older than I, and their Donny and Marie good looks seemed to be winning some pedestrians over. Working their way around the cable cars, they finally got to me. I watched them purposefully plant their feet as they extended a small white card toward me.

"Hello," the girl said. "We're from the Creative Community Project, a progressive forward-looking communal organization working toward a new world order. Please join us for a delicious free meal on our bus as we travel to our utopian farm. My name is Jennie. What's yours?"

Her offer did *sound* pretty good to me. At first, I had actually thought Jennie and her colleague were Stalinists. Creative Cooperative Community Project! CCCP! It had seemed pretty clear. I had been hitchhiking for sixteen hours and had only twelve dollars in my pocket. The offer from these seemingly friendly folk of a ride on a bus with free food was pretty tempting. Also, wasn't this the kind of thing that's supposed to happen your first ten minutes in San Francisco?

I made a decision. "Sure. I'll come with you." I got on the bus with this group of odd, smiling people.

"All aboard for utopia!" the bus driver cackled, pounding the clutch as he forced the beat-up gears to mesh. The doors hissed closed as we drove down Market Street. There were eleven other young people, mostly boys with backpacks, on the bus. While we were stopped for a red light at Castro and Market, I saw dozens of gay men heading into their new neighborhood, laughing and holding hands with each other as they crossed in front of the bus. They looked so bright and life-filled walking past me, almost a commercial for homosexuality. Pressing my face against the window, I worried that I had made an enormous mistake.

On the bus, there was a buffet spread out at the back with some very strange food. The dishes all seemed to be made with broccoli as the main ingredient. In fact, everything was made with wilted broccoli, the kind that you might find tossed in a Dumpster at the back of a supermarket. The million little nubs on the broccoli were all droopy and yellow. There were wilted broccoli muffins. Wilted broccoli sandwiches. Wilted broccoli casserole. Wilted broccoli danish! What did all this wilted broccoli mean?

As the lights of San Francisco faded behind us, I grew skeptical. I found a new mantra: *This is a progressive forward-looking communal organization working toward a new world order! This is a progressive forward . . .*

So, as the mantra took effect, I loaded up my plate and sat cross-legged by myself at the back of the bus. Nothing like this ever happened to Jack Kerouac. Stuffing my fears down with the wilted broccoli, I ate myself silly and fell into the deep-as-the-Grand-Canyon sleep of a nineteen year old who has hitchhiked all day.

Three hours later the bus creaked and grinded over a dirt road a hundred and fifty miles north of San Francisco to what my hosts referred to as their "utopian farm." Rubbing a bad dream from my eyes, I staggered off the bus and found myself in a new nightmare. I had a flash for a panicked moment of barking dogs and German accents in the floodlight-illuminated parking area. Emergency mantra: *This is not Dachau. This is not Dachau. This is not . . .*

Immediately after breakfast the next morning the elders in charge gathered us in a circle in a meadow. I was then tortured with several hours of indoctrination, calisthenics and camp songs. During one lecture there was this heavyset guy at a blackboard drawing incomprehensible diagrams as he tried to explain to us everything we needed to know: the function of good and bad in the universe. The ultimate evil of Communism. How man and woman could be happy and complete only through the union of heterosexual marriage.

"You see," he said with a flourish of his stub of white chalk, "it is clear from this irrefutable interpretation of the Book of Revelations in the Bible that the second coming of Jesus Christ can only occur in South Korea!"

I grew more skeptical.

I finally lost it during one of our many exercise breaks. We were coerced out onto the playing field for a set of volleyball. This was fine: volleyball was one of the few sports I did not imagine had been conceived in the Spanish Inquisition. However, the leaders of Camp Revelations wanted us to chant, "Win with love!" as we played. Even as a native Californian, I found this a bit of a stretch. I tried.

"Win with love," I repeated weakly as I returned a serve.

"Win with love," I said a little louder when my fingertips set the ball in play.

*"Win with love!"* I hollered louder than everyone as I spiked and scored.

I had definitely had enough. I broke away from the game and approached the smiling scorekeeper. "Look, time out," I sputtered out my words. "I don't think I'm cut out to be a member of a cult. I have an appointment with someone in the Haight in just two hours. He is a homosexual gentleman. The minute I get there he will probably suck my dick, so could you please get me my backpack and sleeping bag and then drive me back to San Francisco?"

There was complete silence on the volleyball court. A skinny member of the staff ran off toward the main building. A siren began to wail in the distance. The dogs were let loose. I pulled away as the Boonville camp staff surrounded me, backing me against a California oak. I imagined they all were hiding something behind their backs. A greenish light emanated from them as they pleaded with me to stay. As my breath raced, I saw that the staffers all carried . . . heads of broccoli. These were not merely ordinary heads of broccoli. These were not merely ordinary heads of wilted broccoli. No, these broccoli they now held over my head had minds and souls and faces. I was locked in a battle with the attack of the Broccoli Brain Suckers!

"Back!" I shouted, "I am the Antichrist. I am a Communist. I am a Fag!" (What else can I say to scare them away?) "Get me my backpack and sleeping bag now, or I'll call the police!"

Well, that did the trick. About one second later the camp bouncers dumped me and my backpack out on the dirt road. I was breathing fast. I looked around. The world was still there. Everything seemed to be okay. I had managed to escape from the bizarre clutches of the broccoli brain snatchers.

Once again my thumb was out. I worried I would probably get picked up by one of those Northern California ax murderers that my mom always warned me about. I would be left in little, tiny pieces on the off-ramps of Modesto, Fresno, Delano, San Fernando and Burbank too. But on that day in my life, I didn't care because I knew I had come through something big, some weird kind of trial by vegetable. Now I was back in the world, where I would have to figure out love and God and sex by myself.

And so began about two and a half hours of perfect hitchhiking, where each ride begat the next one and every driver offered a bit of wisdom.

First, an Armenian schoolteacher picked me up right outside the camp. He screeched his pickup truck to a halt and shouted, "Get in before they change their minds!" As we drove down toward Highway 101, he told me, "Kid, forget everything those creeps tried to cram down your throat. Wherever it takes you, ya gotta follow your own star!"

Within two minutes of being dropped by the schoolteacher at 101, four hash-brownie-peddling hippies in an old Saab stopped for me. They told me about an excellent book by Hermann Hesse called *Siddhartha* and graciously got me stoned along the way. The hippies left me near Santa Rosa.

My thumb went out again. An Episcopalian priest pulled over and invited me into his Dodge Dart. Father S. drove me to Mill Valley as we talked about God and Plato, his hand stroking the inside of my thigh. During that ride, I learned so much about the Anglican Communion!

Finally, I was picked up by a Twinkie gay boy in a rugby shirt from Marin County who was going to the Haight to dance at the I-Beam disco. He drove me the rest of the way to San Francisco. At last we rounded those headlands, and I saw the boldly lit Golden Gate Bridge. I wanted to grab each one of those bridge towers and give them a big kiss, thanking them for letting me escape back to my life. If I could have, I would have tap-danced down those bridge cables as we drove into the Presidio.

Scared, shaking but breathing, I braced myself for my second day in San Francisco.

Twinkie Boy left me at the front door of my friend of a friend of a friend. He had been arrested for doing back-alley, fifteen-dollar blow jobs off Polk Street. His housemates were not amused by my knock on their door at midnight. They also didn't buy my story.

"Where did you say this was? Boonville?" one particularly dark-hearted housemate asked, grilling me for flaws in my story. "Hon, you just got swept up by the Moonies. Only an idiot would fall for the old-est scam on Market Street." Oops.

The next day I wandered around North Beach, the direct-from-central-casting fog wisping around my ankles. I felt depressed. Disillusioned. What had I expected? What did I want? I think what I really wanted was to have Allen Ginsberg come bursting out of City Lights Bookstore, give me a big hug and say, "Tim! You made it! How 'bout a cappuccino?"

I thought going to the beach might restore me. I got on a bus and I went out to Land's End. Land's End was the last stop, the edge of a mys-terious continent, the edge of buzzing Western Civilization. This is where I belonged, Land's End.

It was unbearably beautiful there. I walked slowly along the bluffs, casting small pebbles down to the frothy sea. I looked down and saw a beach at the bottom of the cliff. Though this area of sand was approximately the size of a compact parking space, about two dozen people had tucked themselves onto it. I climbed down to this Honda Civic-sized beach. I quickly discovered that it was nude-beach-a-rama here at Land's End.

I took off my clothes, hid my remaining eight dollars in my shoe, and started performing a modern dance: the spirit-of-the-seal-rising-from-the-Pacific dance. Climbing over one razor-sharp rock, I suddenly saw a vision: a sinewy, naked, young man with curly, long, brown hair was dip-ping his foot in the ice-cube-cold sea. He looked directly at me and smiled. I almost fainted. I jumped in the water and strode toward this man through the icy surf. I immediately lost all sensation below my neck.

"Hey! Isn't the water cold?" he shouted to me.

Though I was on the cusp of hypothermia, my mind went into overdrive as my thoughts spoke to me: *What does he mean, cold? Does he mean cold in an emotional sense? Is this a critique of my lack of Freudian oceanic feeling?*

"I . . . um . . . oh!" I sounded like an idiot. I looked at this guy through my dangling water-soaked curls. He was so confident, so sure of himself. How did he get like that?

He pulled me out of the surf. "I'm Michael."

"I'm-m-m-m-m Tim."

I looked out of the corner of my eye, and I saw that Michael had a dog-eared copy of James Joyce's *A Portrait of the Artist as a Young Man* open on his towel.

"I'm a student at San Francisco State," he explained. "I'm taking a class on Joyce. Have you read *Portrait*?"

I trapped my emerging boner between my legs. Sitting at the edge of a continent with a cute boy reading me James Joyce was the height of homo-sexiness to me.

"Would you like to come to my house tonight?" Michael asked. "I live in a small, socialist gay men's commune in the Mission. We compost and everything. Well, we're having a meal tonight. A few of us are thinking about going to Cuba as part of the Venceremos Brigade to help bring in the sugarcane harvest and defeat the imperialist U.S. embargo. Would you like to join us?"

"I'd love to."

"Great," Michael replied. "I better go to class. Why don't you come by around six and you can help me slice vegetables."

Since we didn't have any paper except for the James Joyce, Michael neatly printed his phone number on the inside of my arm with the same fluorescent green highlighter he'd been marking up his copy of *Portrait* with. "There," he said as he capped the pen. "Now you won't lose me."

Michael put on his clothes and climbed up the path. "See you later," he called, waving from the top of the cliff, then walked bouncily toward civilization.

I fell back naked onto the sand looking up at Michael's clear writing on my skin. Naturally, I immediately proceeded to fall in love. The thought of going to Cuba with my new friend began to appeal to me.

Weaving my future with Michael, I drifted into a sun-baked sleep. I imagined our dinner that night. *There will be a brood of dynamic, leftist gay men in attendance. We will eat a delicious ovo-vegetarian meal that Michael and I will prepare. I'll commit to going to Cuba with them. "Venceremos! We shall be victorious!" we will all shout. At the right moment Michael will invite me into his bedroom to listen to his album of whale songs. Michael will kiss me all over and then fuck me gently underneath the poster of Che with the slogan:* Hasta la Victoria Siempre!

The tide came in and woke me up.

Two hours later I was walking in downtown San Francisco killing time before my date. Carefully checking the bright green numbers marked on my arm, I called Michael to get directions to his house in the Mission District.

"Hi, Michael. It's me, Tim, the guy you met at Land's End." As I spoke, I tucked the used copy of an abridged *Finnegans Wake* I had just bought so I could bone up before dinner and impress Michael with my knowledge of Joyce.

"What shall I make for us to eat?" Michael asked. "Do you like broccoli?"

"Sure," I said with a gulp. "I love broccoli."

I hung up resigned to yet another dinner of broccoli. I made a detour on Fulton Street so I could see City Hall before I went to Michael's flat. I wanted to check out the building where Harvey Milk was changing the world. Well, at least my world. Finally, I arrived at City Hall and I looked at the vaulted dome high above me. I thought to myself, *Why is this building so huge? Is it because there is a big idea inside? It looks like it could be the Capitol of an empire or something, not just a City Hall.*

I looked at the huge building and I felt a huge joy. There I was, a foolish, young man, with James Joyce in my hand and a date for dinner. I felt the wheels of the state apparatus, for once, grinding begrudgingly in concert with me. There was a guy named Harvey Milk, a fag like me, inside City Hall tickling the power that be! I felt so strong. It was as if I were in the Paris Commune with the other radical students in 1871. Storming the Winter Palace in St. Petersburg. I felt for once that the world was not an enemy, that society *was* perfectible.

My body was in front of City Hall. I could feel my skin, my feelings, my hopes for the future as tangible as the sidewalk under my feet. For once the big dick of the law and the government would not pull the rug out from under me. I had all these powerful feelings and a date for dinner with Michael, too.

As I walked away from City Hall, I thought to myself, *Well, I guess I'll have to go back to Whittier pretty soon. I only have three dollars left. Maybe I won't go to New York. I want to come back to San Francisco and make a life in this city someday.*

But, for now, I went off to my broccoli.

A few months later, I was working another soul-killing job at a gas station, trying to make ends meet. As I pumped gas into an old man's Buick, I overheard two other people in a pickup truck having this conversation.

"Hey, d'ya hear the news?" this obvious jerk in the truck slurred through his open door. "They got those two guys up in Frisco. Yeah, some ex-cop killed that queer Milk and that dago mayor of theirs, whashizname, Macaroni?"

I dropped the gas nozzle to my side.

I knew it was time to leave California.

I was covered in gasoline.

# John O'Keefe

---

**Introduction** by Mark Russell

John O'Keefe shimmers. You can hear it in his voice, the buttery sounds of his baritone shifting to the high flights of his tenor. His theatre pieces shimmer music. When he performs them they are almost sung. He used to sing in choirs as a boy. His college hero was the experimental composer John Cage.

But John O'Keefe is hardly a choirboy. The politically incorrect, the outrageous action, the dark places where one shouldn't go (even in one's mind)—that is the song John listens to, and sings. When John teaches young playwrights he councils them to shut out their inner critics and write. He is a master at battling his own inner critic to get to the truth.

On my first business trip out to California in the mid-eighties, I was trying to discover what performance art was like on the West Coast. I went around asking all the experts I knew, whom they thought was the most interesting performance artist on the coast. Almost all said, "John O'Keefe." The next thing they usually said was: "But he's crazy."

One day, back in New York, I got a call from some of my friends out at Life on the Water, a theatre at Fort Mason in San Francisco. "O'Keefe has just done a solo show that is amazing. It's called *Shimmer* and it's getting rave reviews."

If I had been richer I would have flown out on the next plane. Soon thereafter a small theatre company brought O'Keefe to New York, and that is where I first got to see him perform. He did two solos *Aztec* and *Sunshine Is a Glorious Bird*. They were simple, gorgeous and frightening. John was a charismatic performer. I could see why the man could be considered crazy. I could see he was a great and gifted artist.

John was a small guy for all the scary hype about him. A bantam weight with piercing blue eyes, the gait of a San Francisco beat poet and a voice that had a light, sweet innocence to it, but could dive down into a raspy bass that sounded like the devil himself was in the room, right behind your ear.

O'Keefe was raised in the Midwest where he was bounced between several boys' homes. He went to school at the University of Iowa and ended up in San Francisco becoming one of the founding members of the Blake Street Hawkeyes, a bunch of theatre rebels that produced David Shein, Bob Ernst and Whoopi Goldberg.

I invited him to give the East Coast premiere of *Shimmer* at P. S. 122 the next winter. As is the case in many of our presentations, I did not see *Shimmer* until opening night. It was a legendary night at P. S. 122. *Shimmer* was a truly amazing piece, dangerous, sweet, poignant, told with passion in a tour de force performance. We were slightly worried that maybe the audience would not take to John's story since they did not know him at all. They gave him a standing ovation.

The *New York Times* gave it a rave. Audiences crowded in. O'Keefe had found his New York home. Although he was never comfortable being a "performance artist," too high art a concept for him. A performer, poet, singer, director, John has always been a playwright first.

*Shimmer* is ostensibly about the young O'Keefe's escape from a home for wayward boys in the middle of Iowa. Many of the events of the story actually happened—he did, in fact, escape the home to his mother, but this is not journalism, what it is is damn good storytelling.

When you read *Shimmer*, think of it as an operetta, a one-man operetta. Listen for the music between the lines, the meter and rhythm of the consonants and sounds, the dynamics of the different voices. This is what makes *Shimmer* such wonderful performed poetry. It is what takes it back to the primal roots of live performance, to Homer's *The Iliad*. One man singing/telling an epic story, though this one is not about a returning war hero, but a little boy running away in the middle of 1950s America.

**Mark Russell** is the Director of Performance Space 122 in New York City and is editor of *Out of Character: Rants, Raves and Monologues from Today's Top Performance Artists* (Bantam Books).

John O'Keefe

## from **Shimmer**

This story is true. Most of it. It was the end of a long, bad time. The Fall of 1956. In the heartland of America, Tama County Juvenile Home in Tama/Toledo, Iowa, just off Highway 30. Had this tall, red brick chimney that stuck up out of it. I can remember others, seven, eight, nine tall, red brick chimneys sticking out of the flat Midwestern landscape, Nebraska, Iowa, Illinois. God and razor straps. Five long razor straps in Tama/Toledo, lined up and hanging on the wall, with holes in the top so that they'd whistle and make tattoos, hanging right where you could see them. Tama/Toledo, the worst and the best—best because it was the last, worst because the razor straps were harder to take the older you got, best because I met Gary Welch and we discovered Shimmer.

Gary was shorter than me. Had sandy-colored hair and a big honker of a nose that hooked out so that you could see up it. I'm glad he didn't have much nose hair because I spent a lot of time with him. Came from Des Moines. The biggest city in the state. Gary was a year younger than me. I was almost sixteen.

I met him during a fight. Kept sticking his chin out at Dewey Wheeler and getting it popped. Dewey had these big, sharp knuckles you could cut grass with. But Gary kept on coming at him. Dewey could have totally dismantled him if Teats Brewer hadn't stepped in and stopped it all. Teats was a big black kid, called them Negroes in '56. He was called Teats because he had the biggest set of pecs in the home. A light-skinned black guy with the fastest hands I've ever seen.

Teats started pushing Dewey back, calling him trash-face and mongo-boy, short for Mongoloid (Dewey wasn't that smart). Dewey backed off waving his hand like he was trying to say good-bye to a girl that didn't like him. And ole Teats, he was strutting and talking like Amos and Andy, flapping his hands around like he was sending signals to a ship out at sea. He'd made his point; he was king of the field, except for Richard Mathison. But Richard Mathison wasn't on the playing field. He was in Lockup and he had two weeks to go, so Teats, he was having a heyday.

After everybody cleared off, I saw Gary sitting on the grass trying to keep the blood off his duds. Ole Mr. White see them dirty and he'd kick him in the shins. Good ole Mr. White, patron of Hoover Hall. That was our cottage. Fast with his hands. Almost as fast as Teats Brewer except he didn't pull his punches. Five-foot-six, mean as mosquito meat. Talk to you one moment, nodding and bobbing his head full of good cheer and confidentiality, next moment on you like a thin cloud of bad gas, hands and feet flying, every one of them too, every one of them reaching their mark and their mark was you, sucker. Went off on Teats a lot. Made him mad as hell the way Teats could cover himself. Tried to pull ole Teats's arms and legs away but couldn't budge them. "You chicken shit, son of a bitch, chicken shit, son of a bitch." And Teats, you could just see him beneath the blur of Whitey's flying limbs, believe it or not, giggling. Teats was an astronaut of beatings. He could enter that dimension and come back like you and me can walk through doors.

"Goddamned Teats. I had that son of a bitch."

He pulled his pants up. His cuffs were over his heels.

"I hate these motherfuckers, ole man White's wife's keeps giving me these long pants. She's trying to turn me into a duck."

"She'll get numb pretty soon."

"Numb?"

"After a while she'll forget you're here unless you remind her. Old man White's another story."

"Yeah, the story of my life."

"I'm John."

"I know, Captain Spacy."

I hated that name. I got it because I wanted to be an astronaut. It was just the beginning of the space age, remember? They were shooting guys down railroad tracks at the speed of sound and blowing up rockets on launch pads but I wanted to go up there.

"Yeah, I'm Captain Spacy."

"Space ain't so bad."

He looked up at the tall, red brick chimney.

"It's gonna blow soon."

"The whistle at the physical plant?"

"Yeah."

"At five o'clock."

"Makes me nervous waiting for it."

"Yeah?"

"It's not because it's loud. It's because I know it's gonna happen."

"Yeah."

"It's neat."

"Yeah."

"I ain't crazy, you know."

"I know."

Just then the whistle at the physical plant blew. We looked at each other as the sound ripped through us, grins of pain and confirmation shifting through our faces. The kids ran toward the cottages, calling out to each other. I watched their heads bob and their hair flash in the summer's sun. The wind came up, could feel it whisper through my hair. I knew it was saying something. I wanted to know what it was saying.

"Race you up the hill."

"All right."

I dug my feet into the grass and pushed off into space. I left Gary behind me. I was fast in those days.

*(Sitting on the floor, Gary talks to Spacy)* "Penguins really live in the ice. Below the water. So do seals. They dive into the water and they go down into the ice and they go far enough that they get to a place where the ice is so cold it isn't cold anymore. It gets hard instead, like super concrete. And it's totally smooth."

"But isn't it dark down there?"

"No, there's light."

"Where does the light come from?"

"I don't know. It's just there."

"Right."

"It's a blue-green glow."

"Like that blue-green you see sometimes in the snow."

"Exactly, it leaks up there."

"Oh."

"Below the ice you find all these places."

"The seals go down there?"

"Yeah."

"What do they do down there?"

"They do everything that we do, but they do it before we do it. We just do it and we act like we did it first."

"You mean there are penguins and seals that look just like you and me and they're in the Home?"

"Yeah, but the Home's different there. It's neat. You get to see girls and drive around."

"Are there people who've ever gotten down there?"

"Yeah. And they tried to bring things up with them."

"What kinds of things?"

"Things they'd never seen before."

"What happened?"

"By the time they got something to the top it had turned into water"

Gary and me found times to make up stories. By the window facing the playing field where we first met, or on the playing field itself, throwing a baseball.

*(Fwack—the sound of catching the ball)* "I don't like to swear." *(Fwung—the sound of throwing the ball)*

"You've got to swear, Spacy *(Fwack)* if you want to talk." *(Fwung)*

"Swearing isn't a sign of good language." *(Fwack/Fwung)*

"Yes it is. Swearing's where you pour the hot iron in. *(Fwack)* Like, look at those *fucking* stars."

"Throw the ball."

"Right. What is it when you say *(Fwung) darn it*?"

*(Fwack)* "I don't want to swear." *(Fwung)*

"Swearing's *(Fwack)* good for you. It's what you say when you mean something." *(Fwung)*

"Deep, Welch, deep." *(Fwack/Fwung)*

"It's true. Just tell it to me *(Fwack)* like you'd tell one of your priesties. What is it, 'Admit it, son, admit it.' What is it when you say *(Fwung) darn it*?"

*(Fwack)*

"Damn it."

*(Fwung)*

"Shadows in the *(Fwack)* night, buddy, shadows. What is it *(Fwung)* when you say *heck*?"

*(Fwack)* "Hell." *(Fwung)*

*(Fwack)* "What is it when you say *shoot*?" *(Fwung)*

*(Fwack)* "Shit." *(Fwung)*

*(Fwack)* "You're getting pure."

"What is it when you say *(Fwung) frig*?"

*(Fwack)*

"Come on."

"Come on, say it."

*(Fwung)*

"Fuck."

*(Fwack)* "What is it when you say *(Fwung) gosh darn it*?"

*(Fwack)* "Come on."

"Come on, say it.""

*(Fwung)* "Fuck it."

"No, that's not it." *(Throws the ball really hard. It stings Spacy's hand)*

*(Fwack)* "Goddamn it!" *(Fwung)*

*(The sound of the ball flying way over Gary's head. Gary watches it as it flies up stage out of sight. He turns back to Spacy and shouts, giving the umpire's signal for "out")*

"Right!"

Gary and me pulled cafeteria. We had to be there at 5:00 A.M., an hour before the rest of the kids got up. Most of the kids hated kitchen duty, but Gary and me, we liked it because we could walk under the Iowa sky, ablaze with its Easter-egg light, the air filled with the sound of roosters and dogs and birds, and our leather shoes as we walked from Hoover Hall to the cafeteria.

> *(Click-click)* "People don't think dogs can think."
> "I think they do." *(Click-click)*
> "So do I." *(Click-click)*
> "I think birds can think."
> "I do too." *(Click-click)*
> "I think bugs can think."
> "So do I. I think worms can think."
> "Me too." *(Click-click)*
> "I think dirt thinks."
> "I don't know, it would be hard on the dirt, all those people walking around on it and digging into it. Anyway, what parts of dirt, the little parts or the whole ground?" *(Click-click)*
> "The little parts think like the little parts and the ground thinks like the little parts when it thinks of itself being the field."
> *(Click-click)* "Well, where does the field end?"
> "Where the fences are."
> "Why there?"
> *(Click-click)* "Because the fences tell the ground when it's a field."

The cafeteria was one of the most exciting places of all because it was where everybody came together, i.e., the boys and the girls. Everyone waited outside the cafeteria. The bell would ring and everyone would file in according to cottage. One of the patrons would begin the prayer.

> Bless us, oh Lord
> for these thy gifts
> which we are about to receive
> from thy bounty
> in the name of Jesus Christ, our Lord,
> amen.

The rustle of chairs, the clinking and clanking of silverware and plates and then, silence. There was absolutely no talking allowed. The sections were patrolled by patrons and matrons who paced the aisles between the tables. Evy, big, fat-faced, black-haired grinner, would roll between the boy's tables with his arms folded over his potbelly, just waiting to give his infamous ear clap, which meant that he would attempt to clap his hands together with your head between them. He could come up on you so quiet you didn't know he was there and no matter how much winking and finger-twitching the guy on the other side of you gave he would inevitably catch you whispering to a buddy or gazing at a girl across the room, and then Pop!—a mind-blackening explosion would send your ears wailing. And ole Evy wouldn't say a word, he'd just float on down the aisle with that same grin.

Going together in the Home meant sneaking glances at each other across the cafeteria.

"Is someone looking at Beatrice? Who is looking at you? Stand up and show us who is looking at you."

She stands up. She doesn't look at him. She doesn't want to get him in trouble. The matron slaps her.

"Who is looking at you?"

She doesn't look. She slaps her.

"I said, who is looking at you?"

She slaps her again and still she doesn't look at him.

Davey stands up and looks at her. Evy strides over to him and says, "What are you looking at boy? Sit down."

Davey doesn't sit. Evy shoves him down in his chair. Davey gets up. Evy slaps him. Davey doesn't sit down. Evy wacks him across the back of the head. Davey's chin smacks against his chest. He lifts his head up and looks across the cafeteria at Beatrice. The fat matron has stopped slapping her. Everybody in the room is looking at him except for her. Davey smiles, blood's coming from the corner of his mouth. Davey's bit his tongue pretty bad. Evy grabs Davey by the collar and pushes him out of the cafeteria. The fat-cow matron tells Beatrice to sit down and keep her eyes to herself. She does. That's love. Love in the Home.

We looked at a lot of codes, Morse Code, semaphore, Braille, the Greek alphabet, sign language. We even made up our own sign language. Teats Brewer caught us signing to each other and made us teach it to him. He was real good at it. The only trouble was he laughed a lot and jumped around on his bed so that ole man White caught us and made all of us hold paper to the wall for two hours. Teats started inventing a new code with his face. Pulling both eyebrows up meant one thing, pulling them down meant another, lifting one meant something else, smiling with both corners of the mouth, smiling with the right side, closing the left eyelid, thrusting the lower jaw out, sticking the front teeth over the lower lip, pursing the lips, wrinkling the nose, crossing both eyes, crossing one eye. It's a miracle we didn't get killed out there, but ole Whitey didn't hear us laughing.

"Whose receiving the code?"

"Anybody who tunes in. They catch this wave and it's talk, and they pass it on."

"And we get it?"

"Right, but we don't know we got it, we just act like nothing's happened. Like static on the radio *(Makes the sound of static)*, we think it's noise but it's really talk. We're not smart enough to get it."

"Like smoke coming off a cigarette, it's like smoke signals for really smart Indians."

"Exactly."

"Who's sending the code?"

"Everything."

"What's it being sent to?"

"To whatever's signaling."

"What is that, God?"

"Yeah, but a weird god, weirder than a jellyfish. You'd throw up if you saw it."

"What would you call this code?"

"I don't know. It's not just a code, it's a language. It's on the edge of things."

"Yeah, it shines."

"Yeah, it shimmers."

"That's it."

"What's it?"

"That's the name."

"Shimmers?"

"No, Shimmer."

*(Gary tastes the word)* "Shimmer."

"Shimmer."

"Shimmer."

*(They laugh with delight.)*

While we were working on the basic principles of Shimmer, Richard Mathison got out of Lockup.

Richard Mathison was a mongrel Hun with a bit of bad Celt mixed in. Biggest fifteen year old I ever saw. Wasn't quite six feet. Didn't weigh more than a hundred and sixty, but all the same, everything about him was big. Sandy-haired, with this huge face and thick, insensitive skin and a mood that could cook and freeze a TV dinner at the same time. His hands looked like they were made out of big dicks. He made Teats look like an exotic butterfly.

And there was Mathison's sidekick, Tony Kemler. Most of the time he just moved around with a convivial grin. But when Mathison was on the prowl he turned into his straight man, a straight man from hell.

And so Mathison was among us again and Welch would have to face him. To let him pee on him, so to speak, the way dogs do.

We walked down the hill together from the Dairy to the Cottage.

"Is he gonna beat the shit out of me?"

"Not as long as you shut up."

"What am I supposed to shut up about?"

"Everything."

"Great. What if he asks me a question?"

"I don't know. Just don't be aggressive."

"What does that mean?"

"Don't laugh. Don't smile. Don't make your face blank. Don't look sad."

"Just look scared, right?"

"Yeah, but not timid."

"How bad is this guy?"

"He's bad."

The whistle blew.

"He looks Italian to me, Richard."

"Why's that, Tony?"

"He's got a big nose and a little dick."

"No shit?"

"But I might be wrong. I ain't never seen it swolled up. Probably when he gets a hard-on so much blood goes down there he passes out."

"Yeah, that would be something to see. Well, what will get him hard?"

"Captain Spacy."

"Captain Spacy, he couldn't get a rise out of nobody."

"He's changed since you been gone."

"Has he gotten tough?"

"He's really gotten tough."

"Could he beat me?"

"Jesus, I don't know."

"I want to know."

"I don't know."

"Don't fuck with me, Tony!"

"Yes, he could beat you."

"Goddamn that son of a bitch, where is he?"

"He's right there, in the shower, Richard."

"Are you in the shower, Space Boy? There you are. Wow, you've grown?"

"He looks tough, don't he?"

"I don't think so. He's really bony."

"You're right, he looks like he's gonna cry."

"Where's his buddy?"

"In the shower over there."

"No shit? Is he tough?"

"No, he's weird."

"Where is he? Oh, he's neat. You're right, he must be Italian"

"They hang out together."

"That's neat. Hey, Spacy, come here. You slicing the biscuit with this boy?"

"No."

"Fuck off, you fat slob."

"What'd he say, Tony?"

"Jesus Christ, I don't know?"

"He say something to me, Tony?"

"I said you're a blimp, muscle-face."

"Did he call me a fucking name, Tony?"

"No, ain't no name ugly as you."

Mathison put his big hand full of dicks right into Gary's face and smashed his head against the shower stall. Gary went down. Everybody backed away. Mathison stepped into the shower stall. And I went off. That's right, I went off on Richard Mathison. Admittedly, his back was to me, but I went off on him. It was all like a dream. I threw my fist (it was my right hand) into the side of his head with all my might. It was crazy, I had this loving feeling mingled with a suicidal glee and this clarity, like riding the rail to a predestined and preposterous act. His head snapped and I distinctly saw spit fly from his mouth. Boxer's spit. I had made boxer's spit fly from Richard Mathison's mouth. I wondered what would fly from mine after he got through with me. But Mathison wasn't doing anything at that moment but going down. I watched him aghast, completely jarred off. So was everybody else. They gazed at me with the disbelief and curiosity of witnesses at an execution. What I did next to Mr. White probably saved me from hospitalization. I got Lockup instead. I slugged him. That's right. His face no sooner appeared around the shower stall than I swung at it. Call it a reflex. His face was bony and hard. Mathison's was meaty and soft. I understood, for a moment, the reason why guys liked to fight each other, it's like petting, except it was hard and very fast. But Mr. White didn't go down. He grabbed the back of my head and brought my face down into his quickly rising knee. Miraculously (I had a butch), he was somehow able to grab me by the hair and throw my face into his left fist. And it was there, I think, believe or not, I had my first Shimmer. And before we struck, that shower drain and me, I entered that place Gary was talking about, where the seals and penguins go, I Shimmered my dad.

Mother's keeping quiet in the corner.

She knows, she knows

ain't no law this side of custody.
Ain't no law. Ain't no law.

Hear the alcohol ripping through his veins.
"This is your dad, Baby. Crossed
the dividing line some years ago,
just before you was born."

"Johnny, Johnny,
sing him to sleep.
Sing him that song he likes.
Goes like this:

> *Tweedle o' twill,*
> *knocking on corn wood,*
> *tweedle o' twill,*
> *knocking on silk."*

"Oh, Jesus, here it comes.
I'm gonna shout,
Johnny,
I'm gonna shout.

Why are you looking at me?
What are you looking at me for?
What are you looking at?
What do you think you see?"

SMACK!

"Hey, Johnny,
why ain't this going right?
Just wanted to give your mama a kiss.
I'm in trouble now, ain't I, son?"

> *Tweedle o' twill*
> *knocking on corn wood,*
> *tweedle o' twill*
> *knocking on rice.*

"Now I'm talking to *you* son,
Now I'm talking to *you.*
Can you hear me?
Can you hear me talking to *you*?

What is he doing, trying to keep me down?
Is he trying to keep me down?

John O'Keefe

175

Is he trying to fool me, honey?
He's singing. Why is he singing?"

SMACK!

What's that word,
they call it?
Surrender.
Yes, yes,

Surrender.
in this big, wide world
full of sin.
Surrender.

SMACK!

My daddy goes a-hunting
He loves those birds
loves those bass.
Why ain't the world like that?
Why ain't the world like that?

My daddy, got to know the other side of his angry face. SMACK! We hit,
that shower drain and me.

## Introduction by Lani Guinier

Using the stories people tell her, Anna Deavere Smith performs and interprets the tough issue of race at the height of racial conflagration. She has borne witness to blacks and Jews in Crown Heights (in *Fires in the Mirror*). In *Twilight: Los Angeles, 1992* she both exposed and then attempted to stitch together the wound left by the riots in Los Angeles following the acquittal of the police officers who were videotaped beating Rodney King. She brings these events to life after the fact, then breathes *new* life into them. She is a fluent translator who inhabits the "moments when speech fails," and then takes us there too, to the "very moments which defy definition and description."

Anna has been searching, she says, for the "American character," mainly looking in spaces we would call the "margins." She has worked as a print journalist chronicling the 1996 presidential election campaign but it is in her artistry on stage that she publishes her most important texts. She is not simply observing and documenting events—she becomes the people who are the events. As she boldly identifies the individual idiosyncrasies within a larger whole, she invites her audience to step back and step in simultaneously. She makes her audience a dancing partner, dizzily spinning us

**177**

around with focal points of recognition even in the most unfamiliar territory. In childlike awe, we rediscover our "I" and, often for the first time, see our "we." It is a balletic tour de force.

While writing *Twilight*, Anna suggested in the fall of 1993 that perhaps I could help her use the Rodney King experience to think about race as well as about the justice system, its powers, its abuses of power. Although she is "first looking for the humanness inside the problems or the crises," Anna came to interview me about "the big picture." We sat in my living room, drinking tea in large mugs. The tape recorder was running and Anna also took lots of notes.

I felt incredibly inarticulate. I knew that Anna was scrutinizing me closely, not just listening to what I said. Each time I took a sip I almost sputtered, cognizant that my cup might become a metaphor for my voice, my ideas, my mannerisms. I could become my tea cup. Not literally, but Anna makes such amazing use of props. She casts an astute eye for the telling gesture, deconstructing her subjects through her gifts of mime, undoing by overdoing. But she also reconstructs the world of her subjects—those who are "other" as well as those that the audience sees as themselves.

Then, in March 1994, Anna interviewed me at the 92nd Street Y about my short-lived, but very public, experience as a Clinton nominee the year before. I was excited and, at first, much less self-conscious than when Anna had interviewed me in my own living room. Somehow being watched by hundreds of people felt less intrusive than being watched by Anna alone.

Anna had prepared diligently. We talked by phone. She showed up with handwritten notes on a large collection of legal pads. Some of the pages were like pieces of origami, creased and ready to become something else.

As we waited, Anna held her stack of legal pads close. She seemed to be studying them. I began to realize that this was a performance, not just an interview. I turned to Anna. "How do you make an entrance?" I asked. Anna looked at me. She said nothing. "How do I enter?" I asked my question again. "How do you walk on stage?" "I have no idea," she replied softly, a note of disquietude in her voice. "I have never done this before."

How could that be? Anna was always fearless; her loud, lusty laugh part of a gutsy talent for public narration. No one is off limits; no idea is too challenging. I looked at her quizzically. She was preoccupied. "I feel," I admitted aloud, "as if I am being asked somehow to 'perform' myself." Finally, she returned my gaze. "I have no idea," she whispered emphatically. "I have never done this before. I have not gone on stage before simply as myself."

She was acknowledging my discomfort and now her own. It made sense. Anna Deavere Smith is a theatrical wizard who magically connects the "I" and the "we." That is why we trust her even as she makes us uncomfortable. In moments when speech fails, she locates our "I" within a multivocal we.

**Lani Guinier** is Professor of Law at Harvard University and author of several books, including *Lift Every Voice* (Simon & Schuster), a personal memoir; *Tyranny of the Majority* (Free Press), a collection of essays on voting; and co-author of *Becoming Gentlemen: Women, Law Schools and Institutional Change* (Beacon Press).

**Elvira Evers**, General Worker and Cashier, Canteen Corporation
**To Look Like Girls from Little**

So it was like a carnival out there
and I say
to my friend Frances
"Frances, you see this?"
and she said, "Girl, you should see
that
it's getting worst."
And I say, "Girl, let me take my butt
up there before something happen."
And, um,
when somebody throw a bottle
and I just . . .
then I felt
like moist,
and it was like a tingling sensation, right?
And I didn't like this,
and it was like itchin',
and I say, "Frances, I'm bleedin'."
And she walk with me to her house.
And she say, "Lift up your gown, let me see."
She say, "Elvira, it's a bullet!"
I say, "What?"
I say, "I didn't heard nothin'."
She say, "Yes, but it's a bullet."
She say, "Lay down there. Let me call St. Francis and tell them that
you been shot
and to send an ambulance."
And she say,
"Why you?
You don't mess with none of those people.
Why they have to shoot you?"
So Frances say the ambulance be here in fifteen minutes.
I say, "Frances,
I cannot wait that."
I say,
"I'm goin'!"
So I told my oldest son, I say,

"Amant, take care your brothers.
I be right back."
Well, by this time he was standing there, he was crying,
all of them was crying.
What I did for them not to see the blood—
I took the gown and I cover it
and I didn't cry.
That way they didn't get nervous.
And I get in the car.
I was goin' to drive.
Frances say, "What you doin'?"
I said, "I'm drivin'."
She say, "No, you're not!"
And we take all the back streets,
and she was so supportive,
because she say, "You all right?
You feel cold?
You feel dizzy?
The baby move?"
She say, "You nervous?"
I say, "No, I'm not nervous, I'm just worried about the baby."
I say, "I don't want to lose this baby."
She say, "Elvira, everything will be all right." She say, "Just pray."
So there was a lot of cars, we had to be blowing the horn.
So finally we get to St. Francis
and Frances told the front-desk office, she say,
"She been shot!"
And they say, "What she doin' walkin'?"
And I say, "I feel all right."
Everybody stop doin' what they was doin'
and they took me to the room
and put the monitor to see if the baby was fine
and they find the baby heartbeat,
and as long as I heard the baby heartbeat I calmed down,
long as I knew whoever it is, boy or girl, it's all right,
and
matter of fact, my doctor, Thomas, he was there
at
the emergency room.
What a coincidence, right?
I was just lookin' for that familiar face,
and soon as I saw him
I say, "Well, I'm all right now."

Right?
So he bring me this other doctor and then told me,
"Elvira, we don't know how deep is the bullet.
We don't know where it went. We gonna operate on
you.
But since that we gonna operate we gonna take the baby out
and you don't have to
go through all of that."
They say, "Do you understand
what we're saying?"
I say, "Yeah!"
And they say, "Okay, sign here."
And I remember them preparing me
and I don't remember anything else.
Nella!
No.
*(Turns to the side and admonishes the child)*
She likes company.
And in the background
I remember Dr. Thomas say, "You have a six-pound-twelve-ounce little
girl."
He told me how much she weigh and her length
and he
say, "Um,
she born,
she had the bullet in her elbow,
but when we remove . . .
when we clean her up
we find out that the bullet was still between two joints,
so we did operate on her and your daughter is fine
and you are fine."
*(Sound of a little child saying "Mommy")*
Nella!
She wants to show the baby
Jessica.
Bring the baby.
*(She laughs)*
Yes,
yes.
We don't like to keep the girls without earrings, we like the little
girls
to look like girls from little.
I pierce hers.

When I get out on Monday,
by Wednesday I did it,
so by Monday she was five days,
she was seven days,
and I
pierced her ears,
and the red band is just like for evil eyes.
We really believe in Panama . . .
in English I can't explain too well.
And her doctor, he told,
he explain to me
that the bullet
destroyed the placenta
and
went through me
and she caught in her arms.
*(Here you can hear the baby making noise, and a bell rings)*
If she didn't caught it in her arm,
me and her would be dead.
See?
So it's like
open your eyes,
watch what is goin' on.


## Mrs. Young-Soon Han, Former Liquor Store Owner
## Swallowing the Bitterness

When I was in Korea
I used to watch many luxurious, Hollywood-lifestyle movies;
I never saw any poor men,
any black,
maybe one housemaid.
Until last year
I believed America is the best.
I still believe it.
I don't deny that now
because I'm victim,
but
as
the year ends in '92
and we were still in turmoil
and having all the financial problems

and mental problems.
Then a couple months ago
I really realized that
Korean immigrants were left out
from this
society and we were nothing.
What is our right?
Is it because we are Korean?
Is it because we have no politicians?
Is it because we don't
speak good English?
Why?
Why do we have to be left out?
*(She is hitting her hand on the coffee table)*
We are not qualified to have medical treatment.
We are not qualified to get, uh,
food stamps
*(She hits the table once)*
not GR
*(Hits the table once)*
no welfare.
*(Hits the table once)*
Anything.
Many Afro-Americans
*(Two quick hits)*
who never worked,
*(One hit)*
they get
at least minimum amount
*(One hit)*
of money
*(One hit)*
to survive.
*(One hit)*
We don't get any.
*(Large hit with full hand spread)*
Because we have a car
*(One hit)*
and we have a house.
*(Pause six seconds)*
And we are high taxpayers.
*(One hit. Pause fourteen seconds)*
Where do I finda [sic] justice?

Okay, black people
probably
believe they won
by the trial?
Even some complains only half right.
Justice was there.
But I watched the television
that Sunday morning,
early morning as they started.
I started watch it all day.
They were having party and then they celebrated,
all of South Central,
all the churches.
They finally found that justice exists
in this society.
Then where is the victims' rights?
They got their rights
by destroying innocent Korean merchants.
They have a lot of respect,
as I do,
for
Dr. Martin King?
He is the only model for black community.
I don't care Jesse Jackson.
But
he was the model
of nonviolence.
Nonviolence?
They like to have hiseh [sic] spirits.
What about last year?
They destroyed innocent people.
*(Pause five seconds)*
And I wonder if that is really justice
*(And a very soft "ah" after "justice," like "justiceah," but very quick)*
to get their rights
in this way.
*(Pause thirteen seconds)*
I waseh swallowing the bitternesseh,
sitting here alone and watching them.
They became all hilarious
*(Pause three seconds)*
and, uh,
in a way, I was happy for them

and I felt glad for them.
At least they got something back, you know.
Just let's forget Korean victims or other victims
who are destroyed by them.
They have fought
for their rights
*(One hit simultaneous with the word "rights")*
over two centuries
*(One hit simultaneous with "centuries")*
and I have a lot of sympathy and understanding for them.
Because of their effort and sacrificing,
other minorities, like Hispanic
or Asians,
maybe we have to suffer more
by mainstream,
you know.
That's why I understand,
and then
I like to be part of their
'joyment.
But . . .
that's why I had mixed feeling
as soon as I heard the verdict.
I wish I could
live together
with eh [sic] blacks,
but after the riots
there were too much differences.
The fire is still there—
how do you call it?—
igni . . .
igniting fire.
*(She says a Korean word, "Dashi yun gi ga nuh")*
It canuh
burst out anytime.


**Twilight Bey**, Organizer of Gang Truce
**Limbo**

So a lot of times when I've brought up ideas to my homeboys,
they say, "Twilight,
that's before your time,

that's something you can't do now."
When I talked about the truce back in 1988,
that was something they considered before its time,
yet in 1992
we made it
realistic.
So to me it's like I'm stuck in limbo,
like the sun is stuck between night and day
in the twilight hours.
You know,
I'm in an area not many people exist.
Nighttime to me
is like a lack of sun,
and I won't affiliate
darkness with anything negative.
I affiliate
darkness with what was first,
because it was first,
and then relative to my complexion.
I am a dark individual,
and with me stuck in limbo,
I see darkness as myself.
I see the light as knowledge and the wisdom of the world and
    understanding others,
and in order for me to be a, to be a true human being,
I can't forever dwell in darkness,
I can't forever dwell in the idea,
just identifying with people like me and understanding me and mine.
So twilight
is
that time
between day and night,
limbo;
I call it limbo.

# Danitra Vance

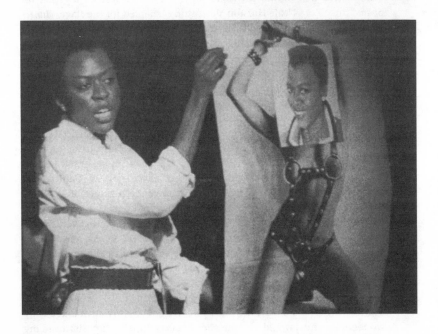

## Introduction by George C. Wolfe

**D**anitra Vance was bar none, one of the most peculiar people I have known. What set her apart from the rest of humanity was not the eccentricities of her personality or dress. No, what made Danitra so truly, uniquely special, was that she lived so completely and comfortably inside of her complexities and contradictions that it only served to expose the rest of us as being small and foolish for trying to compartmentalize ourselves, each other and, God forbid, Ms. Vance.

I first met Danitra Vance in 1986, when she was cast in my play, *The Colored Museum*. In rehearsals, her energy was guarded and cautious—understandably so. She'd just finished a year as part of the ensemble of *Saturday Night Live*. And true to all great colonizers, the producers of that show had tried to suppress her because the T-shirts they wore, emblazoned with the word "Brilliant," would have been rendered pale had they been brave enough to let the true brilliance of Ms. Vance shine through. And during the course of *The Colored Museum*'s nine-month run at The Public Theater and then in London and Los Angeles, she, along with the rest of the five-person ensemble (Loretta Devine, Tommy Hollis, Reggie Montgomery and Vickilyn Reynolds) truly did shine.

In Danitra I found a creative soul mate. We had the same sense of the ridiculous, many of the same demons, and save one or two variations, the same bodies that moved the same way. In 1990 we worked together on *Spunk*, three Zora Neale Hurston short stories adapted for the stage, *Hunger Chic*, a one-act for PBS, and then in 1991, I curated a festival at The Public called, *Moving Beyond the Madness*. It was at this festival that John Leguizamo first presented material from his show *Spic-O-Rama*, Anna Deavere Smith performed *Fires in the Mirror* and for two nights, Danitra performed *Danitra Vance and the Mell-O White Boys Revisited*.

Toward the end of her piece, she introduced to us one of her characters, Harriet Hetero, a feminist stripper. After "reading" the audience, she then proceeded to do her routine which culminated with Harriet/Danitra stripping down to reveal a piece of tape which was covering up the scar from her mastectomy. It was a moment of sheer bravery and unbelievable beauty.

Before she finally succumbed to the cancer in 1994, Danitra, the artist, had taken us to a place we all fear; a place of deep vulnerability where disease secretly enters our bodies and wages a fierce war, a war where even if we end up winning, it is not without costs. She took us to that very frightening place and for a few moments washed us clean of our fear. She did this, not by some New Age mumbo jumbo she uttered, but by the smile on her face and the look in her eyes—a smile and look that revealed, with startling simultaneity, pain, compassion, survival and love.

It was one of the most miraculous performances I have ever seen. Danitra was/is an amazing life force. She was a revelatory artist and a truly wonderful friend. I would say I miss her, but occasionally she visits me in my dreams and we laugh.

**George C. Wolfe** is Producer of The Joseph Papp Public Theater/New York Shakespeare Festival and is author of several plays including *The Colored Museum*, *Spunk* and *Jelly's Last Jam*. Mr. Wolfe is also an award-winning director.

from Vance's introduction to *Live and in Color!*

. . . If white is the highest on the totem pole, I'm not that. If male is the highest, I'm not that. I am a black woman, which is supposed to be the bottom. To me, the bottom is the most powerful position to be in because you can see the sun. If everybody else is so busy looking down at you, they're missing out on what's going on in the rest of the world, while we're looking up and seeing everything there is to see . . . My comedy comes out of looking up from the bottom . . .

In my shows (but not this one), I usually say, "I think of myself as Everywoman and some men." Most shows that I do have a lot to do with gender identification, transsexuality, but this show is more about race . . .

I was exploring my fascination with the talk-show format . . . There's something about the American culture that is expressed so perfectly in [this] format. It's become a way of healing people through the TV. It's very odd that people are so willing to open up their wounds to strangers, especially thousands of people they don't even see . . .

I used to think that some force or some institution could stop you from doing what you wanted to do. Well, actually no one can stop you. You may not be able to do it on HBO or in prime time, but if you have something you want to say or do, you can do it. I think of myself as a hero because I'm the one out there jumping around, saying all these things. People can like me or not like me or laugh at me or hiss at me. Once you're out there on the edge, there's no place to go except over the edge.

## from **Live and in Color!**

Sometimes I wake up screaming.
Sometimes I believe I'm clinically depressed.

Maybe my show is on. *(She turns on the TV using the remote control)* Naaaa. *(She turns off the TV with the remote. She picks up the Singleton Maxwell notebook and reads)*

### Singleton Maxwell M.D./Midol Junkie

This message is for women only because men really don't have a clue, do they. Adam was not a rough draft, Adam was a doodle. Ladies, I am Singleton Maxwell M.D., the woman gynecologist that designed the O.B. Method. I am currently on a lecture tour, with a presentation entitled WARNING: THE DANGER OF BEING A WOMAN. I have spoken before many prestigious groups including most recently a joint meeting of the League of Women Intellectuals and the Sluts Against Smut.

I became a gynecologist because of my gynecological mysteries. Our combined gynecological mysteries prompted me to write a pamphlet (Shows cover) Between Your Legs and You. You can pick it up almost anywhere. In the book, I postulate: "Is there a Capitalist plot against women?" I mean to say . . . Why is it that whenever I have monthly pain the first thing I think of is, Give me strength, give me antiprostaglandins, give me antispasmodics, give me drugs.

*(She puts on her sunglasses. Traditional blues music underscores the following monologue. She sings:)*

In the kitchen barefoot expecting my eighth child
I must take my Midol, so I don't go wild
I'm a Midol junkie and I don't know why
Keeps me feeling funky so I take it all the time
It helps before, during and after
Gives me laughter through my tears
I've been on it for years
It helps my lower back pain
Takes away the strain of being a Woman Woman Woman
WOMAN, WO-O-O-M-A-A-A-N

Yes I'm a Woman W-O . . . W-O *(Forgets lyrics)*
Yes I'm a Woman W-O *(Still can't remember)*

*(Spoken)* Baby, you don't know me. I killed my first husband. It wasn't really my fault, though. It all happened the night before my period was supposed to start and I am sure it was the hormonal imbalance that led me to commit murder. "Did I have to kill him?" "Did I have to kill him?" "Did I have to kill him?" Yes, I had to kill him. He hit me, and I always told myself I would never stay with anybody who hit me. While I packed, the scenario unfolded. I leave him, he finds me, he looks pitiful and boyish, I forgive him, we spend six blissful months together. He hits me again, harder, then he says, "I'm sorry, Baby, I love you more than life itself, doesn't six months of bliss mean anything to you?" He cries, I cry, a year of happiness until he loses his job, bam bam bam, he buys me a puppy, a cute little black springer spaniel, he kicks the dog . . . I'm living the life of the battered wife. I watch Oprah and Phil and Sally and Shirley and Jane and Wilma and Betty and Veronica . . . I started to wonder who would play me in the made-for-TV version of my life. My lawyer said for me to plead insanity, and I said I thought that was just for men. I went to prison.

*(Singing:)*

W-O . . . W-O . . . Oh you know,
Oh you know, o. u. know, all of you know.
I may not be able to spell my name
but Midol keeps me tame
when I'm feeling evil.

*(Spoken)* Take only as directed.


## Television Talk Show

WOMAN GUEST: When I got to LAX, there was no one there to meet me, so I took the shuttle. By the time I got off at Phil and Chris's, a guy there told me Chris had to go to the emergency room and when they came home, Chris went to bed. Phil told me that Chris had AIDS and that he, Phil, was HIV positive.

I thought to myself, it's a good thing I am who I am or this could be . . . not too cute. I didn't know a lot about AIDS. I shook hands with a person with AIDS before I knew what it was. What I'm saying is I never lived with someone with AIDS. I never lived with someone HIV positive and I was afraid. I was afraid I'd turn stupid.

Part of me thought I might throw up my hands and run screaming from the house. I mean part of me wanted to want to do that. That was a few years ago and AIDS was in the paper and on the news every day and everyone seemed to be a little hysterical.

I guess I'm not a hysterical person.

HOST: You say you're not a hysterical person. If there was a time for hysteria, it would have been then. Had you seen something or read something that—

WOMAN GUEST: I had seen you on your talk show.

HOST: You know, I always like to think this show performs a public service, that it enlightens and educates—

WOMAN GUEST: No. You had a PWA on your show and the entire audience hated him. And you never touched him. You didn't shake his hand. You even sat in a chair or two away from him and stretched your microphone over to him. You could have taught this country to be humane but you seemed to side with ignorance. Even your expert doctor said he couldn't guarantee these were the only ways to get the virus. I knew I didn't want to be like you.

HOST: You seem to . . . You've given us so much . . . Let's go to a commercial right now.

*(Camera is turned off.)*

I don't know who you think you are, but this is my show. How dare you get up on national television and humiliate *me*!

WOMAN GUEST: How dare you get up on national television and dehumanize every person with AIDS. Where was all that compassion and intelligence you talk-show hosts are supposed to have?

HOST: Let me tell you something, Miss Holier Than Me, I am famous for my compassion, my sympathy, my empathy, my Ph.D. *People* magazine named me one of this year's "Most Fabulous People" because of my warmth and compassion.

WOMAN GUEST: I used to feel the same way until I saw that show.

HOST: We're coming back from commercial in about one minute and I want you to tell the viewing audience you saw that on someone else's show. Tell them I didn't do that.

WOMAN GUEST: Honey, when you come back from commercial, you won't have a guest to talk to. I didn't come here for this.

HOST: Oh! Believe me, I can run this show without you or any other guest. But let's see how you run the show without me. *(Walks off the set)*

WOMAN GUEST *(To audience)*: How many of you saw that show? It was a few years ago. *(No response)* If the host doesn't come back, will some of you go to the microphones and ask me questions about living with someone who has AIDS or—

VOICE OF THE DIRECTOR: We're back!

*(Woman Guest looks blank, clueless, lonely. She looks toward the wings for the Host. She looks toward the audience. "Help" is written in her eyes. If an audience member gets up, we'll take the question. If not . . .)*

You're turning stupid.

WOMAN GUEST: I didn't want to turn stupid. I gave Phil a big real hug. Not a cheek-to-cheek, hand-on-the-shoulders hug, a *real* hug. And I hugged Chris the same way. But stupidity always lurked somewhere. *(Screams)* The toilet seat! I always put tissue on the seat. That's how my grandmother raised me. Maybe I should sit on the bare seat to prove I wasn't afraid of AIDS. Prove to who? *(Screams)* The shower! I can't get it from taking a shower. EEK! The razors! I don't use other people's razors anyway. Dishes! Couldn't I be the first, the very first person to contract AIDS in some odd, unusual way? I mean, doctors and nurses in hospitals wear gloves and masks and stuff. Yes! No! Maybe. Yes! No! Stop it!

I wasn't having sex with them. I had never had a blood transfusion. I was not an IV drug user. If there was some other way for me to get AIDS, some other way no one knew about, then okay. I would be an innocent victim just like Phil and Chris and everyone fighting this syndrome or that disease or any other malady.

Not long after that, I found this lump in my breast. I had a mastectomy. Then I started this book. All proceeds go to the National Fund for Sick People. *Funny Things People Say to People That Are Sick:*

"I thought you were dead."
"Why don't you have the other one removed?"
"How are you?"

You can ask me questions now.

*(Questions from audience. Pause.)*

Oh, okay, nobody wants to talk to me. I can see some of you are wearing red ribbons. Big deal. What difference does that make? Go hold a crack baby. Go hold an AIDS baby. You want a medal for that? If that ribbon was made out of ten pounds of steel that you had to sling over your shoulder, that might say something. "Count me, too. I'm struggling, too." Fifty thousand women die every year of breast cancer. Wear a ten-pound ribbon for them and one for lupus and one for diabetes and every other life-threatening, life-altering— Since this is a talk show, and since this is *my* talk show. That's all I have to say.

*(Camera holds on Woman Guest for uncomfortable moments, then pans to audience. Blackout.)*

## Flotilda Williams as Juliet

I'm Flotilda Williams. I'm a classical actress. Right now I am in a production downtown with a group called Shakespeare in the Slums. We are doing a play by Mister William Shakespeares call *Romeo and Juliet.* And me, I'm Juliet, okay. Now what I want to do for y'all is to extrapolate and explainate on what be going on in the show. The show starts and a lot of things happen but really we just gonna skip all that and get to the good part, where I come in.

I'm at this party, a lot of fancy people there and I'm there and I'm there with my Mama and the Nurse. Even so, I manage to meet this guy. A very good-lookin' guy, makes me laugh with his funny, funny jokes, probably got some money. So I like him. His name is Romeo. I have thus extrapolated the title—Romeo and me, Juliet, okay.

Anyway the party is not even half over when my Mama and the Nurse say, "Juliet it's time to go." And I say, "Okay, I'll be right with you." So she find Romeo and they say goodbye by touching fingertips like this *(Gesture)* completely missing the point.

After that I go home and I'm trying to be asleep but I can't sleep 'cause I'm thinkin' 'bout this guy. How much I want to see him again. How much I want to talk to him again. How much I want to do things with him I've never done before

Now in the meantime the guy, Romeo, is down in the alleyway lookin' up in my window. Now he not lookin' up in my window because he a freak or nothin' like that, he lookin' up in my window because he like me, okay. Then he start to talk to hisself. Now he not talkin' to hisself 'cause he crazy or nothin', he talk to hisself 'cause it's a play, okay. People in plays talk to theyselves a lot.

And he say, he say,
"But soft! what light throo yonder windo' break?"
That's when I break through the window.

It's nighttime and I'm on my back porch and I'm in a really bad mood because of this whole situation. And I say my first line and stomp my foot and say,
"Ay me!
O, Romeo, Romeo! wherefore art thou Romeo?"
Wherefore mean why. She sayin' why, why, why you gots to be Romeo? Wherefore art thou Romeo!!!

"Deny thy father and refuse thy name;
Or, if thou wilt not, be but sworn my love
And I'll no longer be a Capsulet."
And she thinking,
"'Tis but thy name that is my enemy
Thou art thyself, though not a Montagoo."

What's a Montagoo?

"It is nor hand, nor foot,
Nor arm nor face, nor any other part
Belonging to a man."

You know what she talking about. So she say,
"Romeo, doff thy name,
And for that name which is no part of thee
Take all myself."

Juliet was hip, you dig. She had it going on and she was down. So anyway, you know their families had a kinda Family Feud-type thing going on. Juliet family, maybe like the Crypts and Romeo people could be like the Bloods, you know what I'm saying. And Romeo is not like Michael Jackson, he's a lover and a fighter, okay. Then she see him down in the alleyway and they talk and talk all lovey-dovey, lovey-dovey—back and forth, back and forth, beat beat, beat beat. They got a passionate blood flow going back and forth. I got really good reviews on this part. Spend some money, get some culture.

Then she say to him,
"My bounty is as boundless as the sea,
My love as deep; the more I give to thee,
The more I have, for both are infinite.
*(Hears noise)*
I hear some noise within, dear love, adieu."
That mean 'bye.
"Anon, good Nurse!"
That mean I'll be right with you, Nurse.
"Sweet Montagoo, be true.
Stay but a little, I will come again."

Then she gone. Then she come right back but she has to be really quiet 'cause her Mama 'n' Daddy can't stand his Mama 'n' Daddy 'n' his Mama 'n' Daddy can't stand her Mama 'n' Daddy. So they have to be really, really quiet 'cause if they catch them together, they'll kill him 'n' her, too. So she say, she say,
"Three words dear Romeo, and good night indeed.
If that thy bent of love be honorable,
Thy purpose marriage, send me word tomorrow,
By one that I'll procure to come to thee,
Where and at what time thou wilt perform the rite."
That mean marry me, marry me,
I'm not giving up nothin' till you marry me.
"And all my fortunes at thy foot I'll lay
And follow thee, my lord, throughout the world.
*(Hears noise)*
I come anon—But if thou mean'st not well
I do beseech thee
*(Noise)*
By and by, I come—
To cease thy suit and leave me to my grief."
That mean if you not gonna marry me, don't mess with my mind. I can find somebody else.
"A thousand times good night."

Then she gone again. This time she gone but a little bit longer because she had to talk to her Mama 'n' the Nurse. I don't know why she had to talk to the Nurse 'cause you know she not sick.

She back as soon as she can but she can't see Romeo. But she know he gotta be out there somewhere 'cause they got that passionate blood flow going back and forth, back and forth and she can feel him out there beatin' in the night. What she want to do is holler, "Yo, Romeo, where you at?" But she can't do that because Juliet is a very dignified girl, and hollerin' off the back porch is a very iginant thing to do. So she say, she say, "Romeo, hist, Romeo."

Then she see him.

"'Tis almost morning. I would have thee gone
And yet no further than a wanton's bird
Who lets it hop a little from her hand
Like a poor prisoner in her twisted gyves
And with a silk thread plucks it back again
So loving-jealous of his liberty."

I don't know what that part mean.

Then she say,

"Good night. Good night! Parting is such sweet sorrow
That I shall say good night till it be morrow."

*(She exits.)*

David Cale

## Introduction by Stephen Holden

**E**very love story is also a ghost story. No matter how intimately we know our partners, be they one-night stands or spouses of several decades, it's the mystery of the other, the lure of the unknown and the fantastic that invites us to make that leap into the void known as falling in love. Who and what are we looking at when face to face with someone who gives us that sinking feeling? Are we in touch with the person beside us or spinning a dream of that person to stir up that deliciously scary sensation?

When it comes to Eros, memories, desires and dreams, vestiges of fairy tales, fragments of favorite songs and images from movies converge to conjure up these romantic spirits. Then, if the chemistry is right and the stars and planets are aligned, an encounter can turn into an ecstatic communion that forever changes us and becomes a mystical touchstone in our personal collection of ghost stories.

Few writers in any medium are as insightful into the supernatural aspect of passion as David Cale, the quietest and most reflective of the New York performance monologists who reached maturity in the 1980s. In his spellbinding live performances, Cale, with his mellifluous, slightly insinuating voice and British-American accent appoints himself as an urban camp counselor and erotic shaman telling grown-up ghost stories around a hearth where the music of Frank Sinatra and Joni Mitchell can be heard in the distance.

The lives of the characters who inhabit his stories may be wildly disparate, but all seem suspended somewhere between memory and desire, in a waking dream. Their secret, special memories, Cale reminds us, are the same as ours. These memories are the spiritual equivalent of stored body fat, clutched inside like interior woolen armor against the encroaching night chill.

In his solo masterpiece, *Deep in a Dream of You*, a series of twelve short monologues, four of which are reprinted here, Cale created a collection of dream songs whose form and language extend the diction of popular songs into the realm of dramatic poetry. Cale has the astonishing ability to slip back and forth between male and female characters without resorting to caricature or the benefit of stage costume. Like a millennial E.M. Forster, his evocations of sex are remarkable for their delicacy, even when language is unabashedly explicit. Where most solo performers deal with Eros by assuming positions in the war between sexes, Cale understands that even the basest of lust involves a collision of dreaming souls in search of fusion.

The narrator of "Swimming in the Dark" (what a beautiful metaphor for diving into the erotic unknown!) is a hypnotic conjurer of dreams beckoning us to a blissful, vaguely sinister repose in an enveloping tropical paradise "where the fish are warm and the water barely moves."

"The Dolphins" darkens and extends that vision in its swooning depiction of a sunbather picked up in the arms of a shining stranger who emerges out of the sea to carry her offshore for exhausting bouts of transcendent lovemaking after which she is pulled back to the beach by a school of dolphins.

The metaphysical "Remember" (reminiscent in tone of Harry Nilsson's similarly titled song) is a series of refrains that builds to a revelation that has the terrifying force of a bad acid trip: "I keep forgetting that I'm alive. / I keep losing sight of it."

A similar incantatory intensity propels "Blue Fir Trees," a gay man's elegy to a dead lover who is remembered in specific situations, among them "doing the Jane Fonda Workout to a Philip Glass record." The mourner's ambivalence toward a lover whose flamboyance, he guiltily admits, sometimes embarrassed him, is summed up by an observation that should resonate with anyone who has scoured the earth for true love and found it only in isolated moments: "When we drove through Pennsylvania that night I thought, This may not be it, but it's pretty close."

At the end of the piece we're back in the water. The dead lover, it turns out, is the same person who issued the invitation to go "swimming in the dark."

**Extreme Exposure**

**198**   **Stephen Holden** is a film, music and theatre critic for the *New York Times*.

## from **Deep in a Dream of You**

### Swimming in the Dark

*Whispered into a microphone in blackout.*

I want to take you swimming in the dark.
It's something you've never done.
It's something you'd like to do.

I know a lake
where the fish are warm
and the water barely moves.
There's no weed to get tangled in.

And in this place, money isn't an object.
No one can touch you here.
No policeman will strike you with his billy club.
Smash you in the features.
No religion can harm you.
No nun can get on the television
and make threatening remarks.
And the newspapers won't depress you.
There's no television to reduce you.
Nothing will carry weight.

When people are just another disappointment
I will take you to this place.
Drive you to the water.
Remove your clothes with a tenderness reserved for lovers.
We'll make love till you finally relax.
Under a clear sky and stars
we'll go swimming in the dark.

It's something you've never done.
It's something you'd like to do.
I know a lake
where the fish are warm
and the water barely moves.

Let's go swimming in the dark.

# The Dolphins

*A sultry, English woman in her sixties sitting in a deck chair on an empty beach.*

This is my deck chair. Here is the sand.
You're my Mediterranean.

I never met a soul who didn't love the ocean.
The sea. There is nothing so effective as the sight
of waves for releasing those subtle tensions.
The ones you only realize were there when they're
gone. I come here every day. For the ocean.
And every day children bury my feet in the sand.
The sun moves from the back of my neck to the
left-hand side of my peripheral view.
And the dolphins pass the rock line. Every day.
Same time. Though you only realize they're there
when they leap. Beyond the rock line, three
quarters of the world is submerged.

He came out of the sea.
One minute he wasn't there. Next he was standing
over me. Salt water running down. I pretended
not to notice. Fortunately, I had on my sun shades.
The eyes were out of sight. Still he stood there.
Still. Not speaking. Rib cage heaving. His stomach
was moving in and out of him. I removed the shades.
The eyes met.

> "You are dripping on my magazine," I said,
> "What use is a wet supplement?"

He says nothing, but lifts me out of the deck chair.
I am in his arms! He moves across the sand with
me in his arms! For some reason it did not occur
to shout. The instincts went along. A thin cloud
was moving through the sky with extreme speed.
We pass white houses with signs on them:

> "American breakfast. American beer.
> American language spoken here.
> Have a nice day."

Then this voice began nagging in my head.

> "You look ridiculous being carried.
> You've got legs. You can move yourself."

I chose to ignore it. There was a blue dolphin
on his shoulder.

"He may be dangerous. Dirty.
Have unclean sexual organs."

We move across a parking lot.

"Suppose someone sees?"

Forget people! My face is cornered in his
collarbone. Lips pressed on the dolphin.
His body feels thicker than it looks. Every now
and then a muscle flips. We speak nothing.
Reach a field full of lilies and orchids grown
for export. The air stinks. Lilies crack
underneath us. Salt water runs out of him still.
Down his back. Dripping off the blades.
He lays me down in orchids. My back is wet with
orchid blood. Stains that will never come out.
His head slides down my body. His mouth is shouting
between my legs. My teeth sink into the dolphin.
Dark muscle. Blue heat. No words. Let it go.
Let it all go. Lilies. Blue skies. Salt water.
Tongues.

The next day a plane crossed the sky dragging words
behind it:

"Plan ahead with Nu Form"

I thought my imagination had finally run away with me.
Out of the sea he came. Towards me again.
Lifted me out of the deck chair. Instinctively
I bit his face. Kept his neck in my mouth till
he dropped me down. We wrestled on the ground.
Pulled at each other with such intensity I thought
one of us would be damaged. He held my face between
his hands. The palms cupped my cheeks. He pulled
my lips to his. The breath merged. So gentle were
his fingers along my outline. So sure his hands.
I slid him inside me with such ease that he didn't
realize where he had gone.

Tangled together we drifted into half-sleep.
Unsure of what was a dream and what was actually
happening.

The following day all was peace, tranquility,
at ease. A flying fish flew out of the sea.
With little baby fish flying behind. The fish
flew into a local shopping mall and terrorized
a group of housewives,

"Aaaah, fish!"

Out of the sea he came. Towards me again.
In plain view we just dissolved. So much moisture.
I didn't know where it was all coming from.

As it went it became more extreme. There was an
understanding between us. Still no words exchanged.
This was a landscape beyond language. No human tongue
could touch or make connection to.

Then out of nowhere. Out of the blue. I began to
look forward to him. Release my hair. Paint my nails
in anticipation. If he was late I created reasons why.
Ludicrous notions sprang to mind: I was not attractive
enough to hold his interest. My legs were the wrong shape.
Breasts not large enough. I imagined what he was doing
while he wasn't with me. All kinds of concoctions
filled my thinking. Still no words passed between us.

He came out of the sea.
My body was rigid with anxiety. This time he did not
lift me out of the deck chair, but knelt in front.
Spoke soft words.

"It's so strange, you can see the water reflected
in your eyes. There are waves in your eyes.
Wisps of cloud. I can see myself reflected in you."

And he leaned forward. Closer. And climbed into my eyes.
He was swimming in my eyes. Calling out from inside
my head.

I followed him inside myself. Into the sea. Up to
my knees. Beyond the thigh line. Water lapped my breasts.
Stroked my neck. Till I was out of my depth. Forced to
swim. I was following him. Miles from land. Beyond the
rock line. I became tired. Worn down from following.
I started to weaken. Swallowing water. My lungs were
filling. My body was pulling me under. I was drowning

inside myself. I had to get out. I had to get out of myself.
But I was in the middle of the ocean.

Then something  brushed my leg. Something else touched
my arm. I was surrounded by dolphins. They were nudging
me. Keeping me afloat. I threw my arms around a dolphin.
The dolphin hauled me through the water with incredible
speed. Under the water. Up for air. Under again.
We passed through shoals of butterfly fish. Thousands of
tiny creatures brushed my face. Herds of sea horses.
Scarlet coral. Anemones. Blue Sharks. Manta Rays.
Parrot fish. Triggerfish. Tongues.

The dolphins pulled me back. He went on. Kept going.
Swam away into the back of my mind.

At night sometimes I'll see him in dreams. He moves
around inside my head. From one state of mind to another.
Sometimes he'll be looking at me from the corner of
my eye and he'll grin, and when he grins he stretches
my eye.

Today a small child stood next to the deck chair
looking at the sky and the sea and she said,

> "If the sky's blue, does that mean we're breathing
> blue air?"

And I said,

> "Maybe."

She said,

> "I love the sea."

I said,

> "I never met a soul who didn't love the ocean.
> The sea. There is nothing so effective as the sight
> of waves for releasing those subtle tensions.
> The ones you only realize were there when they're
> gone. I come here every day. For the ocean.
> And every day the sun moves from the back of my
> neck to the left-hand side of my peripheral view.
> And the dolphins pass the rock line. Every day.
> Same time. Though you only realize they're there
> when they leap."

Beyond the rock line, three quarters of the world
is submerged.

## Remember

For Simon Egleton.

Remember when you used to wake up in the morning
and spring out of bed. Without a care in the world.
Without a care in your head.

Remember?

Remember when you used to fall in love with one person
after another. How they would overlap sometimes.
Of course, it wasn't love. Let's call it some kind
of thrilling collapsing of the boundaries. One person
after another. It didn't really matter who.

Remember?

Remember how you liked to tell people you were neurotic,
even though you didn't really know what neurotic meant.
But it sounded mature and sophisticated. It was something
you should want to be. More sophisticated than cigarettes.

Remember?

Remember when you moved into the present tense. How alive
you looked. How for a moment you felt in relation to
everything. The world took on a kind of clarity.  There was
resonance in every action.

Remember?

Remember when fear took a hold of you.
Became part of you. Took up residence. Cramped your day.
Became a feature. Remember when you realized that eventually
you get used to anything.

You'll never amount to anything
with your eyes on yourself all the time.
It'll strangle and contrive you.
It'll leave you where you started.

And with your background it's probably some kind of
achievement that you can even get out of bed in the morning.
A family that's only comfortable with you going down the
same, sad road they're going down.
The same, sad road they've gone down.

Remember

You've got that puffy look.
You've got that tremble in your voice again.

Hang up the phone if your father calls you.
Hang up the phone if your father calls you.

Remember

Put your fists in the air.

Remember

Get out of the house!

Remember

Don't sit still for so long.
Don't let it build up around you.
Don't succumb to what's predictably yours.
Don't succumb to what's predictably yours.

And you say,

> "I keep forgetting that I'm alive.
> I keep losing sight of it.
> I keep losing sight of it.
> I keep forgetting that I'm alive.
> I keep losing sight of it.
> I keep losing sight of it."

But remember when you used to wake up in the morning
and spring out of bed. Without a care in the world.
Without a care in your head.

Remember?

Remember.

Remember Simon.

Remember.

## Blue Fir Trees

I will never forget watching you on the patio next to that
lake in New Hampshire, doing the Jane Fonda Workout to a
Philip Glass record. How the wind blew the music across
the lake. The blue fir trees surrounding the water barely
moving at all. There was one cloud in the sky. Stretching
your pale limbs into unnatural positions and holding them
there.

I read it somewhere that when the body dies, the soul leaves
through the top of the head. I remember seeing my grandfather's
body laid out in my grandmother's front room and thinking
his body looked like a shell and automatically wondering,
Where's the soul gone? and instinctively looking up at
the ceiling as if I was going to see it hovering there.

I will never forget the times I craved you. Couldn't get
enough of you. Wanted you so bad it made my stomach ache.

The times I was embarrassed by your displays of physical
affection. Worried about how it would look. Embarrassed
to be wanting you, or something. Feeling that you weren't
pretty enough and that was ludicrously some reflection
on me. Or that you were too effeminate, and that was somehow
incriminating.

I used to dream of being driven at night by some
anonymous driver. Along an American highway. No words.
Just to be staring out the window like some Garbo creature.
Moody and silent. Deep inside myself. When we drove through
Pennsylvania that night I thought, This may not be it,
but it's pretty close.

In the night the lake looked like it had died.
You wondered if what you wanted in another person is really
what you would like to be yourself.
The trees made sounds. When you shouted your voice echoed
in the mountains. You could duet with yourself.

I will never forget flying in that plane over Boston in the
middle of the night, with a black coffee in one hand trying
to figure out how I could feel something so strongly then stop
feeling it altogether and considering that it was gone for
good.

I will never forget the look on your face when you told
me how you felt and how I couldn't speak, how the words
wouldn't leave me because I felt absolutely nothing.

I didn't realize I had such a vicious streak till you were
kind to me.

I will never forget how soft the skin on your back was.

I will never forget how you laughed at anything I said.

I will never forget how I never believed you when you said
I looked good or what I did was good, thinking that you
were so in love that you would say anything to please me.
That your opinion was invalid.

When nothing makes sense there's always sense of humor.

I will never forget that joke you told me about Ginger Rogers.
When asked how much she weighed, Ginger replied, "145 pounds,
133 without makeup." How every time you told it you cracked
yourself up.

I will never forget how one of your teeth was blue.

I will never forget how when you danced, it looked like someone
else had taken you over.

I will never forget meeting your mother for the first time
and the look on her face that seeing the two of us together
was in some way confirming her most unsettling suspicions.

I will never forget how meticulous you were.

I will never forget that horrible cologne you wore.

I will never forget those kids yelling "faggot" at you
on the street.

I will never forget you saying very quietly,
"Ignore them."

I will never forget one day realizing I knew nothing about you.

I will never forget seeing you in that anonymous hospital.
Laying in the bed with your eyes focused on something that
I couldn't see.

I will never forget you laying there asleep. Still with
your eyes wide open.

I will never forget after visiting you in the hospital
how I sobbed uncontrollably on the telephone and felt relieved
afterwards that I could feel something for someone aside
from myself.

I will never forget not being able to leave that room
because I knew I wouldn't see you again.

But I will never forget when you finished doing that exercise
all those years ago. How the music still kept playing.
You came up behind me. Touched my neck oh so gently with
your lips. Standing there. Miles from anyone. The blue fir trees
still. The water quiet. The one cloud moving very slightly.
Our chests rising. Hearts floating across the lake. Over the
trees. Up into the single cloud. How it moved into the
distance still beating.

And you whispered,

> "When it gets late tonight.
> I want to take you swimming in the dark.
> It's something you've never done.
> It's something you'd like to do.
> I know a lake . . ."

## **Introduction** by Fred Zollo

**I**t was because of Mike Nichols that I met Whoopi Goldberg. And it was because of Judith Ivey that Mike Nichols met her. In the winter of 1983, Mike, Judy and I were in rehearsal for David Rabe's remarkable play *Hurlyburly*. Judy came charging in one day and said we must see this incredible performer, Whoopi Goldberg, who was briefly appearing at Dance Theater Workshop. "What's a Whoopi Goldberg?" we asked. "She's this amazing woman," Judy said, "you'll see." Now the chances were slim that I, not to mention Mike, would spend our one Sunday afternoon off in a downtown theatre, but Judy was adamant—we were going. And we did. And we saw one of the most gifted, not to mention viciously funny, human beings on the planet. Mike promptly took the reigns of the show, worked closely with Whoopi, and the next fall *Whoopi Goldberg Live* opened at the Lyceum Theatre on Broadway. Her life, and in a very real way all of ours, would be changed forever.

When Whoopi moved to San Diego from New York in 1975, she got caught up in the local theatre scene, and by the 1980s was collaborating on improvisational skits in San Francisco's comedy clubs and alternative performance spaces. Her early work included pieces inspired by "Moms" Mabley and Lord Buckley, artists she feared were forgotten by modern audiences. The collection of characters in *The Spook Show*, (renamed *Whoopi Goldberg Live* for Broadway) developed out of improvisations and showcased her as a brilliant observer and mimic, with an extraordinary ear for dialects. After opening in San Francisco, she toured the United States and Europe before landing fatefully at Dance Theater Workshop.

Each of the monologues contained in *Whoopi Goldberg Live* has an originality and power unique to Whoopi, whether she portrayed a Jamaican maid, a New York City junkie/thief/Ph.D. (I'll never forget the character's refrain, "Around the world in eighty motherfuckin' days"), or a seven-year-old black girl dreaming of having "long, luxurious blond hair." Whoopi finds what connects us rather than what divides us. As Susan Dworkin observed, "She never, not once, makes us laugh at anyone's expense—save our own."

As Whoopi shifts abruptly and completely from one character to another, her monologues are in a way always dialogues with the audience members in front of her. In 1984, in two separate interviews, she explained, "A lot of the strength in my work is reactive. I've got these characters, and how they behave on a given night depends on a lot of things: the audience, the kind of day I've had, the mood I'm in. That's why I like to go out into the audience when I do the wino, because I want to know, as much as anyone out there wants to know, what's going to happen next." And, "My work requires the active participation of an audience. They can't just come in and sit. How can you change people if they just sit there? If you're right in their faces and you're fondling them and talking *to* them, they go out of the theatre saying more than just, 'Oh, we went to a show.'"

Whoopi showed an amazing versatility, that overnight, would make her one of America's most sought-after actors. Within a year, she would be nominated for an Academy Award for her work in *The Color Purple*, and just a few years later would win for *Ghost*. And she did something else. She moved us. She made us think. Most importantly, as H. L. Mencken put it so well over eighty years ago, she "comforted the afflicted and afflicted the comfortable."

It's that little girl I keep thinking of, though. She has a white shirt wrapped around her head. No, it isn't just a shirt. It is her beautiful, natural, luxurious, blond hair. I remember being profoundly moved by this moment. That little girl wanted so badly to be part of white America—the America she saw in magazines and on television—the America where young, black children are too often forgotten, shunted aside, lost. I thought of young Whoopi growing up in difficult circumstances, not rich, but richly loved by a strong mother, in New York City some thirty years before. She would not be shunted aside. She didn't need that long, blonde hair. What is beneath the shirt is both more profound and more beautiful.

**Fred Zollo** has produced many plays and films over the past two decades, among them are *Ma Rainey's Black Bottom*, *Hurlyburly* and *Angels In America* on Broadway; and *Mississippi Burning* and *Quiz Show*.

# from **Whoopi Goldberg Live**

## from **Fontaine**

*Fontaine enters, singing.*

"Around the world in eighty motherfuckin' days . . ." *(He is singing, dancing, providing percussion sounds. He breaks into a shoo-bop version of the song)*
    What's happening?

*(No answer.)*

What's happening?

*(No answer.)*

Hey look y'all, I say, "What's happening," y'all say everything's everything, whatever the fuck you say. So we gonna try this shit again. *(He exits. Returns, singing)*
    "Around the world in eighty motherfuckin' days . . ." *(He is singing, dancing, providing percussion sounds. He breaks into a shoo-bop version of the song)*
    What's happening?

*(Audience responds.)*

That was the shit. What's happening, Slick? Looking good. What's happening, Blood?

*(A man in the audience moves to shake hands.)*

Hey, no, let me show you how to do it. Goddamn, your hand's all soaking wet, what you doing there? Shit. Don't make me laugh, now . . . Let me go, Goddamnit. Now here: I go like this . . . *(Initiates handshaking)* Now you do it . . . I don't know, maybe you shouldn't visit my neighborhood. *(He laughs)* What's happening, Cutie? You looking good. Shit, my name is Fontaine and love is my game. And when I kiss the girls, hey, they all aflame. Come on, let me kiss your hand. No, the one with the diamonds on it. Looking good, too. I'm glad to see you here. I'm glad you was cool enough to play. I notice you didn't clutch your pocketbook.
    But you know a lot of people can't handle me. I don't understand it, 'cause like, I feel like I'm a friendly person. But you know, some people's attitude really drove me out of the country a while back. No, they did. But I got the kind of gig that allows me the freedom to cruise, because I am a thief. It's the all-American, traditional gig. People always got stuff; people always want stuff; I provide a service. I service my ass right on up to the Upper East Side, too. Checked out these bad apart-

ments. Found me these gold-plated, digital escargot forks. Cashed them little motherfuckers in, picked up the cash, went on down to JFK 'cause you know on TV they always tell ya, "Come down to pick up your ticket to Europe." So that's what I did.

And I said to the dude real politely, "Hey, where's my mother-fuckin' ticket to Europe at?" And that man looked at me like I farted on his best suit. But he wrote the ticket out. I mean, he handed it to me, you know. I took it and walked away. He come running up behind me talking about how I have ta pay for it first. I said, "What?" I mean, you really expect me to pay *before* I fly? I'm a business person, okay? If I have a product I want you to buy from me I'm gonna give you a taste first just so you know I stand behind my product. Because that's good business, you know? But the airlines, they don't feel like that. They get your money and get you up in the air and then they drop your ass, you know? The dude says he gonna call the police on me and shit and I said, "Fuck it," you know? I gave him $956 and I walked ten steps away over to this chick who is standing there looking at me like this. *(Giggling, he makes a pinched, hyper-friendly face)* I said, "Bitch, what are you grinnin' at?" And she looks at me talking about *(Prissy, condescending voice)*, "We have a bit of a problem. Now what's happened is we've oversold this flight. Now what that means is that we have a hundred seats on the plane but we've sold tickets to three thousand people. So I guess you're not going any-where are you?"

Now I pulled some shit that I'm gonna hip you to just in case you find yourself in the same position. 'Cause I got it down, in effect. I said, "Hey," I say, "I been through your pocketbook and I know where you live." And needless to say I got me a seat on the plane. That's right man. I checked my bags through and shit and like, just as I was going out the door, I passed this big dude walking around in circles with a picket sign talking about "Stop Abortion." I said, "Motherfucker, when was the last time you was pregnant?" And he looks at me, he says, "I don't have to discuss that with you." I said, "Oh, but you should because I have the answer to abortion." He said, "What it is?" I said, "Shoot your dick." I said, "Take that tired piece of meat down to the ASPCA and let 'em put it to sleep." And then hey, I feel better then, 'cause then I know he put his money where his mouth is.

So, I went ahead and got on the plane, you know? And I hate stewardesses. I hate 'em. Their legs' too long and their hair's too big and shit, and they always got their face up in yours. And I'm sitting there and she comes up to me talking about *(In a very measured tone)*, "Fasten your seatbelts." I said, "Fuck you." Because I really did not want to be bothered, you know? And you know how the plane takes off it goes down the runway like this *(Gestures takeoff motion)* and then start moving up? Well, when the plane was moving up, I found myself also moving within the confines of the plane—backwards, feet over head towards the tail—realizing that had I listened to the bitch, I'd still be in my seat. So, when the plane leveled out I creepy-crawled back, you know, buckled my seatbelt, 'cause I don't want her to know she was right.

So you know, I'm hanging loose and I happened to turn around and I see her coming at me again. This time she got this ugly-ass apron on, pushing this rickety fucking cart down the aisle. And they have nerve enough to ask me what did I want to eat. I said, "What do you got?" you know? They said they have steak overdone, underdone and done-done. I said bring me some done-done steak. So she walks away, she come back maybe a couple of minutes later with two big mitts on. You know those mitts you gotta go in the oven with 'cause the shit's too hot? Huge mitts. And she's carrying this little, tiny tray and she put it down and like, dashed away. And I'm sitting here looking at this shit going, "Damn," you know, 'cause I ain't got no mitts. I gotta figure out how to get the aluminum foil off without touching the shit. And by accident my hand did touch it and the motherfucker was cold.

So like, I made the bitch come back and get it. She come back about fifteen minutes later and she had another tray, which she threw at me. Bitch threw the shit at me. I shocked her ass and caught it. That's right. And then I burnt my fingers off. I threw the shit down, I rip off the aluminum foil, I look, I don't see nothing I recognize. The meat was all chewed up and was covered in this sauce, made it look like vumba and gooey shit with green and red specks . . . and then they give me the string beans and the string beans are huddling in the corner looking at you like this *(He looks terrified)* and I said, "Hey," you know, "I'm not eating this shit."

. . . But I was lucky 'cause . . . we was landing. We landed in Amsterdam, and I was lucky because I had a map already, you know, tell you all the shit to go check out. The Diamond Exchange, the Van Gogh Museum, the ballet . . . and in the middle of this long-ass list I see this name that I think I recognize because it said The Anne Frank House. And I wonder if it's the same chick. So I said I'm gonna go check the pad out.

So, like I cruise on over to the street that's described on the map, and in the middle of this block is a white brick building. Has a door and a bronze plaque to the right of it that says The Anne Frank House. So I walk in and immediately I'm hip to the fact that it's a museum. And they got a lady sitting behind the information desk and she got all these pamphlets talking about The Anne Frank House and what to do and why they there. And behind her there were all these huge pictures that look like they suspended in midair. And attached to these pictures are headphones. And the photos are of Amsterdam and Holland during the war, and the headphones give you the narration that goes with the sequence of the photographs . . .

And as I was perusing the area, I noticed a small staircase leading up to a big bookcase, and I'm into books you know, I got a Ph.D. in literature from Columbia. I know you don't think I was born a junkie. I have an education. I got a Ph.D. I can't do shit with so I stay high so I don't get mad. So I went on up the stairs because I want to see this one book. And I pulled on this book, and when I did that, the bookcase opened up and on the other side was this whole other room. Now, wasn't nobody up there said don't go in and there weren't no signs or nothing, so I walked on in.

And the first thing you see when you're cruising into this room is a row of huge windows and all the windowpanes are blacked out so there ain't no sunlight coming in. And you look at the walls that are surrounding these windows and they are covered in this kind of wallpaper, got little flowers on it. And you get up closer and you can tell at one time it was tan but now of course it's old and brown with age and water spots, and peeling off the walls in strips. And on these walls was pictures of movie stars from like, the thirties and forties—Myrna Loy, Carol Lombard—beautiful black-and-white pictures. And when I was looking at that I happened to turn my head and see the skylight and I said, "Oh my, I'm in the room where Anne Frank's family hid." And that kinda like, threw me. 'Cause this ain't something I was really on top of in terms of history. It wasn't; my forte is American history from the twenties to the present time.

Now why is that hard to believe? I mean, I'm a junkie, but I'm not stupid in some respects. A lot of educated people got what I got and that should not surprise you. And don't let this skin tone get you in the trick bag here. See, don't think that that's all there is here. A lot of people are just like me. A lot of people, just like me—Betty Ford. So, in good company, I tell you my forte is American history.

So like, I was checking, you know, the differences because like, here we knew what was happening, things like the Civil Rights Movement. 'Cause we was ready for that. When I say "we" I mean all the people who was involved in making civil rights happen. Because we knew, as soon as Rosa Parks did not get her ass up off that bus, what was coming. We knew. We wasn't quite ready for people getting blown away in cars or little girls getting blown up in churches, but we knew it was gonna be a struggle.

The difference over in Europe is that the Jews wasn't ready. See, they was living and integrating into these areas as well as they could be and they thought of themselves as Germans or Austrians or whatever. And when these people changed on them, started calling them nasty names and turning them in, they turned around and said, "Well hey, we been through this kind of thing before, you know, this is gonna pass." And when they realized what was happening, it was too late. They ended up in the camps, and leaving and going into hiding. And that kinda blew me away, too, because I always thought when you went into hiding it was like moving from one apartment to another. Because everybody I ever knew who went into hiding, I knew where they were. The only people who didn't know was the police. But it was a little bit different 'cause *here* you get nineteen to twenty-five people in one bedroom, but they can all go outside, you know, cruise around.

But these folks was stuck in this room for two years. And it wasn't like they was living. They got in there, they had twenty hours a day of non-movement. Non-movement. No noise. They sat with no sound.

*(Several beats of silence.)*

Nerve-wracking, ain't it? Yeah, and I discovered just like you just did that I couldn't do it. See I'd had to make some noise and mess up and I realized that that was really a stupid way to do things 'cause why cut off your nose to spite your face? And when that hit me so did the fact that I was in an empty room crying. See, wasn't nobody in there saying they was gonna kick my ass, wasn't nothing in there threatening me. I said, "No, this don't have nothing to do with me, get out." And I ran to the door, but I got stopped by a big sign that said: IN SPITE OF EVERYTHING I STILL BELIEVE PEOPLE ARE GOOD AT HEART. I said "What?" I mean, who put this up? Why would they put it in this room? I just couldn't understand it. So I copped an attitude and decided to write a letter to the author of the quote. So I got up close enough to see the author's name and my jaw dropped 'cause it said Anne Frank. And I thought, this is too childish for words! What are you talking about? You didn't even make it! And as soon as I said that it made perfect sense. Of course Anne Frank could say that, she was a child, she was a kid, and you know no matter what you do to children they always able to still see some good in it, see? 'Cause they got that ability to see the light at the end of the tunnel.

I don't have it. I'm what you call jaded. And I thought, yeah, man. What can I say? And I started examining my own shit, you know. What are my day-to-day worries? I mean what grinds my ass to the bone on a daily basis? Things like, Why can't I get an American Express card? Why can't I find a hairdresser to mess with my coif? These are my big day-to-day worries, but then you go into a room like this and you hold your coif and your card up against life and death and you know the true meaning of trivial pursuit.

So, I decided what I was gonna do was try to adopt this philosophy somehow, this "in spite of everything . . ." because it might help me in case I got home and I caught some motherfucker in my house ripping off my stereo. Yes, I would still break their legs, but I would remember that in spite of everything this person is still good at heart and that would save their life. So I decided, and I figured that it was cool, and I needed to see the other side of that, 'cause this is only half of the story.

So I took the train from Amsterdam into Germany, and going to Germany was a whole other trip 'cause I didn't go to big cities. I went to little, tiny towns, places in the Schwarzfeld which is the black forest, and me and the black forest was it. You think I'm bullshitting? Some of these people ain't seen no black people since Hannibal. And as a matter of fact, I get off the train, I have five or six little kids running up on me biting on my arms talking about *(In a German accent)*, "Ooh, choco-latte." And you start talking to all these people and you find out that a lot of these folks are born in these villages, raised in these villages and they gonna die in these villages. And they don't go nowhere. And you know, further up in the forest you get, don't nobody go there. All they know about America for the most part they get off the TV set. And you know what the biggest shows in Germany are? . . .

*(No response from the audience.)*

Let's take five. There ain't no fourth wall here. That means, probably, if I'm posing a question, I'm talking to you. See, 'cause you notice there ain't nobody else up here but me. And these opportunities don't present themselves very often in this area. This is not *Dream Girls*.

So tell me, what do you think the biggest shows in Germany are? Dallasty . . . Dallasty? *Dallas, Dynasty* . . . the big three . . . Say what? No, I tell you . . . *(Responds to a call from the audience) Cosby?* Don't you wish? Shit no, I'm gonna tell you what they are. I'm gonna tell you what they are: *Dallas, Dynasty* and *Bonanza*. Yeah, *Bonanza*. And you ain't lived till you see *Bonanza* in German. *(In a German accent)* "Pa? Where is Little Joe? Little Joe is in the toilet. And Hoss? Hoss come zee here . . ." *(He continues with German gibberish)*

And then you sit there and people come up on you and say weird shit like, "We see how, on the American documentaries, see how it is for the black people in the United States. Please to tell us how it is for you to live in the ghetto and please eat this watermelon, we got it special for you." And you know I have to say I was really surprised to discover such . . . to hear those people say watermelon shit kinda freaked me out . . . to discover such rampant ignorance in the world, 1983–84, especially coming from the United States where such a thing would never happen. I mean we're beyond that subject, right? Yeah, yeah . . . Well tell me, what was the last contemporary German you seen on American TV consistently outside of the Olympics? *Hogan's Heroes*, yeah. We're talking contemporary German, jack, and when that realization hit me, I said, "Oh my, I got to get my ass home." Because I'm there with the wrong attitude, you know. 'Cause I'm walking around looking for bombed-out buildings, saying shit to people, talking about, "Why you fighting this terrible war?" Could not even see 1983. I said, "I gotta get my shit together."

I had a lot of time to think . . . I'm one of these people, you know, where if you don't speak English don't come up to me in the street and ask me where shit is. Yeah, you the same way, right? "Yeah, go talk to somebody who know what the hell you talking about . . . come over here take my job . . ." Yeah, well you know, it's real hard to be that cold once you been the alien. See, and once you been the alien, you find out how hard it is to have to ask somebody where some shit is. And you find out what it takes to be able to tell them. It don't take nothing but a little bit of graciousness, that's it. Just a little bit. And that coupled with everything else that happened to me kinda freaked me out. Because I realized that life is a constant thing, it's constant live and learn. Never get over that shit, not even a junkie. Not even a junkie.

## Girl with the Long, Blond Hair

*Girl enters with a white shirt draped on her head.*

This is my long, luxurious blond hair. Ain't it pretty?

*(Audience responds: Yeah!)*

I can put it in a ponytail. Wanna see?

*(Audience responds: Yeah!)*

No. You do?

*(Audience responds: Yeah!)*

Okay, let me get it off my shoulder. Wait. See, look? See? And look, now it's in my eyes. And my mother made me go to my room 'cause she said this wasn't nothing but a shirt on my head and I said, "Nuh-uh, this is my long, luxurious blond hair." And she said, "Nuh-uh, fool, that's a shirt." And I said, "You a fool, it's my hair." And she made me go to my room.

But I don't care, 'cause when I get big I'm gonna get fifty million trillion million million elephants and I'm lettin' 'em go in the house so they can trample on everybody and then she gonna want me to make 'em stop, but she ain't even gonna know I'm there because I'm gonna have blond hair, blue eyes and I'm gonna be white. I am. Uh-huh! Uh-huh! For they said on TV, all you got to do is go to the optometrist office and he got blue eyes in his desk drawer. And then I'm gonna have a dream house and a dream car and dream candy and a dream horse and me and Barbie are gonna live together with Ken and Skipper and Malibu Barbie. We are. And then we gonna buy stylish clothes 'cause we wanna go somewhere, 'cause we gonna go somewhere exciting, 'cause we gonna get on the *The Love Boat*. But you gotta have long hair to get on the *The Love Boat*. You do. And I wanna be like that lady on TV who live in that big house. You know, that lady and then a big old car drives up and there ain't nobody even driving in the car except some tap-dancing shoes, and then the tap-dancing shoes get out and they tap-dance up the walkway and they tap-dance up the side of the door and they ring the doorbell and then they tap-dance back down. Then the lady open the door and she ain't even surprised that there's nobody in them shoes and then they tap-dance right in the car and drive away.

Now I want that to happen to me. But you still gotta have long hair. Now I told my mother I didn't want to be black no more. I did. 'Cause she don't never do nothing exciting. She just go to work all the time. She work on Wall Street. That's all she do is work, work, work and she don't even know nobody exciting and nobody exciting know her and she don't even look like nobody on TV, not even on *The Justice League*, not even on *The Smurfs*. And she says she don't wanna look like no damn Smurf. And then she said, "Even if you sit in the vat of Clorox until hell freeze over, you ain't gonna be nothing but black." And she was right because I sat in the Clorox and I got burned. And she said I just have ta be happy with what I got. But look, see? *(She takes the shirt off her head and holds it at her side)* It don't do nothing. It don't blow in the wind and it don't cas . . . casca . . . casca . . . cascascadade down my back. It don't. And I put that bouncing and behaving stuff in it and it didn't even listen, and I want some other kind of hair that do something else. I do.

*(She speaks to audience members)* Hi. You got hair like mine, huh? How come you don't have your shirt on? You came outside without it? Nobody said nothing? No? Can I touch your hair? Huh? *(She picks her nose)* Oh look, a sticky one. I use another hand. Your hair's soft. My hair's soft too, feel. It's dusty, but it's soft. And your friend? You don't care that he don't have no shirt on his head? How old are you? *(The woman responds: thirty-five)* I'm gonna be seven on Wednesday. Yeah? Thank you. I'm big for my age 'cause we live near a nuclear reactor. My granny said we have ta move soon or we all gonna glow in the dark.

*(Speaking to a different woman)* Ooh look. She got that kinda hair too. Is that your hair? On the top? Somebody in your family look like me? It just naturally like that? I guess nobody look like you on TV neither, huh? And she got it and he got it and nobody got no shirt on. And

no nobody on TV look like none of y'all. Well, who do those people look like? Huh? Don't have to wear no shirt on my head. Then if I'm lucky I grow up and be cute. I be cute like you and I don't even care if I look like you, except I don't want no mustache 'cause my aunt Ernestine got a mustache. Oh. we not supposed to talk about it.

*(She drops the shirt on the floor)* So look, see, see, I put it away over there, see. I'm not thinking about it, see. I'm not! I'm thinking about something else. Thinking about cotton candy and I'm thinking about the New Edition and I think about all the new clothes my granny got me 'cause she got me new shoes and new stockings and she got me a brand new shirt that I'm supposed to hang up . . . That's my shirt. *(She picks up the shirt)* See, I just picked it up. I just picked it—I'm just holding it see? I am. I'm just holding it. I'm not gonna put it on 'cause they said I'm gonna be cute. See, I'm just holding it, for real. And I'm never— I know I'm never gonna put it on again, never, never again. But I'm gonna keep it just in case you lied to me.

# John Fleck

## Introduction by Ryan Hill

John Fleck has the boundless physicality of a rock star. The kind of energy that can transport an audience. So, it is difficult to describe exactly how his body is missing from this excerpt. Without the wet, wild moments of his motion, we're left with our own interpretations.

Interpretation has been both a boon and a hindrance to Fleck's work. A show's meaning can change from nightclub to theatre, from gallery to museum, from documentation to media sound bite. But his work still belongs to the loud, smoky bars and nightclubs of L.A.'s early punk scene. Trained in theatre and song, Fleck's early works were scrappy operas mixing holiday themes with self-effacing humor. These smaller works responded to the punk/gay scene that had accepted him. His involvement with other artists, theatre directors and musicians pushed his work to become psychic travelogues exploring themes of sexual ambiguity, Catholicism and dysfunction.

Fleck's personal themes were demonized in public during the cultural wars of the early nineties. Along with three other performers—dubbed the "NEA Four"—Fleck's work was given a mainstream flogging that had nothing to do with the rapport he shared with his audience. Coincidentally, all four performers use their bodies, along with words, as expressive tools. The use of their bodies was key to this period of national exorcism—reminiscent of Hitler's "Degenerate Art" exhibit—in which artists were used to focus attention on the religious right's agenda. The print media dutifully reciprocated by fanning the flames of scandal. In effect, Fleck's piece *Blessed Are All the Little Fishes*, a work about an alcoholic's moral confusion, became a "performance artist urinating on a picture of Christ." This was understandably an easy mistake to make for those unaccustomed to performance art.

Fleck's performances are grounded in the skills he has acquired as a working actor. He ties together rants, raves, songs and sound with a nuanced delivery and a keen visual sense. Varied subjects are collaged together by a singular voice in shifting situations; he is truly a master of the transition. An information junkie, Fleck sprinkles his shows with both media trivia and breaking-news items. His performances evolve from conversations and things read in the paper or seen on television.

These works are meticulously scripted from extensive acting and writing exercises, and yet, in each live performance, Fleck deviates from the script through improvisation. Built into every piece is his interaction with audience members. Playing with his audience allows him to break the fourth wall, win over individuals and manifest his themes through role-playing. This technique heightens and celebrates the risk of live theatre.

*DiRT* becomes an amusement park for the audience. This piece continues his interest in creating a hybrid between art and commerce; professionalism and mock amateurism; message and sheer entertainment. Before each performance, his chorus members sell T-shirts and solicit applicants for "Paydirt Fellowships." These grants are awarded to audience members at the show's finale. Each audience member is able to make up to one hundred dollars for a one-minute performance and is then treated to an onstage picnic with beverages and backrubs. Fleck also wears a costume with a money tree that audience members are encouraged to pluck, and he auctions costume fragments from a previous musical number to support his grant program.

The work practices what it preaches by leading the audience through a "Survival Seminar for the New Millenium," a financial seminar that teaches the audience how to make money off their personal "dirt." Throughout *DiRT*, money is circulated back and forth from the audience by underwear-clad assistants while Fleck sings, cajoles and dances around a mound of dirt. Both silly and sad, Fleck's *DiRT* defies expectations, pushing some audience members to reject and others to embrace him. I have seen people walk out after the first five minutes and others loiter in their seats basking in the show's afterglow. John Fleck is a body in motion, colliding with ideas and feelings we have about ourselves. What's missing from the following excerpt is the intensity of that body, what's left is the acceptance of it.

**Ryan Hill** is an artist and professor of mass communications in the art department of a private college in Los Angeles. He directed the mockumentary *Me—The Video*, part of an exhibit at the Museum of Contemporary Art in Los Angeles.

## from **DiRT**

### Act Two

God's in the Dirt.

*(John is on his knees picking the dollar bills and other debris out of a pile of dirt, center stage)* Now you can find God in any dirt—a garden, a cornfield, on a mountaintop—but I, myself, have found God out in the desert dirt. *(Indicates his pile of dirt)* This is dirt from Joshua Tree National Monument—it's part of the Mojave desert about two and a half hours east of L.A., above Palm Springs, high desert—and this here is sacred dirt from there—well ya know, the Indians worshipped the dirt—and I plan on taking it all back after this run's over 'cause ya gotta respect the dirt. *(Walks away from the pile)*

So what I do is I try to get outta town at least once a year if I can—away from the striving for something—and I drive on out to ole Joshua Tree and I park my car in the middle of nowhere and I look for a big pile of rocks in the distance. Ya know, they've got those big-ass rocks out there—they look like . . . giant . . . dinosaur—potatoes—stacks of 'em and I start walking towards this pile . . . always looking back to see where I'm coming from, 'cause you don't want to lose your way out in the desert. *(He has slowly walked to the pile of dirt)* And I walk until I don't hear one man-made noise—oh, it had been over two years since I'd not heard one man-made noise—and I know it sounds like glasses tinkling—or footsteps *[At the time of this writing, I was performing in a nightclub, so I had to improvise around the club noise.]* but it's only the sound of the wind on the rocks—all I can hear is my heartbeat. *(His hand on his chest, thumping like a heart beat)* Oh, it'd been so long since I'd heard my heartbeat—Ooo, you can feel it on your skin—the silence—it's heavy. And I peel outta my clothes, like a banana out of its yellowed skin . . . and I'd peel outta my clothes right here, but I'm not feelin' real good about my body right now, plus I don't think nudity is allowed here at Luna Park, is it? Uh uh, ya gotta pay more for nudity, but out there, *(Sings à la that seventies song)* "In the desert, there ain't no one for to give you no shame, la la la la la la la la la la laaaaaa. *(He mimes stripping off his clothes)*

And I fold them nicely and place them next to my water bottle and I sit down in that dirt—Oh, *(Sings à la Oliver)* "Dirt, Glorious Dirt . . ." This is good dirt, *(Grabs a handful)* this is clean dirt—virgin dirt, no one's ever walked on this dirt before. This is God's dirt—and I start to rub that dirt all over my face. *(He is rubbing his face with dirt)* Oooh, talk about a great exfoliant. I always come back from the desert lookin' real good, and I rub that dirt down my tits, and down my belly—and I know I gotta lose a little weight in my belly, but it's still a mighty beautiful belly—and I rub that dirt down my dick and my balls, my beautiful dick and my beautiful balls—and I wish my balls were a little bigger, but they're still mighty beautiful balls—and I rub that dirt down my asshole—Oh, and it feels good, the dirt on my asshole . . . and I realize my asshole had never seen the light of day before. Never felt the sun shine on my asshole before, God—oh, and it feels mighty good, the sun on my asshole—God loves my asshole, don't ya God? God loves my asshole as much as my mouth, don't ya? *(Sings an old Marvin Gaye song)* "It takes twooo, Baby . . . it takes two, Baby . . . me and you . . ." God and me. Oh, God and me, that's the show I wanna be in—God 'n' me . . .

And I stick a little finger in my ass—just a little, 'cause it's real dry out there, ya can't get much more than a little in there—oh, and please don't give me that garbage that real men don't like a little finger in their butt every now and then. It doesn't have to happen that often. But many a smart lady *(To someone who is there that night)* Mary Sweeney, included, knows how to keep her man happy with a little finger action sometimes. Yeah, assholes need lovin', too—assholes need lovin', too—I love you, God. Oh God, oh God. *(His hand thumping on his chest as he simulates an orgasm)* I love you God!! God . . .

And I shoot for what seems ten minutes—I hadn't shot like that in years. Hadn't used those muscles in a long time, *(His chest thumping slowing down and disappearing)* and I look down and see all these little golden puddles in the dirt—puddles of honey—and I'll be damned if this little dragonfly-like creature doesn't land right next to a puddle and starts drinkin' my honey. And this big, red ant comes up and starts drinkin' from another puddle . . . and then, a few more of 'em come—and they're all drinkin' my honey, God—I'm inside them, God. And you're inside me, God— *(Indicating audience)* and I'm inside you and we're all inside each other, God. There's no separation, God, there's no separation . . . *(He is looking up in profound ecstasy)*

And I look up and I see this rock above me—and ya know, it was right after the heavy rains we had last year, last April—and this rock's got all these different colors of moss on it, it's like lichen. It clings to the rocks and it grows in these strips of colors . . . and I swear there's a good thirty-one flavors of color there—there's a lime green, firehouse red, crimson peach, Angelyne pink, tangerine orange and chartreuse and fuchsia and rust and taupe and violet and mauve, and it looks cheap! Uccck, it's so garish, too many colors . . . it looks like it was made at Kmart. I could buy a better lookin' rock than that. *(Realizing the horror)* And I know it's a real rock, God . . . and I know it's real moss—but it looks fake—it doesn't look real. I could buy a better lookin' rock than that . . . *(He gets up and brushes off the dirt from his bottom)* And this just takes me out of my experience completely—and that sky, God! I saw a better lookin' sky last month in *Gone with the Wind*!—and that flower, it's too perfect—there's no such color—it doesn't look real—I could buy a better lookin' flower than that. And that cactus, I've seen a better lookin' cactus in a magazine . . . *(John starts to gather together the corners of the plastic tarp on which the dirt is sitting)*

And this body, please, I could buy better than this. And I could buy a better face than this—I could buy better skin. I could buy a better nose. I could buy better teeth. I could buy a better life than this, God. I could buy better . . . I could buy better . . . *(He is a horrific sight, clutching his plastic tarp of dirt. He catches a tear on his little finger)* I gotta tear. I love it when that happens. But ya know, this is getting a little too maudlin, don't ya think? A little too self-indulgent—I don't want to give performance art a bad name—this is a work in progress, "Please be patient, God isn't finished with me yet." Let's do a little rewriting, shall we? Let's dramaturg this puppy. Lets chop off about ten minutes and let's go back to the desert when I'm on my hands and knees thanking God for all this dirt— *(He is on his knees in the dirt praying to God)* Oh, thank you, God for all this dirt . . . And I look over and I see this rabbit about fifty feet off— a big one, up on its hind legs, just staring me down. Both of us starin', not moving a hair. *(Aside to the audience, quietly)* Ya know, I'm a sign of the rabbit—that's what it says on the place mats at Tem Tem House of Thai, this Thai restaurant on Sunset and Poinsettia—food's mediocre, but the place mats are great. They match up what year you're born with what sign you are—you know, there's the "Year of the Tiger," or "Year of the Dragon"—but, I was born in the "Year of the Rabbit"—and it says, rabbits are the luckiest of all signs.

And I'll be damned if that big ole rabbit doesn't start to dig—and I start to dig—and we're both diggin'— *(Sings)* "I can dig it. He can dig. She can dig it—can you dig it baby?" And then my hand hits this object buried in the dirt—it's hard, smooth . . . and . . . I dig out this magnum of Andrè champagne—ice cold, in the middle of the desert—and I realize I am a lucky, motherfuckin' rabbit!!! A toast—a toast!! *(Music cue: a bongo version of "Tonight" from West Side Story. John does a dance shaking up the champagne and uncorking it. But there is no mighty explosion—it's a dud, filled with water. [It's always good for a cheap laugh 'cause it's a phallic symbol and looks like it's gonna shoot all over the audience])*

*(John sings)* "Tonight, tonight, there's only you and me tonight." A toast—a toast to you and me—a toast to the dirty bunch of us—'cause ya know ladies and gentlemen, no matter how much we scrub, no matter how high we climb that corporate ladder—that stairway to heaven— we're all as dirty as the next guy. Come on, if they vaporized us right now, you'd still be sittin', I'd still be standin' here. There's this layer of

dirt all over us—have ya ever looked under a microscope? There's hundreds of billions of dirty, little critters crawlin' all over us—and that's the problem with this antibacterial soap we're using. It's killin' all the good dirt. *(He runs back up to his pile of dirt and grabs a handful)* Oh, it's Good to be Dirty!! It's good to be dirty—a toast to the Good Dirt! And if you can make a buck off it, so much the better!! Hey, I'm a man of the nineties, what can I say?

Hey, they finally named the nineties. Ya know, every decade has a name—the sixties, the seventies, but nobody's officially coined the nineties yet . . . So, I was channel surfing a month ago and I landed on C-SPAN, and they were interviewing Tom Wolfe, the writer-guy, he was at some press conference promoting his new book and this reporter asked him, "Would you please name the nineties." So, Mr. Wolfe, in his usual dapper fashion, said that, "The eighties will be remembered as the Decade of Fevered Money." I'll buy that—Reagan and all. And he said that, "The nineties will be known as the decade of Fevered Morality." Hmmm . . . right on Tommy. I think it's a combo actually—a parfait. It's still a decade of Fevered Money. Oh yeah, lotsa bulls out there—money, money, money!—and it's definitely a decade of Fevered Morality—dirty, dirty, dirty—so you got *(He does a little dance)* money, money, money and dirty, dirty, dirty and . . . if you can't lick 'em, join 'em. Make some money off your dirt. Hey, it's the only way. Dirt's gonna survive. *(He grabs a handful of dirt)* Hell, we woulda blown this shit to kingdom come if we weren't makin' some greenbacks off this.

*(He walks down into the audience)* So, this is where I conduct my "Survival Seminar for the New Millennium"—where I teach you how to make money off your DIRT, grassroots style. 'Cause, Honey, when that old Y2K comes crashing down on us, hell, dirt is going to be a very valuable commodity. *(He takes out a fistful of dollars, ones and fives)* Now, I've got a fistful of ones and fives here. I'd like to pay for someone's dirt, if I may? *(John interviews an audience member or two. Not for too long, keep 'em wanting more. Theoretical questions:)* Hi, what's your name? *(Perhaps it's a woman?)* Is this your date? No, is he a friend? Uh, uh. A close friend? How close? Ever had sex? No. Are you into girls? *(If the answer is, "Yes," that's worth two dollars, and probe deeper. Or, if she says, "No, I'm not into girls":)* Then what are you into? *(If she answers, "No one":)* Then you must have a very reliable vibrator. Hmm?? Yes. *(Give her a dollar)* Now, when you masturbate, do you concentrate on the clitoris or do you go for penetration? *(Give a couple of dollars more. Or, perhaps ask a man: Is he with a date? His wife? Has he ever cheated? With whom?—that's worth two dollars. Find out how big his dick is, is he a good lover, what kind of sounds he makes when he orgasms?—a bonus of three dollars. Does he have any masturbatory techniques he'd like to sell—the sky's the limit)*

*(John runs back on stage)* OK, you get the point. 'Cause, I'll tell ya, there's no more funding for this kinda stuff anymore—so we've gotta fund each other—that's right—you pay for my dirt, I pay for yours, and then you pay for somebody else's and now it's my turn to pay for *yours*— *(The assistants come out and to his back attach a money tree with real and fake dollar bills on it)* you see, it's the Farming Theory of Free Market Economics. Once you plow the fields, you gotta irrigate 'em, keep that water circulatin'. Oh yeah, that irrigation makes the grass grow green— a toast to the green, green Grass. *(An assistant rolls out fourteen feet of Astroturf down into the audience)* A toast to the green, green grass of home. A toast to Los Angeles! Oh yes, there's lotsa green, green grass here. And ya know, I'm the first to poo-poo Los Angeles. Ooo, I hate it—it's all about money, it's all about appearance, it's still a cultural wasteland. Bla bla bla. Hell, I sound like a New Yorker . . . some folk hate the very dirt we walk on. But ya know, "L.A. has been bery, bery good to me." *(Sound cue for "The Green, Green Grass of Home," the Karaoke version of the Tom Jones hit. There is a long musical introduction which John talks over, and then he starts singing)* My grass has been bery, bery green in L.A. My roots are very deep here—and I hope your grass is green too. Oh, I hate you, L.A. *(He turns to run away, up on the pile of dirt)* No, I don't . . . *(He starts to step down from the pile and is accompanied by back-up dancers dressed as his Mom, Dad and Mare-ey, his horse—wearing a mopped wig and riding on a broomstick)*

*(He sings)* "The old home town looks the same—as I step down from the train—and there to meet me is my momma and my papa. Down the road I look and there runs Mare-ey." *(One assistant now runs out on a broomstick with a mop on her head)* Get it? Mare-ey *(He gives out a horsey neigh)* "Hair of gold and lips like cherries, it's good to touch the green, green grass of home. *(He walks down his Astroturf carpet out into the audience)* Yes, they'll all come to see me—they'll be reachin', smilin' sweetly—yeah, it's good to touch the green, green grass of home." *(He is in the audience with his money tree)*

The old house is still standing, though the paint is cracked and dry, and there's that old oak tree that I used to play on. You wanna play on my old oak tree—touch it—go ahead. What's your name? Mary? Touch the green, green grass, Mary. Touch it—Touch it—Touch it!!! *(He rips off his money tree and stands still in the audience)* "And then I awake and look around me—at four black walls that surround me—and then I realize—yes! I was only dreaming." For there's a God. And there's a sad, old Padre. On and on, we'll walk at daybreak. Again, I'll touch the green, green grass of home.

*(During the above verse, one female assistant, dressed as a preacher in a simple Pilgrim hat with a Bible, and a male assistant dressed as God in a long,*

*long blond wig appear center stage on a ladder with a dowel that has four rolls of toilet paper on it. John walks over and lies down on the grass in front of them. God unrolls toilet paper all over John as he sings the finale.)*

"Yes, they'll all come to see, in the shade of that old oak tree, as they lay me 'neath the green, green grass of home . . ." *(John gets buried under a pile of toilet paper)*

*(The End—with a fabulous curtain call, of course.)*

**Reno**

## Introduction by Ellie Covan

I consider myself extremely lucky to have witnessed Reno work literally *hundreds* of times in my living room, better known as Dixon Place, a laboratory theatre located in downtown Manhattan. In all those years, I never left the room; I tried, but I never did. I think it's because her work is so completely organic that each moment feels spontaneous and unpredictable.

When asked to think about Reno and her work, my first impulse was to make a drawing of her. A drawing that would capture her movement, her gestures, her inimitable voice. Her arms are outstretched, every finger is engaged, her head is thrown back; and her lips are a whole separate picture. Just as she's doing psychic cartwheels and back flips, so is her body in constant motion. Her dog Lucy is in the drawing too, and like Reno, always makes her presence known. And Reno's laugh—I think I could even draw her laugh. Her hair and her body are flying in all directions—she's outta control!!

But, of course, she's not. She actually knows what she is doing, and for a very good reason. She has worked her ass off for nearly fifteen years. When I first met Reno in 1986, she was traveling around town and performing every night of the week, sometimes two or three times a night, from downtown performance spaces to uptown comedy clubs. She started with five-minute bits at the WOW Cafe in 1984 and put her first full-length show together in 1987. She worked *all* the time and not always successfully. I remember the days when you couldn't get her off the stage. In fact, I got so mad at her for taking too much time at Dixon Place that I banned her from the space. That didn't last long; she was relentless.

The first of many people in New York's downtown scene to permanently change her name and her hair color, Reno has always been at the forefront of the "comedy-performance movement." Reno makes us laugh at both our own expense and hers until we are all sniffling and wiping our eyes. Perhaps only the late Frank Maya (a brilliant performance poet and songwriter) ever made me laugh that hard, and Frank's comedy was very similar in that autobiographical, vulnerable, totally revealing way.

But people are not just captivated by her humor. Reno has a very smart wit—sharp, hard, she cuts to the quick. Her audience is flattered. She respects their intelligence. But the quality I'm most drawn to is her fearlessness. And I don't mean lack of stage fright. She's unafraid to speak her truth, to open herself up, to make people angry, to fail. She's not afraid to *not* be funny. And for a comedian, that's courageous. I think of Reno as a comedian, but in fact, she doesn't tell jokes. Unlike mainstream stand-up comedy, the form and syntax of her work does not use the patented punch-line formula. Her work has been called "radical comedy," but that seems mild to me.

Everything Reno does is both personal and political. Not unlike social satirist, Lenny Bruce, her work is her life. Reno doesn't waste any time on stage, but makes a beeline for government, domestic violence, public policies, sexuality, abortion—and I'm not talking about making easy jokes about politicians and celebrities here. She addresses the important issues of our day and doesn't care if she's totally funny or politically correct. At the same time, she can take the most mundane circumstances, like a weekend in the country or sitting in traffic, and go way over the top with her physicality and her outrage.

I remember seeing my father wipe his eyes at a Reno show. When my dad laughs really hard, his whole body shakes and I could see his back vibrating from the kitchen. Afterwards, I was dumbfounded when my mother said, "She's a darling girl!" In retrospect, maybe Reno *was* sort of "darling" as she was pulling her hair out, raging about the mayor's quality-of-life campaign.

Reno has spoken of laughter as being like a doorway, like something extra, something on top of time. Whether it's personal or political injustice, Reno empowers the audience by uniting us in our feelings of outrage and frustration. Making people laugh has been her salvation. I really get that.

**Ellie Covan** is Founder and Executive Director of Dixon Place, a New York City presenting organization dedicated to the development of literary and performing artists.

## from **Reno Once Removed**

Performed at the end of the Reagan era, referencing President Bush's follies.

*A "P" in parenthesis means I do some physical messing around—that is, more than the normal level of such.*

I've spent an enormous amount of energy attempting to embargo myself against the elements. And anything Adam Smith ever mentioned. Division of Labor. Accumulation of Wealth. I think I was just waiting for that Invisible Hand to come my way.

I came from that Find-Yourself-But-Never-Did generation. Around about eighteen, we heard we should go out and find ourselves—or at least be on the lookout—I heard I was out in Lubbock where Route 40 meets the 8 Interchange. But by the time I got there, I had gone. So I followed the skid marks and slipped into a big ole pool of bourbon—eighteen years later, "Hi, how are ya?"

I just started to have to go to meetings with executives and the first thing they say is: "So, Reno, how is it we're just hearing of you now for the very first time and you come to us fully formed and you have lines in your face already? What have you been doing?"

What am I going to say on my résumé? You know how vampires don't photograph? I don't résumé. I just don't read on a résumé. There would be all these gaps.
"Where were you for this . . . *decade*??"
I was diving into the gaps in what would have been my résumé.

What was I doing all these years?
I made a few phone calls.
Went to some memorial services.
I was making tragedy, young man. Someone has got to do it, otherwise there would be no miniseries.

What do you say to these people? I mean, after a while it dawns on me. These are the people who have never thought of suicide. Do you know anyone who has never thought of *suicide*? And these are the people who run the world!

So eventually I end up making some kind of euphemistic statement: "I was living an alternative lifestyle. And *you* weren't there!!"

Yuppies! They appeared in 1980. We'd been setting up for their party. They came down, did a few lines, got some fake energy, made some fake money and now we can't do drugs anymore! Thank you!

Yuppies, man, it's not like they came to drugs for feelings. It wasn't: "I just don't know what my role in life is supposed to be. How will I contribute to the woof and warp of the human fabric? I guess I'll just go . . . join Drexel Burnham Lambert!"

Drexel Burnham Lambert—it was a show. And the show closed.

Nobody could criticize the eighties while they were actually happening. It's like we were victims of our own measurements of time. We had to wait until the PENDULUM swung—October 1989, November 1989, December 1989, January 1, 1990—that REAGAN, what a motherfucker!

Some of us had already seen the hands coming out of his back, but no matter. The man was screaming and yelling about getting rid of Big Government, he had to get rid of it. That was the scourge of America—Big Government. You know, maybe we needed a little bit of Government. Maybe we needed to try to keep the fingers out of the frankfurters, so we had that OSHA, the Occupational Safety and Health Administration. But, Reagan was so excited about the possibility of parties in Washington again, he probably thought: Ah, finger sandwiches, that's a GOOD thing, get rid of those party-pooping, regulator liberals.

I don't know if it's accurate to call the eighties conservative. Didn't people used to vote conservative so they'd keep a little money in the bank?

It was the age of the New Prosperity? Yeah, six or seven investment bankers made five billion dollars each. I don't know if it's going to filter on down to the rest of us. I mean how many waitresses can they tip?

This was not the era of prosperity, this was the decade of denial.

I'm using the word "denial" to mean an upper-class version of lying:
"I didn't really know I was lying. I was in denial about it."
"Well then, you can't be indicted for it."
"Exactly, that's what I was thinking."
I know you were, that's what we all were thinking you were thinking, which is why we were not thinking at the same time.
I don't know whether you noticed that, but it really was what was happening.

The major amount of the New Prosperity, the cash made in that decade, twenty-seven percent was land that we sold to other country people. Not that I'm a nationalist, but is that not like a junkie selling her plasma?

It was wild. The Death of Communism and Capitalism in the same decade.

As we know—ffft, ffft, ffft—things aren't the same as when in civics class they had those big old "Products Maps."

*(P—invisible sketching of U.S. map, with product symbols.)*

And you had . . . oh, each state had a picture of the product it was happiest about making. There was Vermont with the maple syrup—your feet were cold, but you did not care because your mouth was so happy. And Texas with its Eiffel Towers, their brand of culture, the black gold pumping out of the ground. And in the middle of the nation was steel.

For the last ten years, the whole country, Uno Producto: *The Deal*. A
  handshake with a devil's sign behind it.
This country's become one big pyramid scheme:
You buy the rights
To sell the rights
To take a lease
On the option to buy
The purchasing agreement
For what? FOR WHAT?
We never found out. But down at the bottom of the
pyramid there's still that lady with the airbrush:
"It's all over! It's all over!" And she's running out of paint.

Every day we hear banks are merging, folding, people are being forgiven. Donald Trump got forgiven, what, two, three hundred million dollars of loan. A consortium of banks got together to forgive him, what are they, the Pope? "We forgive you, Donny." Do we ever get forgiven? Can we carry a fifty-dollar balance on our electric bill? No, we're in the dark. But Donald Trump, he's too big to fail—we, we're too small to succeed. They're trying, they're reaching, they're too small—fuck 'em.

Everyone's in deficit. No one's in proficit. Even Japan is in deficit. Everyone's in this forgiving mode. Brazil calls up Mexico. "We forgive you." "Gracias." Where is this minus money? Where is this big ole hole with minus signs? Apparently, it's not sexy to be in the black. It's sexy to be in the red.

It's like, "Hey Baby, let's Debt. I want you to get into the red with me. The first time I saw you I knew I wanted to have your debt. C'mon Baby, let's grind, let's grind, let's . . ."

LET'S GRIND THE ENTIRE ECONOMY TO A HALT.

*(P—Screeches.)*

But don't worry, we'll bring out the yellow ribbons and nobody will even notice.

I didn't know what to do. I wanted to wear a yellow ribbon. I supported the troops. I supported the troops so that they'll go home. All of the troops, not just the American troops, but the Iraqis, the French, all of them. So that they'll live. Of course, if they get home and fall off a bridge when it collapses because we spent all our money making Patriots, that's a whole other story.

I just don't want to be lied to anymore. Just tell it to me straight: We want to dominate the oil reserves of the world. We want to be on top of the new world order.

I can believe that, it will not be a problem if you actually utter the word, O-I-L. OIL! I will get it. But I hate this, "We've got to liberate Kuwait because they're torturing the people in the streets there."

Oh yes, every time there's torture we're right there. The United States in Chile, El Salvador, Tehran, the Chinese in Tibet . . . we were right there. Of course—we were on the other side, but it's not like we weren't there.

The Bush-man—he was up in Kennebunkport sending what, 200,000 people to their possible deaths. It's a hundred and forty degrees over there, they've got flea collars on each and every one of their openings to the outer world. And he's up in his holiday lair shouting pronouncements from a golf cart, in his boat; he's pitching horseshoes, shooting archery, playing baseball, softball, badminton, tennis. What the fuck!

And remember, he was in that boat, that boat? The *cigarette* boat, they were calling it, and every five minutes it was Ffffllllggg, spewing out ten gallons of that whatever it is—secret—that we were over there for in the first place. Ffffllllgggg, I'm the Environmental President, fffllllggg.

We have no eyes, we have no ears. We are stupid!!! . . . *(Chants à la Tommy)* "Take my eyes, I can hardly SEE. TAKE my ears, I can hardly . . ." I cannot . . . Lie to me! Lie to me!

*(Now chanting "Give Peace a Chance":)*

"Everybody's talking about . . ."
Saying one thing and doing another. Yes!

*(Beat. Lets it stand. Then, quietly . . .)*

So, I took *my* point of light to the bank.
Only a hundred of us make any money in this country.
The rest of us are volunteers. After all, People, we are the FDIC. We are the Federal Deposit Insurance Corporation. We put our money in the bank, they use it. We put it back again.

*(P—Bends over motioning them to get on her back.)*

"Come on little rich people, come on, come on, come on rich people, come on. Come on, get on my back. I know you need me, 'cause you would have to work if it wasn't for me. You go ahead, get right on there. I wouldn't want you to have to work. It would be hard. There's no jobs anyway, 'cause a couple of you shipped them all out of the community, but other than that it's no problem. I'm not worried about that at all, not at all, not at all, not even a little bit am I worried about that . . ."

## from **Reno Finds Her Mind**

*This piece is performed like a screaming rock anthem. A "P" in parenthesis means I do some physical messing around—that is, more than the normal level of such.*

MY FRIENDS ALWAYS SAY TO ME:
"COME ON RENO CAN'T YOU JUST RELAX?"
*(P)* DOES IT LOOK LIKE IT?

"WHY DON'T YOU COME WITH US THIS WEEKEND?"
AND SO THEY INVITE ME TO THE COUNTRY.
THE "COUNTRY." I LOVE THAT.

BUT I DON'T LIKE THE COUNTRY.
EVERY TIME I GO TO THE COUNTRY,
IT'S THE SAME GODDAMN THING.
FIRST OF ALL, IF IT'S THE SUMMER,
THERE'S NEVER ANY AIR-CONDITIONING,

THEY'RE ALWAYS LIKE:
"OH, THERE'S NO NEED FOR AIR-CONDITIONING.
WE'RE IN THE COUNTRY.
WE'VE GOT SO MUCH AIR ALREADY."

YES, BUT IT'S STICKY, UGLY, MOSQUITO-RIDDEN AIR
WITH THOSE BUGS THAT LIGHT UP
AND YOU SMASH 'EM
AND YOUR HAND SMELLS
ZZZEEWWW FOR THE NEXT SIX WEEKS
AND *THAT* IS NOT RELAXING.

AND THE SAME THING IN THE WINTER.
IT'S ALWAYS FREEZING IN PEOPLE'S HOUSES
IN THE COUNTRY,

"YOU KNOW, WE'RE WORKING ON THE HOUSE."
YEAH, FOR THE LAST TWENTY-SEVEN YEARS!

THEY SAY:
"OH, WE BOUGHT THIS HOUSE,
IT'S JUST THE SWEETEST HOUSE.
WE PRACTICALLY *STOLE* THIS HOUSE . . ."

YEAH, 'CAUSE THERE'S NO ROOF
AND PLANKS MISSING
IN THE WALLS AND THE FLOOR.

"CAN'T PUT THE HEATER ON—THE HOUSE IS SOOO BIG—
THE HEAT'LL GO OUT."

WHY'D YOU *BUY* THIS HOUSE????

YOU'RE SPENDING THE WHOLE WEEKEND
IN ONE LITTLE 5 X 7 FOYER
BECAUSE THAT'S THE ONLY ROOM
THERE'S A HEAT REGISTER ACTUALLY WORKING.
"THIS IS VERY RELAXING
*(P—CHATTER TEETH)*
I'M REALLY HAVING A GREAT TIME."

YOU HAVE TO WEAR A DOWN SLEEPING BAG
LIKE A JUMPSUIT ALREADY.
*(P—HOPPING, SHIVERING)*

AND ALWAYS THE PIPES BREAK
SO NOW THERE'S NO HOT WATER OR HEAT.

RELAXING?? *(P—SHIVER)*
I DON'T WANNA LIVE LIKE THAT!
CAN'T MAKE LOVE *(P—SHIVER)*
EVER HAVE SEX WHEN YOU'RE FREEZING?
"HARDER. I CAN'T FEEL ANYTHING, GET THE HAMMER."
IT'S ONE LONG . . .
IT'S PURGATORY, BABY.
JUST KEEPS GOING . . .

NOT THAT IT MATTERS ANYWAY . . .
BECAUSE EVERYBODY GOES TO BED AT FRIGGIN' *NINE O'CLOCK.*
WHAT IS THE GREAT BIG WONDERFUL THING ABOUT THE COUNTRY;
IF YOU'RE GOIN' TO BED AT FUCKING NINE O'CLOCK AT NIGHT,
IT MEANS YOU'RE BORED!!

AND THAT'S WHAT THEY DO UP THERE!
THEY PLAY *BOARD* GAMES!
*(YELLS)* OOOOH!! THEY'RE ALWAYS WITH THE SCRABBLE,
MONOPOLY, SHUTES AND LADDERS . . . I GAVE THAT CRAP UP WHEN
I WAS SIX YEARS OLD.

OH! OH! AND THEY'RE OPENING ALL THESE FUNKY,
ANCIENT DRAWERS—
AND EVERY ALLERGY KNOWN TO MANKIND
COMES SLIDING OUT INTO YOUR FACE.
*(P—SHIVERING AND SNEEZING)*
THEY GOT MOLD AND PICCALILLI
AND WHATEVER THE FUCK THEY GROW UP THERE!
MISS HAVISHAM, SHE'S RIGHT THERE.

AND YOU'RE WALKING THROUGH THE HOUSE
*(P—FRANTIC GRAB AT INVISIBLE STUFF ALL OVER FACE)*
FEELS LIKE YOU'RE OBSESSIVE/COMPULSIVE,
BUT, NOOOO—IT'S JUST THE *COUNTRY*!
YOU EVER GET COBWEBS IN YOUR APARTMENT *IN* TOWN—OOOHH!!

EVERYBODY SAYS:
"IT'S SO UNNATURAL LIVING IN THE CITY."
EXACTLY! BECAUSE *NATURAL* HURTS!
*NATURAL* HAS ALWAYS PRESENTED A PROBLEM FOR THE HUMAN RACE.

UP THERE, YOU GET POISON IVY, POISON OAK.
WHEN WAS THE LAST TIME YOU GOT POISON SUMAC ON 42ND STREET??
"I GOT THIS HORRIBLE ITCH AT *ICEMAN COMETH* THE OTHER NIGHT."

MOTHER NATURE DOESN'T BOTHER—
SHE WALKS AROUND NEW YORK CITY.
WE HAD THIS GIGANTIC HAIL STORM LAST JUNE.
PPFWW, IT WASN'T A PROBLEM.
"THIS IS JUST A LITTLE SHOW, JUST A LITTLE ENTERTAINMENT."
EVERYBODY WAS CATCHIN' 'EM,
PUTTIN' 'EM ON OUR WALLS—
'CAUSE WE KNOW WE DON'T GET WEATHER IN NEW YORK CITY!

*(THE FOLLOWING CRESCENDOS UNTIL "PICKLED CARROTS.")*

IN THE COUNTRY, HAIL STORM?
PEOPLE ARE RUNNING FOR THEIR LIVES!
THEY'D BE, "BATTENIN' DOWN THE HATCHES!"
"WHAT'S A HATCH?"
"I DON'T KNOW, BUT WE BETTER BATTEN 'EM."

THEY'RE DIGGIN' STORM CELLARS—DEEPER! DEEPER!
"DO WE HAVE ENOUGH PICKLED CARROTS?"
*(TO THE AUDIENCE)* I HATE PICKLED CARROTS!!

*(PAUSE.)*

AND THEY NEVER LOCK THEIR DOORS IN THE COUNTRY.
ANYWAY, IT DOESN'T MATTER IF THEY FUCKING LOCK THEIR
    DOORS OR NOT,
BECAUSE THEIR FRONT DOORS IN THE COUNTRY ARE LIKE BATH-
    ROOM DOORS!
THOSE DOORS WITH THE LOCK IN THE KNOB.
YOU DON'T EVEN FEEL LIKE YOU'RE INSIDE!
"OH, I FEEL SAFE! NOW THAT YOU TURNED THAT LITTLE TAB IN THE
    KNOB."
NO FOUR YEAR OLD IS GONNA BE ABLE TO OPEN *THAT*.

I DON'T EVEN PEE BEHIND A DOOR LIKE THAT.
I'M GONNA PEE, I GET "THE CLUB," *(P)* I GET THE BIG GUARD DOG,
THE GERMAN . . . UH . . . DALMATIONS . . . UH GERMAN . . .
PEOPLE! I GET **GERMANS** OUT THERE!

YEAH, THEY NEVER LOCK THEIR DOORS IN THE COUTRY BECAUSE
THEY ALWAYS SAY:
"WE DON'T NEED TO LOCK THE DOORS,
THERE'S NOBODY AROUND FOR *MILES*."

**EXACTLY!!**

BECAUSE *THEN*, WHEN THE MALCONTENT CASHIER THAT YOU
UNWITTINGLY INSULTED WHEN YOU CHANGED YOUR MIND AND
CANCELLED YOUR COFFEE ORDER AFTER IT TOOK HIM SEVERAL
MONTHS TO FIND IT AT THE 7-ELEVEN LAST WEEK.

AND HE'S PISSED.
AND HE TAKES DOWN YOUR LICENSE PLATE NUMBER,
AND CALLS DOWNSTAIRS TO HIS SISTER'S HUSBAND'S BROTHER . . .
WHO'S *HIS* BROTHER,
AND IS RUNNING THE ENTIRE VILLAGE OUTTA THE BASEMENT OF
THE 7-ELEVEN.

AND HE FINDS OUT WHERE THE HELL YOU LIVE.
AND HE GOES DOWN THE MOST RURAL, RURAL *(P—BACKSTROKE)*,
RURAL, MOST RURAL ROUTE,
LIKE, BACKWOODS RURAL INTO THE CENTER OF THE FOREST,
1967-BEFORE-CHRIST ROUTE.

AND HE SHOWS UP IN THE *MIDDLE* OF THE NIGHT . . .
I DON'T KNOW, LIKE 9:15 OR SOMETHING.
OOOHHH!!
AND HE'S THERE, HE'S ONE BY ONE TAKING EVERY LITTLE HAIR OUT OF YOUR SKULL.
AND YOU'RE SCREAMING, AND NO ONE'S COMING TO HELP YOU! WHY??? BECAUSE:
"OH, DON'T WORRY, THERE'S NOBODY AROUND FOR *MILES*."

YES! NO ONE EXCEPT FOR THAT SICK FREAK FROM THE GODDAMN 7-ELEVEN!

PLEASE! IN NEW YORK CITY, THEY DON'T TORTURE YOU.
YOU COME IN—THEY'RE: "BAM. BAM." GONE.
GONE. YOU KNOW? IT'S OVER, TEN SECONDS, GONE.
THEY GOTTA GET OUT OF THERE, THEY'LL MISS THE 5:17 TRAIN!

# Heather Woodbury

## Introduction by Marcia Farquhar

Although Heather Woodbury's stage is bare—a couple of chairs and a microphone—and the clothes she wears, oddly nondescript (leggings and faded tie-dyed dress in one episode, sleeveless T-shirt and overalls in another; Doc Marten's in one, bare feet in another—the clothes of "rehearsal"), this is not simply the aesthetic of low-budget, downtown theatre. Woodbury's aesthetic is more akin to Peter Brook's concept of the stage as "empty space": a space which she fills as she conjures with language and movement. As *What Ever* unfolds, the audience is introduced to over one hundred characters: fictitious, "ordinary" people, whose lives interweave in this odyssey like so many signs across a geographical and allegorical map of the U.S.A. in the late twentieth century. In front of our eyes she leaps, physically and verbally, between these characters. The journey as metaphor provides the stories and encounters of *What Ever* with a grid of highways and byways and external or internal locations onto which the nomadic wanderings are mapped.

The difference between the original form of *What Ever* (or *The Heather Woodbury Report* as it was known in 1994–95), at the point of its genesis, performed week by week for nine months in half-hour episodes at The Sidewalk

Café in New York, and its final, edited form, performed in eight episodes over four nights, has recently been articulated by Woodbury: "It was originally more open-ended, and simultaneously more topical." So, for instance, weather catastrophes or political events would impact on her characters. When Newt Gingrich said that women shouldn't be in the army because they got infections, Woodbury responded by including a new character, an "Army lady with a recipe for ditch itch." The characters that appear in the four hundred, as-yet-unpublished pages of *What Ever*, or in the studio recording of the eight episodes, or in four nights of live performance, are now *fixed*—their tales part of an unfolding whole. Yet the structure encourages the viewer to experience fluctuating levels of interest in and fondness for individual characters.

Violet Smith is such a character—an octogenarian, Bostonian, free-thinker, at times hilariously overbearing, at others poignant and poetic. In the first excerpt, she tells her maid a story of the not-so-good "old" days. In the second excerpt we learn of a strange haunting in Carlito's letter home: written and spoken by Woodbury, these tender messages to his wife tell not only of the absurd apparitions but also of his everyday experiences of injustice in the U.S.A. That Woodbury manages to bring Cobain the Friendly Ghost into a short monologue, which also refers to a fear of deportation and tuberculosis, without mawkish sentimentality, is indicative of her ability to speak as others, with dignity.

The third excerpt introduces Skeeter, a counter-cultural teenager who, speaking in an antiquated, courtly language replete with words such as "veracity" and "mendacity," exposes corporate cynicism as he crosses the States in pursuit of magical assistance for his predicament—namely his love of two girls. In this scene, Skeeter has a conversation with Wayne, one of the many incidental characters he encounters on his journey. In the fourth excerpt the two "babe dudes" Clove and Sable are found writing notes regarding Kurt Cobain and Skeeter, their shared love interest, in a "learning impeded" school class on Bosnia. It is Woodbury's talent to write and perform characters who are not coyly sanitized that make the odyssey so alive.

As is usual with the serial form, from the novels of Charles Dickens to TV soap opera, there are always clues in the monologues and dialogues as to the "backstory." In these three excerpts there is a lot of background information to assimilate, that serves to locate the newcomer and to reiterate the narrative to a contemporaneous point for the initiated. Heather Woodbury playfully mixes up conventions in an entertaining form. *What Ever*, referring to television but performed with little or no technology, offers the audience not only compulsive viewing, but also work for the imagination in a way that TV can never do. As Edward Said has pointed out, if serious thinking is confined to an audience of specialists, it leaves popular culture open to appropriation by apolitical and right-wing forces.

**Marcia Farquhar** is an artist and cultural critic who lives and works in London. She mainly exhibits and performs in Europe and has recently completed a master's thesis on the work of Heather Woodbury and Rose English.

### Violet Tells Cora Sue of Smuggling Diaphragms

VIOLET: Cora? Cora Sue? D'you think you could stop vacuuming deah? Could we not have the vacuuming today a'tall? The racket is fraying the hell—I'm sorry, I know you don't like profanity—fraying the hell—the hooey, the hooey out of my nerves.

CORA SUE: MM-hmm. If you don't wont it, we won't have it.

VIOLET: Thank you, Cora Sue. I'm not feeling very well today. The doorm'n that I get on with wasn't in, and the other doorm'n wouldn't walk Balzac, and that's why he did his dirty deed on the cahpet. I'm AWfully sorry you had to clean it up, Cora Sue. If I'd felt a'tall better I'd've cleaned it myself.

CORA SUE: Don't be ridiculous. *(She exits to the kitchen to make tea)*

VIOLET: Why don't you take a breathing spell, deah? We'll have a cup of tea. *(Calling to Cora Sue)* D'you know, I think I might've gotten a strain of flu that the doorm'n has because I feel like a violet today. I've always thought my name was pahticulahly unsuitable f' someone of my tempehment, but t'day I feel like a little shrinking Violet.

CORA SUE *(She brings tea and sits)*: Here you go.

VIOLET: Thank you, deah. You're not a'tall like my mothah, Cora. But my mothah didn't like profanity eithuh. Personally, I think a convehsation withOUT profanity is like SOUP without salt.

CORA SUE: Well, you—you shouldn't be havin' that eithuh, I keep tellin' you, SALT is bad for you.

———

VIOLET: Did I ever tell you the story about smuggling birth control into the states before the war?

CORA SUE: Mn-mm, no, you haven't told me that one.

VIOLET: Eh, do—you do believe in birth control, right deah? Your church isn't one of those that—

CORA SUE: Well, I don't know what my church's opinion is, but yes I do believe in birth control.

VIOLET: Good Cora, I'm glad that you've got good sense.

*(Cora Sue stiffens and looks Violet up and down. Violet blushes.)*

Well, eh, um, my first husband Bill and I used birth control because I was nineteen and I didn't want to have any children. So

**Heather Woodbury**

we were going back to the States for the winter—turned out to be miserable, most of the time we spent with uh Bill's family in Chicago. Dreadful sort of people. Terrible time. —But first we were starting at Boston Harbor. We were to arrive by ship in Boston, stay with some relatives of Bill then take the train to New York and make all the gay rounds for Christmas pahties and I thought what more wonderful stocking present for a few of my bosom friends but to bring them some diaphragms, deah. And then I'd distribute the rest to the Sangerites to give them out to all the, eh?? To the public at lahge. Can you believe that diaphragms were illegal: can you believe that STILL they're complaining about teen pregnancy and we still have to smuggle birth control out to the young! Can you believe that? What do these idiots think? Cahn't they see the connection?

CORA SUE: No, 'cawse they can't. Didn't you watch the State of the Union Address last night? Did you see them making any type of connections?

VIOLET: That's why they're idiots, deah. So, I got in touch with a doctor in Lyons and he sold me a satchel full of diaphragms. All different sizes. I'd round three dozen. And we get off the boat and theh's Bill's relatives in Boston and they're waving from the docks—very staid old staunch Boston—they're going t' put us at Beacon Hill for the weekend. And we come off, come through customs without a hitch and then Bill's cousin takes a strap of my satchel, says allow me, Missus, I said, no it's quite all right, he says, allow me, I said, no, that's quite all right, says allow me, I said quite all right and I was trying to hold it and then don't you know, Cora Sue, it ripped apaht and three dozen diaphragms came streaming out onto the docks in Boston. And theh were people swirling all about, passengers and—and everyone froze, came to an absolute standstill and just stared at these diaphragms littering the dock. I turned a very dark shade of bordeaux (which was my favorite wine at the time). And then d'you know what happened, Cora Sue?

CORA SUE: Mmn-mm.

VIOLET: Right. Suddenly—these Boston Irish Catholics made a MAD SCRAMBLE for the diaphragms! Ev'ry father's daughter, ev'ry mother's son went DIVING for these diaphragms. A riot broke out! Scrambling! Policemen had to be summoned?! Women were sticking the devices between their breasts t' keep them from being confiscated. One man jumped, into th' harbor and swam for it! We were driven directly to the train station in the highest dudgeon and put directly on the train to New York. I s'pose that

Extreme Exposure

might've been the beginning of the foundering of—my marriage with Bill, though I think even he found it funny at the time. America is a funny place, isn't it Cora Sue?

CORA SUE: MM-hmm.

VIOLET: Yes it is. Isn't it?

CORA SUE: Hmmm.

VIOLET: Well that's really all I have tuh say.

CORA SUE: That's all that you CAN say.

VIOLET: Yes. I s'pose.


## Carlito Writes Home

Dearest Elisabeta,
Listen sweetheart, it is cold here in the north of California. Now we get a ride to Mr. Schmidt's brussel sprouts farm in the truck of Danny, one of the Chicano guys. The sea wind comes like cold hands from over the cliffs and seizes us by our necks and shakes us like puppies. It rains much. The brussel sprouts are glazed with frost each daybreak when we arrive. The Chicanos say it is the first rains like these in many years, it is good for the farm. But we are chilled to the bone of our bones. Another thing is making us shiver and that is, we have a ghost. Do not worry, Elisabeta, because he has told us he comes for friendship. Immanuel was relieving himself on the other side of Danny's truck when the ghost came behind him in the mirror. In Ingles he told him, "Do no be fri-hyan, I yam Cobang the Frangly Kos." The Chicanos translate this as meaning he comes as a friend but anyway, they don't believe he is there. For some strange cause, they have not laid eyes on him. Ever since we found the little nude gringa talking to herself in the brussel sprouts, this ghost has been visiting. He is blond and skinny and walks the cliffs. We have seen him many times, especially at daybreak. He likes our singing or humming. This has brought him twice. He stands, in his cloak of ice plants, covered only by a thin layer of sand, and his figure wobbles, as if we are seeing his reflection only in the stiff grass. We Mexicans have started to scatter crumbs for him at lunch, just a few tortillas. The Chicanos laugh at us but they don't know anything, the pendejos. He must be hungry, no? Helacio agrees with me that the gringa brought the ghost. The sheriffs said she was taking drugs from a dance on the beach and she walked into the sea. I think she wakened him from the place where the dead are sleeping. Helacio has hurt his leg and he may have to go back home. We are afraid to go to the hospital now they have voted a law to deport us if we go there. The Chicanos say, don' worry, they never enforce their laws, but still we don't trust this. Little Joe has a bad cough and it will not go away.

He had to stop working the fields but he is lucky because he found a good job preparing salads in a good restaurant in Sacramento. Hopefully his cough will improve there. We hope he will stop coughing blood and it isn't tuberculosis. Pray for him and for me also and for this lonely ghost to find his peace. I pray for you and for Nilda and Miguel and Ester and Daniel. Kiss them for me. Here is your money. Did you buy them candy for Christmas, as I asked you to? I wish I could be there at this moment to drink a coffee in the sun and watch you wash your face and neck while outside all of our little donkeys are braying.

Love Always,
Su Esposo, Carlito

## Skeeter Hitches a Ride with Wayne

**WAYNE: I'm doin' an all-nighter to Pittsburgh, that take ya anywhere ya goin'?** SKEETER: Shure. **WAYNE: Careful.** SKEETER: Yeh-up. *(Gets in)* **WAYNE: Slam 'er hard. There we go. Where ya headed?** SKEETER: New York City, tuh visit my Aunt Jeanette. **WAYNE: You a hoosier?** SKEETER: Er, nuh. **WAYNE: Me Neither. Illinois.** SKEETER: Oregon. **WAYNE: What you doin' in Indiana. Just passin' through?** SKEETER: Wull, wull I tried tuh visit my dad, Bruce. **WAYNE: Oh yeah?** SKEETER: He's in Marion. **WAYNE: Penitentiary?** SKEETER: Yeah. **WAYNE: Oh yeah.** SKEETER: Marijuana smuggle.

**Name's Wayne.** Skeeter. **Oh yeah?** Yeh-up. *(He is crying)* **Are you upset, Sneezer? You look like yer . . .** I am. **'tsokay kid, pour yer heart out, I've heard everything, 's entertainment for me, keeps me awake, go ahead. Let Uncle Wayne have it.** Dey wouldn't even let me see 'im. This's been one taxatious hitch. I mean, I grew up hitchin' rides. But this west tuh east ride's been rackish . . . I been frozen, I been bored tuh tears, I been nearly raped. *(Wayne looks)* By a woman. **Call it sexually coerced by a rampant female, Skeezer, sounds more masculine.** Shure, but anyways I got stuck in Injun territory. **Oh yeah?** Yeh, 'at was pretty hectic, but then I got immersed in it. From a cultural stand-point. **Mmm-hmm.** Then in Wisconsin I near qualified for the frozen foods section, till I got picked up by a girl in a stolen pickup. **Hold on—ten-four good-buddy. Got a fourteen year old here on a cryin' jag, call ya back, over and out.** I'm sixteen. **I knew you weren't eighteen.**

Anyways, this girl picked me up was drivin' four hundred miles to get an abortion. **I'm pro-life, but I can sympathize with your situation.** Yeah? **Yeah! Go on. This is good.** So I'se hopin' on makin' Marion by Xmas, since this half-breed dude who gave me a ride in South Dakota knew my dad Bruce from prison and said that he was goin' to be in Section C 'cause in addition to smugglin' marijuana he, subsequent to his imprisonment, wrote letters to media officials regarding his sale of reefer to this Senator Flinch Whitcomb in 1975. **Woh dear!** So they would not let him have visitors, but if I made it by the holy days they might make an exception. But then he reckoned I got lost in these back roads of Wisconsin and went way north, almost froze and then I met Camille. **Who?** The girl gettin' th' abortion, dude. **Right.** And I got all waylaid by her. **Wait, you got laid?** Naw, nuh, she was having an abortion, Wayne. **Wouldn't have to worry about gettin' her pregnant.** She was vomitin' an' all, dude. **I see your point.** 'sides, I'm already stricken with love for these two babe dudes in Cali., Clove and Sable. I thought about fallin' in love with Camille but it would a just been overmuch. **Right.** Seein' as I fall hard. **Oh yeah?** So I went tuh Milwaukee with Camille and I waited for her tuh get her abortion an' den we consorted fer a few days apropos of her trauma an' all. **Did you get laid?** Nah, we couldn't. **Dry humpin'.** Yep. **Dry humpin' in the pickup, yer alright, Keifer.** Skeet. Er.

**So why yuh cryin'?** I'm not anymore, dude, cuz yer tangently gettin' me distracted offa my chagrin. **But why were yuh cryin'?** Cuz I wanted to see my dad. **When's a last time ya saw him?** Nine years old an' before 'at, four years old. **You only saw him twice.** Wull, till I's three he hung out with me an' my ma Linda but after 'at— **He split.** 'at about summarizes it. **So what happened?** Dey tol' me at Marion dat he was in Section C an' I couldn't see him, couldn't even so much as write 'im a fuckin' note and when I said det must be on the illegal slope of the criminal justice climb, dey started tuh ask if my age was of legal tender, an fer ID, so I told 'em my ma was outside in the car but she didn't want tuh come in, den I gave 'em my fake ID an' I exited rapidamente. **Good lie. Good escape. You did good.** Yeh, den I just walked a real long ways, till I thumbed down yer massive vehicle— **Debbie.** *(Skeeter looks askance)* **The truck. Her name is Debbie.** Oh. Hello, Debbie—and the rest is contemporaneous, Wayne.

**That was good, Jeeper. Time for a doughnut break. Crack open that Hostess box and hand me that thermos. And let me tell ya somethin'.** Whut? **Yer better off.** Whut? **Yer better off you didn't see him. Yer old man's a trouble-makin' loser.** 'at's what my ma Linda sez. **Mother's always right, Jeep.** Skeeter. **Mother's always right.** Tuhhhhh. **Gulpa joe?** Thankee. **Yep, it's a long haul, it's a long haul, but we're gonna make it, we gotta.** Tuhhh, yup. **Yup, we gotta.** *(Blows horn, passes someone)*

## Sable and Clove Write Notes in Class

SABLE: **Why were you so late for class and why didn't Posner say anything?**
CLOVE: Cuz I was talking to that hectic counselor. They all think I'm all

suicidally tendacious ever since I walked into the ocean at the rave. They think I'm all Generation X and influenced by Kurt Cobain. It is so dull. **SABLE: What did you say?** CLOVE: I say no, duh. *(Draws doodles in the air)* Star star star. **SABLE: But it is true you do have those fiendish dreams about K.C. Spiral Spiral Spiral.** CLOVE: Yah. But that is the ghost of Kurt Cobain. That's not Cobain himself. You know we were never all fan-like. I only started to like *In Utero* recently and you even disagree with me about that. Anyway, that's different. He's haunting me because he saved me from drowning and he wants something. It's not the same as being influenced, this note is way too fucking long. **SABLE: Yah it really was. We have to start a new sheet of paper and we hardly did any drawings. Posner is so dull.** CLOVE: I know. I hate when he gets all hectic about Bosnia an' stuff, I get all—more than agged—I get all—like I can't breathe and all complex like bolted. **SABLE: All bolted?** CLOVE: Like all, I can't breathe, I just can't think about all those people in that country too much all trapped in a city like that and all those armies and all. **SABLE: Right! So, don't think about it. But are you sure you're not all influenced by Cobain and stuff? You look a tad fiended. Are you still sleepwalking?**

I think so cuz yesterday I woke up in my little brother's room scratching his guitar with an onion. **An onion? What were you doing scratching Kyler's guitar with an onion?** Sleepwalking, duh. Gah, you're agging me to excess today. **Right, so then let's talk about Bosnia with Posner.** This class is so learning impeded. **Null that—whose idea was it to take this for our history credit?** Wull, it was a good name. **"This Century in the News" is a good name? Boing Boing Boing.** Yah. Wull I thought so at the time. Dude, I've been gettin' ragin' headwaves about that boy we met at the Rave, Skeeter. **Did you get a letter from him?** No, I was arrested how could I give him my address? Did you? **Good. Yah, he sent me a postcard.** What do you mean "good"? What did it say? Flower petal. **It said he thinks of me all the time. Tear drop on flower petal.** Wull, I'm sure if he had my address he would've written me too. That's funny cuz that's what he says in my dreams. Penis near tear drop. **That he thinks of me all the time? Ooo I'm so ultra-planted!** No, that he thinks of me all the time. **Wull he sent me the postcard. Lips next to penis.** Wull, Did he ask for your address? Fangs underneath lips. **No, I put it in his pocket when he hitched off.** So you threw yourself in his pocket. How was his pocket? Gnarly hand with long sharp fingernails dripping blood droplets covering the entire page. **New sheet of paper. It doesn't matter. Never mind.** I'm going to get stoked in the bathroom after class? You want to come? **No, I want to be alone.** She vants to be alone. Lady wearing veil. **Yes, she does. Blackout.**

*(Clove walks to restroom, smokes joint, puts on lipstick, looks in mirror and jumps.)*

Cobain, is that you? He went out the window.

*(Notices lipstick smearing her wrists and begins to write on mirror in lipstick.)*

Take a look at that blue vein
Shining through my pale skin
Like the vein
Of Cobain
Who died in pain
Blowing bullet through his brain
Take a look at my blue vein
Tree is bare, branching branching
Sew it to his blue brains
Like thread winding winding
Turning and split
Branching and bent but never slit
Still spun from the heart
Bare branch blue vein, carry it with you to the beat
Blue blue blue vein, enwrap
Blue blue blue vein, spin out
Blue vein run bold, blood fast, blood sweet
Blue vein unfold, unclasp, unseat
Blue vein run wild without puncture
Blue vein run ravenous deep but do not rupture
Bare branch blue vein, entrance me with your dance
Practice my pulse, enchant me in your chants
This is no ode to sad Cobain
Who died in vain
This is the ode to my blue vein
Shining through
Pale
SKIN!

# Robbie McCauley

**Introduction** by Vivian Patraka

Robbie McCauley's performance career began in the avant-garde theatre of New York in the sixties and seventies where she performed at The Joseph Papp Public Theater and at La MaMa E.T.C., as well as with the celebrated Negro Ensemble Company. These theatre experiences prompted her to create her own solo performances. McCauley views her work as a continuing performance serial entitled *Confessions of a Working Class Black Woman*. The series includes *Indian Blood, My Father and the Wars, Sally's Rape* and, her most recent offering, *Surviving Virginia*.

The performances that comprise *Confessions of a Working Class Black Woman* are intended to "bear witness to racism" and to enact the contradictions of living in a racist America, which disavows the centrality of black people to American history from its very beginnings. Her monologues intertwine personal memories and family narratives with historical statistics and accounts of pivotal events. She recycles and revises a number of key "signature stories" from her life history. However, the larger context of *Confessions* isn't the narrative of that personal history, but the political perspective she has on it, and on how past events have shaped present ones.

Because of her commitment to make visible these connections and to revitalize the act of remembering, her performances are always an evolving dialogue. As the critic, Lucy Lippard, noted in response to *My Father and the Wars*, "There is no politics without memory, and one reason events seem uncontrollable is that we have forgotten how to remember." To remember, for McCauley, is to witness, and what is critical is that the audience witnesses history along with her.

McCauley's performances are multimedia events including slides, live music, dance, songs and video. Her performance style is direct and diverse and ranges from galvanizing voice to silence; rapid movement to stillness; and intense interaction to retreat. She addresses questions to the audience, sometimes has them chant parts of her pieces ("Massa is we free?") and sometimes stops a performance to hold a dialogue directly with them. One gets the impression of an enormous power and urgency held in check by a finely honed calm operating to keep her audience with her.

In *Indian Blood* she explores her grandfather's career fighting Indians (and Latinos and Filipinos) with Teddy Roosevelt, the militarism that was passed down to her father, the effects of her family's moving "up South," (i.e., North, from Georgia) and the treatment of Indians in the U.S. ("Indian land and black labor made this country.") The thread running through *My Father and the Wars* is her father's experience in the military; the piece scrutinizes his patriotism ("Daddy believed in America.") and explores her relationship to him in the context of her increasing radicalism. *Sally's Rape* weaves together narratives of African-American slaves, particularly the rape of McCauley's maternal great-grandmother (named Sally) on a Georgia plantation, and that of Sally Hemmings, Thomas Jefferson's slave with whom he fathered one or more children. The piece challenges the status of "having white blood as if it were somethin'," by powerfully evoking the violations which produced it.

*Surviving Virginia* continues McCauley's exploration of the contradictory history of racism and its effects. Generations of the family's men reenlist in the military to avoid worse discrimination outside it and to contain their rage in response to it. The family moves from state to state—Virginia, Kansas, Georgia, Maryland—and from one military base to the next. The geographies of racism and segregation continue even after death—where to live, where to work, but, also, where to die and be buried. This migration of the family constitutes an internal diaspora that continues the enforced diaspora by which their ancestors came to be here. It exposes the fiction of citizenship as a stable property and reveals it as an ongoing struggle for survival, safety and inclusion. The central historical contradiction with which McCauley explores citizenship is located globally in the year 1619: free elections (the hallmark of citizenship) for propertied whites and the enterprise of slavery come into being simultaneously in Virginia that year, conveying that the roots of citizenship and democracy are deeply entwined with those of slavery and enforced diaspora.

**Vivian Patraka** is Professor of English and Theatre at Bowling Green State University and Director of the Institute for the Study of Culture and Society. She is author of *Spectacular Suffering: Theatre, Fascism and the Holocaust* (Indiana University Press).

# from **Surviving Virginia**

## Prologue

*Slide: Aunt Jessie. Steps left, Aunt Marie's cube right, a chair up center and a 1619 chair down left. Robbie enters to steps.*

*(Sings:)*

> . . . I am old now as those old women were back then . . .
> feel like sand on my feet, feel like brick pillar porch . . .

*(Lights down center.)*

I'm
older
and family stories continue, get deeper.

*(Slide out. Robbie down center.)*

"Surviving Virginia" . . . is a metaphor for "Family Stories,"
which is a metaphor for a black family surviving Virginia,
which is a metaphor for any black family surviving America . . .
which is a metaphor for any family surviving Virginia and America
since we're all privileged and damned metaphorically coming from Virginia.

Oops! "We all . . . "
well, democracy cries and *(Does step/circle dance)*
we all do dance
between contradictions
of individual and
ancestor identities.
I like to play on phrases.
I like language.
Talking stuff damned different ways
keeps me well.

*(Stands right of cube.)*

My Aunt Marie said Grandma P. used to say,
Lawd, the world! Horses and elephants can think
but they can't talk. That's the way people are.
If they don't say anything, don't mean they ain't thinking.

*(Sits on Aunt Marie's cube.)*

My best thing Aunt Marie said is to take myself back to when I was a child, and listen to my parents.

Keeping your job. My father believed in work. When they take you on the carpet, hear everything they say and don't answer. Focus on a picture. If you don't have anything to say, they think you're gonna zig. And you zag. That's what they learned in the military, when the enemy gotchu.

*(Robbie crosses down center. Lights change.)*

I want to get back to the part about the grandfather and the band. That was in Norfolk.

## Part II

*As Aunt Marie.*

Papa was a good dancer. He'd always dance first with Mama
at the dances, then he'd dance with me. He'd pick me up,
and I'd wrap my legs around him. Later he taught me
to dance on my toes. "Dance on your toes," he'd say,
"good dancers dance on their toes."
Dances like the Snake Hips. Boogie.
You just shake yourself. Lindy-Hop.
Then that dance where you shuffle along,
come back, clap your hands, go on your heels
and then you come back and shake your heinie.
Dance.

*(Music: Ragtime style. Lights cross up left. Robbie dances with cloth.)*

For Grandfather and 'em, Norfolk was a stopover from Kansas.
Fort Riley. On the way to Georgia. Fort Benning.
Thomas Jefferson had bought Kansas with Louisiana from France
with our money. Excise taxes back then.
Kansas was the center of this land. Center of country's controversy over
    slavery.

*(Lights on Story Area. Gathering cloth. Gossipy.)*

In the 1850s, Kansas had like, a state civil war.
John Brown was there. "Bleeding Kansas" it was called.
Finally fought for the Union.
Per ratio, more people from Kansas were killed than anywhere.
My Daddy was born in Fort Riley.
1915. My father a baby, traveling from there.
On wagons and horses.
Grandfather was such a horseman and

Grandma P. did the laundry on dusty roads. She also took her crocheting needles.

*(She starts to gather and wrap the cloth around herself.)*

We heard the San Juan Hill hero stories,
but the heroic act
for the black men
was standing down in the contradiction
of fighting for other people's freedom. *(She completes the wrapping)*

They moved to Norfolk after the Spanish-American War. Grandfather kept reenlisting to get family benefits. In Columbus, the army town we considered home, during the war, the women talked about the allotment all the time. "Marrying somebody who was going oversea . . . get the allotment." I never heard anybody herself admit that she was doing that, but I heard others accuse 'em of it. Funny, how women get those reputations. *(She pulls off the cloth)*

*(Lights change. Aunt Marie's cube.)*

*(As Aunt Marie)* Helen was eleven and a half. Mama had gone to town to get Alvin's first hard-bottom shoes. Helen had an earache. She was trying to heat sweet oil. Those Sterno stoves people had. Her dress caught fire. She swallowed. She ran out the house. Inhaled. The other kids were there. *(As Robbie)* My father was younger than Helen. He used to always tell us, years later, to never run if you're on fire.

   *(She turns out; as Aunt Marie)* How Papa formed the band was in Norfolk. He'd retired and reenlisted over and over since the Spanish-American War like many soldiers did, reenlisting to take care of their families. He was also patriotic. Camp Alexander, Newport News, Virginia. The Major didn't expect Papa to do anything about it when he told him to form a band. Papa was already feeling free. He'd served with honor. Had his self-respect. Fought with Teddy Roosevelt. Now was "The Great War," 1917.

*(Music: John Philip Sousa music up and fades down.)*


# Part III

*In the 1619 chair.*

*(With wonder)* 1619 was the first election in Virginia. The Virginia Company. The company and the colony both named for a sixteenth-century British queen who was supposed to 'a been a virgin.

Her l'il cousin, son of a scandal-ridden mother, became king after the so-called "virgin" died. He gave a charter to the company to run the colony. And in 1619 this company allowed colonists to elect representatives to help make the colony's laws. They were called Burgesses.

This House of Burgesses continued. Even after the l'il cousin had taken the charter away, 1624. 1624, became a royal colony. By 1660 resentment had risen against British rule. And the rest, of course, is history. Did you know that?

*(Lights down center. A slave trade dance with hands moving.)*

A young man on a little ship, somebody said
a Portuguese young man on a little Portuguese ship,
first in 1443
on an adventure in Africa in 1443,
sailed further South than others, other traders.

South of the Sahara. South of the Saha, South of the Saha, South of the Saha. Th-the first Africans from the first Africans from, is-is-is-is-is the first Africans from the first Africans from . . . *(She kneels)*

Is thinking about the slave trade taking me off the deep end? . . .

*(She gets up)* Back to Portugal. Trade in Africans went slowly back and forth, back and forth to Spain and Portugal. Africans provided other Africans—good business. Overland is. Peaceful, they say. Trade got more profitable. Furious by the 1600s. Developed furiously in the eighteenth century. Lotta countries in Europe. Directly. Especially Holland. France. Africans sold Africans—good business. Is good business. Then Sweden. And Germany/Prussia. Of course, England. The famous port at Liverpool. The Beatles as social icons were overrated—so were we all. All getting deep into the trade.

Anyhow, the l'il cousin, James VI, changed his name to James I when he became King of Scotland and England. I wanted to learn all of this. *(Slave trade dance with chained legs movement)*

Anyhow in 1618, he gave a charter to thirty London merchants to trade in parts of Africa. The Company of Adventurers of London into Parts of Africa. Reminds me of a British actor in a car with a working girl. Before that, somebody said Europeans and Africans were both feudal societies, but Africa was pretty stable. After so many wars, Europe was unstable, like us now. Unstable people either move fast or get destroyed. The slave trade developed furiously.

*(Lights change. She stands on steps. Slide: Hospital.)*

If I'd grown up in Norfolk, we'd've lived in one of the black sections—Lindenwood, Huntersville or later in one of the more upper-crust black sections like Broad Creek Shores (where blacks petitioned to buy in 1957) or, still later, in Brambletown (where whites moved out when blacks moved in) over by Virginia Boulevard and Princess Ann Road, where blacks moved in in the sixties. Engleside used to be white. Greenhill used to be white. Segregated cemeteries, of course. Cavalry was black. But some are buried together now in Woodlawn, and Roosevelt is opening up.

*(Lights change. 1619 chair. Slide: Chains.)*

1619. The same year 'tis said, that African people were first sold to the shores of this country to work as slaves—to Virginia. Am I the only one who hasn't recovered?

*(Slide out. Lights change. She walks in Story Area. Reflective.)*

The Virginia stuck in my memory?

One of the sources of my black fury? I don't think you can fix anything by denial, certainly not marriage. Thomas Jefferson was brilliant it seems, a real Liberal which back then was Republican, a real slave holder, a real lover we're told. Never married Sally Hemmings, his slave mistress whom romantics claim he loved . . . and could've. He defied the King, but could not defy his countrymen. On this. They were "all" doing it. Didn't even free her. Everything would've been different. I think the contradictions made him crazy.

Virginia, like its character is gorgeous and slippery,
It's wet grounds and hard mountains, and new now up North.
But sleepy foothills, peanuts, tobacco, the sea and greenery . . .
Aah! My father lived to be buried in Arlington National Cemetery.

## Part IV

*Lights change. She is eating an apple on Aunt Marie's cube.*

So after Norfolk, Papa, Mama and the boys went to Fort Benning. Helen and Bill had been born in Fort Wachuka, Arizona. Bob and Alvin in Kansas. That's where they learned to speak Spanish. I was born at Fort Benning. The twenty-fourth Infantry was the first company there with two others. Blacks are first in a lot of things we don't get credit for. My brothers ran all around the base shouting, "We have a sister. We have a sister." Your father, my brother, loved me, taught me to braid my hair. We were in Georgia, the deep South, with all those rules against black people, but when I was born, my brothers were happy.

*(Lights change. She moves down center.)*

After Helen was buried, Papa's hair turned gray.

*(Lights on 1619 chair. She remains down center.)*

A funny thing Aunt Marie told me. One time there was a social event at one of her jobs. Everybody was asked to stick a tag on themselves saying who they were. Aunt Marie said she wrote on her tag: I DON'T KNOW WHO I AM. This comforted me because I don't think it's easy to identify ourselves.

*(She dances to the music in her head.)*

She said, "I do know Papa is part of history. Anybody who fought a war."

*(Lights change. She takes 1619 chair, places it down center and sits.)*

Arlington National Cemetery. Stuck in traffic on Memorial Day. The hot, little Nash car. 1950-somethin', Daddy sweating. I don't remember finding Grandfather's grave. It had to do with the drink, being late all the time, being on edge. But there were plenty behind us. Being 'shame' all the time about being colored, I knew it was our fault. Nobody said it wasn't. Nerves always on edge, and then the whiskey. If I don't tell these stories, the tension remains.

But Grandfather was buried there. Somebody said Medgar Evers was the first black man buried in the main part. But I knew my grandfather was buried there. I have a picture of it. Daddy by the tombstone. Mother laughed when I said that day in the traffic that there wouldn't be any room for Daddy when he died. And when he died, there wasn't.

A black man came to our house. Mother, too grieved, too tired. The black man said Daddy could be buried in another army cemetery. Buried in another part of another cemetery that had special part for the army somewhere out in Maryland—not Arlington. They played *Taps*.

*(Slide: Daddy at the tombstone. Music: a dirge. Lights change. She replaces the chair and stands.)*

"Sic Semper Tyrannis": Thus Always to Tyrants. What does the Virginia motto mean? Do you say it giving the finger? . . . I don't know.

*(Slide out. Music out.)*

## Part VIII

*Lights on the steps. Robbie walks to the steps and stands.*

My mother said Oak Leaf Park had just been built. It was a nice place. We lived on Greenleaf Drive. It was all new. Projects. For the defense workers. For the black workers, Mother said. *(She sits)* July. I shoulda been born in June. Ma Willie came up to Norfolk to be with Mother. She hated the government housing, the colored housing for the workers at the shipyard. When I came, they assumed I'd be a boy. Robert Jr., since Daddy was at war and Mother was romantic. But out I came. My sister said Mother put Vaseline on me, put me in the carriage out in the sun. *(She stands)* All the McCauley boys were good with tools like their father.

"Your father applied from an advertisement, in Washington D.C. where we were living, in a bulletin for jobs at the navy yard, and was accepted. He was married with one child and another one on the way— you. So, he didn't have to go to war. When we got there, you know they realized he was black. He didn't get the job he wanted. He ended up in the boiler room which made him angry. We'd only been there since February. That's why he left for the army outta Norfolk. He went to the war while I was pregnant with you to keep from getting in trouble. He didn't have to go but he went, to keep from getting in trouble, I think." *(She sits)*

My sister ran when mother brought me home. That was her first memory except for some vague recollections of hiding under the bed with our other grandmother during the air raids. Ma Willie. Living in the projects had a good connotation back then, Sister said. It was 1942.

*(Lights change. She walks down center.)*

The birth certificate had "Baby Girl" on it for the longest time. I guess they were wondering how I got to be a girl . . . Mother didn't like the name Roberta. Ma Willie got real tired of Norfolk, no place to sit out. "A park for the colored don't mean nothing! You supposed to have a house with a yard . . ." After about two weeks, Ma Willie said, "Anything! R-O-B-B-I-E! Write that!" And she packed us up and got the first thing smoking back to Georgia.

*(She moves to Aunt Marie's cube and sits.)*

*(As Aunt Marie)* Everything changed after we had to leave Georgia, 1934. Everything was different after that. Those men in white sheets stood outside the house that night when Papa told the white men he wouldn't buy whiskey for them. They threw whiskey on him. And we packed up and moved out soon after. It was sad because Mama was settled and we had beautiful furniture. She told the other women on the base to just come get whatever they wanted. Look like nothing was ever like that again, 1934.

Some folks ain't hurting for nothing.

# Lisa Kron

## Introduction by Peggy Phelan

Lisa is a founding member of The Five Lesbian Brothers, a theatre collective that grew out of the WOW Cafe in 1990 and extends the legacy of the Split Britches Company and other "first generation" lesbian performance artists.

Like many performance artists working in the U.S. now, Lisa's work is autobiographical. But unlike many other performance artists, the point of Lisa's work is not about the discovery and achievement of a usually under-represented identity. (The sit-com *Ellen* dramatizing the main character's coming out consolidated about ten years of performance art plots into one hour.) Lisa's work begins with the assumption that we are all under-repre-sented, all in search of an image of ourselves that forever eludes us. Her work does not fall into too easy universalist claims such as: "O Jews and lesbians and fat people are all the same," but much more intriguingly suggests that art comes from the slow, often comic, often agonizing attempt to ask oneself a question. The structure of that inquiry sets in motion a series of political and philosophic propositions that gives Lisa's work its dizzying, often antic, energy. If it is an achievement to ask oneself a question, it is an achievement that first requires that one become a spectator to oneself—and this in turn allows Lisa to find an unusual intimacy and sympathy with her audience.

It seems to me that we will be unable to put this century to sleep until we construct a bedtime story that acknowledges the bright blinding light of the Holocaust. Lisa's *2.5 Minute Ride* is one of the most compelling versions of that story I've seen.

The performance begins with Lisa narrating a slide show, family pictures. But no images appear on the screen. *2.5 Minute Ride* is about enduring events we have not directly witnessed. Lisa's father's parents were seen by a witness boarding a train to the concentration camps. Lisa's father did not himself see this; nor did he see their deaths. And yet the force of that unseen sight governs what he knows of his parents, and by implication, of what Lisa knows of her grandparents.

In Lisa's *2.5 Minute Ride*, the trip back to Auschwitz is juxtaposed with her family's annual outing to an amusement park in Cedar Falls, Michigan. Enveloped within a family quite literally limping and clutching onto frail and near-blind bodies, Lisa's father insists on trying the new 2.5 minute roller coaster ride. He wants to experience the borderless exuberance of joy, the simultaneously thrilling and nauseating proof that he can survive history's mad roller coaster.

Lisa's performance brings her spectators to the lip of death; makes us all lose our glasses, and groping in the dark, she asks us to accompany her as she goes further into the architecture of our collective past's trauma, into the barracks that are inscribed with graffitied prayers sprayed across languages we cannot ever fully translate. Remembered and recited in a contemporary performance art piece by a Jewish lesbian living in the Lower East Side of New York, these illegible inscriptions give testimony—if not to God or redemption or forgiveness—then to the astonishing power of language to endure, especially when it is beyond our ability to digest its meaning.

Perhaps only in the willful pursuit of that which makes no logical sense (juxtaposing the trauma of the Holocaust with the banality of the amusement park), do we begin to glean, however dimly, the possibility that joy is, in the end, the most courageous response we can offer to the disaster of our lives, our prayers, our loves, our dreams. This joy is not nihilistic, absurd or existentialist. Based rather on the conviction that to act and to perform is to do much more than survive and endure, Lisa's performance turns her spectators into artists, insisting that they too shape and revise the disasters of our history and present.

Paul Celan, perhaps the greatest of all German poets of this century, wrote: "Once when death was mobbed / You took shelter in me." Lisa Kron's *2.5 Minute Ride* provides one place from which to make a sheltering approach to the borderless tragedy of this century. And to my great joy, part of that shelter is pure comedy.

**Peggy Phelan** is Professor of Performance Studies, Tisch School of the Arts, New York University. She is the author of *Unmarked: The Politics of Performance* (Routledge) and *Mourning Sex: Performing Public Memories* (Routledge). She is currently writing a book entitled *Death Rehearsals*.

Several years ago I went to a big, family party at Peggy's parents' house. There were hundreds of them there—Healeys, Dohertys, Flahertys . . . They were all healthy and Irish and good-looking. They all played sports—all day. And at one point in the afternoon another one of the in-laws asked me, "Does your family have parties like this?" And I said, "No, my family's all either crippled or dead.

———

I'm trying to remember how many times we really went to Cedar Point as a family when I was growing up. It's occurring to me that it's one of those fake "traditions" my mother uses to get me to come home more often. Like how she asks me every year, "Are you going to make it home for Christmas this year?" And I say, "I do not come home for Christmas. I have never come home for Christmas. We are not Christians! Stop trying to trick me!"

———

Elizabeth drives like a demon over pitch-dark Polish roads. Dad sits in the back and tells us stories. I ask questions. I keep my voice firm and my crying to myself.

"Were you looking for your parents?"

"No, I had done that the summer before."

"And was it hard to accept it? Was it shocking?"

"No, I don't think it was hard to accept it because I don't think I did accept it. I knew, but I think somewhere I thought maybe they were still alive. I don't think I accepted it until just a few years ago, in Lansing. It was the winter and it was so cold and I was shivering. In my coat. And I realized this would only happen to them once. They were old and they stood outside, lined up in the cold and they were of no use to anyone and they were killed."

———

At the entrance to the Magnum there are signs all over which say under no circumstances is this ride suitable for people who are elderly, diabetic or have heart conditions. I look at my father. He can't read the sign because, in addition to having all the conditions listed, he is also legally blind. I tell him what it says and I say, "Are you sure this is a good idea?" He says, "I don't have to do anything. All I have to do is sit there." And then he pops a nitroglycerin in his mouth. "Well, then, why are you doing that?" I say. "Just in case," he says. I try to get him to pretend to take another one so that Mary can tape him doing it. This might make a very nice video moment. But he says no because he is worried that if the girls who run the rides see him taking a pill they won't let him on.

———

A horrible moment in the parking lot. We think they're going to make us pay to go in. No way. No way, no way. In the car we don't say anything to each other, but it's clear to all of us that we can't pay an admission fee for Auschwitz. Oh. They're only charging us for parking. Well. Okay.

———

Under no circumstances would they let us take a video camera on a roller coaster, but one of the girls told us that Mary could go up the exit stairs and shoot from the platform on the other side. When she got there, though, they gave her a hard time and she was really pissed off because these little high school amusement park girls were getting all snippy with her and making her stand in the sun, and she already had that kind of aggravated look that lesbians get in amusement parks in Ohio. So, she told me that I would have to go first and convince the girls to let her onto the exit platform. I found a method that worked pretty well, actually. I'd say, "Can my friend shoot here?" And the girls would say, "Well . . ." And I'd say, "We're doing a documentary video about my father. He's a seventy-four-year-old, blind, diabetic, Holocaust survivor with a heart condition." And they'd say, "Oooh. Okay." It's painfully easy to place the weight of the world right on a teenage girl's shoulders.

———

There's nothing like watching someone else watch your family to really give you some perspective. I keep catching Peggy and Mary staring at various members of my family like this . . . *(Puts hands on face in gesture of horror)* They don't understand why my family likes to come here. Now that they bring it up, I guess I don't really either. Three members of my family are, to use an expression I think you are not supposed to use anymore but it is the expression my family uses to describe itself, "crippled." As in the phrase, "So crippled up we can hardly walk." In addition to being crippled they are also in great, great pain. They gasp and moan with pain all day. It is in this state that my family, once a year, tackles a fifteen-acre amusement park. This year, along with her wheelchair, my Aunt Francie is also dependent on an oxygen tank which must be wheeled alongside her. It's so hot that the park is nearly deserted. And my mother and my aunt consider anything above fifty degrees a heat wave. The sad truth is that my family comes to Cedar Point for the food. I can't bear it. A few years ago, after a little therapy, I began to be aware that the women in my family say things like, "Oh, I'm really not hungry. I just can't eat a thing. I think I'll just have some pudding." Or, "I just need a little something light, maybe some pie." And as soon as we arrive at Cedar Point my Aunt Francie, true to form, says, "I really don't feel good. I think I need a hamburger." The day has just begun and already I'm feeling trapped, trapped, trapped with my family. I involuntarily leave my body and squish my whole self into my brain where a voice in my head is ranting: "A hamburger will not make you feel better! Shut up! Shut up about hamburgers! It's ten o'clock in the morning for godsakes! Eating the hamburgers at Cedar Point is probably what put you in that wheelchair in the first place!" My therapy brain kicks in. I think, Now, Lisa, this reaction seems a little extreme. Is it your aunt you are despising or the part of you that is capable of eating a hamburger at ten o'clock in the morning? These thoughts must be leaking out of my brain onto my face because I see Peggy giving me the "chill-out-it's-only-ten-o'clock" look! I try to reenter my body, but when I do I see that Aunt Francie is eating, from out of her purse, several cold sausages left over from breakfast at the Bob Evans. I concentrate on making my face blank and just following Peggy, and I try not to think about how last night at the Friendly's my aunt went on for ten minutes to the waiter about what foods make her choke.

———

What month was it? October. It's so cold. Elizabeth's car has separate controls for heating the driver and the passenger. On my side I've pushed the little lever all the way over to hot. I don't think we listen to much music. Oh yes, we did. Bach. Seems appropriate for the night before Auschwitz. Dinner at the Orbis Hotel. Dad says, "How funny, tonight we are having a beer with dinner and tomorrow we'll be at Auschwitz." Dad and I, we've been waiting for this our whole lives. We don't know how to feel. Tomorrow we'll be at the place where his parents' bodies lie. No, they were burned. Will we step on their ashes? Will we see a wooden pallet where they slept? Will we kick a stone they also kicked? Will they be hovering above the place, watching us? Are they waiting for their boy? Have they waited all this time for their little boy to come and say good-bye to them? I almost had a nervous breakdown before this trip. I lost a friend over it. She told me she was sick of hearing about it. She is an asshole, but I did sound like a broken record, I'm sure. But what will I do, I thought, if my father cries. I've never seen him cry. What if he falls to the ground and sobs and curses the heavens? On the one hand, I think I have maternal feelings toward him and on the other hand, I don't think I can handle it if I really have to hold him as if I were his mother. Oh. The room is full of hair. Is that my grandmother's hair? Is she here? Elizabeth is just pregnant and she feels sick.

If you believe a baby can be marked, you shouldn't come to Auschwitz. A room full of eyeglasses. They stumbled off blind to their deaths. A room full of suitcases. The smell, oh the smell. A room full of artificial limbs. The Israelis are here. A big group with a huge Israeli flag. Huge enough for my father to easily see, all day, the big blue Mogen David. What a blessing they're here today. He doesn't say too much, but I know these Israelis are his little safety valve. A reminder that the world of Auschwitz is no more. I'm glad they're here too, although after my initial feelings of comradeship I am just irritated all day with these irritating Israelis. If I get shoved one more time . . . We read every word of every exhibit. I have to read them out loud to Dad. "Okay. This is a poem by a woman named Zofia Grochowalska Abromowicz." I'm sorry. *(Repeats a little louder)* "Abromowicz. It says: 1944. Wheels speed along the track, rushing toward the victory of crime, transporting, transporting people to gas, people to a crematory, people to a petrol-sprayed pyre. Smoke floats, thick, foul smoke . . ." *(Instead of the next words, a sob comes out)* I bury my head in my father's shoulder to hide my contorted face. He pats my back. He's okay. He's a good dad. He might be crying a little too and he might not. I can't tell. I feel shaky and helpless. I pull myself together. Really! The day is just beginning. I repeat the line that has undone me: "People burn people here."

———

We go on the Mean Streak. It's a new, wooden roller coaster with a 2.5 minute ride. As soon as we take off, I know that it's a mistake. Dad is clinging to the bar and he has a look on his face like a horse in a fire. I feel like my teeth are rattling out of my head. I hold onto my dad's arm. Trying to pump some kind of rays into his body that will keep him from having a heart attack. I think, Oh, my dear God. What have I done? This is really going to kill him. 2.5 minutes is a really long time on a roller coaster if you are having a good time. If you think the experience is killing your father it's a really, really long time. For a split second I can see Mary selling this videotape to *A Current Affair*. The lead-in will read: "Bizarre murder!!! Lesbian forces blind Holocaust victim on roller coaster!" I am so relieved when we get to the end, I am almost weeping. I want to carry him to the first aid station. I wonder if he can walk. He stumbles out of the car, walks right up to the video camera, as if for a post-game interview and says, "That one was the best!"And asks me if I want to go again.

———

The first Auschwitz camp is like a college campus. Red brick buildings and swaying birch trees. A beautiful wrought iron fence with a sign that says, ARBIET MACHT FREI—WORK WILL MAKE YOU FREE. You have to use your imagination here to comprehend what went on. In the afternoon we drive the three miles to the second camp. Birkenau. Here, you need no imagination. This one looks like what it was. It was sunny three miles away. Here there is no sun. This is malevolent ground. On the way in I ask Dad and Elizabeth if they want something to eat. "No," they both say. They can't eat here. I can. I feel defiant as I shove a cracker into my mouth and walk through the gates. They give us a map and we go exploring. The day alternates between a feeling of horror and a feeling that we are at Disney. We look at the map and say, "Where should we go next? To the pits where they buried bodies in mass graves or the fields where they piled them up and burned them." We have to laugh. We especially laugh at the bookstores which we refer to as the Auschwitz gift shop. They sell postcards there. "Greetings from Auschwitz, wish you were here." We make gruesome jokes about what gifts they sell . . . lamp shades and soap. I actually go into one of the shops to buy a book but it's full of pictures of the Pope and I turn around and walk out. I had been so afraid I wouldn't feel anything here. I think that was my biggest fear. But, when I enter the crematorium, for the first time in my life I feel horror. Physical repulsion. I can feel my face contort, my lips pull back. In the gas chamber, my father stops to take his two o'clock pill. This breaks my heart. I stand to the side and cry. Hard. I can feel . . . I can feel the bottom. It's clear to me now that everything in my life before this has been a shadow. This is the only reality—what happened to my father and his parents fifty years ago. Elizabeth sees me crying and says, "Oh, no."

———

The park is closing in ten minutes. We split up a little at the end so that some of us can ride the Mantis, a new stand-up roller coaster, and some of us can get one last batch of Cedar Point fries . . . and maybe a shake for the ride home . . . and maybe some fudge. The caravan of cars is parked right at the gate, in the handicapped zone, of course. Then we've all made it back except for Dad and Aunt Kitty. I've reached my Family Day limit and I am ready to go. "Buckle your seat belts." I say to Peg and Mary, "They'll be here in a minute." And we wait. "Let's go, go, go," I say. And we wait some more. Finally they wander into the headlights of the cars. Peg says, "Oh my God, Lisa. Your dad doesn't look so good." "He's okay," I say. Peg says he looks a little green. Their walk out of the front gates of Cedar Point to the front seat of the car is torturously slow. Peg and Mary watch intently and send Catholic prayers with every step. I slump in the back seat and mutter impatiently, "He's fine." About six months later Dad has triple bypass surgery. Somebody, he or my mom, casually mentions that he thinks he probably had a little heart attack on the way out of Cedar Point last summer. Peg says she is not going to Cedar

Point with my family again. "You people are insane!" she says. My mother always says, "You know the doctors told us that your grandmother was near death at least a hundred times and she turned out to be fine. Well, okay, eventually she did die but that was the exception, not the rule."

———

At the end of the day I'm feeling giddy, almost euphoric. We've done it. It's over. Check. Dad says, "Where is my bag of glasses?" And I say, "I'm sure they're in the car. I must have left them in the car, Dad. I know they're in the car." They are not in the car and now it's nearly dark. We can't leave without them. Dad says it's all right but his face is ashen. Elizabeth talks to the guard in German. He says we can drive in, along the railroad tracks. It's pitch dark. We drive to the end of the tracks. Now there's Auschwitz dirt on Elizabeth's car. We leave Dad in the car and take two little flashlights to look on the monument where I changed film in the camera. I have to be careful and look where I'm going so that I don't fall into the ruins of the gas chamber. Elizabeth has lost her mind. She's racing all over the monument and screaming. "I don't see them. Do you see them, Lisa? Oh, God, oh, God, I don't see them. Are they here? Do you see them?" We get back in the car. We drive back to the front gate. The other place I could have left them was in the barracks. I had stopped to take pictures in the barracks where there was writing on the rafters in old, German script that said things like, "One Louse and You're Dead." And "Honesty Endures Longest." And "Cleanliness Is Healthiness." We can't drive the car over the tracks. So I go with the guard on foot to look. He is taking me into all the barracks. There are a hundred or so. He speaks a little German. I speak none but I manage to put together the sentence, "Barrack mit schrieben." He takes me right to the barracks with the writing. I have to run to keep up with him. When he gets too far ahead I am in pitch dark. How does this man work here? All day the air has smelled like smoke and we've heard dogs barking in the distance. My dad says that Jews and dogs don't get along. I have never in my whole life been so frightened. The glasses are not here. We will find them the next day at the visitors' center but tonight we don't know that and we are feeling broken. We thought we could walk away from this. I can't bear that there is a piece of us left here somewhere. I know that my dad has lost much more important things than his glasses in this place, but that was a long time ago. I have an image now that he has a bubble around his life that is complete and apart from this place, and now I've broken the circle and lost a piece of him here. I thought I could come here for a day and then get on with my life. And now we have to come back in the morning.

## **Introduction** by Robert Hurwitt

**W**ith the snap of a fan and the arch of a brow, a burly, Japanese fisherman is transformed into a regal mermaid. With a slight shift in stance, vocal register or rhythm, a Samoan matriarch becomes a young African-American boy, a Kentucky yarn-spinner becomes a Japanese *sensei,* or a frightened and confused young woman trades places with a fiercely single-minded demon.

Brenda Wong Aoki bills herself as a storyteller, but she's as much actor as narrator, dancer as monologist, and as innovative and fresh as she is steeped in tradition. She is the storyteller as shape-shifter. And as much as she draws on ancient Japanese folklore for some of her work and on Japanese performance traditions for all of it, her performances are as quintessentially representative of contemporary multiethnic America as she is herself. Born in Salt Lake City and raised in Los Angeles, Aoki is of Japanese descent on her father's side, Chinese, Spanish and Scottish on her mother's. Her artistic training was as eclectic as her ethnic heritage, beginning with lessons in ballet, hula and piano as a child (courtesy of a barter system her parents had set up for poor, older customers at their west-side Long Beach pharmacy).

Modern dance followed, as did voice. Aoki became a founding member of San Francisco's Asian American Dance Collective and of the Asian American Theater Company. She trained in commedia techniques with the Dell'Arte Players, and in Noh and Kyogen forms with Yuriko Doi's Theatre of Yugen, then went to Japan to study with Noh master Nomura Shiro. In the mid-1980s, she co-founded an extraordinary, if short-lived, zen-jazz performance ensemble called SoundSeen with jazz musician Mark Izu (now her husband) and Dell'Arte director Jael Weisman. Since the 1990s, she has worked principally as a solo performer—usually under Weisman's direction, with Izu providing accompaniment—though elements of all these various forms continue to infuse her work.

At first glance, Aoki is a performance minimalist. She works with a simple set (sometimes enhanced with projections), with one costume (a fine, embroidered kimono for her traditional Japanese folktales; T-shirts and trousers for the story of her wild youth among Asian-Pacific-Islander gangs, *The Queen's Garden*) and only a classic Noh fan for a prop. Even her characterizations are effected with a minimalist's attention to the choice of key details. But that attention to detail is also what contributes a sense of depth to each moment on stage. Working from a still, concentrated center, Aoki shifts quickly from one character to another, conveying each change with a clear, concise, but simple, gestural or vocal choice. Her voice is remarkably flexible, both in accent and in pitch. Her gestures, informed by her Noh training, pinpoint a key physical characteristic—the placement of arms, the cock of a head, the center of gravity, the angle of a brow—to express the character. At times, she seems to be acting as much with her thighs as with her voice.

At first, Aoki focused her solo work on dramatizing Japanese folktales, such as the ghost stories that make up *Obake!* Starting with *The Queen's Garden*, in 1992, she has increasingly worked in a more autobiographical mode. *Mermaid Meat* (1997) is a prime example of her more traditional work. *Random Acts* (1994) is a multilayered tale of her transition from one form to the other, the story of a single woman on the solo performance circuit, consumed with worries about aging and her own ethnopolitical relevance, and beset by Christian fundamentalist protesters who suspect that her Japanese children's songs might be satanic incantations. (Yes, it really happened!) More recently, in *Uncle Gunjiro's Girlfriend* (1998), Aoki has begun to explore some of the more fascinating aspects of her own family history. The story, a secret family shame she only recently discovered, concerns a great uncle—her Japanese, immigrant grandfather's younger brother—who fell in love with and eventually married the Mayflower-descendant daughter of the archdeacon of San Francisco's Episcopal Grace Cathedral, and the riots, persecution, antimiscegenation legislation and family tragedies that ensued. It's a big story, packed with historical details that need to be told and—like the idiosyncratic combination of performance traditions that make up Aoki's art—quintessentially American.

**Robert Hurwitt** is theatre critic for the *San Francisco Examiner*. He was awarded the George Jean Nathan Award for Dramatic Criticism in 1996.

## from **Random Acts**

Dedicated to the memory of Lia Toailoa
and the love of Lisa and Fala Toailoa.

### To Fa, Lia

I'm looking at the beautiful face of my nephew
Captain of the football team, All City,
Most Valuable Player
All dressed up in his letterman jacket
Lying in his casket

      Dead

Shot through the heart by a fourteen-year-old stranger the day before he
      was to go to college
And we've been sitting here for almost a week now
My family
His friends
Hundreds of kids from the high school and we've been looking at Lia.

Behind Lia,
Up where the preacher usually speaks,
Sit the chiefs
All dressed up in their lavalava suits

They've been listening to us
First we were shocked
Then we were angry
Now there's nothing more to say

So, the football team stands up
Beautiful young men all the colors of the rainbow
They take off their jerseys and
Place them gently inside the casket
So Lia will know his team is always with him.

A young boy sings a cappella in a sweet, clear voice:
      "We don't have tomorrow . . . We only have today."
Then the family goes up
First Lia's grandparents
Then Lia's aunts and uncles
Then my brother-in-law and my sister.

My sister and them went to every one of his football games. Lia'd run
out on the field—#35. Take off his helmet. Look up into the stands and
bellow, "TOAILOA!," and his little brothers, Puka and Josh, would holler
back, "LIA!!!" Then all together they'd roar, **"SAMOA!!"**

Lia, the first in the Toailoa clan to go to college.
Lia, our hero.
Lia, dead.

The family unfolds lace
Yards
       and yards
              of lace

Lace that flows through the church,
       weaving through the people,
              flowing down the center aisle

The family walks in a circle
       around the casket
       'round and 'round
       swaddling Lia in our love . . .

       Clomp! Clomp! Clomp!

Two midget clowns parade down the center aisle.

       Clomp! Clomp! Clomp!

One is wearing gigantic shoes
       with cleats
              His face obscured by an enormous football helmet.

       Clomp! Clomp! Clomp!

The other is wearing a long, red dress
       a football jersey
        #35

It's Puka and Josh, the little brothers
Wearing Lia's uniform

       Clomp! Clomp! Clomp!

Never breaking stride,
They march to the casket.

       Clomp! Clomp!

Too small to see inside

They stand on tippy toe

> Clomp!

They look at Lia . . .
> and they begin to cry

>> GREAT
>>> BIG
>>>> SOBS

Like I haven't heard them cry
> since they were little babies

Now hell is breaking loose.
One of the football players is kicking over the chairs
Another is pounding his fist into the wall
Again
> And again
>> And again

Lia's grandmother breaks free
Dives into the casket
Clutches Lia to her breast and wails

"Lia, oh Lia! We sent you fo da mainland to get education. But, if you'd stay Samoa you'd be ALIVE!!! Forgive us, Lia. We only want best fo you."

Now everyone is wailing
In Samoan
In English
The children are freaking out
They scream too.

I look at this mess and I just want to get
A GREAT BIG GUN
AND BLOW AWAY THE KID WHO DID THIS
BIT BY BIT
PIECE BY PIECE
SO IT TAKES A REAL LONG TIME
AND REALLY REALLY HURTS
BECAUSE I HATE HIM, I HATE HIM, I HATE HIM!
I WANNA KILL THE MOTHER WHO BIRTHED HIM
I WANNA KILL THE FATHER WHO'S SEED SPAWNED HIM
I WANNA TAKE OUT HIS WHOLE ENTIRE FAMILY!
BECAUSE I HATE HIM, I HATE HIM, I HATE HIM!!!

**HAAAAAAAH!!**

Brenda Wong Aoki

An old man is beginning to shout.

**HAAAAAAAH!!**
A deep,
> low sound
>> other men join him.

**HAAAAAAH!!**
> We are begging the ancestors to give us strength
**HAAAAH!!**
> We are asking the ancestors to take this young warrior's spirit home.
**HAAAAAH! HAAAAAH!!**
**HAAAH!!! HAAAAAH! HAAAAAH!**

And the highest chief stands
> Raises his arms and roars:

"DEATH IS THE NORM!!!

Everyone stops

"Life . . . is the miracle."

Tears stream down his wrinkled face. But, he's smiling at us. Puka and Josh are still sobbing quietly. He goes to them, this wizened old man in a lavalava. He puts an arm around Puka in his helmet and Josh in his jersey and says:

> "For Lia
>> For the children
>>> Go in peace"

We rock
We moan
We hold one another
And we listen to our chief.

> To Fa, Lia

> To Fa, O'e

## from **Mermaid Meat**

A work for symphony.

### Passion

The Fisherman sat in the dark, in the cold, in the heart of the midnight sea . . . Waiting . . . Watching . . . There! . . .

The Fisherman cast out his net. A large man, he planted his feet firmly in the bottom of the boat, hand over hand, muscles straining, he hauled in his catch. Wiping the sweat from his brow he looked at the massive load of quivering seaweed. A monstrous tail emerged, phosphorescent, silver green. My God, it was the biggest fish he'd ever caught!

But wait! . . . It wasn't a fish, well it was a fish, but it was also a woman . . . A wild, savage woman with full, ripe breasts, luminous skin. And her eyes—eyes so deep, so dark they could suck a man's soul right out of his body . . .

The Mermaid! . . . She rose up and the Fisherman saw that she was easily his size. He grabbed his spear. With one blow, she knocked him down. The Fisherman sprang to his feet. Fearing for his life, he rushed at the creature. She struck him. Harder. Dazed, he lay in the bottom of the boat.

She approached him cautiously. She touched his hair. His face . . . the roughness of his jaw. She looked into his eyes. They were the color of the sea before a storm. She ran her hands over his limbs and felt his body—warm, like rock.

She bent over him. Her long, thick, curling hair—like seaweed, falling in his face. As her fingers continued to explore him, the Fisherman realized she meant him no harm. Then he realized she was more woman than fish.

She took in his scent of earth and musk. The Fisherman began to shiver. His breath to quicken. The Mermaid was fascinated. She licked him. He moaned. So she licked him again, all the while stroking him with her hands. She had never before felt such heat from an animal and she was obsessed with the smell of him.

The Fisherman looked up at this wet, voluptuous creature. She smelled like clean, fresh, sea water. Without thinking he grabbed her hair and pulled her full mouth to his. They drank deeply of one another and a violent shock rolled through them. Tumbling over and over in the bottom of the boat, they were animals caught in a struggle, devouring one another, panting in their frenzy.

They licked and kissed and bit and rolled, again and again.

**Brenda Wong Aoki**

**271**

The Mermaid had never before felt the embrace of a human—surrounded, enveloped, tormented with a thousand caresses. Burning with pleasure she began to undulate wildly—and then to lash and lash with strange wave-like movements.

Then the Fisherman plunged into the innermost darkness of her and felt a sensation like a huge sea anemone sucking and sucking.

The Mermaid let out a melodious wail and like a giant python contorted violently. Then their cries began to mount in endless spirals, widening, deepening—expanding out over the sea . . .

When it was done, they lay shuddering, rocking together with the waves.

## The Deed

Then the Mermaid rose to return to the sea. But, the Fisherman said, "Wait! Please—stay with me."

Now, the Fisherman knew that what he asked was not a light request for it was well known that eating the flesh of a Mermaid is the secret to eternal youth and what human can resist the temptation? For man's siren song is to stay forever young.

The Mermaid looked long and hard at the Fisherman and said, "One day. I will stay just one day."

So, the Fisherman took her home to where he lived with his daughter at the edge of the sea. The Mermaid gave the child an exquisite comb of coral and pearl. She told her tales of an enormous turtle who lived in the depths of the waves. And when the child had fallen asleep, the Mermaid and the Fisherman again knew one another—in a quiet, gentle way.

The day had passed.

The Fisherman and his daughter begged the Mermaid to stay. But the Mermaid said, "It is forbidden!" The little girl began to cry. The Mermaid lifted her, rocking her gently saying, "You and I are not the same. You will grow old and I will remain forever young. Only grief can come of it."

But, the little girl threw her chubby little arms around the Mermaid's neck and wept the harder. "But . . . the sea took Mama, and now the sea gave us you." The Mermaid looked at the child and knew it was too late. The die was cast.

The Mermaid moved into the little house by the sea, and in the evenings, when the day's work was done, they would tell one another stories and laugh while the Mermaid combed the daughter's hair with the comb of coral and pearl, singing:

Blood, Tears, Sea Salt,
Mama loves you.

**And the Daughter would say: "Mama, when I grow up, will I be beautiful like you?"**

**And the Mermaid would laugh, "Daughter, when you grow up, you will be magnificent."**

**Years passed and the crinkles around the Fisherman's eyes grew deeper for he was growing old, his daughter grew ripe and luscious and became, indeed a magnificent woman.**

Time passed. The Mermaid's shimmering tail grew dull and useless; her golden skin—pale and dry. Sometimes, late at night, a cry came floating on the mists and the fog. *(The Mermaid's call is heard—sorrowful, longing)* A keening from the heart of the sea. It was her sisters, calling her. But, looking at her beloved old Fisherman and her almost-grown daughter she'd think, It's only for a little while.

One evening as the Mermaid combed the daughter's hair—the daughter noticed *tiny tendrils of gray* curling at her cheek, velvety furrows wrinkling her brow! She turned to the Mermaid, "Why is it you never age? Tell me this secret you kept from me!"

Then one night as the Fisherman slumbered deep in his dreams . . . *(A horrible scream)* It was his Mermaid screaming. Her exquisite face contorted in pain and blood . . . blood everywhere. Blood that dripped from a gaping wound carved deep into her back. And there, holding the Fisherman's very own knife stood his daughter. "Why!? Why!? Why?" shouted the father. But the daughter never answered, she was too busy gnawing on the flesh of the Mermaid.

Then the door flew open and in stormed an enormous bald-headed woman. She picked up the Mermaid and swept out. The Fisherman followed. The bald-headed woman walked straight to the sea, waded through the waves and transformed into an enormous sea turtle. *(The Sea Turtle roars—wild, savage, animal)* The Fisherman tried to follow, but huge waves pushed him back. The Turtle and the Mermaid rode the angry waves as the blood-smeared daughter watched from the shore. In a terrible voice, the Mermaid called out to her, "The Pity!! Oh, the Pity . . ." and dissappeared beneath the sea.

## The Price

Years pass, generations pass, one hundred generations pass . . . One full moon, a lone woman hunched against the wind makes her way to an ancient burial ground at the edge of the sea.

It's cold and the woman grieves.

Stumbling, half crawling, she comes closer.

Finally, she arrives at a labyrinth of graves. Graves outlined with shell, rock, bits of wood. Graves marked with stones piled into strange formations. Finding a place in the midst of the dead, we see her in the moonlight.

She's young, but her face . . . limbs . . . everywhere—hideously scared. And there, glinting in the moonlight, embedded in her matted hair—a comb of coral and pearl. She takes a crude knife and begins a macabre ritual: she slashes her arms, her legs, her face and her hands. Then she spins wildly, sprinkling the graves with her blood. When all the graves are marked, she crumbles to the ground exhausted. After a time, she rises to her knees and addresses the dead:

Happy Death Day, my Darlins! It's Mama! The Queen of the Dead, unable to die. The Fisherman's foolish, foolish daughter! For one hundred generations I have lived and loved and borne you, my children. So many children—pushing through this body into the earth.

I've shed a sea of tears and blood because I'm cursed to watch each of you—my babies . . . die. Your husbands . . . lovers . . . depart . . . And even when we were together—as you grew old and I remained forever young—you hated me!

I tried to hold on to you. Tried to keep you with me . . . but your lives slipped through my fingers . . . And I'm left alone with this— *(She holds up the Fisherman's knife)* To help me feel the pain and see the blood and then I know . . . I'M . . . STILL . . . HUMAN!

She takes the ancient knife and once again begins to stab herself, singing with a mother's love:

Blood, Tears, Sea Salt
Go to my babies
Blood, Tears, Sea and Salt . . .
Tell them—
Mama loves you.

She begins to cry. The cry becomes moans. The moans seem to carry to the heart of the earth. Until the woman's voice resembles . . . the Mermaid's call. *(Gradually, we hear—contorted, mutated, mottled with agony—the Mermaid's call)*

## Forgiveness

Remembering that call, the woman ran down to the sea. Standing on the shore, she cried out over the waves *(We hear the same horrible Mermaid call, but this time much stronger)*

A storm began to gather. From the depths of the waters appeared an enormous sea turtle. The woman begged, "Please, let me die!"

The sea turtle began to thrash and thrash, churning the surf into an angry tide of dark icy sea. And there, riding the back of the turtle—wild, black hair, luminous skin, deep, deep eyes—the Mermaid!

"Remember this?"

And running the length of her back—a hideous scar.

The woman standing on the shore, shouted back over the storm, "And for that, I've been cursed for a hundred existences!"

Stinging rain struck her face, raging waves pushed her back, thunder roared and lightning split the blackening skies . . . but the woman held fast and stood her ground. With all the strength left in her soul she cried out, "FORGIVE ME! PLEASE, FORGIVE ME!"

Then the Mermaid looked at this woman, who once she'd considered her very own daughter—the daughter who had wounded her so deeply—and beheld a woman of scars. Just like herself.

"It is not in my power to grant you death, I can only grant you peace." *(She sings the Mermaid call—rich, full of forgiveness and healing)*

A warm rain began to fall and gently caressed the scars in the woman's face. A huge wave rose up and engulfed her. And the wave continued to crest and crest until a tsunami swept down upon the beach and embraced the woman and all her loved ones in their carefully tended graves. Then it gathered them up and carried them back to the sea. And when the waters receded, nothing remained. Nothing . . . but pure, clean, golden sand . . .

In time, marking the place where the woman had stood—there grew a great pine tree. A pine made all the more beautiful for its gnarls and scars. And the pine remains by the sea, by the source, by the place of the beginning. Ever more, ever green.

## Guillermo Gómez-Peña

**Introduction** by Lisa Wolford

**O**ver the past ten years, Guillermo Gómez-Peña's writings and performances have been recognized with numerous honors, including a National Book Award (1997), a Bessie Award (1989) and a MacArthur Foundation Fellowship (1991). A visionary artist and cultural critic who refuses to let his work be circumscribed within preexisting categories, Gómez-Peña is as likely to be found performing in community centers or marginally funded alternative arts venues as in the museums and galleries of Mexico City, New York and London.

The allure of Gómez-Peña's politically astute solo pieces lies in the power of his poetic language, along with the warmth and charisma of his performance persona. Whether flamboyantly costumed in a zebra-striped suit as "El Quebradito" or in traditional black pants and embroidered jacket as "El Mariachi Liberachi," Gómez-Peña establishes complicity with his audiences by means of humor and playful wit, fostering tolerance of his politically charged message even among spectators most directly implicated in his critique of xenophobia and U.S. imperialism. Gómez-Peña has suggested

that the effect of his performances on certain audience members can be similar, metaphorically, to being "stabbed in the back with an invisible knife; they only find out that they've been stabbed the next day when they wake up and find blood in their sheets."

Each of his performance events is to some extent site-specific, adapted to speak to the particular concerns of the community to which the work is being presented. Drawing from a wide range of poems, performance monologues and spoken-word pieces, Gómez-Peña weaves selected elements into a distinctive textual montage. By adding transitional texts that highlight certain aspects of meaning within a piece, he subtly frames each performance in such a way as to more directly address a given audience. This strategy of recycling is typical of the *rasquache* aesthetic as articulated by Chicano art theorist Tomás Ybarra-Frausto, an oppositional and distinctively working-class style of art that makes use of humor and irony in order to critique dominant cultural paradigms.

Whether working as a commentator for National Public Radio, engaging in street interventions at Ellis Island and the Statue of Liberty or organizing performative town meetings in Toledo, Ohio, or Washington, D.C., Gómez-Peña epitomizes the role of the artist as citizen-diplomat and public intellectual. He uses performance as a tool to initiate dialogue on a range of complex issues, including censorship, immigration and Anglo-American attitudes toward Latinos and indigenous peoples. His work is characterized by a type of artistic and political strategy that he describes as "reverse anthropology."

In both his performance texts and his critical writings, Gómez-Peña seeks to appropriate and reverse the direction of the ethnographic gaze, in his words, "shifting the notion of center and margins and creating a space for the South to become the speaking subject and the U.S. to become the object of analysis, adoration, criticism, etc." His work explores situations of radical historical, political and cultural contingency, strategically occupying a mythical center from which he is able to explain the dominant culture to itself.

Moving from the familiar landscape of California under the xenophobic administration of Governor Pete Wilson to a utopian future in which the peoples of the Americas peacefully coexist in a landscape without recognizable borders, Gómez-Peña examines structural and political inequities. His performances alternately deploy and destabilize familiar images of the "rrrrroomantic Mexican" as seen on picture postcards and in tourist brochures, using humor and irony to guide his audiences through the millennial cartography of his "performance universe," a world in which essentialist notions of identity collapse and geopolitical borders fade in the wake of an irreversible process of cultural hybridization. Whether evoking the specter of a U.S. economy in ruins following the massive migration of Mexican workers to the South, or a nation in which the first Chicano president addresses the country from the Brown House, he articulates the complex range of tensions and projections, desires and fears, that characterize U.S./Mexican relations at the end of the twentieth century.

**Lisa Wolford** is Assistant Professor of Theatre at Bowling Green State University and Resident Dramaturg of Theatre Labyrinth in Cleveland.

## from **Borderstasis**

A performance monologue.

*Dressed in either my Postmodern "Pachuco" outfit, or in my "Mariachi Liberachi" suit, I grab a megaphone. I subvocalize while looking at various audience members for about a minute. No words come out. I nod repetitively while looking at the audience.*

## Introduction

It is a pleasure to be here in [name of city]. Tonight I will attempt to occupy a space equidistant from performance, activism and [    ]. I cannot guarantee you I will succeed, but I'll give it a try.

My multiple repertoire of hybrid personae includes El Mexterminator, El High Tech Aztec, El Naftazteca, El Designer Primitivo and El Quebradito But tonight I have chosen to come as [    ].

Dear foreign audience:
welcome to my conceptual set
welcome to my performance universe
welcome to my border zone
welcome to the cities and jungles of my language
las del inglés y las del español
kick back, light up your conceptual cigarette
*(I light up a cigarette)*
and breathe in, breathe out,
breathe in, breathe out
rreelllaaaxxxx
now, reach over,
grab the crotch of your neighbor
and massage
yes . . .

## I. The Larger Context: A Post-Democratic Era

We experience the end of the world . . . and the word, as we know them, and the beginning of a new era. Perhaps our main frustration is our inability to envision its new characteristics and features. It's a bit like being drunk in the middle of an earthquake and not having a language to express it.

We live in a world without theory, without ethics and without ideology. Our spiritual metahorizons are rapidly fading, and so are our geopolitical borders. The nation state collapses in front of our swelling eyes and is immediately replaced by multinational macro-communities governed by invisible corporate boards, trading partners and computer firms. The new political class believes, or perhaps pretends to believe, that free trade and a healthy economy are the solutions to all our problems, even to the cultural and social ones. In this unprecedented, may we call it "postdemocratic era," basic humanistic concerns are no longer part of their agenda. Civic, human and labor rights, education and art are perceived as minor privileges, and sometimes as dated concerns. Artists and intellectuals don't seem to perform any meaningful role other than that of decorators of the omnipresent *horror vacui* and entertainers of a new, more tolerant and cynical consumer class.

As far as I am concerned, we have no real government looking after the human being. Left to our own civilian fate, it is entirely up to us to figure out which are the new models of survival, citizen collaboration and multilateral cooperation—the new terms for a new social contract. In this sense, the nineties to me are about citizen responsibility, community action and a civilian *logos*. This presentation is a humble contribution to the imagining of a true citizen action.

Let's exercise our political imagination for a moment.

## II. The Self-Deportation Project

*(Normal voice)* It is the immediate future in a typical U.S. city, that is to say, a city full of immigrants, people of color, and people who speak other languages . . . like Spanish. You perceive yourself as an "angry white male," but no one knows about it. Not even your beautiful "Hispanic" wife or your interracial kids.

*(Nasal voice—à la Walter Winchell from Tijuana)* You wake up one day and go to work. You need to stop for gas, but the gas station is closed. (You don't know that all the attendants went back to Old Mexico the day before.) You drive around looking for an open gas station until you run out of gas. You call a cab, but there are no cabs because the drivers, mainly Latino, quit the day before.

Somehow you make it to the office to find your colleagues watching TV in total disbelief. A nervous President Clinton is pleading for all unemployed Anglos and African-Americans to show up immediately to the closest emergency labor recruitment center. The country is paralyzed. The disappeared Latino labor force must be replaced overnight.

At lunchtime you discover that most restaurants are closed. Someone explains to you that the chefs and the waiters were all part of an epic self-deportation program. Since you are fairly apolitical, you still don't quite get it. Many stores and hotels are closed—for obvious reasons—and the banks are going crazy. All across the country, millions of Mexicans, with their suitcases in hand, are lining up at bank counters to withdraw their accounts on their way back to their homelands.

You begin to worry about your family. You decide to go home, walking of course, because your car is parked somewhere on the other side of town without gas.

Your Hispanic wife is devastated. Most of her relatives chose to go back to the old country. She is also furious because Juan, the gardener, and Maria, the babysitter, are nowhere to be found. She explains she had to stay home to take care of the kids, and missed all of her work appointments. She even had to take the kids to do the shopping, which Maria normally does. They stood in an eternal line at the supermarket, only to find that there was no fresh produce. According to the supermarket manager, there were no truckers to deliver it.

Now your kids are crying because they miss Maria.

You go to bed in total perplexity, and you dream . . . in Spanish. Or better said, you have a nightmare in Spanish: you see yourself picking fruit under a criminal sun for ten hours a day, your hands covered with a monstrous skin disease produced by pesticides. You wake up sweating.

Next morning, you turn on the TV. A panicked president delivers the bad news: very few people responded to his desperate call for workers. The unemployed "citizens" were clearly not inspired by the idea of working for minimum wage and no benefits. The nation's tourist, construction, garment and food industries are all in disarray. San Diego, Los Angeles, Santa Barbara, San Jose, Fresno, San Francisco, Phoenix, Tucson, Santa Fe, Albuquerque, Denver, San Antonio, Houston, Chicago and myriad other smaller cities have declared bankruptcy. And so have many national banks. And if this weren't enough, the president concludes, within days, crops across the country will begin to rot because there's simply no one to pick them. Luckily, Mexico has offered to send some emergency food supplies and maybe even some Mexicans. In very broken Spanglish, or rather gringoñol, a desperate President Clinton proceeds to beg the remaining Mexicans to stay, "Queridous amigous: querremos que ustedis recapaciten y nou abandounen sus trajayos mas, les subiremimos el salary y les dareimos muchious benefits y su terjeita verdi instantánea. Por favour."

*(Normal voice)* Now, take a deep breath and slowly come back to the present. It's the spring of '98. Nativist politicos and citizen groups across the country are doing everything they can to stop illegal immigration and to take away the few rights left for immigrants, including access to education and medical services. They conveniently make no distinction between "illegal" and "legal." They blame all immigrants for

crime, drugs and especially the lack of jobs. Their inflammatory rhetoric appeals to your fear of an uncertain future, but not to your intelligence. You feel manipulated and angry. If you could ask one question of the political class, what would that question be? *(Long pause)* "Are you guys truly, truly aware of the logical consequences of your anti-immigrant politics?"

Now, you cool down. It's been a hard day, que no? You sip your delicious coffee . . . from Chiapas, and turn up your favorite Latin jazz.

## III. P.S.A. #187: El Año del Niño

*Two voices.*

Dear American Citizen:
Has the weather in your city changed dramatically in the past year? Have you experienced torrential rain, unprecedented blizzards, tornadoes or record breaking heat waves?
**It was probably El Niño.**
Did you witness on TV the biblical scenes of devastation in Florida, New England and California?
**El Niño, pues, who else?**
Did a sudden tornado spoil your last vacation?
**That was certainly El Niño.**
Are your allergies unbearable this year?
**It's El Niño . . . for sure!**
Do you know that 200,000 illegal aliens cross the U.S./Mexico border each month to take your jobs?
**It's definitely El Niño . . . with hordes of other niños.**
Aren't you shocked by the amount of drugs crossing through that very border right under the nose of the INS?
**A.k.a.: El Niño . . . and his seditious connections to the Tijuana Cartel.**
Were you surprised by those paramilitary kids in Jonesboro who gunned down their schoolmates and teacher?
**Niños will be niños.**
On another issue in current affairs: what do you suppose is the cause of your president's uncontrollable libido?
**That would be . . . las niñas.**
Si señor, El Niño is to blame for all your anxieties and fears, and it's no coincidence that he's got a Spanish name and comes from the South. Who invited him anyway! Despite all our legislative efforts to stop him from crossing the border, El Niño is here to stay, and will never say Adios . . . ajua!
**If you see El Niño himself or any other niño with a similar ethnic phenotype roaming around your neighborhood or mind, please report him to 188-Mexi-fobia.**

## V. Returning to America After Black Tuesday

*The following is a clumsy attempt at storytelling.*

I fly back to the U.S.
a few days after "Black Tuesday,"
the sad April first when the new anti-immigration legislation came into
    effect.
It's Thursday night at a hectic LAX
as I wait for my luggage.
I am sniffed by two humongous police dogs.
A border guard approaches me,
no big deal—
I always get stopped 'cause I've been told
I just have this archetypal "suspicious" look,
a cross between a border dandy
and a generic Latino outlaw.
"Excuse me sir, where are you coming from?"
"Mexico City," I reply.
"Why?" he asks.
"What do you mean?
Why Mexico City as opposed to Hong Kong?
Or why am I coming back?
'Cause since I live here in California,
I am condemned to always come back."
He finds no humor in my logic.
"What do you do?" he asks
"I'm a performance artist . . . and an occasional commentator for NPR."
"No, I-am-asking-you . . . what do you do," he insists.
"You mean, you want me to describe my aesthetics and cosmology?
Or are you simply implying I am lying to you?"
He is now visibly upset and demands to see an ID.
I show him an art press card.
"What do you write about?"
"Crossing borders, U.S./Mexico relations, immigration, situations like
    this one . . . "
He pauses and then continues more aggressively:
"So what do you think about your country's government
being so involved with those big-time drug dealers from Juarez?"
"It's bad," I say. "But what about the fact that there is evidence
to support that the drugs coming from the Contras a decade ago
were introduced to communities of color via the LAPD?"
He takes a step back: "Where did you get that crap?"

"It was international news last year," I reply.
"But nowadays the drugs are mainly coming from Mexico."
His insistence in demonizing Mexico sets me off:
"Sure," I answer, "precisely because there is a market here in America;
or are you so naive as to think that the production of drugs
creates the market?"
He doesn't get my point. Neither do I.
Instead he writes a mysterious note and sends me to secondary inspection
where I spend the next two hours watching a bored customs agent
inspecting every inch of my suitcases,
including toiletries, props, costumes,
performance scripts, my phone agenda,
and all because of my big mouth
and my thick mustache.

*(I nod several times while looking tensely at certain audience members.)*

Fear . . . America is the land of irrational fear. We are all suffused in a culture of fear, and we love it. This is perhaps what separates us from the rest of the world.


## VI. On Fear of The Other

Do you hear the police sirens? Beautiful, eh?
Ammmeeeeeeerica, what a beautifully scary place to be,
but then living in fear is normal for us,
we are all scared shitless of the immediate future.
By the way, are you scared of me?
Of my accent, my strange intelligence,
my obnoxious capability to articulate your fears?
An articulate Mexican can be scarier than a gang member,
¿que no?
Are you scared of my mustache?
My unpredictable behavior?
my poetic tarantula,
my acid politics,
my criminal tendencies,
my tropical diseases,
my alleged ancient wisdom?
My shamanic ability to exorcise the evil out of white people?
Yes or no? Que si que no; que tu que yo.
'Cause I am scared of you,
of your silence pinche mustio

your silence makes you really scary!!
And the distance between you and me makes it even worse.

## VII. Neo-Nationalism

*Second exercise in political imagination. Now, let's imagine the first Chicano President of the U.S., addressing the Brown House. He is a nationalist, but he's got a good sense of humor.*

*(Ultra-militant voice—with reverb)* We witness a resurgence of ultranationalist movements, together with the rise of the New World Border globalist rhetoric. Québec, Puerto Rico, Aztlán, South Central Los Angeles, Yucatán, Panamá and all the Indian Nations have seceded from the new Federation of U.S. Republics. Independent micro-republics are popping up everywhere in the blink of an eye.

Verbigratia: The twin cities of San Dollariego and Tijuana have united to form The Maquiladora Republic of San Diejuana. Hong Kong has relocated to Baja California to constitute the powerful Baja-Kong, the world's greatest producer of porn and tourist kitsch. The cities of Lost Angeles and Tokyo now share a corporate government called Japangeles, which oversees all the financial operations of the Pacific Rim. The Republik of Berkeley is the only Marxist-Leninist nation left on the globe. The Caribbean populations of the East Coast, including Nuyo Rico and Cuba York, have merged to form the Independent Pan-Carib Nation. They willingly accept refugees from Haiti and Miami. Florida and Cuba now share a corporate junta that has the cryptic name of "Lenin, Mas Canosa & Associates." The nation/city of Mexico D.F. (Detritus Defecalis) now called Tesmogtitlán (from the Náhuatl nouns *tesmog*, pollution, and *titlá*, place), with its fifty million inhabitants and its eight hundred square miles is presently negotiating its independence from the F.U.S.R.

## XIV. Free-Falling Toward a Borderless Future

I see
I see
I see a whole generation
free-falling toward a borderless future
incredible mixtures beyond sci-fi:
cholo-punks, cyber-Mayans
Irish concheros, Benetton Zapatistas,

Gringofarians, Butoh rappers, Hopi rockers . . .
I see them all
wandering around
a continent without a name,
the forgotten paisanos
howling corridos in Fresno and Amarillo
the Mixteco pilgrims heading North toward British Columbia
the Australian surfers waiting for the big wave at Valparaiso
the polyglot Papagos waiting for the sign to return
the Salvadorans coming North to forget
the New Yorkers going South to remember
the stubborn Europeans in search of the last island
Zumpango, Cozumel, Martinique
I see them all
wandering around
a continent without a name
el TJ transvestite translating Nuyorican versos in Univisión
the howling L.A. junkie bashing NAFTA with a bullhorn
El Warrior for Gringostroika scolding the first World on MTV
Cholo warriors pointing their camcorders at the cops
AIDS warriors reminding us all of the true priorities in life
Lacandonian shamans exorcising multinationals at dawn
yuppie tribes paralyzed by guilt and fear
grunge rockeros on the edge of a cliff
all passing through Califas
en route to other selves
and other geographies
*(I speak in tongues)*
standing on the map of my political desires
I toast to a borderless future
with . . .
our Alaskan hair
our Canadian head
our U.S. torso
our Mexican genitalia
our Central American cojones
our Caribbean vulva
our South American legs
our Patagonian feet
our Antarctic nails
jumping borders at ease
jumping borders with pleasure
amen, hey man.

## Introduction by C. Carr

**H**olly Hughes began her theatre career at New York's WOW Cafe, that "home for wayward girls" featuring work by lesbians. There she developed her first play, *The Well of Horniness* (1983)—now a classic in certain circles. At WOW, Hughes had found a "great sense of permission," as she once put it. This applied to both its casual acceptance of the politically incorrect tropes of dykedom (like butch/femme) and to its aesthetics. WOW was part of the East Village club scene in the early-to-mid 1980s, a milieu unique in performance art history. This scene was fluid and playful, run by artists for artists, with everybody sharing the same trash-and-vaudeville style, the same post-punk, anyone-can-do-it spirit. The most direct ancestor to the East Village aesthetic was actually "queer theatre," the exhilarating, tawdry, preposterous, vicious, ingenious work done by the likes of Jack Smith, Charles Ludlum and Hot Peaches. Queerness crossed over in the East Village, influencing almost everyone. Hughes's work appeared not only at WOW but on whatever was passing for a stage at Limbo Lounge, Club Chandelier and the Pyramid. The club scene, however, was just about dead by 1986.

Hughes wrote *World without End* in 1989 after the death of her mother.

It's a pivotal piece in the Hughes oeuvre for two very different reasons. First, it marks a break with the "dyke noir" style she'd developed at WOW. Early plays like *The Lady Dick* (1985) explored relationships between women but were steeped in the essence of pulp fiction. They were detective stories without crimes about gun molls without guns and women driving each other to emotional extremes. Hughes's characters were preoccupied with "the killer inside"—rage, lust, love and pain—while putting their sexuality up front where everyone had to acknowledge it. This hard-boiled world cracked open though, as Hughes attempted to make sense of her relationship with her mother—her original up-front sexuality role model and the central enigma of her life. In one memorable scene from *World without End*, the mother flirts with a paramedic while on her deathbed. "What a set of buns," she tells her daughter. "I can't do anything about it. But you could."

"My mother was sex to me," Hughes once said of her impulse to write this piece, "and I had to think again about what sex meant to me and how I could express it in my life after my mother's death." Here begin the ironies. Soon after she had written this first autobiographical piece, Hughes was catapulted into the surreal political discourse surrounding the National Endowment for the Arts. As NEA chair John Frohnmayer described her, "Holly Hughes is a lesbian and her work is heavily of that genre." Meanwhile, because *World* includes an account of a one-night stand with a man, certain lesbian critics concluded that Hughes was going straight. Never interested in offering simple answers or definitions—especially for a word like "lesbian"—Hughes suddenly found such simplifications demanded of her and projected onto her. Then, while touring with the piece in the summer of 1990, Hughes and three other performance artists—Karen Finley, John Fleck and Tim Miller—were defunded by Frohnmayer.

In an article that may have helped precipitate the defunding, the right-wing *Washington Times* declared that Hughes's character in *World without End* "demonstrates how her mother imparted the 'secret meaning of life' by displaying her body and . . . placing her hand up her vagina." This complete fabrication was soon being repeated as fact by the likes of David Gergen in *U.S. News and World Report*. Audiences began to show up expecting Hughes to take her clothes off and when she didn't, reviewers complained that the work didn't go far enough.

Perhaps by now, enough time has passed for *World without End* to be understood as a eulogy to the unruly body—that is, to a woman and mother who thought with her body. Like all of Hughes's work, it has an undercurrent of dark, comic rage and features a character trying to understand her own identity. Art reflected life in a way never intended, as Hughes, on stage and off, was simply not as the world (without end) defined her.

**C. Carr** is a staff writer at the *Village Voice*. Her book, *On Edge: Performance at the End of the Twentieth Century*, was published by Wesleyan University Press/University Press of New England in 1993.

## from **World without End**

*The following section is directed at specific members of the audience. If performed in some fancy-schmancy sort of theatre, you know, with a proscenium and real lights, not clamp lamps, which is quite unlikely, but in case it should happen, the performer addresses imaginary people in the audience. That's acting.*

Did you have enough to eat?

How did you sleep? I'm sorry I got in bed with you. It was an accident. It used to be my bed. You kept on dreaming. I'm glad.

Should we lock up then? I don't think I have a key.

Should we leave a light on?

Did you go down to the water one last time?

What did I leave behind? I always leave something behind. I just don't know what it's going to be this time.

I can't tell you how happy I am you decided to come with me.

But this is where we split up.

You have to follow me. Take the red car.

I should have made a map. Do you mind getting lost?

I'll tell you what we can do. I can describe the important landmarks so that when we go by them you'll know—we *are* on the right track.

> *(She walks upstage, talking.)*

So we'll head out about two miles north, out by the Dixie Highway.

The first thing you'll notice on your right is a Denny's.

> *(She turns downstage.)*

Not just any Denny's! This is the very same Denny's where I used to have dinner with my mother on my father's golf nights.

> *(She sees the Denny's, floating somewhere just over the heads of the audience.)*

Oh my God! There we are!

Hunched over the menus, lost in the smell of fresh Formica, potato salad, and things in general frying.

My mother straightens her bifocals, she folds up her menu:

"I want to ask you a question, young lady. Do you like

boys

or girls

or both."

> *(She giggles nervously. But I guess that's really the only way anyone giggles.)*

I lean forward, my nipples grazing the shrimp in a basket:

"Both," I said. "I like both."

"Well no wonder you can't hold down a full-time job," my mother says.

And the waitress overhears! She swoops down, apologizing, cocktail
sauce in one hand, tartar sauce in the other:

"Oh forgive me, I should have asked! You can have both! Here you go,
help yourself!"

And we'll pass by Apple Mountain.

It's not really a mountain. It's a pile of landfill they seeded over with a
few diseased elms. I know what you're thinking. You're thinking it's
really tacky to have a mountain made of garbage.

Well, you say that now, but you're new to Michigan, you live here as
long as I have you'll crave any kind of mountain you can get your
hands on!

There's a little too much sky out here.

This is my favorite mountain because I went riding here when I was two.

I know I was two, I had to be two because my grandfather took me and
he was dead by the time I was three.

There must have been some kind of remission.

It was September, late. The light was something you could taste.

He walked ahead, his cane clobbering the goldenrod, the Queen Anne's
lace.

He picked me up and put me on his horse. I wasn't afraid.

I was two inches from the sun.

I can still feel it.

The slow curve of the earth, a dying man's hand on my body, seven hundred pounds of palomino between my legs.

Let me feel it again.

"Giddy-up!" I moved, the horse moved, the earth moved. Separately.

*(She addresses a member of the audience at point-blank range.)*

Do you realize the entire solar system is moving twelve miles a second
towards the constellation Hercules?

Is that news to you? I knew it the first time I touched you. Back then I
laughed. I asked him to take my shirt off. I thought I would never fall.

If you're hungry we can stop. Really. I wouldn't mind. I know a place. A
great place. The H&H Bakery in Pinconning.

I used to think it was named after me.

So did my sister. She didn't care for the place.

I stopped there with my sister, my mother, two friends of mine.

Where was my father?

My mother was being so nice to me I didn't recognize her. She let us sit in a booth. She let us order milkshakes. She even promised to take us to—DEER ACRES!

Then, out of the woods, a porcupine started waddling across the parking lot.

"Look girls! A porkie!"

My mother called porcupines "porkies" and skunks she called—"wood pussies."

"You wait right here." And Mom dashed out to the Buick and popped open the trunk.

And she lifted out an axe.

Porcupines have no natural enemies. Nothing in the world wants a mouthful of quills and the porcupine knows this. They don't even know how to run.

Unfortunately.

I don't know how many times she must have hit the damn thing. Long after it was dead.

Maybe someone in the restaurant kept count. They were all looking. Then my mother came back into the restaurant, her hands were full of bloody flesh and quills. "Here you are, girls. Something for your class. Science!"

It could have been worse. It could have been a lot worse.

She put down the axe.

If you look quick, you'll see the house I grew up in, the house she almost died in. The day the ambulance came it was hot but her hands were ice.

She was just lying there, moaning, little x's where the eyes should be. You know, like in a cartoon. It was . . . funny.

When the paramedics came into the room she started fussing with her bedclothes, she ran a blue hand through her hair. She opened her eyes.

"Are you going to check me out?" she said to the tallest.

I couldn't believe it! My mother was flirting on her deathbed. I hadn't seen her that frisky in a year.

They took her vital signs then they asked to see me in the hall.

Where was my father?

"Your mother's very sick."

"I know that. That's why she needs to go to a hospital."

"No she doesn't. Not anymore."

I went back into the room, I bent over her. The last of the peonies lay facedown in the dirt. I could hear the men waiting in the hall. I could smell them wanting a cigarette.

"Holly," she said. "Holly."

"Did you check out the tall guy? What a set of BUNS on that guy! I could almost taste them. I can't do anything about it, but you could."

Then the paramedics came back into the room and my mother turned to the tallest one and asked: "Why don't you just pick me up?"

And he did.

That's how she went out of the house the last time, in the arms of the ambulance man, talking dirty to him in her emphysemic wheeze. Her voice was like stale air forced through a bellows one last time.

I was the fire she fanned.

*(She sits down again in the armchair.)*

Just for the record, he did have a nice set of buns. But that's another story.

————

All I really wanted from my mother was her French.

*(The woman leans back in the chair and closes her eyes. From offstage left comes the faint sounds of an accordion. I'd really prefer a set of bagpipes, but the accordion is more reasonable. The song is sweet, like a remembered childhood song, something upbeat, por favor. The woman smiles, the song is part of her reverie. Suddenly, her eyes open. She realizes the song is not part of the dream, but is really happening. A woman enters playing the accordion. She is tall, with broad shoulders and good bones, elegant and eccentric—a Midwestern Marlene Dietrich, let's say. She's wearing a smoking jacket and very little else other than the accordion. She reminds you of those Saturday mornings when your dad would dress up like Clark Gable and chase your mother around the breakfast nook with his semi-annual hard-on. As the song progresses, the woman in the chair relaxes and dives back into her dream. She speaks as though she's dictating a letter into a foreign language, one she barely knows.)*

I'd say . . . Oh, Mama, I can't sleep at night. I smell the ocean. Not that far-off Atlantic, not the unbelievable Pacific. I'm talking about that old ocean, that blue blanket that used to cover this country, all of us, from the teenage anorexics to the Burger King evangelists, all of us sleeping with the dinosaurs, the black-capped chickadees, our heads full of fish, waiting to be born.

That's the ocean that floods my bed each night and what can I do about it, Mama?

I get up in the morning and the world is just flat and dry and there is no hint, in the parking lot, at the mall, at the 7-Eleven, of why I am so full of ocean. Do you know what I saw?

I saw a boy grab a cat and sit on it and pee all over it. I saw a man hit his wife so hard the whole house cried, I swear. The big, blue Colonial was weeping to see this woman down on her hands and knees, picking up the three-bean salad, picking it up, bean by bean.

All I want to do is sleep, Mama. I'm just like everybody else.

But I'm sinking, I'm turning to stone because of what I saw that night: that woman's blood and tears on the dining-room shag, snaking out of her, spelling out curses in a language NOT English. She was saying: "I'm sorry, I'm sorry," but her blood was singing another tune. It was singing . . .

Sorrow. Death. Death to all of us in this woman's tears. Mama, am I the only one who can read tears?

Oh, I can't watch TV anymore, I can't watch TV. There's always some guy on TV laughing and everyone is laughing with him, except for this one woman and me. I know she's gonna cry enough in the next week to flood all of us out of our houses, even the ones who are laughing.

Am I the only one who's afraid of drowning?

Teach me to swim, Mama! Teach me how to read this sorrow so I can resist the common current. Mama, teach me that French!

Mama says, "What makes you think I know any French?" Her voice is cool and blind, but, and this is a big but, she puts her hand on her hips and I see those hips move under her wraparound skirt so heavy and full, I can smell the memory of ocean drifting out from between her legs. Oh there is *power* in my mother's hips! I tell you what I've seen! I've seen her hands with their tapered fingers run from her hips down to her thighs, I've seen her tongue sneak out of her mouth to wet her lips when everyone else was just watching TV and I know, oh, yes, I know, my mother is *full* of *French*.

The two of us? Two of a kind. She gets up when the rest of us are sleeping to do a slow and sultry striptease for her private audience of African violets and oh! How they bloom. And me? Well, the thing you got to remember about me is I was born feet first, that's right, after forty years of living inside her I came out of her feet first, wearing this dress, high heels and this bracelet. I guess you could say I was *born* to speak French.

Mama took me to the bathroom and started asking me questions. Taking off her clothes and asking me questions. With every garment I got a new question. She unbuttons her blouse and asks: "Do you want to know where babies come from?" She shimmies out of her skirt and says: "Are you ready for the meaning of life? I'm talking about the secret life, the

French nightclub where we're all dancing? The hidden room where we stash our gold." She says this and VOILÀ!

My mother's got no underwear on. Her pantyhose . . . it's down there on the ground, sulking, feeling sorry for himself, then that old pantyhose just slinks on out of there, belly to the ground, and my mother is standing in front of me . . . *(She mimes to the audience)* NAKED. Uh-HUH. NAKED. And glistening. Bigger than life, shining from the inside out, just like that giant, jumbo, Rhode Island Red Hen in front of the Chicken Palace and Riborama.

*(The woman's attitude is extremely important throughout this section beginning with the strip in the bathroom. Her tone should be one of an initiate witnessing a sacred ritual, a mystery revealed. The tone is awe, which can be misinterpreted as fear and lead to a reading of this passage as an incestual event. But no matter what a girl does, there will be those nuevo puritans among us who see something dirty in this. I suggest they read Joe Campbell or the Great Mother, hell, even the* World Book *probably talks about "Fertility Rites." See it's in all the classics.)*

And she's smelling of salt, and she's promising me grease, something to suck on, and she's asking me in, oh, she's asking me in. And my legs are trembling, just like a diver's legs, because I'm high above that sweet, pink ocean, that body of water that is a body, the body we call Mother, and I'm about to go in. Oh, I'm about to go in.

Mama says: "Holly, if something's bothering you, and you want to know the answer to it, just remember the answer is inside you." And with that she reached inside herself and then she took her hand out and oh! I could see how wet she was! And that smell! Let me tell you about that smell! That smell made me want to do the mashed potato! Just me and my mother, my naked mother, dancing in the split-level.

She said she liked to smell herself. She liked to see herself open to nothing but her own eyes. It made her a better gardener. It's true. It's like her purple lips gave her a certain sympathy for the tomatoes. She could get them to go red when everybody else had a yard full of little green fists of fruit. She knew she was a tomato. Crawling through the mud. Or a rose, trained to climb up the sides of houses.

She said: "Holly, I know you're afraid of the world, and with good reason. My father was a trout fisherman! And what did he use for bait? Mice! Live mice. He'd chop off their legs and tie them to a hook and oh! They were so attractive before they drowned! That's what fish like. And I started to beg for those fish, those were my favorite fish. That's what's scary. I know you're afraid of the world and with good reason. But Holly, this is your clitoris, let me tell you what she does for a living! It doesn't do any good to be afraid of the world!

———

When you think of me, why don't you just eat an apple.

Chew very carefully, I am still your apple. Lick every drop of juice that drips down your chin and say: "Help me. I want to change. Let me be changed."

It could happen. Didn't it happen at least once?

Didn't it happen that night I held you and ate you until your singing golden skin was all the way inside me? Weren't you changed then? Weren't you an apple then?

It's not always February. We don't always drink this weak tea.

Even for my father and my mother, there was a late August.

When she got sick he took very good care of her. He could understand her at last, she was like work to him.

See my mother on the last night of her life? My father bends over the scrawny bed. I could see the bones in his face for the first time. He feels like a farmer towards her. "Help me," she says.

And he does. He kisses her.

Not gently. Her mouth is open and I see her tongue.

Apples are suddenly everywhere! The fly is out of the amber, the teapot boils down in the western sky. Help me, I am dying to change.

She pulls him on top of her. His hand goes between her legs. On the last night of my mother's life my father's hand is red. Red! Red from the light of apples falling. Suddenly apples fall like rain outside the bedroom window.

Oh. I get it. After she's gone we'll still have pie.

And now I see my mother touch my father. I see him shimmy. I see him change. I see him, oh I see him.

He is an apple in her hands.

*(Exit. Blackout.)*

## Introduction by Morgan Jenness

**N**ew York, fall 1998. I walk up the oft-trodden steps of New Dramatists, to attend their yearly induction of four new members. I am here to see a new client—Luis Alfaro. Luis's work has been well known on the West Coast since the mid-1980s, but few here in New York know his work as either a performer or writer, and there is a real sense of curiosity and anticipation.

The presentations of actors reading from the new members' plays begin. I feel that pleasant comfort of being in a familiar place, located at the center of something I know well. Then Luis is introduced. "I'm going to do something a little different," he says. He gets up from the audience and starts speaking as he walks forward, carrying a sheaf of loose papers: "A man and a woman are walking down Broadway in downtown Los Angeles . . . The man looks at the woman . . ." Luis grabs a music stand and places his newly completed pages on it. "Can I use this?" No one stops him. "Bitch, shut up," he continues, thrusting his hand commandingly in front of him, pointing his finger at us. "The woman looks at the man and says, 'Aw honey, you know I love you. I just wish you wouldn't hit me so hard.'" And Luis Alfaro proceeds to create a world in front of us, and around us, a world where a man

295

gets slapped, a woman gets slugged, a drunk staggers, an earthquake shakes, a clown throws toys that hit children in the head and people desperately search for a hero or a saint outside a Circus Disco with a three-hundred-pound drag queen.

Suddenly, we are no longer sitting in cozy, familiar comfort in a converted church on 44th Street, but are on the very real streets of L.A. and my heart is starting to do the "cucaracha dance" of some of Luis's characters. "See this finger? I cut it at work making another pamphlet critical of those who would like to see us dead. Four gay Latinos in one room. They're afraid to touch my wound. Would prefer to see it bleed and gush, than to question mortality and fate." The power of the words and the sizzle of Luis's impromptu performance have relocated us. We are no longer observers looking at a world we might previously have seen as other than ours, but are now looking at ourselves as an "other" within a world, at this moment, more real than where we are. He shatters our belief in what we think we know and reorders our assumptions.

His work has been described by the John D. and Catherine T. MacArthur Foundation as having the power to "eloquently challenge race relations, sexual orientation, gender and poverty"—the types of things that, in America, so often tend to place people on the edges of society. In his extraordinary poem *Orphan of Aztlan*, he talks about throwing one's identity in the face of others, making oneself fabulous, daring to tell the truth, to tell one's own story, "because we are at the edge / We are at the border / We are at the rim of the New World and there is no place to run or hide."

Luis also says one must go "back to the very beginning and speak a neighborhood language, like speaking in tongues." It is this defining and redefining of the real American neighborhood—whether it is the corner of Pico and Union streets or a thousand other corners—and the defining and redefining of the shape and form of what our language is to be, that thrusts Luis Alfaro forward as one of the most important forces of our current cultural landscape. As an artist and as a human being, Luis manages somehow to change our center of gravity by repainting the accepted landscape. The edges do become the center, the narrow cultural assumptions of otherness shift and the white-washed face of America itself is turned inside out to reveal the intricacies of the bone, blood and inner skin underneath its thin veneer. We ARE at the rim of the New World and, thankfully, there IS no place to run or hide.

**Morgan Jenness** was formerly an associate producer at The Joseph Papp Public Theater/ New York Shakespeare Festival, and is currently Creative Director at Helen Merrill, Ltd.

# from **Cuerpo Politizado (Politicized Body)**

## Abuelita

*Luis appears in a circle of light made up of twelve votive candles, each one repre-
senting a different story in the mystery of Christ. He is in a black slip. Against the
upstage wall there is a large slide of Luis's finger. As the stage lights brighten, Luis
is heard singing. He holds up his hand showing the audience an injured finger.*

I've been redeemed
by the blood of the lamb
I've been redeemed
by the blood of the lamb
I've been redeemed by the blood of the lamb
Filled with the holy ghost I am
All my sins are washed away
I've been redeemed

See this finger? I cut it jumping into my mother's rosebush. Suicide
attempt or accident? I don't know, I'm just ten years old. I did it because
of *Abuelita*. Us kids, we hate *Abuelita*, my mother's mother. Hate her
more than Mrs. Polka, our fifth grade teacher. You know it's the ultimate
hate when you hate your grandmother more than a fifth grade teacher
named Mrs. Polka. Besides the usual complaints, *Abuelita* pinches our
cheeks too hard, gives us too little money along with those boring stories of the depression: "We ate dirt burritos . . ."

The world stops when *Abuelita* comes to visit. Rules the house
with an iron fist. Potatoes and beans for breakfast and Channel 34, the
Spanish-language station, day and night. *Novelas* with adulterous housewives during the day, and *Lucha Libre* with masked wrestlers fake-hitting
each other all night long. *Abuelita* loves it.

I don't know if I did it on purpose or if *Toro* pushed me. Another
in a long list of dogs that we have owned, ranging in name from *Oaxaca*
to *Mazatlán* to *Puebla* (named after ideal vacation spots for Dad) is running on the porch. This one's name is *Toro*. Later to be run over by a car
on a busy Pico Boulevard morning and renamed *Tortilla*.

*Abuelita* sits on the porch reading yet another installment of
*Vanidades*, a sort of *Cosmopolitan* for the Latina set. Completely even
more unrealistic than *Cosmopolitan*, *Vanidades* has pictures of beautifully
trim, dyed-blond Latinas, making *tortillas* or *chile rellenos* in gorgeous
Ann Taylor outfits at an outdoor, Mayan-designed, wood-burning pit.

I rise out of my mother's rosebush and immediately plunge into
the Latino dramatic effect—the painful *ai yai yai yai yai*. There's a gash

on my finger and it starts to bleed pretty badly. *Abuelita* turns on the hose and runs my hand under the water. Inspecting my finger, she laughs, pinches my cheek, thanks the *Virgen* for the minor miracle, does a sign of the cross and applies primitive Latino first aid.

She looks at me, smiles and raises my bloody finger to her face. Closely inspecting my afflicted digit, she brings it up close to her eyes. I can't tell what she is looking for. As if holding it up to the eyes she might find some truth, some small lesson or parable about the world and its workings.

Her eyes canvas my finger, probing with her vision, slowly and carefully. And then quickly, and without warning, she sticks my finger inside of her mouth and begins to suck on it.

I feel the inside of her mouth, wet and warm. Her teeth lightly pulling. Equally comforting and disgusting at the same time. Being in this womb feels as if I am being eaten alive on one of those late night Thriller Chiller movies: *Vampira, Senior Citizen Bloodsucker!* But it isn't that at all. This is the only way that *Abuelita* knows how to stop the bleeding.

*(He begins to sing again. During the course of the song, he holds up his other hand and begins to show a different injured finger.)*

I've been redeemed
by the blood of the lamb
I've been redeemed
by the blood of the lamb
I've been redeemed by the blood of the lamb
Filled with the holy ghost I am
All my sins are washed away
I've been redeemed

See this finger? I cut it at work making another pamphlet critical of those who would like to see us dead. Four gay Latinos in one room. They are afraid to touch my wound. Would prefer to see it bleed and gush, than to question mortality and fate. I could go on about being tested, but it seems so futile. As if we don't all know that one little HIV test could be wrong.

I hold the finger in front of me. Stick it close to my mouth. Drip, drip, drip all over my desktop. I hold it close to my face. Quickly and without warning I stick it inside of my mouth and begin to suck on it. Tears roll down my cheeks. Salty, wet tears roll down my face. I can feel my teeth lightly pulling, and I wish.

I wish for an *Abuelita* in this time of plague.
I wish for an *Abuelita* in this time of loss.
I wish for an *Abuelita* in this time of sorrow.
I wish for an *Abuelita* in this time of mourning.

I wish for an *Abuelita* in this time of shame.

I heal myself.

I heal myself with primitive Latino first aid.


## A Mu-Mu Approaches

*Luis walks over and stands behind a table. On the table there are two large boxes of "family size" Hostess Twinkies. He is dressed in a black slip. He picks up one of the boxes of Twinkies and opens it. He slowly turns over the box as the Twinkies fall on the table. He picks up one, opens it up and shows it to the audience. He puts the entire Twinkie in his mouth and eats it. Luis begins to eat all of the Twinkies on the table as a voice-over of his voice begins to play. Voice over:*

My father says that when he first came to this country that there wasn't enough. That's why he married the Mu-Mu. Hips as wide as a river, she was abundance personified. As the years wore on, this was the role that the Mu-Mu reflected: quantity and prosperity. The Mu-Mu informed us of our wealth and kept hidden all traces of our poverty. The Mu-Mu gave us hope and security.

And the Mu-Mu embarrassed us. It seems that the Mu-Mu was interested in every aspect of our American lives. From parent-teacher conferences to Boy Scout outings and altar boy affairs. The Mu-Mu was always there. There to remind us of how good a life we had in *Los Estados Unidos*.

Once, a strange man walked into the Mu-Mu's house and took the only television we had, a small portable in the living room. The Mu-Mu grabbed my brother's pee-wee league baseball bat and walked down to the corner of Pico and Union with slippers and curlers in her hair, *endiablada* and cursing. The Mu-Mu was seen minutes later, curlerless, panting a heavy breath, smiling the devil's smile and holding the portable television in hand. Swinging the pee-wee league baseball bat, the Mu-Mu whistled a happy tune while a robber's blood dripped off the bat and onto the downtown pavement. The Mu-Mu was serious, *gerl*.

Years later, the Mu-Mu's husband assimilated and decided that the Mu-Mu was too abundant. That the hips of Mexico were the hips of the past. The Mu-Mu should reflect a more American point of view. The Mu-Mu of Mexico was no longer desirable. The Mu-Mu of Mexico was holding us back. The Mu-Mu of Mexico was too big, too wide, too fat, too much. Too much for our new American sensibility.

This sudden shift in border nationalities threw the Mu-Mu into a deep and dark depression. The Mu-Mu began to wear darker shades of colors. Eventually giving up patterns altogether. The Mu-Mu began to dream of a Mexico of visions: a body wide as a river and a view of the world gleamed from novela watching.

The Mu-Mu attempted suicide courtesy of Hostess Manufacturing. Kitchen cabinets, sewing rooms and garages carefully concealed packages and boxes filled with cupcakes, Sno-balls, lemon pies, doughnuts and Ho-Hos. The secret bakery was never mentioned.

Sometimes, late at night, far from the breast of the Mu-Mu, the nightmare that is the Mexico of my youth haunts me. I clear the kitchen of all traces of my bicultural history: the Mexican novela and a sweetener called America. The nightmares continue. A Mu-Mu approaches.

*(Luis finishes eating the Twinkies. The audience can hear his heavy breathing. Luis swallows the last of the Twinkies. He staggers off the stage. The lights slowly dim on the empty Twinkie box.)*


## Bachelor Party

*Luis appears on stage with an "assistant" that he has recruited from the audience. They bring out a table. On the table there is a loaf of bread, a bottle of tequila, a shot glass, a pack of condoms, a glass with water and Alka Seltzer. Luis picks up his text from the table and begins to read it while the assistant pulls apart the bread and gives small pieces of it to Luis, who eats it.*

The first time I slept with a woman was in 1979.
I was seventeen and already "out,"
But to the guys of my Pico-Union neighborhood in downtown Los Angeles,
It was just a matter of the one good experience.

*(Luis continues to eat the bread while trying to read his text.)*

The consummation happened by default.
My childhood neighbor,
Rafas Rincon,
was getting married and it was up to us,
the neighborhood boys,
to put together a bachelor party
to beat all bachelor parties.
There we all were,
The Jose Garcias
The Raul Chaveses
The Elias Martinezes
The Efraim Rodriguezes,
just like when we were in kindergarten.
Just like when we were in Explorer Scouts.

Just like when we were altar boys
at Immaculate Conception Parish.

*(Luis eats more bread.)*

I was in charge of the stripper.
My dad rented a Masonic Temple hall on Figueroa
next to the Mexican Alcoholics Anonymous storefront,
which we, of course, called *Áh-Áh.*

I found a stripper in the yellow pages.
Where else?
She cost a hundred and fifty dollars.
Her name was Tiffany Amber.
I swear.
I chose her because the company's byline was:
"Nasty As You Want Her to Be!"

That night was a special night for all of us.
You could say that it was our parting of the ways.
Everyone knew it. But no one said it.
You stay in Pico-Union and you work the factories.
We were the children of assembly line immigrants,
but we wanted more.

Rafas looked beautiful that night.
All *Mexicano* with his caramel-colored skin and that mole on his cheek.
And God, how he wore those 1970s Izod shirts so well.
He was Rafas.
The closest thing we had to a barrio hopeful.
He had just started UCLA and joined the rowing team.
The trail of muscle and hair on his arms said it all.

Quique Pastor got the idea for the bread.
He said it would soak up most of the liquor.
So, we all got there half an hour early to get the yeast going.

*(The assistant opens the bottle of tequila and pours it into the shot glass. Every time the assistant fills the shot glass, Luis slams it on the table and drinks it. He begins to get very drunk, very fast, and continues trying to finish his text.)*

When the stripper arrived,
she was everything we thought a Tiffany Amber should be:
big, fake, California tits,
a peroxide blond in dolphin shorts
and a tube top with tie-dyed palm trees.
It was too much.

We were too young,
too Mexican.
I wanted to pray with her.

*(Luis takes another shot of tequila.)*

And the music?
Oh, the music,
Donna Summer's "Four Seasons of Love."
Hey, I was gay. I noticed the music.

*(Luis takes another shot of tequila.)*

It all started innocently enough.
Tiffany Amber took off her clothes so fast,
like they had ants on them, or something.
For five dollars, she squirted whip cream on her breasts
and we got to lick it off.
She walked down an aisle of horny teenagers
with sweaty hands nervously holding five-dollar bills,
as we licked, licked, licked.
She made a hundred dollars easily.

*(Luis takes another shot of tequila.)*

Then there was a game called "Shoot the Kitty"
where Tiffany Amber lay on the floor
as she lifted her legs and spread them.
We crumpled up ten-dollar bills and aimed them
in the general, drunken, pussy area.
She made another two hundred dollars.

I don't know.
It was fabulous.
It was decadent.
It was disgusting, and I was down a hundred bucks.
I was gay and learning all about
what it meant to be straight by the minute.

*(Luis takes another shot of tequila.)*

What can I say?
The night went on.
The Tiffany Amber show continued on.

*(Luis takes another shot of tequila.)*

Extreme Exposure

We lay on the floor with rolled up twenty-dollar bills in our mouths,
while Tiffany Amber straddled our faces
and used some amazing muscle control
to pick up another three hundred dollars
off of us drunken fools.

*(Luis takes another shot of tequila.)*

It was now A.M.
I cried.
We sang Mexican *rancheras*
with our arms around each others' shoulders.
We looked like short versions of our fathers.
We pulled together the rest of our resources, $324,
towards what we assumed was the obligatory
Groom's-last-screw-with-a-stripper-before-the-wedding-the-next-day.
But it was not to be.

*(Luis takes another shot of tequila.)*

That day, Rafas Rincon,
our barrio hopeful,
celebrated the act of reconciliation confession
at Immaculate Conception Parish.
There would be no time to reconfess
before the wedding
if he went to bed with a stripper now.
He couldn't go through with it.

*(Luis takes another shot of tequila.)*

Everyone looked at me.
The pride of Pico-Union.
It wasn't just a fuck,
it was a neighborhood's reputation at stake.
It was civic duty.
It was peer pressure.
The guys were hoo-hoo-hooing me.
I didn't want to fuck Tiffany Amber,
I wanted to do her hair.

*(Luis takes another shot of tequila.)*

Rafas took me aside.
He handed me a condom and told me it was time to grow up.
I cried drunken tears.
I wanted boyhood.

I wanted Boy Scout jamborees.
I wanted roller derby.
I wanted G.I. Joe.
I wanted midget wrestling on cable.

*(Luis takes another drink and finishes the bottle. The assistant pulls out the secret second bottle, opens it and begins to pour.)*

Rafas smiled a drunken, sweet smile
as he leaned forward
and kissed me on the lips.
His calloused UCLA row team hands
slowly rubbed the back of my neck.

*(Luis takes another shot of tequila.)*

I had no choice . . .

*(Luis takes another shot of tequila.)*

Tiffany Amber was great.
Patient and instructional.
Mostly, I got through it with the memory of
Rafas's kiss
and the electricity of his hand
on the back of my neck.

*(Luis takes another shot of tequila.)*

And the song.
Oh my God, Donna Summer's
"Love to Love You Baby."
Sing it with me, won't you?

*(The audience is encouraged and begins to sing "Love to Love You Baby." They continue throughout the rest of the piece.)*

> Ooh, love to love you baby,
> ooh, love to love you baby.

And my ten minutes with Amber went something like this.

*(Luis stops drinking tequila. He opens the condoms while the assistant opens the Alka Seltzer tablets. The assistant puts the tablets in the glass filled with water and Luis puts the condom on the glass. The carbonation fills the glass and the condom expands and eventually "takes off" from the glass. Hopefully, it takes flight toward the audience. The lights fade. Luis is drunk and pathetic. The assistant wanders off. Lights out.)*

John Leguizamo

**Introduction** by Gregory Mosher

The Goodman Studio is a 135 seat theatre with a remarkable history. Among the many playwrights who have premiered work there are David Mamet, David Rabe, Spalding Gray, Elaine May and Tennessee Williams, whose final play opened there shortly before he died.

I was lost in memories of Tennessee Williams while waiting for an early performance of John Leguizamo's new play *Freak*. My reverie was interrupted by an explosion of hip-hop, while a young fellow dressed in camouflage pants and a Knicks jersey tore up the aisle and onto the stage. Two hilarious, intimate, scatological and courageous hours later, John waved good-bye to a stunned and delighted audience. The first thing that occurred to me was that Tennessee would have loved it. It had that rarest of theatrical qualities—life.

My second thought was that I had to invade backstage, where John was conferring with director David Bar Katz, and ask them if they would like to do the show on Broadway.

Three venues, ten months and a billion rewrites later, *Freak* opened at the Cort Theatre and played twenty-four sold-out weeks to a thrillingly young audience, most of whom were seeing their first Broadway show.    **305**

Like his great predecessor Richard Pryor, there is just no place John won't go, and no personal disaster out of which he can't get a laugh. But John had more than a comedy act in mind, so for almost a year, *Freak* struggled to find itself as a *play*. Plays sustain an audience's attention by asking a question (Can Oedipus lift the curse on Thebes? Will Louie ever get laid?) and working out that question through meticulously structured conflict. John (and David) had to find that story in a surfeit of good material. But once a story—John's liberation from his father—existed, the episodes could be hung on that clothesline.

For instance, John's expedition to lose his virginity at a Kentucky Fried Chicken restaurant is a hilarious anecdote and, as you are about to see, stands on its own. It works as a scene in a play because he suffers the indignity to prove something to his father. If you're a tragic genius like Eugene O'Neill, breaking free of your old man becomes *Long Day's Journey into Night*. If you're a comic genius like John, out pops *Freak*. The obsession with dramatic form was rewarded when the show received Tony Award nominations not only for Best Actor, but for Best Play.

John plays forty-nine characters in *Freak*. They do not appear sequentially, as in his earlier pieces *Mambo Mouth* and *Spic-O-Rama;* instead he plays scenes with five or six characters onstage *together at the same time*. This rather astonishing illusion began with instantly recognizable voices, bodies and psyches. Then John and David created, with a choreographic ingenuity that Jerome Robbins would have envied, a moving physical presence for each character—a presence we sensed without actually seeing. The epitome of this wizardry was the scene in which John sat on a box within the audience while he—and we—watched an imagined scene from *A Chorus Line* taking place on an empty stage: "There was a Latin person in the show. And she didn't have a gun or hypodermic needle in her hand and she wasn't a hooker or a maid and she wasn't servicing anybody so it was hard to tell if she was Latin, and everybody's respecting her and admiring her . . . I was lost in this amazing moment, singing along as loud as I could."

I've never asked John what was "true" in *Freak*. It's not important, and even John probably doesn't know anymore. I do know that John's father, after not speaking to him for years, surprised him by coming to see the show late in the Broadway run. When John emerged from the stage door, his father greeted him with, "How could you do that to *me*?" John, startled and shaken, said, "How could you do that to *me*?" And for the next three hours they drove together, weeping and raging, through rainy New York streets before embracing in hard-earned reunion.

As Samuel Beckett said, "There's nothing funnier than unhappiness."

**Gregory Mosher** is a director and producer. He has presented new work by such writers as Samuel Beckett, Tennessee Williams, David Mamet and Spalding Gray. He produced *Freak*, with Arielle Tepper and Bill Haber, on Broadway.

## from **Freak**

Now our apartment was so puny it wished it were a project. It was a seventies nightmare; our walls were avocado green with brown linoleum and a nuclear orange shag rug; we were trying to re-create the papaya of our tropix and those seventies lamps that hung like an alien eyeball staring at us. And the centerpiece, the pièce de résistance of this mess, was our TV, my dad's pride and joy. It was sacred to him, because my pops could Latinize everybody in America; we would let the screen get real dusty so that everybody looked nice and dark and Spanish. And my father was the only one allowed to watch TV, 'cause he thought the more you watch it, the more you wear it out. Dad was operating under some kind of third-world logic.

He'd say, "Don't use my television and don't sit on my furniture unless we have important guests. Use the floor for sitting and the kitchen sink for eating. And we're not gonna buy any more food if you keep eating it! Food, I repeat, is for the guests and the animals. And I just brushed the dogs, so don't pet 'em! And get the hell off the rug, I just vacuumed it. And stop sucking up all my oxygen—I'm breathing it."

My brother and I would be like, "Okay, Dad, okay."

I was a prisoner in my own house. I felt like . . . Anne Frank. Except she only had Nazis to deal with. And every time my father had something important to say, the subway would go by. And it wouldn't have been a problem, but we shared a wall with the number 7 Train.

He'd start lecturing us, "I'm only gonna say this once. The most important thing I want you to do is . . ." and sure enough the train would roar by, drowning him out ". . . or I'm gonna kick your ass!"

Paralyzed with fear, I'd say, "Okay, Dad—no problem."

But as soon as my father was out of the house, my brother Poochie and I would be like a Navy SEAL operation. "Now, Poochie," I'd say, "it's 1800 hours, and the *Prince of Darkness* will be . . ."

Poochie freaked out. "Prince of Darkness? You didn't tell me nuttin' about no Price of Darkness. Na-ah, I'm not listening. Mamaku mamasa mama mamakusa . . ." He put his hands over his ears and closed his eyes.

"Poochie," I'd have to yell, "the Prince of Darkness is the man you know as Dad. Now you go put the bubble wrap under the rug so when Dad comes through the hall we'll hear him. Now we're punishment-proof. We outsmarted that ignor-anus! What a maroon! What a sucker-butt! Ha ha! *Ungawa ungawa, Dad's away for two hours. A beep beep, we're TV freaks. Get stupid.* Poochie, turn the TV on." Then we'd settle down for a TV frenzy—*Spiderman, Underdog, Gigantor* the space robot. Everything was great until I messed with the antenna. I'd be swinging around in time to the *Spiderman* theme when suddenly . . . SNAP! The blood drained out of my body and into the ground and back to Latin America. "Poochie, I broke the antenna!"

"And just then, "John!" Luckily it was just my moms.

"Mom. Why are you climbing in through the window?" I wondered.

"The rent is due. What the hell are you doing? You're sitting in the furnitura. You're eating the food. Ay, dios mio, you broke the antenna!! Oh my God! I'm looking into the face of a dead boy." Moms had a knack for calming me down.

"Mom, use me for cruel animal experimentation, sell me to child pornographers, but don't let him get his hands on me!!!" I begged, throwing myself around her legs.

"No, don't, don't. I'll miss you. But now I must distance myself," she said. "Come, Poochie, you're an only child now. Ciao. Get off me, John. Get off."

Then all of a sudden we hear the sound of snapping bubble wrap and Pop's voice, cursing, "Coño, qué es toda esta mierda de bubble wrap, hijo de puta."

So I'm blowing and fanning the TV 'cause my pops would feel it for heat. And my moms goes into rescue mode, "I'll take care of your father," she whispered to me as Pops came in. "Fausto, you look so ultra sexy. You look so sexy. Yes, you do. Let's have a game of one-on-one?" Moms flashed a breast at my father, pulling out all the stops. "You and me. One-on-one."

But my father wasn't taking the bait. "Woman, put that nipple away. I just wanna watch my television. C'mon fellas."

My moms tried another approach. "Good, good. Okay, then, why don't you go downstairs and play some pool. Hmm? Okay? Play some pool?"

God bless my moms. We didn't have a downstairs.

Pops turned on the TV. "I said no, woman. What the hell's all that static. I can't tell Sonny from Cher."

"I'll fix it! I'll fix it!" I offered, right away. So I moved the good piece of antenna for all I was worth. "Like this, Dad? Or this? Here?"

"Move the other one!" Pops barked.

So I pretended to move the broken antenna. *Trompe l'oeil*. I frantically shifted my body around while holding the broken antenna in place. "There? Like so? Perfect? I was using up all my available cuteness.

"Move away from that television," Pops ordered.

"Okay, I am away," I said, inching over a bit.

"Get the hell out of the room, you little shit!" Pops yelled. I stayed in the same place but moon-walked.

"Okay, I'm leaving the room, the neighborhood . . ." and as I head for the door, I trip. He sees the antenna came off in my hand. "It's a spear and I'm a hunter?" I offer meekly. I know what's coming next.

My pops field-goals me with a kick across the room. Luckily, the nice hard brick wall broke my fall. And my head opened up like a piñata. "Dad, look at the pretty candy," I cooed. Then everything went black. And as I was waiting to die, my life started flashing before me. Yachting on the Cape, debutante orgies at Vassar, Monet sunsets on the Riviera. Wait a minute—that's not my life. And I felt my soul leave my body and hover over, and I looked down and—"damn, why didn't anybody tell me I had such a flat face," and I sailed out the window toward the light higher and higher, and I remembered my comix and how Spiderman once said to Ironman that "to escape the pain, one must move toward the pain." And my soul thought, "Fuck that noise!" and sprinted the hell outta the house, and into the sky . . . and as I flew closer to the light, I saw a divine being, a beautiful woman standing there naked, her pert breasts glistening in the moon beams, and I wanted to suckle the breasts of all nurturing unconditional loves, and her arms were outstretched, beckoning me toward her . . . and just when I was about to touch her, I caught a whiff of my favorite Chino-Latino restaurant, shrimp fried rice and platano maduro, and suddenly I wanted to live. If only for the plantanos, I wanted to live and—*boom*, I was back in my body with all this new-found wisdom. The first words out of my mouth said it all:

"Poochie broke the antenna."

Poor, slow, chubby Poochie. I watched him go off screaming and yelling, "No! Don't! Anything but that. I'm your favorite. Remember, Dad?" And I just stood there watching, the only brother I had, beaten senseless with the antenna, and all I could think was, "Thank God it's not me." But I don't wanna leave you with a bad impression of my pops. 'Cause he wasn't always this brutal. No, sometimes he drank, too.

———

So we had to move again. Now as much as the Irish and the Italians hated me, I finally found a girl who loved me, and my grandfather said to me, "John, you have three loves in your life. Don't waste them. Now pull the plug." I knew she was going to be the first one. She was my ebony princess, my Nubian bucket of love, my Africanus romanticus. She was black and her pops was a Black Muslim, so when it finally came time to meet him, I thought, This guy might be my future father-in-law. I came over in my best Elijah Muhammad bow tie and said, as nerdily as I could, "Hello sir, I'm here to pick your daughter up for a date."

Her black pops met me at the door, sucking on his teeth and popping out his cheek. "You don't fool me, boy. You don't look like a Muslim with that bow tie—you look like Pee-Wee Herman, and when I look at your white skin I wanna kill you."

"But I'm not white, sir, I'm a Latino."

"Well, then I definitely don't wanna get caught up in an illegal-alien Mexican situation. I heard about you Mexicans, buying up all the Cabbage Patch dolls just to get the birth certificates," he said.

So I would have to sneak up to her window at night to avoid her pops, and I'd stand there and profess my undying love. "I love you, Yashica."

"What did you say?!" she yelled.

She lived on the fifty-eighth floor.

"I'll love you forever!!" I screamed again.

Then the neighbors called out, "Yeah, we love you, too—now shut the fuck up and go to sleep." So she met me at the service elevator, then snuck me into her room. And it was so romantic—we put on some Al Green, she turned on the black light, we took off article after article of clothing till we were in our underwear only and I was about to finally lose my virginity. I looked at my beautiful black Venus. She looked at me.

Then she said, "Oh, my God, you are the whitest motherfucker I ever saw. You glow in the dark."

"I love you, Yashica," I responded.

"Yeah, whatever. You don't get it, Translucent Man. Oh, my God—turn around for a second. I can see your intestines, like a guppy. I can tell what you had for lunch. Hold on, hold on, I want my sister to see your blue, veiny ass, guppy boy. Shanté, Shanté, come here, girl."

———

With Dad unavailable, my moms had to take up the slack. And times were tight—every day of the month we ate Shake 'n' Bake. Right out of the box. We couldn't afford the chicken. When they came out with Shake 'n' Bake Barbecue, it was a fucking national holiday in my house. And since my moms was working so much, my uncle Sanny became our surrogate moms. Now, my uncle Sanny was a little unconventional. He was what you'd call a triple threat: Latin, gay and deaf. And he was so wise he was dubbed the Einstein of Jackson Heights.

"*Ay, fo,*" Sanny exclaimed. "I know things even God doesn't know! *Ay, puta, que escándalo, me jodí.* At Christmas I always made a lousy Santa. Instead of filling the stockings, I was always trying them on, *Ay, fo!* Poof, bad thoughts be gone. *Ay, que escándalo, me jodí, la loca dame huevo.*"

I loved him and I told him so. "I wanna grow up and be just like you, uncle Sanny, except for the liking men part."

"I know your father doesn't respect me," Sanny said, "but that's bullshit. Because feature this: many highly respectable individuals of ancient and modern times have been homosexuals: Plato, Michelangelo, Disney. Oops, I outed him. *Que escándalo, lo jodí.*"

Just 'cause we were poor didn't mean we didn't get culture. 'Cause one day my uncle Sanny took us to Broadway, The Great White Way. He finessed this technique he coined "Second Acting." First we mixed in with the intermission smokers and then we tried to slip into the theatre undetected to catch the second act.

"John, Poochie, here, smoke these," uncle Sanny said. "Uh-uh-uh, menthol for you, Poochie. You're only twelve. No, they're not children, they're midgets."

So with stolen programs in hand we waited for everyone to sit down, then we ran down the aisles and grabbed the empty seats.

I wasn't sitting with anyone I knew and I'm scared of being clocked and I'm peeping at this ridiculous musical *Chorus Line* thing when I hear somebody called Morales on stage. There was a Latin person in the show. And she didn't have a gun or hypodermic needle in her hand and she wasn't a hooker or a maid and she wasn't servicing anybody so it was hard to tell if she was Latin, and everybody's respecting her and admiring her . . . I was lost in this amazing moment, singing along as loud as I could. Then I felt a hand grab me and I was yanked up out of my seat by one of those Pilgrim ladies, and beat with the flashlight. My brother got caught, too, 'cause he was still smoking his Kools, and Sanny got busted, 'cause he was lip-synching along too loudly. And I'm still like, "She's singing to me, she's singing to me!" And uncle Sanny's yelling, "Shut the hell up and run! Run!" And that's how I got culture.

———

So I was still a virgin. So for my sixteenth birthday, Dad, seeing his son's miserably failed attempts at becoming a man, decided to give nature a little push.

He got the car out and loaded us in. "Hey, John, Poochie, get in back." My dad suddenly got serious. "John, you know since the average pinga is six inches and the average vaginga is eight inches, there are two miles of unused vaginga in New York City and I'm gonna find some for you. Okay, here we are. Poochie, wait in the car."

"Kentucky Fried Chicken. How's the Colonel gonna make me a man?" I wondered.

"Not the Colonel, stupid. It's a lady who works here. She fries/batters chickens by day and chokes chickens by night."

And the next thing I know I'm in the back of the Kentucky Fried Chicken and this mad, fine, stout German lady in her late forties comes out. "Your swarthy looks are so dark and I feel sorry for you, so I will fuck you. I'll think of it as war reparations."

So she has me over the fryer and we're sucking face. Then she reaches down and touches my Thing. It was the first time someone other than me had touched it, so as you can imagine, my Thing's buggin' out.

I can hear it talking to me. "Uh, Johnny, what's she doing?"

"Just relax. We're getting some," I try to reassure my Thing.

"Uh, she's being a little rough—she's pulling, Johnny!"

"She's German. Now will you shut up?!!"

My Thing is not giving up. "Johnny, can't you just do it? I like how you do it. You know where to touch, what I like . . . What I need . . ."

Then she put the whole thing in her mouth.

Suddenly, my Thing is singing a different tune. "Ooh! Why didn't you ever do this?"

I told him, "I couldn't reach!"

Now, you know how people always say that time distorts memory. Details change. Exaggeration occurs with the retelling. But not in this case. Before I could think, she'd stripped down and put my hand on her little vertical smile. Her coochie was a failed experiment from *The Island of Dr. Moreau.* Now I'm man enough to admit that I've been confused about female genitalia. You never know what you're gonna get. You're always in dark light. And you always have to pretend to know what you're doing, so you never really get a good look. If I saw one coming at me in the light of day I'd probably take a snow shovel to it. Then she does the international cunnilingus sign and coaches me.

"It's like a flower. You have to unravel it."

So with the courage of Jacques Cousteau on his last expedition, I started to unravel and unravel and unravel her huge coochie lips. It was like Dumbo. If she could flap them she would be able to fly out of the room and back to Germany. When I opened it all, it made a Tupperware burp.

And then my Thing, the little general, gets scared and starts talking to me again. "No. Hell no. I'm not going in there. I like the mouth."

But I didn't want to disappoint my pops, so I had to sacrifice the little general. In he went. I was like a porn star: "You like that street dick. That nasty Latin seed." So I started working her right in the fried chicken batter, this way and that way, up and down. And she's like, "No, over *here*, Honey." "Oh, I'm sorry. It's my first time," I explained. Breasts and thighs are flying up in the air—not hers, the chickens'. We're in a cloud of flour. And finally in her moment of orgasm, a stream flew out of her. I was soaking. Marinated in her juices.

"Hey, did you just . . . No, you didn't just . . . did you? I can't believe what I'm gonna say. Did you just pee on me?" I asked.

"No, it's the way I come. It's another gift. See, my urethra is connected to my clitoris, and when my pubogeneous muscles contract . . ."

"You share too much, lady," I interrupted. "I just want to cuddle."

But my time was up, so she went over to the window, grabbed a coochie lip in each hand, and jumped. She flew away into the night like a giant pink bat. 'Bye, Mothra.

When I came out to the car, Pops was all questions. "How did you do? Give her the eighth ingredient, hijo?"

"Yeah, I did it!"

"But how do I know? I need proof," Pops persisted.

"Proof? Proof?" I wrang my shirt out and wiggled my toes, which made a squishy sound. "There's your proof."

"That's my boy!" Pops beamed. "Now we've shared this!"

**Josh Kornbluth**

## Introduction by Scott Rosenberg

I first encountered Josh Kornbluth's working style when we were collaborators on a zero-budget, radio variety show in Boston called *The Urban Happiness Radio Hour*. The theory was that Josh would devise some skits, and we'd rehearse them before the live show's broadcast. But Josh usually wound up writing the scripts at the last possible minute before air time. Back then, I thought this was Josh's calculated ploy to get fresh readings and spontaneous performances out of his troupe. Later, as we became closer friends, I understood that he just has a hard time putting words to paper, and a boundless capacity for procrastination.

When I first met Josh in the early 1980s, he was a TV critic with a reputation at the *Boston Phoenix* for possessing a writer's block of Hoover Dam proportions. Just a few years later, Josh was writing with seemingly effortless profligacy, producing one marvelous full-length monologue after another. Something had happened to him on the journey from TV reviewing to the solo performer's stage: by connecting with a live audience, he'd found a way to uncork his voice.

I'm not talking here about how the experience of standing in front of an audience affects artists' delivery and helps them ground their work. "Being in the moment" is everywhere the goal of meditators, athletes and method actors alike. But, outside of jazz clubs, there aren't many artists who can actually create ambitious original material the way Josh does: live, in public, from scratch.

When Josh delivers his stories of growing up Communist in New York City; coming to terms with a loving but maddening father; apprenticing in math at Princeton or flailing through life as a legal temp in San Francisco; he weaves comic threads and serious themes through the narratives with a casual expertise. He loves to digress, to charge down some side alley that leaves you wondering, How can he ever find his way back to the central story? Each time, right at the moment you've concluded he's completely off the rails, he turns a corner that puts him back on track, but with some new dimension layered on the yarn. Like the great farceurs of the nineteenth century, he ends his shows by tying up every loose end with a precision that's satisfying but never pat.

It had never seemed possible to me that such disciplined writing could take place on stage, "in the moment," but that is how Josh creates: he develops each new monologue in workshops that set out with some general theme and gradually coalesce into polished works. The funny thing is—and this is where the sheer uniqueness of Josh's talent lies—the tales told in these embryonic improvisatory shows are typically just as entertainingly intricate as the final product. The dance of digression and return isn't entirely the result of forethought and rewrites; it seems to commence the moment Josh and audience collide.

Kornbluth is not a sketch artist; the long form—ninety minutes or more of a single narrative, laden with ironic wordplay—has always been his home. And his body of work—from *Red Diaper Baby* and *Haiku Tunnel* to *The Mathematics of Change, Ben Franklin: Unplugged* and the forthcoming *Oboe Minus One*—has always been autobiographical at the core, though his later shows venture more confidently into wider realms, like calculus or the nature of historical research. With such a focus, charges of narcissism always lie in wait: the great fault of the narcissistic solo performer is to lose sight of the audience's needs, and behave as though every traumatic hangnail must be lovingly chronicled for the crowd. But Josh's creative method ruthlessly weeds out material that's too self-indulgent to connect with listeners; and his unquenchable, self-aware humor transforms even mundane personal details into unexpectedly illuminating epiphanies.

Kornbluth is a big, exuberant guy who always seems to have a surplus of stories and words inside himself, lined up and ready for the light of the stage. There's really no substitute for seeing him live—with great performers, there never is—but reading his words will at least offer a taste of his unusual talent.

**Scott Rosenberg**, now senior editor at *Salon* (www.salonmagazine.com), was the *San Francisco Examiner*'s theatre critic from 1986 to 1992. He won the George Jean Nathan Award for Dramatic Criticism in 1989, and has worked sporadically and enjoyably with Josh Kornbluth over the years on various projects.

# from **Red Diaper Baby**

My father, Paul Kornbluth, was a Communist. He believed there was going to be a violent Communist revolution in this country—and that I was going to lead it. Just so you can get a sense of the pressure.

And anything my father told me I'd believe, because my father was such a physically magnificent man: he was big, and he had this great big potbelly—not a wiggly-jiggly, Social Democratic potbelly; a firm, Communist potbelly. You bopped it, it would bop you back. It was *strong*.

And he had powerful legs, from running track at the City College of New York. And he had these beefy arms. And he was naked—virtually all the time; naked in the apartment. And all over his body he had these patches of talcum powder—you know, Johnson's Baby Powder—I guess because he was a big man and he would chafe. Especially around his private parts.

And he had me on the weekends. I would have loved to have slept in late on the weekends, but I couldn't because my father wouldn't let me. He would wake me up.

This is how he'd wake me up: he'd come bursting into my room and then he'd stop in the doorway; and when he stopped, the talcum powder would come bouncing off of his balls—it was like the entrance of a great magician. And then he'd come running up to my bed, and looming over me he'd sing:

Arise, ye prisoner of starvation!
Arise, ye wretched of the earth!

I didn't know that was the "Internationale"; I didn't know that was the international Communist anthem. I thought it was my own personal wake-up song.

Check it out: "Arise, ye prisoner of starvation"—it's time for breakfast. "Arise, ye wretched of the earth"—it's five o'clock in the morning and I'm being woken up!

And if I didn't show the proper signs of life right away, my father would lean down over me—and his long, graying hair would straggle down, his beard would flutter down into my nose—and he'd yell, "Wake up, Little Fucker! Wake up, Little Fucker!"

That was his nickname for me: Little Fucker. Nothing at all pejorative about it, as far as my father was concerned. For my dad, calling me "Little Fucker" was like calling me "Junior" . . . "Beloved Little One" . . . "Little Fucker."

I knew from an early age that one day I must grow up and become . . . a Big Fucker. And I assumed that that would be around the time that I would lead the Revolution. Because my dad had told me over and over that all the great revolutionaries were also great fuckers.

But for now I was just lying there in my bed, my father looming over me with his—to me—enormous penis . . . swinging around, spewing smoke, powder, whatever . . . while I just had this little, six-year-old . . . training penis, if you will.

"Little Fucker." I didn't realize at the time that my father had his own language—not only his own English, but his own Yiddish. I used to think it was real Yiddish, but then my mom would say, "That's not Yiddish. What your father speaks is not Yiddish. I went to Yiddish school in Bensonhurst—and what your father speaks is not Yiddish."

I'd say, "You mean, *ouska* is not—"

"No. There's an *oyska*, but there's no *ouska* . . ."

Well, in my father's Yiddish, there was a term *ouska. Ouska* was a prefix, meaning "a lot of," "very"—as in, "I am *ouska*-cold, my son!"

I'd say, "Of course you're ouska-cold, Dad; you're ouska-naked. The window is ouska-open."

As it would be in the kitchen, where we'd go for breakfast. Dad and I would sit around the kitchen table having hard-boiled eggs (my father, not a soft-boiled kind of guy). And never little eggs: when Dad went shopping for eggs, he always got ouska-jumbo-large-size eggs, so we would not want for eggs. And we would smear on our eggs, in my father's language, "salad dressing"—meaning mayonnaise. And we'd drink juice —apple juice, orange juice . . .

And Dad would regale me with his stories of organizing in the South with the Henry Wallace campaign. (That's *Henry* Wallace. *Henry.* Okay?) And he'd drill me over and over in the catechisms of our faith— of Communism. Like how society has been driven from one stage to the next, driven inexorably by the forces of dialectical materialism, until . . .

I sense I'm covering old ground. But just to review: according to Marx and Engels—and my dad—the first human society was Primitive Communalism: everyone's just kind of dancing around, like at a Grateful Dead concert.

The next stage after Primitive Communalism was Slavery—which must have been a bummer of a transition.

Then from Slavery to Feudalism, and from Feudalism . . . Well, we've learned from history that it's very important after Feudalism to stop in Capitalism before moving on to Socialism. Very important to stop in Capitalism. Because that's where you get your appliances.

So you stop in Capitalism, you get your stuff, and *then* you move on to Socialism, and finally to Communism—and you're back at the concert.

After breakfast, me and my dad would move from the kitchen into the living room—although when I say "kitchen" and "living room," I'm being euphemistic. There was one basic room—except for my bedroom: Dad always insisted that I have my own bedroom for my privacy—he'd just come bursting in at any moment. But aside from my bedroom, there was just one basic room. That's because when my father moved into an apartment, the first thing he'd do is he'd knock down all the walls. I don't mean that metaphorically; he'd *knock down* all the walls.

The first time he did this, we had to move—right away. Because we lived on the first floor, and the building came . . . ouska-down.

So we moved into the next building—same landlord, who insisted on giving my dad a lecture on the crucial architectural concept of the supporting wall. That's the wall you must not knock down.

So my dad went knocking around with his hammer to find the one wall that wasn't hollow, left that wall up, knocked down all the other walls. And all along the external walls of our kitchen-cum-bathroom-cum-living-room-cum-dining-room area were posters of our heroes, our gods: W. E. B. Du Bois, Malcolm X, Dr. King, Ho Chi Minh, Bertolt Brecht, Emma Goldman . . . And then, at the end of all these posters: my height chart. See how the Little Fucker measures up.

And then we'd go outside for our walks. When we went outside, my father—in his one true concession to society—would put on clothing. This is back in '65, when I was about six years old. Dad wore this one-piece, bright orange jumpsuit—a parachute outfit—with a broad collar and a big zipper with a peace symbol pull-thing that would seal in the freshness of the powder.

Being Communists, we had songs associated with every activity. But me and Dad didn't just have generic walking songs; we had specific going-up-the-hill songs, specific going-down-the-hill songs.

We had learned our biggest going-up-the-hill song off an album by Paul Robeson, a great Jewish folksinger. It was a record my dad had borrowed from the public library, and then—as a revolutionary act—refused to return. (And my mom was a librarian . . .)

Going up the hill, me and my dad would sing:

> *Ey yuch nyem*
> *Ey yuch nyem*
> *O Volga, Volga*
> *Ey yuch nyem.*

Very hard to walk fast while singing "*Ey yuch nyem*."

A lot easier on our going-down-the-hill song, which we had learned off an album by Doc Watson—a great Jewish folksinger from the Appalachians (another record that my dad had liberated from the library).

Going down the hill, me and my dad would sing:

> As I go down in the valley to pray
> Studying—

—as we went down in the valley to pray on East Seventh Street, between C and D—

> As I go down in the valley to pray
> Studying about that good old way
> And who shall wear the robe and crown
> Good Lord, show me the way.

My father couldn't hear me. He thought I wasn't singing. He didn't connect it with the fact that he was singing so ouska-loud he was drowning me out. So periodically he'd turn to me on the sidewalk and go, "Sing louder, my son—I can't hear you!"

> Oh, fathers, let's go down
> Let's go down, come on down.
> Oh, fathers, let's go down
> Down in the valley to pray.

"Try singing even louder, my son—and perhaps with more . . . melodic invention."

> Come on, fathers, let's go *down*!
> Down in the valley to pra-a-a-ay . . . to pray-yee!

"And a child shall lead them!" my dad would say, and then we'd hit the flatlands of Manhattan, as we continued north on our walks towards Herald Square. And along the flatlands we'd sing what, for us, were "flat" songs—rounds—which were easier for me, more even between the two singers. And along the flatlands we would stop at the bodega to pick up supplies, and we'd stop at the pharmacy to get Dad's pills—and we'd continue north along the flatlands, singing rounds like:

> Come follow, follow, follow, follow, follow, follow me.
> Whither shall I follow, follow, follow
> Whither shall I follow, follow thee?
> To the greenwood, to the greenwood
> To the greenwood, greenwood tree!

A nice, cheerful walking song—though confusing lyrically, to an urban child. "Follow thee to the greenwood tree—why? I'd much rather follow thee to, say, Chock Full O' Nuts."

Which was the kind of place we had to eat, me and Dad, because we had to live ouska-cheaply. Because my father . . .

Well, he was a schoolteacher—he was a very good schoolteacher. But my dad would get a job and be teaching his students with great passion, but at the same time he would be developing this *anger* towards his bosses: the principal, the assistant principals, the school board. And this anger at his bosses would build and build, until finally Dad couldn't take it anymore. This would take about two weeks. And at the end of those two weeks, Dad would go storming into the principal's office and yell, "Fuck you!"

Often the guy would never have seen my dad before. And he'd say, "You're fired! . . . If you work for me, you're fired!"

And then Dad would get another job, and he'd be teaching his new students with great passion but developing this anger towards his new bosses. And at the end of two weeks he would storm into his new principal's office and go, "Fuck you!"

And the new principal would go, "You're fired!"

So Dad would find another job—perhaps a little farther away from New York, as he lost his license to teach in this gradually growing radius. And at the end of two weeks at his new job:

"Fuck you!"

"You're fired!"

And another job:

"Fuck you!"

"You're fired!"

And another:

"Fuck you!"

"You're fired!"

This went on for years and years; my father never saw . . . the pattern. He never saw the cause-and-effect between "Fuck you!" and "You're fired!"

So we had to live ouska-cheaply. Which was fine with me: I loved eating at places like Chock Full. You could have a nice hot dog, maybe some coconut cake . . . then we'd continue north for further ouska-cheap adventures, like the Museum of Natural History—where at the time the admission was whatever you would care to donate. They've since changed that policy—I think because of my dad. ("Pay them a penny and not a penny more, Fucker!" "You're right, Dad! We're not gonna give in to those imperialistic paleontologists!")

We'd go running up to the dinosaur exhibit, where Dad would give me a tour. I don't think he was an expert in the field, but he did have his bright orange tour-guide outfit. "The Tyrannosaurus rex, my son—one of the largest . . . reptilian fuckers ever to walk the earth!" And other little kids would break away from their field trips and join us. The field was a lot more interesting the way my dad described it.

And then, after a weekend of this kind of ouska-fun, my dad—as the courts had mandated—had to return me to . . . my mom.

My mom, Bernice "Bunny" Selden: also Jewish, also a New Yorker, also a City College grad, also a Communist—but so different from my father in temperament. If my father was an out-there, ouska-Communist, my mom . . . *inska*.

And she had her own inska-wake-up song for me, too—and like I thought Dad had written the "Internationale" for me, I thought my mom had written *her* wake-up song for me; I only found out years later that Irving Berlin wrote it.

My mom would be getting ready to go to work at the library across the river. She'd go into the bathroom in her nightgown and come back out with her hair in a bun. Then she'd go back into the bathroom and come out . . . with *another* bun having been added, from some mysterious source. And she'd stand in my open doorway—which was easy for her to do, because for some reason she would not let me have a door. And she'd tiptoe up to my bed and she'd lean down and sing:

> Oh, how I hate to get up in the morning
> Oh, how I'd love to stay in bed
> For the hardest blow of all
> Is to hear that bugler call:
> "You gotta get up, you gotta get up,
> You gotta get up in the morning.
> You gotta get up, you gotta get up,
> You gotta get up in the morning."

A pretty nice wake-up song. Unless you know the second verse, which to me gets to a surreal level of violence that I find almost Sam Peckinpah-esque:

> Someday I'm gonna murder the bugler
> Someday you're gonna find him dead
> I'll amputate his reveille
> And stamp upon it heavily
> And spend the rest of my life in bed!

I thought she could snap at any moment. So I'd get out of bed; I didn't want my reveille amputated!

But I still didn't have that get-up-and-go that the "Internationale" gives a kid. So she'd guide me gently up from my bed and lead me into the living room and sit me down on the couch, and then—this goes back to when I was at least four or five—she had this little motherly trick she'd play to get me going in the morning: she'd serve me a tall cup of double-espresso—with whipped cream and a maraschino cherry on top, because I'm a little kid!

And I'd sit there sipping my double-espresso on the couch, beneath the half-dozen or so ceramic disks that she bought in Mexico, where she went to divorce my dad—which, by the way, was when I was six months old.

They were married for nine years, then I was born—then, when I was six months old, they divorced. From time to time I'd wonder why.

But then, a few months ago, I was reading this article in the *Village Voice* about a guy named Saul Newton, a crazed psychoanalyst who ran this psychoanalytical cult called the Sullivanians. They had a co-op on the Upper West Side. I was reading about this Saul Newton guy, and how he told his patients that the family is evil—parents are intrinsically evil, and they can only wreak havoc on their children; you must break up the family.

Reading about this guy—Saul Newton, Saul Newton, Saul Newton—and suddenly it hit me: Wait a second! My *dad's* therapist was named Saul! So I called up my mom and said, "Mom, I'm reading about this Saul Newton guy," and she said, "Yeah, that was your father's therapist."

Evidently Dad was an early patient of Saul's—sort of a test case. And after I was born, Saul convinced my dad that now that he had a family, and families were evil, his family must be broken up. So Dad left me and my mom up in Washington Heights and he got an apartment down on the Lower East Side.

And then, according to my mom, after a couple of weeks Dad started to miss us. He came running up the island to try to reconcile with us. But Mom saw him coming and escaped with me down to Mexico, where she got the divorce, bought big, floppy hats, danced around in circles with strangers, and got the half-dozen or so ceramic disks—each one of which depicts a woman escaping from slavery.

So I'd sit there under the disks on the couch, sipping my double-espresso, as my mom went up to the old radio console and turned on WBAI—listener-sponsored, sometimes listener-taken-over WBAI. The morning disc jockey at the time was Julius Lester—he of the ouska-deep voice. And supposedly, Julius's program was a classical music show. But what Julius would do is, he'd play about five minutes of a Baroque oboe concerto . . . and then speak for hours, about his various ex-wives and their sexual peccadilloes.

And I'd listen real carefully to Julius, and I'd sip my double-espresso, and I'd listen to Julius, and I'd sip my double-espresso . . . and then I'd go running off to school—jazzed!

I was so excited my first day of kindergarten. After spending the first five years of my life exclusively in the company of my parents and their friends, that day—for the first time—I was going to get to mingle with the masses.

Boy, was I disappointed! That first day, I walked into my kindergarten classroom at P.S. 128 and I saw all these little kids running around screaming, pulling hair, bopping each other, crying. I thought, How will I ever organize *these* people?

# Deb Margolin

---

**Introduction** by Lynda Hart

As I write, missiles are exploding over Baghdad and the impeachment of President William Jefferson Clinton is marching right along. Some might say that the Phallus has been dethroned; I, on the contrary, would say it has risen to all new heights. I am tempted to say: "Make Love, Not War," but we've already said that and John Lennon is dead. So is Michel Foucault, would that he were alive to write this particular moment in the history of sexuality. On the art front not much happens between women in the American theatre that doesn't make the return to lesbian-feminist ideals of the 1970s—two women floating over each other in a pool of water waving their breasts as they pass by—seem downright hot. Margolin's *Indelible Flesh* has recently closed after an extended run at Dixon Place; it is a play about death, desire, the intolerable sufferings and exquisite pleasures of the body— a poignant, breathless, tour de force mingling of tragedy and comedy. Deb and I have just finished editing her book of performance pieces, *Of All the Nerve: Deb Margolin: Solo*. And we have been pondering the deep irony of "queerness" in North American theatre where there was little, if any, "lesbian" theatre to be taught or performed until Deb Margolin, a founding member of Split Britches Theatre Company, began writing for them in the early 1980s.

Margolin came out of her de-sexualized closet to take on what has been perhaps the biggest sex scandal in U.S. history; what I've referred to as an "international, linguistic sex orgy," in the Clinton/Lewinsky multimillion dollar fiasco—which reached its climax, not unsurprisingly, with the deaths of "third world people." At the same time, Margolin continues to write about the making and unmaking of love; holding her peace-in in a performance world that remains resistant to penetration by work that refuses the easily assimilated formulas wedded to implacable identities.

When Margolin performs *Bill Me Later*, her contribution to this anthology, she begins with a comment from Lewinsky that is also an issue that every woman performer must address, consciously or not, the moment she walks onto the stage: "I am not a fat, cheesy, slut," or some version of such preconceptions. Margolin plays "Lewinsky" as a woman in love, with the only power that the dominant order allows women—the seduction of a powerful man—in this instance, our commander-in-chief, wringing from this paradigmatic, come-to-me-daddy story all of the pathos, yearning and sobering hilarity that this oldest of stories writ large on the American unconscious permits to be seen. Other characters come and go throughout the performance in juxtaposed free associations—Margolin's Aunt Dodo, whose arthritic back gravitated her so curved toward the earth in her last twenty years that the only view she must have had was of her own crotch, is one of the most memorable cameos. Clinton (hanging onto his presidency by the skin of his teeth or the cellophane on his cigar) is a man who will do it with anybody, even Margolin. She sighs with an admixture of lust and contempt—if only she could get invited to the right parties.

As in all of her performances, *Bill Me Later* exemplifies Margolin's unique way of making political/philosophical commentary at once farcical and deadly serious, giving even more clout to her piercing critiques of a culture so dissociated from itself that the few of us shrieking the question: "DID YOU SEE THAT?" can scarcely be heard.

Margolin has scored some eighteen years in the theatre, as playwright, performer, dramaturg, director. She has taken her shows on the road all over the world and into the hallowed halls of such academia as New York University, Yale and UPenn. But most of all, Margolin's inexhaustible voice of feminist consciousness, her daring incursions into all manner of views that were "not-to-be-seen" relentlessly push at the stage's continues. We have been framed she calls out to us again and again—stop, look, listen—the pageant is passing us by and we are part of it whether or not we are willing to participate. Margolin is doing something about it. Let us go watch and learn.

**Lynda Hart** is Professor of English and Theatre at the University of Pennsylvania. She is author of *Fatal Women: Lesbian Sexuality and the Mark of Aggression* (Princeton University Press) and *Between the Body and the Flesh: Performing Sadomasochism* (Columbia University Press).

# Bill Me Later

I'd like to talk to you tonight about Bill Clinton.

There's a picture of him, in *People* magazine, from about seven years ago. He was on the campaign trail with his saucy wife, his running mate Al, and Al's Aryan centerfold Tipper Gore. This photo caught them, with the tyranny of all spontaneous photos, in a misleading, yet deeply revealing, moment of giddiness. On the left side of the photo sit Hillary and Bill on a bench, side by side. Hilly is laughing her head off, almost literally; the width of her face, already endless, is too narrow for her smile. Sitting across from them on the camper bus are Al, with a grin on his face that looks like a wince, as if lizards were biting his buttocks, and Tipper in his lap, her head thrown back with a schoolgirl's abandon. Her dress, in all this hilarity, has risen perilously up on her ample thighs, and had the light been better or worse, her womanhood would have belonged to all of us. Meanwhile, the only face, the only singular face, is that of our president, Bill Clinton. He is not laughing; it isn't funny. At all. His eyes are effulgent, they have the focus of a whole campaign and all its magnificent pretensions, a greed and hunger, a whole constellation of scam and idealism. The weight of his aching testicles is in his eyes—the white heat of desire—and they are fixed on Tipper's body. I'm telling you, ladies and gentlemen: he wants her.

The beauty of this man is, he wants all of us. An American can have a piece of his ass without so much as an in-store coupon. He'll do it with anyone. And that means *me*. And he takes sex very seriously. And that's like me. Monica Lewinsky's Jewish. And me too. He's a sex addict. And I've heard of that. My passion for Bill Clinton is as old as his national public life. So this is a classic case of not being in the right place at the right time. Here's a man who'll do it with anyone, and I just can't get invited to the right parties. I took that picture, cut out Tipper's face, put in my own and wept.

At night, none of that matters. I have him. At night, there is nothing left undone. At night, I meet him for the first time, every single night, and we experience that rush, that movement which is eternal and without progress, like the dangerous movement of a full, powerful river, and it carries us the full length of its own expanse. Now, Gennifer Flowers has remarked that the full length of his expanse isn't particularly considerable, but size is both a literal and a figurative thing. And figuratively, he's monolithic. He's got the figurative thing down. And in. And near every hand and mouth he can grab between briefings. That's my man, my only, my love, my entreaty, my destiny and my oral executioner: Bill Clinton.

**Deb Margolin**

Let me tell you how it goes. And why. It's a scenario, complete in every episode. It's the only newspaper that brings out the same issue every day and still reads like a dream and is full of surprises. Let me tell you how it goes.

It begins without beginning. Everything does. You conceive a child in the dark of your body and without your knowledge. Everything momentous begins without beginning. I'm young: I'm nineteen. About three or four years younger than I am now. I'm in that flush and burst of sexual life, which also begins without beginning. I can barely walk, though I walk quickly and with grace. I am in love with myself, with my own form and insinuation. When I look down at my own breasts, my blood rushes inside to fill them to bursting, and my mind rushes outside to objectify and ache for them; I am paralyzed with the twin forces, being and desiring. The cups of my lace bra are like a lover's hands, and the ecstasy caused by their slightly painful touch on my nipples could cause a plane to crash. I am drowning in the beauty of my own body. Often I have to duck into a bathroom or an alleyway to release these warring forces, to render them briefly irrelevant; one touch and I explode utterly, and then pull down my dress and walk away from the one-night stand with this woman I am and am in love with.

I've lived in Maryland, been raised there, and now, between my sophomore and junior years at whatever that prestigious college is down there, I've landed a White House internship of some sort. I know I've landed it because I have big tits, and I feel that's justice. I'm a political science major with a minor in women's studies. Very minor. And now, after a few interviews in tight shirts and a couple of security questions regarding my arrest record, I'm *in*.

The night before, I shave my legs as though performing surgery on a head of state, and select my outfit in communion with God. It is, I decide, to be the von Furstenberg-like wrap dress, which shows cleavage as if by accident, and clings to every curve as if it were just too beautiful and too rich to do anything else, to manifest a shape of its own. It's short, and so my legs are their own fashion, and these I glove in stockings with a touch of glitter in them, daytime glitter, nothing gaudy. And to showcase the muscles in my calves—twin fists under silk—I've got high-heeled, black shoes, business-like, with a T-strap; sexy shoes that deny sexiness, so you're forced to blame *yourself* for how they make you feel when you see a woman sashaying down the sidewalk in them. Blame and credit, indistinguishable in carnal love.

I get my first glimpse of him that very day, after lunch. No one's looking into my eyes, and I know why. I've already met senators, secretaries, reporters, security personnel, and they all look eighteen inches below my eyes when shaking my hand, but with him, it's immediate and it's full eye-contact. I'm in one of the executive antechambers, being shown an elaborate computer filing system by a plain woman in a skirt and blazer, when all of a sudden I feel a jolt of energy, like a quick change of weather by the shore, a sudden wind and sound and voltage. I look up, and I see he's come in the room, followed and surrounded by a dozen or so men, all talking urgently; they remind me of a swarm of bees suddenly disturbed in a hive. His back is to me, his head is turned, and I catch his profile. Then, he senses it. He senses snatch. He's got eyes all over his body, he senses snatch, he turns full-on towards me and gives it to me right in the eyes. Our eyes lock; it makes a sound, a mechanical sound, a loud click, it's audible, I know it; he knows it too, we both quickly look around to see if anyone's heard it. It's always like that; when we fall into carnal love, we worry not that we'll be seen, but that we'll be *heard*. Vision doesn't tell the lover half enough. It's *sound* in love, pure music. The way someone breathes, the way they murmur, the way they come. Saxophone, he plays the saxophone, Jesus Christ. We hold eyes that way for what seems like years, and then our eyes fall onto each other, hungry. He bursts out laughing at something one of the wonks has said, and his eyes twinkle, they have left my eyes and are roving the landscape of me. They don't get far; he's smiling, still talking, he's staring at my breasts, adorned as they are by the lovely feminine hieroglyph my collarbones make above them. His hands twitch, in his mind he's touching me already. I am frozen, suspended. The file woman is still talking to me; I can't hear her, I'm in a prison of adrenaline, estrogen, panic.

His hands. I fall upon his hands. I remember reading once that the hands and heart of a developing fetus are formed at exactly the same instant. I have never seen anything so beautiful, so annunciatory, so articulate, so rapacious as his hands. They're huge, just immense. He uses them the way a painter uses color. They're exquisitely hewn, they make me wonder where they've been, they make me want to smell them. I've never seen anything so ravishing. I want his fingers under my dress. I know that he could put his two hands all the way around my waist and touch his own fingers; I know that he *will*. He's a terror. I'm completely in love with him. A moment later he's gone.

The next ten days are a blur of accidents and coincidences. We *happen* to run into each other in the hall, he *accidentally* brushes my arm with the small of his back; he *suddenly* has endless business in the dull green, windowless room I've been assigned. And then one day, it's over. No more accidents. I'm typing one day, I've got classified documents on my desk concerning the adultery of an army general and the homosexuality of one of his commanding officers, and I'm opening a file, I'm typing in *commands*, when there before me, there before my downcast visage, I see the hand, the left hand. I can't tell you of its beauty any better: it made a mockery of the shape of Michigan, it redefined desire, it rendered the shovel nugatory. The left hand, laid down on my desk like a gauntlet. I don't look up. I can't; there's no point, no possibility. I don't know how much time passes in this explosive stillness; I pick the hand up and bring it to my lips. Then I move it far enough away to see it again. It's lying in my two hands, obscuring them completely; I look like an amputee. I consider this hand. On the fourth finger is a huge, gold wedding band—*full of sound and fury; signifying nothing*; this is what I think. Reaching up with my trembling right hand, I turn the ring slowly on the massive finger, once, twice, three times, I can count the rotations it makes by the reappearance again and again of a scratch on the band that looks like teeth marks, like someone tried to bite it off, this is what I think. A phone rings somewhere. I pick the hand up again, it's weightless this time; I bring it to my lips again. This time, holding the hand by the ring, I slip the fourth finger all the way into my mouth, my eyes fall shut and can't open; I'm biting it, I'm trying to cause pain, trying to cause the pain I feel. I feel the full length of it, I slide it between my gum and my upper lip, I bite it hard; he winces, moans. I hear the Commander of the Free World *moaning*.

He pulls me to my feet. Standing thus before him, I have the feeling of having stood before him a thousand times already. I have no strength; he catches me in his arms. He puts his hands around my waist, and his fingers touch. No one's saying anything, doing anything. We're in the eyes again, we've disappeared a little bit into each other's eyes. At this moment I remember the way Guess Jeans or Escape for Men perfume or one of those companies whose ad agency specialized in artsy, haunting commercials used an F. Scott Fitzgerald quote that went something like:

*Before he kissed her, he knew that kissing her would change his life forever, so he waited. The silence around them was such-and-such and blah-blah-blah, as if a tuning fork had been struck against the stars . . .*

Or something like that. I realize that, in using Fitzgerald's lyricism to hawk toilet water, the clever ad agency had both *trivialized* and *nationalized* this beautiful language in a single strophe. That's how it felt to stand there in front of him. I swear to God.

And then he kisses me. He knows how to do it; it's as if he knows how to do it but doesn't have time, his lips are chapped and his teeth seem to be placed in front instead of behind them. I can taste my own blood, and I can't hear anything anymore, it's because his starched white shirt sleeve is wrapped around my head, all I hear is the slow movement of this opulent linen hissing. The kiss is brief, unsatisfying. He pushes me backwards, guiding my body; I fall backwards onto my desk, my head is resting on my computer keyboard, which miraculously makes a perfect pillow. Now I think of *Midnight Cowboy*, of Jon Voight fucking that older woman in the middle of a Scrabble game, each of them thinking they'd be paid by the other for the favor; the tiles with letters on them are sticking to his back, digging into his flesh. I burst out laughing. He's got my skirt up, my panties down. His lips are on the soft, swollen skin of my belly, and that hand with the ring, the ring finger itself, is inside me, reshaping my future.

Suddenly he pulls me upright, and with a dazzling continuity, places my hand on his Manhood while reaching under my shirt simultaneously, unhooking my front-fastened brassiere with a fast, circular flick of thumb and forefinger and sampling the pendulous bait for good and ever. As for his Manhood . . . well . . . it defies the usual calculus; as I said before, size is both a literal and a figurative thing. It's clear to me right then and there that I'll focus figuratively. So he was ENORMOUS. Oddly cool, full of pulse. He picks me up suddenly and carries me to the door. Instead of locking the door, which makes a sound, that mechanical click of eyes meeting, he blocks the door with his enormous back and buttocks, pulls down his fancy pants and uses some part of me for the fullest expression of the most creative aspect of his life as a man.

Afterwards—and a brief afterwards—we drink. We drink something sweet and bitter from a cut glass bottle, and we whisper. I feel like I'm back in college. He's laughing, finally; it's as if he's finally united with those others in the bus picture in a moment of youthful and sexual mirth. Released, he's laughing, but the tension builds again violently and quickly, and this time he locks the door. The click sounds like a gunshot, the sound the door makes, locking. I've pulled my clothing back together, it's neat against my body; now he lunges, places his hand at the scoop neck of my dress, and pulls; it falls off my body, completely wounded, and in tearing makes a sound like someone choking. For a moment I'm in my underwear, but he tears the bra off my body in the same way. It's a technique he's obviously perfected. He takes my nipples between his thumb and forefinger, causing me shock, and he growls: *fuck me*. He growls: *fuck me*. We're on the floor now. He's taken it out of his pants, and it's against my pubic bone, between my breasts, it flickers past my lips, and now it's between my legs, and now it's breaching my boundary, small but endless. I'm dreaming, I must be dreaming. His teeth are around my nipple, he's all the way inside me, he's so beautiful, like Achilles he's beautiful, he's murmuring to me, he's way above me, he's all the way inside me, my cervix is aching from the thrust of him, his heels are burning the smooth, green carpet, and finally I lose vision, I think I'm screaming but it turns out I've been silent, contracting and expanding around him, my life shattered, my lipstick still in place. I've been dreaming. He doesn't fuck.

He calls me. Late that week. I know he's in love with me, that I have achieved a temporary eternity in his thoughts, in his groin. I know he's been over it all, again and again, that he's come again and again, empty for thoughts of me, of my absence, of my impossibility. I'm just a silly, little whore with a lot of new stockings. How in love I am with my slavery to my own body, to the feelings it inspires in men: in him. That is all I am. He calls me, and that is all I am. Someone says: *the president would like to speak to you*, and I'm thinking *duh*, and I'm thinking *I want to feel you again, all the way inside me*, and I'm thinking *never*, I'm thinking *never*, I'm thinking *I own you completely*, I'm thinking *my life is nothing but cunt and so is yours, how doomed we are, how we've died together*, and then I hear his voice. I hate his voice and I need it. It's breathy, urgent; it's the voice of an addict talking to a dealer, it's passionate, it's on the verge of hallucination. And all he's said is my name. He says it, he's looking for me, like a pair of hands, he's seeking me like a blind man reading a bomb warning in Braille, seeking me, he says my name. I say nothing, I'm seeing the ocean for some reason, he says my name again. He keeps saying it. He doubts I'm there, and then he says my name again, sensing the worst, that I am there, and I am, and I'm descending. I will never answer. I begin hanging up, and it takes an hour, it goes out like a tide in sunset. He's saying my name, and I let the receiver come to my lips and I stick my tongue on it, and it tastes salty, and then I bring it down to my breasts and put the speaking end on my left nipple and the talking end on my right, and I feel like I'm going to come, right then, but I withhold. He's saying my name, in anguish, he's saying it again and again and I can't hear it, just feel the vibrations of it, now on my lower back, my stomach, and now it's between my legs, and inside me, and I'm coming, the best come, the final orgasm I'm to have over him, stimulated by his belittled voice and my own name; he's speaking to my womb, to the flagella and filth and life and smell of me, and for once he doesn't know it, he doesn't even know where his lips are, he doesn't know what he's got, and then, after all that time and feeling, I hang up on him, quietly, like a whisper, like a deep kiss.

Now good for you: you've noticed he's a hypocrite, a liar, a trivial thinker. You feel betrayed after watching him play saxophone blues during his inaugural celebration and then allowing his government to slash arts funding to the bone. You've surmised that he falsified his entire approach to government; you've fumed that he promised an end to military homophobia and gave us "Don't Ask Don't Tell"; that he criticized George Bush for failing human rights advocates in China and then walked smiling into Tiananmen Square to be photographed next to a Chinese car; you're shattered that he promised health care for all Americans and has left people dying without health care of a disease that could have been cured with the forty million dollars we've spent to investigate who sucked his dick and in what order.

But you know what? That's the *truth* of the matter, and truth is not what sells. In America, it's sex that sells, and he is an American; he is America, O God, is he ever, and honestly, secretly, after midnight, so, forever forward, am I.

# Roger Guenveur Smith

## Introduction by Margo Jefferson

**W**e are a nation of obsessed monologists—stand-up comics, tragedians and commentators, pushing to make our voices heard and our identities known. But the solo American voice doesn't just convey solo thoughts and feelings; on the page or the stage it can embody a social type or an entire group's longings, furies and absurdities. Think of it as a voice crying aloud in the wilderness, yes, but joking, dreaming, debunking and tale-telling as well. Think of the wilderness as American life and history, and think of that life and history as a thicket of racial facts and fantasies. Now you are ready for the work of Roger Guenveur Smith.

Certain elements are always present. Race is never static, it's a psychological and ideological jumble that Smith is always pulling some trick or truth from. As his alter ego asks in the hilarious two-man vaudeville *Inside the Creole Mafia*, is he a black man or a Creole? An actor too light to play black characters and too dark to play white ones? A highly trained performer who can go classical highbrow then streetcorner lowlife in a flash? All of the above. The performance turns the questions into a series of brilliant strategic moves. Every stage is a world, and one man in his life wears many masks.

Just consider the opening lines of *Blood and Brains*, his most recent piece.

I am a fugitive slave
I live underneath the Hollywood Freeway
Or the Brooklyn Bridge
Somewhere
Under the Rainbow

The first two lines yoke the slave narrative to the Hollywood crime drama (*I am a Fugitive from a Chain Gang*); the last three move from Hart Crane to *The Wizard of Oz*, from manly poetic bravado to female torch-song yearning.

This writer and actor is a time traveler and shape-shifter. His pieces draw on all kinds of linguistic and dramatic styles. To start with the most obvious, Mr. Smith draws on white formal, white vernacular, black formal and black vernacular forms of speech. But there are all sorts of subtleties to be found within these categories, which in any case overlap more than convention would have us believe. I think of these works as multi-voiced monologues. No character speaks in just one voice, be he the willful, noble Frederick Douglass or the incandescent, self-devouring Huey P. Newton.

*Blood and Brains* takes this practice still further. Every line signifies a shift of time, stance or self. The most grotesque facts and the most clear-sighted hallucinations join forces. Every horror has its bitter comic dose.

I went into space and blew up
I went into hiding up your family tree:
Don't look now
I'm an American slave
And I've got my own sitcom
Millions of laughs per century
with no commercial interruption

History is all bound up with literature, and it is also as intimate as sex or family life. "I've gone underground," the narrator says, true to the ghosts of Dostoyevski and Ellison:

Got an inventory of all Confederate flags
and colored jockey statues
Closely monitoring the activities
of the brother
who took my mom's car keys on Crenshaw
and the brother
who put a knife to my lady's neck on Wilshire

The final line of *Blood and Brains* is, "I'm ready." Ready for his close-up, Mr. DeMille and Mr. Lee, and ready for anyone with a passion for theatre that takes no prisoners and goes for broke.

**Margo Jefferson** is a cultural critic for the *New York Times*.

Roger Guenveur Smith

# Blood and Brains

I am a fugitive slave
I live underneath the Hollywood Freeway
Or the Brooklyn Bridge
Somewhere
Under the Rainbow
My coalition kept warm
by blazing barrels of trash
scraps from the cane fields
and the fast food establishments
I'm on the run
Up and down a basketball court
and into the bush
You can't touch me
I am a maroon
Chilling high above
the smog line
and the tourist enclaves
The North Star
visible every night
My guide into a Philly groove
The Delfonics
Soundtracks to my most intimate moments
Ain't no stopping me now
I'm on the move
Up the Chesapeake
and into the Mississippi
inventing jazz and blood plasma along the way
I'm wearing a hat
a brim
a new attitude
and I'm ready for a new century
so bring it on
serve it up with mush
crumbs
from the table of discontents
*I'm going to the Great House Farm*
*O Yea*
and I can't decide if I want dreads
or an Afro
or a skinhead

or a conk
so I'm shopping for wigs
Do you have the Henry Box Brown look?
He was shipped North in a box
and wound up with a flat top
Henry Box Brown
I'm on the run
In a white Bronco disguised as an ex-football player
Through the streets of Virginia Beach
and into a boxing ring
battering my brother to death
grinning at the press conference
proclaiming victory
and misquoting some dead leader
I'm a movie star
gun at the ready
plastered on plantation walls
next to the malt liquor ads
Drunk
on my own infected blood
Strong
stronger than the jackass and the circus elephant
that get more respect than I do
No I'm not registered to vote
but still I'm running for office
For the Canadian border
For some hovel in South London
where I can make a living
a better living than I'm making now
cutting cane
with this rusty machete:
My master is my father
My father my master
Note my resemblance to this wooden nickel
Isn't my grimace the same as his?
I whipped my overseer
Didn't you see it on *Cops*?
I whipped Rosa Parks
She forgave me
I know how to do
the Black Panther Stomp
and the Charleston
and don't forget the Texas Hop

Disguised myself as a tap dancer
Entertained on the White House lawn
All the while tapping the phone
and getting out the message
to the barbershops
and the Lodges
The Howard University School of Law
Never go outside
without wearing my root
tucked into my right Nike boot
I'm a fugitive slave
running in Hitler's Olympics
gold chains and medals dangling
on the cover of a box of Wheaties
constructing ships for my imminent departure
moored in the Harlem River
or Lake Michigan
When it's frozen over
My kind of town
Quiet
No slave catchers in sight
Just a soft neon glow
from the *taquerias*
Someone wants to sell me a green card
I'm in the Grand Canyon
listening to Bob Marley tapes
Smoking the peace pipe
with Osceola and the Wild Tchoupitoulas
Jumping up at Mardi Gras
and carnival
and on the first and fifteenth of every month
I'm sitting on the dock of the bay
watching the luxury liners go by
and it's New Year's Eve
and they're playing the blues
and Public Enemy
and I'm trying desperately not to believe the hype
All I need is my Thorazine
I'm not a violent person
Just terribly misguided
I went into space and blew up
I went into hiding up your family tree:
Don't look now

I'm an American slave
and I've got my own sitcom
Millions of laughs per century
with no commercial interruption
I wear three-piece suits
and penny loafers
I've read the classics
I've been to Yale
and I've been to jail
Trumped up charges
They gagged me
Then they made me a news anchor
on the Titanic
Reporting live from a disaster in progress
Swam to shore with Cuban refugees
only to be shipped to Panama
where we swam the Canal
after we dug it
The Rio Grande
The Nile with Langston Hughes
Caught the mock slave auction
in Williamsburg
Took a couple of licks
just for old times' sake
Gave a couple
to show my versatility
Personally escorted Nelson Mandela
throughout the fifty states
Showed him where the Civil War started
and never ended
The Underground Railroad
upgraded for the 1990s
Let's just say it runs from here to there
and it's not a straight path
I'm moving
to the beat
of bare feet
Shackled and perfumed
Pedicured
for the front row patrons
who love public executions
Yeah I ran with Fred
Knew him from the projects

Even back in the day
He had his own talk show
Guests like Nat Turner
and Denmark Vesey
Theme song went:
*Learning will spoil the best nigger in the world*
*So let's get spoiled y'all*
That's how I learned my ABC
Wrote my first book
Gave my first lecture
Recorded my first platinum CD
Conferred with Dr. King
at the Lorraine Motel
*Told* him to duck
Now I'm at large
My portrait on the post office wall
and the cover of *Time* magazine
A tremendous reward for my capture
Because I'm the most valuable player
One of the world's great men of color
Taught Hendrix how to play "Foxy Lady"
Yet invisible
in my Eleganza ensemble
My tuxedo
My butt-nakedness at Attica
My tears frozen
in some rerun sequence
on somebody's telethon
I'm eating my pass to freedom
Once carefully forged
and now digested
My only meal for days
WILL WORK FOR FOOD
my latest poem
scrawled on Henry Brown's discarded box
A liquor company told me
I'm descended from great Kings and Queens:
forty ounces of black history anybody?
You can't catch me
I know all the black roads and alleys
The best restaurants
How to live high
on the hog

I invented chitlins and crack cocaine
A secret lab
behind where Thurgood Marshall plotted civil rights
and political casualties come to be consoled
Where the dismembered get stitched
And everything is everything
Doorman
to the best club in the world
where the passwords are
Freedom
Now
Changed my name
From Bailey to Stanley to Johnson to Douglass to
Ida B. Wells
Plotted with John Brown
Narrowly escaped the noose myself
Still running
All those European tours
Applauded and lauded
till they mistook me for an Arab
Got hooked on heroin and bebop
Started my own import export concern
Got busted for trafficking in literacy
Still doing time on that charge
Never should have preached about
David or Goliath
or how we need to boycott Denny's
This is written by myself
in blood if necessary
No Westside abolitionist
furiously working the laptop
on my behalf
scripting my punch lines
and designing my wardrobe
This is written in my mother's milk
Stronger than any formula
or synthetic decongestant
My voice is my own
No Richard and Willie act here
I write my own music too
The only tune I've ever covered
was the "Star Spangled Banner"
1983 NBA All Star Game

Remember?
I've gone from Jamestown
to Trenchtown
to Jonestown
Never did like Kool-Aid
Fought in every war invented and then some
Right now I'm fighting for the right
to peddle this knowledge
on this particular corner
at this particular time
Dime bags of truth, anybody?
Fugitive
In the jungles of Surinam
and the hills above South Central
awaiting an earthquake
or an insurrection:
whichever comes first
Meanwhile making myself heard
on the far end of the dial
in between
the shouts and screams
the grunts and sighs
the sirens and helicopters
Dogs
lapping at my scent
Chasing me since 1838
Up and down Malcolm X Boulevard
Somebody tell me
It's just a Spike Lee movie
Somebody tell me
why I just fired two rounds
into my own reflection
like some Narcissus gone mad
I've read the classics
Remember?
Spray painting my name
any name
on any wall that will have me
Outlaw
Gangsta rappa
Ph.D.
My dissertation lies unread
Trampled underneath the crowd

as they file out of Madison Square Garden
or the unemployment office
or the 4th of July celebration
where they just hanged two niggers for sport
Still I rise
From this nightmare called history
Cold sweats
in my cardboard box
my concrete crib
my room without a view
Dreamless nights
and endless days
Punching this heavy bag
like Louis
or Ali
like James Brown at the Apollo:
Out of confusion
Out of bondage
Up from slavery
Up from Maryland
Up from Mississippi
Up from the gutter
in which I'm lying right now
choking on my own filth
and the automotive exhaust
See me in your rearview mirror?
Now look into your future
Snap
into that virtual reality
Am I still preaching the gospel
on late night TV?
Pushing pancake batter?
Reading old slave narratives
as bedtime stories?
Putting America to sleep?
Fugitive
I've gone underground
Way underground
Burrowed underneath Mount Rushmore
and Stone Mountain Georgia
Got an inventory of all Confederate flags
and colored jockey statues
Closely monitoring the activities

of the brother
who took my mom's car keys on Crenshaw
and the brother
who put a knife to my lady's neck on Wilshire
and the brother
who pulled a gun on me
claiming to be an off-duty cop
in search of a stolen bicycle
and the brothers
who stomped my friend to death
in front of the Hollywood Palladium
and laughed
Something about a black leather jacket
Are my references too obscure?
Can you follow my drift?
In the Atlantic?
In the Caribbean?
In the creek
in chapter four
of Frederick Douglass's *Narrative*?
*In an instant*
*poor Denby*
*was no more*
*His mangled body sank*
*out of sight*
*and blood*
*and brains*
*marked the water*
*where he had stood*
The deed was done by a religious overseer named Gore
Hell of a baptism
But still I have risen
To fight the negro breaker
Jim Crow
Naysayers
and doomsayers
Enemies within
Supremacists of every stripe
My own self doubt
and suicidal tendencies:
*You have seen*
*how a man was made a slave;*
*You shall see*

*how a slave was made a man*
Armed with two fists
one mind
and a semi-colon
Dangerous
Devious
Made it to Tribeca in one day
feeling as if I'd escaped a den of lions
One of the lucky ones I suppose
So many more to follow
So many more to lead the way:
Now take me to the bridge
I'm ready.

# Anne Galjour

## Introduction by Steven Winn

**G**reat solo artists can make an audience see, hear and feel the world they evoke. Anne Galjour makes her listeners smell and taste it, too.

When Sherelle Dantin and Urus Arceneaux get together in *Alligator Tales*, Galjour's lush comedy set in Louisiana's cajun country, it's the roux that does it. Hot, smoking oil, browning flour, the sudden perfume of onions in the pan: a captivating seduction is underway. By the time Sherelle adds eggs and freshly shelled peas, Urus has hauled himself off the couch and come to the kitchen. "I could feel him behind me with that smell of his cow pasture he always has on him," Sherelle murmurs to herself.

Galjour layers sensory impressions and sense memories to create characters with both a vivid present-tense reality and a persistent hold on the past. Her pieces emerge as richly textured solo plays, with interwoven plot lines, social commentary, mythic overtones, plenty of weather, local superstitions and a few eruptions of magic realism. Eight characters and one perspicacious dog appear in the narrative sweep of *Alligator Tales*. Six years pass between its first half, "Hurricane," and its stormy conclusion, "Mauvais Temps."

In her early solo works, first performed at San Francisco's tiny Climate Theatre in the early 1990s, Galjour turned to the Brothers Grimm and Scottish folktales as structural models. In *The Krewe of Neptune*, she spun a gaudy and violent prelude to a Mardi Gras ball. *Alligator Tales*, which premiered at the Berkeley Repertory Theatre as *Hurricane/Mauvais Temps* in 1996, brought her work a new amplitude.

Galjour's wellspring is located in Cut Off, Louisiana, her hometown on Bayou Lafourche, ninety minutes southeast of New Orleans. Born in 1957, Galjour, like Eudora Welty, remembers a childhood steeped in the storytelling of a small Southern community. She taps her mother's devout Catholic faith, too, a belief that "touched everything with reverence." One of the characters in *Alligator Tales* devotedly tends to the makeup on a plaster Virgin Mary. Sherelle's body registers the approach of a hurricane or some other force of nature when the saints' medals pinned to her bra rise up against her blouse.

Galjour's characters inhabit a kind of fallen paradise, where oil rigs loom over the marshland. A cook defrosts a frozen turtle in a microwave. A plague of alligators and water moccasins follows the dredging operation for a new levee. In one mordantly comic scene, Sherelle's sister Inez casts her line for redfish and snags a scuba diver instead. "Let me take you back to shore," Inez says of her bleeding catch, "before you attract a shark."

Nothing can match the fury of the natural world. Hurricanes bear down on Galjour's townsfolk and the delta's delicate ecology with unremitting force. But "hurricanes are good," as Inez points out. "They clean out the mouth of the Mississippi and push out the silt that builds up the marsh."

Grace arrives in wondrous ways in *Alligator Tales*. When lightning strikes Urus a second time, it turns his hair a purified white. One baby in the story appears in a pasture, a cow licking the infant clean when Urus finds him. Another is born during a hurricane. Creation and destruction come together at the climax of the piece, new life beginning in the ferocious wind and rain.

Galjour left Louisiana in 1980, after graduating from Nicholls State College with a major in theatre and a minor in liberal arts. She moved to San Francisco with her husband, John Mayne, a television and theatre set designer. Galjour's career as a storyteller began in her son Ian's nursery school class.

Her performance skills now rival her narrative gifts. Moon-eyed and balletically lithe at 5'3", Galjour moves on stage with a fluid efficiency. Her sets are minimal, with the visual splendor reserved for the shifting, watery hues of the lighting. Galjour's voice covers a chromatic spectrum, too, from the breathy flutter of a child's first words to Urus's booming, French-accented cadence.

She changes roles by spinning lightly on one foot, tightly squinching up her face or letting it go slack. With that, as her characters come and go, Galjour connects a fictionalized Cut Off, Louisiana, to the rest of the world.

Anne Galjour

**Steven Winn** is the theatre critic of the *San Francisco Chronicle*, where he has worked as a critic and reporter since 1980. He is co-author of *Great Performances: A Celebration* (Bay Books).

# from **Alligator Tales**

## from **Part One: Hurricane**

### Scene Two

*Inez Dantin and her dog Michael are fishing along the Gulf of Mexico.*

INEZ: I took a deep breath. The air smelled like Coppertone and salt. I pulled on the line a few times and thought, If that hurricane's bad enough, it'll suck up the sand dune, the road, then the island. Before you know it, I'll be casting my line from my back porch.

Then it bit. At first I thought it was seaweed 'cause I didn't feel that jerk of life trying to get away from me. But then it pulled so hard the line was zigzagging from the struggle. But I held on tight. I jerked the line a few times to tire it out. But it pulled harder. So hard it dragged me in the water up to my knees. Just when I thought it had me, up out the waves pops a scuba diving man. And he was screaming.

Michael swam out to help get him up to the sandbar. When I waded out to them the scuba diving man was standing there holding onto his mask.

He was gasping so hard I couldn't see his face with all the fog in his mask. When I lifted it, I could see he was hooked. The hook was lodged in his head not two inches from his right eye. And he was bleeding. "Let me take you back to shore before you attract a shark." Me and Michael waded back to shore with that scuba diving man at the end of my line.

I sat him on a piece of driftwood. I got my scissors from the tackle box. His poor fingers were shaking trying to find the hook in his head.

"Let me. I've unhooked hammerhead sharks and catfish in my day. I can unhook you."

I cut the line and looked at the wound. The skin had torn some from the struggle. Michael sat beside him while I soaked a towel with water from the waves. I was just gonna pour it on his skin to see the wound when he put his hand over the hook and cried,

MARLON: "NO! No water, please!"

INEZ: "Come on now. Everybody knows salt water's the best thing for a cut."

But he shook his head so hard the little lead weight kind of knocked him in the eye.

MARLON: "NO! Not that water."

INEZ: I looked out at the oil rigs. Then down at the tar on the beach. I ran to the car to get the first-aid kit out the trunk. Michael stayed beside him the whole time to help keep him calm. He looked like one of those Jesuses with the blood dripping down the side of his face . . .

I stretched out my towel and laid him on his stomach with his head turned to the side. He was a red-headed man, lean and freckled all the way down to the tops of his flippers. I looked him in the eye. It was green and bloodshot. "Lie still. I'll get this hook out your head, but you have to lie still."

I pressed my hand on his face and stretched his skin. I must have hit a nerve because he started to jerk. So I had to press his face harder. "No flapping. Lie still."

I pulled out that hook so slow it came out the same way it went in. I looked him in the eye and showed him the hook. "No meat. What I told you."

His eye started blinking and he spit out some words.

MARLON: "Pretty deep, eh. Is it deep enough for stitches?"

INEZ: "Well you had a hook in your head. As long as you've had a tetanus shot I think you'll be all right . . . Did you see any redfish when you were down there?"

MARLON: "No. Just a few flounder, some catfish, an eel."


## Scene Four

INEZ: When I got back to the house the kitchen smelled like roux . . .

I went down the hallway to find Sherelle. There she was in the bathroom, sitting in front of the mirror, adjusting the pad in her new bra. She was so white she looked blue. She took a comb through her stringy, brown mop. I watched with my own eyes, strands of her hair float down to the floor around her ankles. It made me forget all about what I caught at the beach.

"Sherelle, the bra that prosthesis company made for you looks so natural. Let's get you another one, Honey, so you can have two. And if you let me give you a protein-conditioning shampoo treatment with Urus's eggs, I bet your hair's gonna be so shiny and thick, you won't be able to fit it all in the rubber band."

She looked at me in the mirror. She put her hand over her pad and smiled.

SHERELLE (Sits in chair): "Inez, Rosetta says the Virgin Mary appears in Galveston every year for the Feast of the Assumption. She said a man who had a brain tumor went there. He was told to wash his head with the sand. He did. And when he went back to the doctor the brain tumor was gone. I was thinking about asking Urus to take me. If we left today we could get to Galveston in time."

INEZ: I knelt down and picked up the hair from the floor.

"Sherelle, if you want to be healed you have to go to the refrigerator. I got fish in there that'll make your hair thick. I got cow's liver that'll build up your blood. Trying to find the Virgin is not gonna make you any better. Besides we gotta go to the grocery store. Hurricane Wanda's coming. We gotta get canned food and water in case the power goes out."

SHERELLE: "You don't believe in miracles, Inez, because you don't have to. But if you're going to the grocery store, would you get me a box of Little Debbies and a case of Hawaiian Punch for when Wanda comes."

## Scene Seven

ROSETTA: When Wanda hit we were ready . . .

While I was heating up the leftover turtle sauce piquant for our anniversary I could see Grady in the living room. He was in his Lazy Boy with his hand in his pants watching Wanda on TV. I went to the china cabinet and pulled out the tumbler with the gilded ducks flying on it. I filled it with two fingers of Wild Turkey and three cubes of ice.

When I handed him his drink he wouldn't even look at me. He just sat watching Wanda blowing down trees and ripping all the roofs off in Galveston. "Grady, I know you mad 'cause I don't like the dishwasher you bought me for our anniversary. But it don't match my kitchen. All you have to do is go back to the store and get it in aqua. You hear me? Grady? I mean it. I'm sorry."

But he wasn't listening. He had sucked up that Wild Turkey. And with his hand in his pants he was in his LazyBoy talking to all his deers.

GRADY: "That damn woman. Always got to have what she wants in this house. I'm so sick of this French Broque furniture. The sofa ain't long enough for me to lie down in. The glass I'm holding don't even fit in my hand. If it wasn't for ya'll, and my ducks, my sailfish, my alligator and my LazyBoy you wouldn't even know I live here. But I tell you what fellas. If they find oil, I'm investing in an alligator farm and hatchery. We can sell the skins to those Frenchmen and get twenty-five dollars a pound for the tails. So keep your wings spread open boys 'cause if we hit, we'll all be flyin' out of here."

ROSETTA: I pulled the cake out the microwave and put the old bride and groom on the top. While I was putting the food on the table I watched Wanda blowing a church away leaving nothing but the altar and the tabernacle standing. I looked at the old bride and groom all wide-eyed on the cake.

"You know, Grady, I was thinking, if we do strike oil, I saw a long sofa at Maison Blanche that has a pattern of ducks flying over a pond on the cushions. It's available in teal or rust."

He stirred his Wild Turkey with his finger. He scooped an ice cube and sucked it in his mouth.

GRADY: "Rust."

ROSETTA *(Sits)*: I sat on the arm of his LazyBoy and pulled just a little all the hairs on his wrist. "And maybe we could take down this picture of Jesus at the Last Supper and you could go up in the attic and bring down that barracuda you have with the teeth showing."

GRADY: "What we gonna do with Jesus and his men?"

ROSETTA: I took his drink from his hand and slid onto his lap. "Whatever you want. 'Cause I want what you want. I do."

The wind was picking up speed and pulling the shingles off the roof. I bent over to kiss him. Then the front door slammed open blowing in hard rain and Inez Dantin. *(She crosses downstage)*

INEZ: "I can't find Michael and Marlon."

In the wake of Hurricane Wanda, Michael dies, Marlon is hospitalized and Urus finds a baby lying in his cow pasture. He brings the child to Inez. She names him Beau.

## from **Part Two: Mauvais Temps**

*Six years later.*

### Scene Two

SHERELLE: I walked around back. There Urus was in his pasture talking to his cows. One of the Holsteins was pregnant. He rubbed her belly. Her tail started wagging. He bent over and pulled her ear. She parted her lips and licked him. Then she lifted her tail and let go a sweet, putrid mound that smelled like the first time Urus stood behind me in my kitchen.

I turned around to leave. All of a sudden the air got heavy. My head started buzzing. Then a crack from the heavens split open my ears. The next thing I remember, Urus and the Holstein were on top me saying,

URUS: *"Mon Dieu* Sherelle, your blouse is smoking."

SHERELLE: There were two streams of smoke rising from my medals. I could smell the burning foam in my bra. Urus and his Holstein looked at me wide-eyed.

URUS: "Had I known this would happen I would have worn my watch to take the hit."

SHERELLE: He lifted me up and carried me across the pasture with his cow following behind till she got to the gate.

When he opened his back door I was surprised. His kitchen was tidy, but it smelled like an overripe cantaloupe. He laid me on his sofa and covered me with a crocheted blanket. My scalp felt like it was burning. I lay there staring up at his walls. There were pictures of him in his F.F.A. jacket. His cows were wearing ribbons. There was a mirror framed by a pair of steer's horns. Urus sniffed the air. By the look on his face I could tell he smelled the burnt foam in my bra.

URUS: "Be glad, Sherelle. If I woulda had that kinda protection, it mighta stopped the lightning from striking my palm."

SHERELLE: Urus soaked a towel with cold water. He rubbed my neck and my ear. I could feel blisters rise. "Urus, I think I saw Jesus."

He looked me in the eyes and lowered his eyebrows.

URUS: "Was he alone, or with family?"

SHERELLE: "It was just Him, standing there with Inez's old dog, Michael. I could hear crickets. Then you came."

I took his hand. I felt the soft, shiny patch of skin in his palm. Urus started sweating. I put his palm over my blisters.

Then the sky flashed white. Our hair flew up. We couldn't move. The shock from his hand popped open my blisters. The water and the current kept him stuck to my skin. When our hair fell we stayed there rigid and steaming. I unbuttoned my dress for him to touch my skin. Urus fell down to his knees. I opened wide my lips and let his tongue touch me. It felt like a sharp jolt that sizzled all the way up to the roots of my hair. Then he stood up. He held my face in his hands and he kissed me. I tasted myself in his mouth. The rain started falling hard on the window. I pulled Urus toward me and I let him in like the ground takes the rain.

Then the sky emptied. My head stopped buzzing . . . We got up and looked at ourselves in his mirror underneath his steer's horns. My hair wasn't white like his. But it was full and frizzy. Urus stood behind me in the mirror.

URUS: "Don't be afraid. I know how you feel. The second time I got struck and my hair turned white, I thought, Why me? But if you ask me Sherelle, I think yours looks professional."

# Scene Five

*Inez has just learned Sherelle is pregnant.*

INEZ: There were scenes of the Mississippi River swelling against the levees. Then the TV went to static.

URUS: "I got some flounders in my little Igloo. If ya'll got some red sauce, I could make a court bouillon with one. I got some onions, garlic, bell pepper and rice."

INEZ: "Urus get away from my TV. The river is rising. We gotta see what's gonna happen to the levee."

> Urus put the ice chest down on the table. When he touched Sherelle's stomach, their hair flew up. Sherelle held down her hair and grabbed his arm.

SHERELLE: "Let's go in my bedroom, Urus. Then we can cook." *(She turns around)*

INEZ: I decided I would make the court bouillon. I didn't want to take any chances with having Urus Arceneaux anywhere near my appliances.

> I opened the ice chest. It smelled like fish oil and marsh. I could hear Sherelle and Urus laughing in her room.

> I pulled a big one from the top. It was slippery and heavy. I laid him on the table and passed my fingers so softly down his side it made his tail slowly curl. Urus started cooing. I slit him open. Lightning struck. The rain started falling. I heard Urus and Sherelle hit the bed.

> I turned the oven on 375°. I rubbed his skin with olive oil and removed his fins. He lay in that pan, clean, shaven and smooth. I decided he was too meaty for a red sauce. It would just water down his flesh. So I buttered my fingertips and passed them slowly down his slit. Sherelle's bed started creaking. I stuffed him with basil and shoved him in the oven.

> The rain was blowing through the screen door like a sieve. Someone came running up the steps. It was Web Pitre holding his briefcase over his head. He came inside dripping on the mat.

> "Take off your loafers before you come in my kitchen, Web." I wiped my fingers and handed him the dish towel. He dried his face and his arms.

WEB: "I was driving out to the levee. It was raining so hard I couldn't see."

INEZ: I turned to the TV. Roger Spaulding was kissing another man's wife. Web stood behind me smelling like Old Spice and fish.

> The flounder was heating up. I fixed a glass of iced tea for

Web and one for me. Web took his seat at the table. Lightning struck and Sherelle cried out to the Virgin. I stuck the glass in his face. "My sister's very religious. Especially in a storm."

The fish was sizzling. Through the window the rain was coming down in rumpled sheets. Sherelle started moaning. Web put down his glass and looked toward the hallway.

WEB: "I hope she gets what she's praying for."

INEZ: I felt so embarrassed. I tried to distract him from what was going on in the bedroom. "Web, caught any dolphins lately in your net?"

WEB: "*Non.* But I keep my cast net in my truck for in case I see a girl."

INEZ: I couldn't help but stare at Web's toes. It stopped raining. I was just gonna ask him if he wanted to go fishing. But, he stood up and looked past me toward the hallway.

*Sherelle enters.*

SHERELLE: "Web Pitre. You're sweet-talking my sister when you should be sweet-talking me. Inez, Web wants to buy the old hunting camp out in the marsh."

## Scene Nine

INEZ: I didn't know where Beau was when the water hit . . .

The wind picked up speed. It spit rain in my face. The rain tasted like salt. The rumble got louder. But it wasn't thunder. It was from the ground, like a strike on an oil rig. It grew louder and louder. Then I saw it. It was a wall of water rolling toward our home. I dropped the contract and ran to the oak tree. The trunk was so slippery it was hard to climb. When the water hit the yard I climbed to the second branch. Oh my God. Where's Beau? The water ran up the back steps into the door. It carried redfish and water moccasins too stunned to fight. The wind kept rising. I felt myself slipping. So I tied myself to the branch with my belt. The water was swallowing everything in the yard. Dogs and horses and duck decoys swept past me. When the water rose to my branch I had nowhere to climb. I saw Grady's deer's head, pieces of candy and a coon's cap. Oh my God. Oh my God. Beau! I untied the belt and tried to grab for some antlers. Everything in the water was moving so fast. Little alligators swept past. Their eyes were blinded by the salt. Cows were trying to catch up their calves. I could hear people screaming. Their voices were being swallowed by the water. I swam with all my might to get to this Holstein. I held onto her neck till we got to Urus's house. The water had climbed to his roof. I saw his boat rocking in the waves. I let go of her neck. The current swept me to the stern. I could feel stunned fish and snakes around my legs. Oh my God! Oh my God! Then I saw Beau. He held out his hand to pull me in the boat. I held him in my arms. His body was trembling. For the first time in my life, I heard Beau speak.

BEAU: "A baby. Baby."

INEZ: There underneath the canopy was Urus and Sherelle. She opened her flannel shirt. Her baby nursing at her breast. It had a head full of wet brown curls. The boat was rocking so much it was hard to keep steady. Sherelle looked tired. She raised her lazy eyelids and smiled.

SHERELLE: "It's a girl, Inez. Her name is Marie Henriette."

## Introduction by Laurie Stone

**D**anny Hoch belongs to the street. The street where Euro-nomads, junk peddlers and drug dealers mingle; the street that harks back, with its spray of ethnic eateries and social clubs, to immigrants who thronged the Lower East Side and Brooklyn. The street where pan-global *luftmenschen* mix with the stigmatized and exiled.

I was lucky to see Hoch early on. The show was *Some People*, the year 1994. What screamed out wasn't raw talent, but craft and concentration. Hoch is a junkie for the way people reveal themselves without knowing it. He has an agile body and a super-powered ear. His mimicry doesn't condescend; it signals no arduous leap. He can slip into otherness, because it's not *so* other. His voices come from the Queens neighborhood in which he grew up, a section that included Jews, Italians, Puerto Ricans, Asians, Dominicans, Cubans, Sierra Leonese and West Indians. There was no ethnic majority.

*Some People* features eleven characters. Every figure is desperate to speak—language is a soul print and way of bursting through isolation. It can also be a stamp of dislocation, as throats choke on alien words. Yet, even the most constricted keep up a natter, like the Polish immigrant, Kazmierczack, who has been sent on a plumbing job to the apartment of a teacher: "Halo eh, you something broke? Something you break? Something you always never very good?" His strain is as valiant as it is absurd; Hoch capturing his bent-head shame but also his bright-eyed search for a bridge. His vocabulary exhausted, he's reduced to groans and sputters.

Blanca's garrulous, tell-it-like-it-is attitude is, for Hoch, the universal urban voice—searching for truth, often misinformed, but consistently street-smart. While being hypersensitive to any signs of AIDS in her gay roommate, she denies it could possibly touch her. When her boyfriend suggests using a condom, she protests, "You ain't sticking no fucking rubber shit up inside me, I don't know who touched it. You might as well put on a rubber glove and do some Spic and Span in that shit . . ."

In his next piece, *Jails, Hospitals & Hip-Hop* (1998), Hoch has unsettling, revealing things to say about young males who aren't slated to own the world, or even their own fates. The mood is hooded, wary, spitting. Flip, a white teenager affecting the persona of a rap artist, Flip-Dogg, interrupts his Rupert Pupkinesque interview with Jay, about his group Montana Gansta Blood Thugs, to tell his mother that he returned the bottles and left the money on the counter. Victor, a young Puerto Rican crippled by cops who mistook him for a criminal, flirts with a woman from Czechoslovakia and wishes he could enter the military: "At least here we got democracy, and everybody's protected."

Flip, with his infatuation for race drag, is one extreme that Hoch portrays. Another is Emcee Enuff, an actual black rapper with gold teeth and Versace shades, making his first appearance on *Letterman* and plugging his fourteenth album, *MC Enuff: Where Is the Joy* on Murder-U Records. Hoch sees the romantic self-delusions in both characters, but he loves their confusion and yearnings as much as he pokes at them.

*Jails* is vibrant and gutsy—Hoch's roller-coaster tongue and morphing body are ratcheted to high gear. He looks at hip-hop as an art of reclamation, turning the less-than-zero poor kid into something better; the boasting rhymes concocted from coded language and egos on respirators, the dances from martial arts postures and erotic juice, the graffiti from an insistence on visibility and a desire to hurt what's been placed out of bounds, and the baggy clothing from over-large prison requisition.

**Laurie Stone** is author of *Starting with Serge* (Doubleday); *Laughing in the Dark: A Decade of Subversive Comedy* (Ecco Press); and *Close to the Bone: Memoirs of Hurt, Rage and Desire* (Grove Press). She has written for the *Village Voice* and the *Nation*.

# from **Some People**

In the following excerpt, two sets of ellipses ( . . . . . . ) indicate the response of unseen characters.

## Blanca

*Blanca, a young, pretty, twenty-something office worker stops by her friend's house to borrow shoes.*

Listen Lisette, lemme borrow your shoes? The short black ones . . . . . . No, because Manny gets off Foot Locker in twenty minutes and I have to take the bus . . . . . . But I can't be looking ugly in the bus . . . . . . So find them! Don't stress me more. All right? My life is already stressed enough, can I tell you? The other day, right? I was at Manny's house, and we was fooling around, and like, you know how guys be getting all shy like when they wanna say something really important but they don't say it? Or like, they say it, but like, their voices be getting all low so you can't hear what they saying? So he was doing that, right, and like I don't be playing that. I was like, "Hello-excuse-me-I-can't-hear-you-what-you-saying," right?

So I figure he's doing that because he wants to ask me to marry him 'cause already we been together one year, nine months, seventeen days and he ain't asked me nothing. So I look, and he got this thing behind his back, and I figure it's a Hallmark card or something saying like, "Hello Blanca, how you doing, I love you, will you marry me?" Instead, he got a condom right? . . . . . . Right? So I was like, "Excuse me, who's that for?" He was like, "That's for us." I was like, "Excuse me, I do not think that's for us." But he goes, "No, we have to use it," because he said that he had seen some thing in like Channel 13 or something, like some thing. He goes, "No, you have to be careful, you don't know what's out there." I was like, "Excuse me, I know what's out there, I'm talking about what's in here," right? I was like, "You ain't sticking no fucking rubber shit up inside me, I don't know who touched it. You might as well put on a rubber glove and do some Spic and Span in that shit, 'cause I ain't having that." . . . . . . No, 'cause, one year, nine months, seventeen days we been together, now he comes to me with it? *Now* he thinks I'm dirty? I ain't fucking dirty.

And he thinks like I don't know nothing. Like he thought that I thought that you could get it from mosquitoes. Plus it ain't like I just met him. I know his whole family, his parents, his sisters. They're nice people. If I would have got something, I would have got it one year, nine months, seventeen days ago, right? . . . . . . No, we talked about it, but you think we used it? . . . . . . We started fooling around, I was like, "You seen *this* in Channel 13? He was like, "No." I was like, "Mmm-hmm."

. . . . . . Not those, the black ones you wore last Friday! The short ones with the bows on it. I'm telling you though, Manny be driving me crazy sometimes for the dumb reasons. Like, you know Manny's father's Puerto Rican and his mother's Spanish. So he's Puerto Rican, right? And he's dark and his last name is Sorullo. So when people ask him, he always says Sorulo. 'Cause he says he wants to work in business in Wall Street, and that nobody wants to hire a Sorullo. So I be telling him, "Manny, that's your last name, you can't do that." And he be getting angry at me like, "That's my last name, that's how it's pronounced!" And like, "You got it easier than me, Blanca, 'cause you're lighter than me, 'cause you're a woman." And I'm like, "Excuse me, I'm Puerto Rican too," right?

So it was the Puerto Rican Day Parade, and I had gotten us these T-shirts with the Puerto Rican flag in the front, and in the back there's a little coquí and it says, "Boricua and Proud." So you would think that he would be like, "Oh, thank you, Blanca, that's so sweet, I love you," right? Instead he starts screaming, "I'm not wearing this shit! I can't believe you got me this! It's ugly!" I was like, "Excuse me, it's not ugly." So he puts on a Ralph Lauren shirt. I was like, "Manny, you think somebody's hiring you for Wall Street at the Puerto Rican Day Parade?" So he goes to me, "Look Blanca, I might be Puerto Rican, but I don't have to walk around looking like one." . . . . . . I was like, "Excuse me. You think that people think that you Swedish? You Puerto Rican." I couldn't believe it. It's like, he wants to wear a condom, but not a T-shirt.

. . . . . . Not those ugly heels, the short ones with the bows . . . . . . So find them, don't stress me more! It's like I be nice to people and they be having temper tantrums. You're like Lemington. You know my room-mate Lemington, right? . . . . . . I know, his name is Lemington, that's weird, right? So you know he's gay, right? And you know if you see Lemington, you be like, "Oh my God, this guy is gay." But if you see his boyfriend, you be like, "Oh my God, this guy is not gay." 'Cause he's like six foot and all muscular. Like when I first had seen him I was like, "Mmm." Like that, right? But he's gay. And they're not only gay, they're black and gay. Can you believe that? I couldn't believe that . . . . . . No, 'cause they don't look like those guys from *In Living Color*. At all. But you know I don't care 'cause I'm very liberal. But I think that his boyfriend be beating him 'cause one day Lemington had a cut right here, and I seen those signs in the subway that like, if you're gay and your lover beats you call that number . . . . . . Right . . . whatever.

So we be getting along, except this one morning I'm getting ready to go to work. It's like seven-thirty in the morning and I'm sitting there eating breakfast, I look up and he's wearing my skirt. So I was like, "Lemington, what you doing with my skirt?" He was like, "That's your skirt?" I was like, "Yes that's my skirt, Lemington, where you got it?" He goes, "In the closet." I was like, "Well that would happen to be my closet, which would happen to be in my room, so that would happen to be—ding!—my skirt," right? I was like, "Lemington, you can't be wearing my skirt." So he starts crying, right? And he's like, "Fine, I won't wear it!" And I can't have him crying in my house at seven-thirty in the morning 'cause then the neighbors be thinking like *I'm* beating him or something, right? So we had gotten over it, right. Except that he be leaving me these pamphlets all over the house like I should read them. Like in the dishes he puts them, in the freezer. So, should I go to get a ice cube, I'll read a pamphlet. Meanwhile I got frozen pamphlets in the freezer. It's this one pamphlet, it's called, "Getting to Know Your Body." It's these drawings of these women, looking at themselves, in you know, there, with instructions. Excuse me, but I don't need to be looking in there. For what? It's money in there? Plus, what if somebody comes over and they go to get a ice cube, they'll be thinking that I'm looking in there with instructions like, what's this? He thinks that I'm like one of these women that doesn't know nothing about her body and goes and does whatever. *(She puts on her lipstick)*

But he's sweet though, he got me this cute shirt with all these pictures of famous womens on it. Clara Barton, Nefertiti, Mother Teresa is on the shirt. And he gives it to me and he goes to me, "Rejoice in your womanhood, Blanca, be good to yourself 'cause you're a warrior." I was like, this is some black, gay thing or something? He called me a warrior. I picture myself like, running through the jungle with a machine gun like, "Look out, it's Blanca coming!"

But the thing is, now he got this little dog, right? And a) he don't be feeding it, so the dog be eating my curtains. Now I don't have no curtains, people could just be looking at me naked through the window. And b) he don't walk it. So the dog be shitting all in my house. And let me tell you, I don't know what the dog be shitting because it got nothing to eat but curtains. It's like, little curtain shits is in the floor. The other day I'm getting ready to go to work and I get out the shower in my towel, I step in this little macadamia nut shit. So he goes to me, "Wipe it." So I wipe it, I took a Bounty but I don't have time to go back in the shower and scrubbing shit out my foot twenty-four hours. So I go to work. People at work are like, "Ooh, you smell like shit." And when I explain to them that, "Excuse me, I do not smell like shit naturally, but I happened to *step* in shit," they're like, "Oh, you stepped in shit? You must be stupid then." And I'll tell you right now, I can't have people calling me stupid, 'cause I ain't stupid.

. . . . . . No, I wanna kick him out, but then he'll think it's 'cause he's gay. I mean it's not that he's gay that his dog shits in the floor, it's that he's irresponsible. Things are so complicated. Plus I think he got AIDS too . . . . . . No, 'cause he's all skinny . . . . . . Yeah, Manny's skinny too, but Manny's just skinny. Lemington's gay and skinny all right? . . . But them people be getting that shit anyway, right? . . . . . . They do though, right? . . . . . . Right. You got them? Finally, gimme. I hope they fit. I'm telling you, you know what is it? *(She puts on the shoes and checks herself in the mirror)* I think my life is stressed because I have to learn to be nice to myself. 'Cause if you think about it, nobody's being nice to me. You included. But listen, I have to go because you're making me late. And these shoes are too tight but I'm wearing them. And let me tell you something. If Manny comes to me with that whole condom thing again, I'm gonna tell him like this, "You think I'm dirty? Who do you think I am? Do you even know who *you* are?"

## from **Jails, Hospitals & Hip-Hop**

In the following excerpt, two sets of ellipses ( . . . . . . ) indicate the response of unseen characters.

### Bronx

*A man in his mid-twenties loiters in a hallway of the C-74 building on Riker's Island, New York City. He conversates with a new inmate.*

. . . . . . Really? That's messed up, man. I hear you . . . . . . Yeah . . . . . . Wow. Hey yo, do me a favor? Take a walk with me for one second? I gotta get a toothbrush. Just take a walk with me to get a toothbrush for one second. *(They walk)* But for real, man, if I was you, I would talk to your lawyer and tell him that you wanna plea-bargain. 'Cause even though you was just an accomplice, if you plead not guilty, and it goes to trial, they could decide to make it a first-degree felony against *you*, and that's it. I'm sayin', whatever, even if you not an accomplice, whatever, bee, I wasn't there, I ain't sayin' you did nothin', man. I mean, I just met you yesterday. But, especially 'cause you're black . . . I mean . . . are you black? Oh, I wasn't sure, I thought you might be, whatever. Still, just plead guilty, guilty, guilty. I seen it happen before. Even if you didn't do it. Otherwise they start makin' deals with all your peoples, make it look like you're the one that pioneered the whole shit. Then they get you for conspiracy when you was just an accomplice—or you just happened to be there, like I said I wasn't there, I ain't sayin' you did nothin'.

*(He calls an officer)* On the gate! On the gate! Officer on the gate! . . . . . . Nah, to inmate services—for a toothbrush, they took his toothbrush in the dorm. Right? Right, they took your toothbrush in the dorm? They took his toothbrush in the dorm! . . . . . . That's my ID card right there. Show him your ID card, pa . . . . . . So we'll wait right here then. Damn, where we going? Right?

*(Back to the guy)* I'm tellin' you, if I was you, I would just say guilty, take the bid, do your little one-to-three, whatever, politic, you know. Me, I got different problems, man. See, I try to do the right thing, they lock me up. Giuliani's like, "Oh, people on welfare are lazy." I'm tryin' not to be on that shit. I'm workin', right? I'm in Fordham Road. I'm sellin' Bart Simpson T-shirts, and um, what you call it—O.J. Simpson T-shirts, right? This cop come up, arrest me 'cause I don't got a license. I'm not selling drugs! I'm not selling drugs! I'm selling Bart Simpson T-shirts, O.J. Simpson T-shirts. That's work, man. You think that shit is easy? That shit is hard, man, I don't even wanna go into it . . . . . . Nah, but that's illegal? They said it's illegal. You know, I'm tryin' to do right in my life, man. I wanna be a entrepreneur, or whatever you call it. You know if I was that little girl that they show on TV in that commercial selling lemonade in front of her house, you think the cop gonna arrest *her*? Nah-ah! Nah-ah! But see, if you think about it, the little girl, she's a entrepreneur, just like me. She's a businesswoman. She got—what you call it?—Overhead. She gotta get her sugar, her lemons, her cups, she makes her stand, then she stand outside all day. Me? I got my shirts, my stand, I stand outside all day. But you know if that cop see her in front of her house with her little white picket fence or whatever, he'd be like, "Oh . . ." —all jolly and shit—"that's so cute, lemme get a lemonade, sweetheart?" Right? And then he'd drink his lemonade and then he'd say, "Mm, tasty . . . whatever, whatever." Then he leave. Then he go beat up some people. Then he go home and fuck his wife, and feel like, it's not really such a bad day today. God bless America, right? But he see me in Fordham Road? Nah-ah, different story. He step to me, "Hey you! Where's your fucking license?" He gonna say, "Where's your fucking license?" to the little girl? Nah-ah! Nah-ah!

See, what is it, he don't care if I got a license, or I don't got a license. He don't like the way I look. I live in 163rd Street, I got a certain look. People in Park Avenue, *they* got a certain look. But the cop gonna see somebody from Park Avenue or Tribeca, hauling three kilos of cocaine to their girlfriend's house, on their designer fucking rollerblades or whatever, he's not gonna get disturbed by their look. He'll say, "Hey, how are you? Have a doughnut. Okey-dokey, buddy." Or whatever. But then he see somebody that appears—I don't even know—*unprofessional*, or whatever, he automatic think criminal.

So this cop, he gets out the car all with his cop shit. But see, he had sunglasses, so when he look at me first from the car, I look darker. When he get out, he like—"Uht, uht." He get *confused*. 'Cause if you put me next to the cop, I'm whiter than the cop. He start askin' me, "What are you? What are you?" I say, "That's not your business, you wanna buy a shirt?" Then he knock over all my shit in the street, the shirts is dirty. Now I have dirty products. I have to pay for that shit. And peoples is laughin' at me, man.

Next thing, he throw me down in the ground, he got his night-stick in my back, with the spit and the gum from the sidewalk is in my face and shit. He say, "What are you, what are you?!! Are you Puerto Rican, are you Puerto Rican?" I say, "Nah, I'm not Puerto Rican yo, I'm selling Bart Simpson, O. J. Simpson T-shirts, what's the problem officer?" But see, he wanna know, what am I? I mean, my color is white like Bill Clinton, but that's not good enough for him, you know, in the way that I'm speaking, or I don't even know. He got a complex, he needs to see a therapist 'cause he's confused. Then, he look at the T-shirts, and he get more confused. 'Cause he don't know who's Bart Simpson. He knows Bart Simpson is Bart Simpson, but he don't know Bart Simpson is Dominican, Jewish, Greek, Puerto Rican? What is he? He don't know, but he know that Bart Simpson and O. J. Simpson make more money than *him*, so he feel threatened. Then the cop look at me, and he see somebody that's a entrepreneur, that's trying to start a business from nothing, that I'm busting my ass. He see that I have the possibility to better my situation. That I have the opportunity to increase my status, or whatever you call it. And then he looks at himself, and he sees that he's just a servant and that's it. Even if he turn captain, lieutenant, police chief, whatever, he's just a *servant* and that's all he *gonna* be . . . So he feel threatened. And 'cause he feel threaten, that day he gonna decide capitalism is illegal. And 'cause I got a prior felony on my record, they put me in here. *(To another guy)* You got a cigarette?

*(Back to guy number one)* See, if you analyze it with the little girl and the lemonade, that's supposed to be America, right? That you could stand outside your house and sell whatever. If that's not true that you could do that, don't advertise it then. Don't put it in the TV, you know? To be honest with you, I seen that commercial, I got inspired by that shit. I said yo, shit ain't really that bad, I got chances and shit. Now I'm in fucking jail, bro. I feel like *suing* them lemonade motherfuckers, man. Or suing somebody . . . . . . For false advertising . . . . . . I know I wasn't selling lemonade, that's not the—Hey yo, shut up, bro. I didn't really ask you to respond and shit, damn.

*(To another guy)* You got a light? *(Back to guy number one)* . . . . . . Nah, they arrested me a month ago, I ain't even had a hearing, nothing.

First they had me in C-73, I was there for two weeks, but I got in a fight, this guy tried to cut me. Motherfucker tried to assassinate me right in the TV room and shit, 'cause I wanna change the channel in the TV. So they transferred me to 74, lock me here . . . . . . Nah, this kid tried to step to me 'cause I tried to get them to watch something else, man. They sitting there for two weeks watching that Tonya Hardy/Nancy Kardigan shit. How you gonna tell me that shit interests you, man? You don't even know what's figure skating, I told them, man. What the fuck is that? That concerns you? Ice-skating got nothing to do with my life. Once my mother took me ice-skating to Rockefeller Center when I was three years old, I fell in my ass and I cried, I said, "What's this shit? A sport?" Now I'm in jail and I sit there every day, I have to watch that shit. That shit is punishment for real, man.

I don't give a fuck about one girl don't want the other girl to win the World Ice Medal, then she gonna start scheming and get some kid with a golf club to hit her in the fucking knee. That shit is cartoons, man. They in there debating over that shit, fighting. "She did it!" "No she didn't do it!" I told them, "You in jail, man, fight over your shoes or some shit!" Goddamnit. But you know what is it? I figured it out. It's that people like to see these smiling cornflake-type women fucking each other up. 'Cause if you think about it, you never really see, or you rarely see, nah, you might see like in a soap opera or some shit. Like, one lady's like, "Oh, I'm gonna take her man," or "I'm gonna stab that bitch," or, ". . . poison her tea . . ." or whatever. But in real life, they're all sitting around the sofa drinking ginger ale and shit. So when it happens in real life, people eat that shit up. They're like, "What?! Two white ladies fighting? Where?!" and shit. They pay money to see that shit. In cable. In pay-per-view.

Every single day for four months, in the news with that. Right? . . . . . . Who you trying to play? You know you was watching. But see, they make that ice-skating/golf-club bullshit the number one story. They try to make you think that that's the most important shit that you should be concerned about, so that you forget, they try to distract you, to make you ignore, from that you can't feed your kid and shit, that you can't fulfill your dreams 'cause people won't hire you 'cause you got a felony on your record. Fuck that, I had to change the channel man . . . . . . Nah, this kid wanna act hard rock with me, pull a razor. Pssh. I cut him before he cut me . . . . . . Nah, he wanna force me to act like a criminal. I ain't in here 'cause I'm a criminal. I'm in here 'cause I'm poor, that's why I'm in here!

*(To the officer)* . . . . . . Huh? A toothbrush . . . . . . Yeah. That's what we're waiting for. *(To guy number one)* Go get your toothbrush . . . . . . Nah, he ain't gonna let me. He ain't gonna let me. Yo, see if you could get two . . . Tell 'em they took two . . .

## **Introduction** by David Román

The first time I saw Marga Gomez perform one of her full-evening solo performances was at Josie's Cabaret and Juice Joint in San Francisco. It was the spring of 1993 and she was workshopping *Memory Tricks*, her tour-de-force solo piece about her vexed relationship with her mother. I remember being immediately struck by how Marga was able to maneuver deftly from high hilarity to quiet poignancy. Since then I have seen her perform in a wide range of venues throughout America, from neighborhood coffeehouses and benefits for grassroots, progressive organizations to prestigious regional theatres and hip performance spaces. Whatever the venue, Marga playfully baits the audience with a kind of "can-you-believe-this?" rhetorical wonder and before we know it, the entire audience has fallen under her appealing spell. If we're not at the edge of our seats it's because we've already fallen off them from laughing. A gifted storyteller, Marga's performances combine the high energy of stand-up with the focused intensity of a poet.

Her first two full-evening pieces, *Memory Tricks* and *Marga Gomez is Pretty, Witty & Gay*, explored questions of sexual and cultural identity. *Memory Tricks*, like *A Line Around the Block*, tells the story of Marga's child-

**363**

hood and her relationship with her parents who were both active participants in the thriving 1950s Latino entertainment milieu of New York City. The daughter of a Cuban comedian and impresario and a Puerto Rican exotic dancer, Marga grew up in New York City in the midst of this Latino performance world. *Memory Tricks* is about her effort to understand and forgive her mother after a history of disappointments. In it, Marga performs both herself and her mother, and in the process begins to conjure a lost world of Latino popular culture. This world is embodied more fully in *A Line Around the Block*, where the vaudeville culture of forgotten Latino entertainers serves as the backdrop for Marga's homage to her father.

In these works, Marga pays tribute to her parents by recycling both their public performances and private anecdotes. In doing so, she records this legendary, if largely undocumented, Latino entertainment scene. The individual memories that compose her stories are thus recirculated as the collective reenactment of a lived cultural heritage. In this sense, memory is not merely a nostalgic longing for a previous moment of cultural stability. Rather, memory is a means to investigate the individual and collective meanings of identity.

Marga's work provides, at once, a social context for her audiences to consider her self-representations as a Latina lesbian and the historical context for her career as a solo performer. But unlike other solo artists whose work is defined by identity issues, Marga's work is as much about performance itself as it is about identity. *jaywalker*, Marga's latest solo piece, makes this point beautifully as it hilariously chronicles Marga's adventures as a Latina lesbian in Hollywood. Can Marga be any more marginalized? Well, it turns out she doesn't even drive. In *jaywalker*, "pedestrian" suggests the lowest rung in the social hierarchy. *jaywalker* charts Marga's picaresque adventures; along the way it satirically comments upon Hollywood's immediate commodification of marginalization. But like her father, "La Jaywalker" is also a believer.

*Memory Tricks* and *A Line Around the Block* set the personal and cultural foundation for Marga's own contemporaneous struggles as an artist. And yet these performances not only capture the struggles of Latinos but they capture what we might call a kind of "Latino resilience." If *A Line Around the Block* moves us to restore the fading legacy of her father's artistic vision, *jaywalker* reminds us that a woman without a license can still drive the show.

**David Román** is a professor of English and American Studies at the University of Southern California. He is the co-editor, with Holly Hughes, of *O Solo Homo: The New Queer Performance* (Grove Press).

# from **A Line Around the Block**

MARGA: My father was a believer. When every *teatro* in New York was going out of business, he started his own. He bought the old Triboro Theater in Harlem. He got a loan and a lawyer and new publicity photos. I still have one. He's wearing a white tennis sweater and an ascot. His mustache is perfect. His hair is fluffy. There's a Parliament cigarette dangling from his lips. At the bottom of the picture you can see the lit match burning down to his fingers. His expression is tough, like he knows he's about to get burned but it's worth it.

    With the grand opening of the Teatro Latino a week away, my father was getting extra productive. Usually he didn't change out of his pajamas until show time, but now he was up and dressed and ready to go in the morning.

WILLY: Good Morning, Miss Gomez. I have a big surprise today. Your father is taking you to Orchard Beach. We can take some fresh air. Sunday is the big day for Orchard Beach. We need to be seen. Think of the publicity for the show. What do you think?

MARGA: We went. My father's beach attire was less than fabulous. Instead of sandals he wore his bedroom slippers and socks to the beach. He used the same pair of brown-and-white swim trunks he brought from Cuba as a young man. Now they were faded and stretched out and I looked up into them accidentally and saw his balls, but he didn't notice 'cause he was thinking again.

WILLY *(Sitting on a beach towel)*: We need shows for the entire *familia* to share. The old *abuelitas* and the teenagers together, that's how it used to be. Now there's trouble with marijuana. We have juvenile delinquents. They don't listen to their parents. That's why I say to you don't let me catch you with marijuana, Miss Gomez. Because if I do then it's over. I'll kill you. Okay? *(To a passerby) Hola.* Nice to see you. Are you coming to my Grand Opening? Okay. Next time. God bless you. *(To Marga)* This beach is no good anymore. When the money comes in from Teatro Latino, I'm going to put a swimming pool in the backyard. What do you think? And I'm going to build a cover over the pool so the neighbors can't throw bottles at us, don't worry. Tell your mother about the pool. I bet that Italian palooka she married doesn't make a pool for her. How's your mother? Does she ever talk about me? Hmm. She will . . . She was the most beautiful girl in any of my shows and so talented too. *Que se yo.* I don't think I'll find another one like her . . . *Dios mio!* I'll be right back. *(To the passerby)* Hello, how are you today?

MARGA: Right then a tall and tan and young and lovely girl walked over. She could have been from Ipanema until she opened her mouth.

BABE: Excuuuse me are you Willy Chevalier? Wow! You're the one who's doin' that big show with Bobby Sylvio? Wow! All right! Thank you. They're daisies. *Mira*, I wanna give you my telephone number. Can you tell Bobby Sylvio to call me? Anytime. Tell him I love the way he dances when he sings. Wow! He's so groovy. I'm serious.

WILLY: Okay I'll give this to Bobby Sylvio. ASAP. You can count on me, Baby. 'Bye, 'bye. *(He rips up the number and stomps on it)* Marga, get the towels. It's time to go.

MARGA: We went to City Island for dinner. My father swallowed a dozen raw clams and finally relaxed. At sundown we walked to the pier and he climbed into an empty motorboat and got behind the wheel.

WILLY: Miss Gomez would you kindly take my picture. I want to show Petra. You remember I told you about my friend Petra. Very nice girl. She don't believe I have a boat.

*(A flashbulb pops.)*

———

*Two years later. Willy enters carrying a box.*

WILLY: Did the magazine people call? Are you sure? Were you talking on the phone, Marga? Did you go out? Is the phone working? How do you like that? They are going to ignore my birthday spectacular. Ah! That was eight months ago. You think these magazine guys remember when was my last birthday spectacular. They can't remember to call me back. When the Teatro Latino goes down then they'll write the same baloney. "What happened to the *artistas*? What happened to the shows?" Now I have to compete with that garbage on Channel 47. Everybody's watching TV in their panties, eating *chicharones*. I'll fix that. *(Pulls out a parking ticket from the box)* How about this? A guy walks to his car and he sees a parking ticket there. He thinks, "*Conjo. Que paso?*" But the ticket says, "You are hereby summoned to Teatro Latino. To answer a charge made against you by Police Officer Willy Chevalier." I printed five thousand of them. We'll put them on cars all over the *barrio* while people are sleeping. I should work on Madison Avenue.

*(House lights up. Marga hands out parking tickets to the audience.)*

MARGA: Come to Teatro Latino! Here, pass these down the row please. I was supposed to give these out when I was sixteen but I didn't feel like it. "What did you do on your summer vacation, Marga?" I put fake parking tickets on cars in Harlem with my father. How queer. Fantastic show at the Teatro Latino! See the world's only Garcia Lorca impersonator! He was a major buzz kill, let me tell you. But my father got him cheap. You are hereby summoned to Teatro Latino! Which isn't there anymore 'cause it got torched in a riot. My father lost everything except for his Café Pico gigs and Petra who moved in after the Teatro burned down. She was a country girl from the mountains of Puerto Rico. She killed flies with her bare hands. She wore her bellbottoms too short. She hardly knew any English and if she wanted a soda she'd ask the waiter, "What kind of Coke do you have?" What a hick. All she needed was a rope belt. We'd have to do stuff together. Go out to dinner. My father always took us to the same place, Blanco's Spanish Restaurant in Greenwich Village. It sucked. You could get better *paella* in Alabama. I hated Blanco. I hated Petra. I hated my hair.

BLANCO: Petra, how incredible you look tonight. You don't deserve her, Willy. And Marga, what's wrong? Are you bored, Darling? What can we do for La Marga? Maybe the boys at the bar can invite— Okay, okay, Willy. I just thought . . . but she's not my daughter. How about a nice *paella* tonight? Would you ladies like that? Or Petra, if you prefer, you see that lobster tank over there? Pick out the three biggest ones you find. We'll take them to the kitchen, boil them alive and serve them to your table. Because as I say to Willy, "Blanco's *casa es su casa*." *Mira*, Willy, your money is no good here. Save it for your next *teatro* and this time get insurance, eh. Always the *comico*. And to drink, Petra? We have every kind— orange coke, grape coke, Pepsi coke and Coke coke.

---

## from **jaywalker**

Hello. They call me The Jaywalker. In Spanish I am known as La Jaywalker. I want to share something with all of you tonight. But first, by applause, who hates Los Angeles?

*(Applause.)*

That's too bad because hate isn't spiritual. I used to hate L.A., then I learned that it takes much less energy to love it. There are so many reasons. The culture, the surgery is unbelievable. The quality of life and the air are second only to Bombay and the caste system. I see the beauty of it now. Just like the first day I got here.

It was pilot season. There was a carnival atmosphere all over town. And right here on Hollywood Boulevard I saw John Tesh get his star on the Walk of Fame. And it made you feel like anything was possible. I had big dreams. I believed that if I worked hard and played by the rules I could make a difference. Someday I would play the first lesbian on *Baywatch*. I did everything you're supposed to do for a career: I studied my craft, I quit smoking, I joined a gym. I read . . . very little. I wore an itty-bitty backpack. I got a boob job . . . just one, they're expensive. I hired a photographer to take the perfect composite shot. Every serious actor should do this. It was like getting four head shots on one 8 x 10 that showed off my acting range by the different outfits I was wearing. I was a doctor, boxer, hitchhiker and a burn victim. I mailed this masterpiece off to every agent in town, and to make a bigger impression I slipped candy bars in the envelopes with a funny note, "Hungry for candy? I'm hungry for success." A trade secret I picked up from reading *Dramalogue*.

I did my homework. I was doing all I could do to succeed in L.A. except for one thing—I couldn't drive. I never learned.

*(In a lousy Spanish accent)* Because where I'm from, in my country, Manhattan . . . it doesn't matter.

So, I walked everywhere. And I felt good about it. L.A. needs pedestrians. On every crosswalk there's that sign with the arrow and the button that makes the light turn green. If it wasn't for the pedestrian who would push those buttons? How would the traffic flow? That was my job and I pushed that button like this, with pride! Drivers would call out their windows to me, "Thank you, Lady. Thank you."

I think that's what they were saying. And I'd say, "You're welcome, Isuzu," and haul ass across the street before another actress could sneak up behind me to push the button and get me killed. It happens all the time, but nobody talks about it.

Pilot season attracts a certain amount of homicidal talent. And they get away with it. "Oh I didn't see her, Your Honor, I'm blond."

You must look out for the other pedestrians here. Just because somebody's not behind the wheel doesn't mean he can't be an asshole.

Like the day I was walking down La Cienega admiring the carpet displays. And this guy with a gym bag cuts me off . . . And he says, "On your left," as he passes me like there are lanes on the sidewalk, like he's a Jaguar and I'm a dented Chevy.

"Hey, we're all equals on the sidewalk, Mister." But he couldn't hear me 'cause he had the windows rolled up inside his head.

*(Walking music.)*

Mostly, it was just me, walking alone for miles and miles of pristine sidewalk. Like Lawrence crossing the desert. That's when I felt free. I'd take giant steps, skip to my Lou, Moonwalk, La Bamba, James Brown, Vertigo, Riverdance! I'd walk on the wild side but when I reached the corner I'd stop. Push. And wait for that ever-loving green light to shine down on me. Yup, it's a metaphor. While I waited, I practiced the creative visualization techniques I learned from *Dramalogue*. *(Breathing deeply)*

I saw myself not as a star, but as a working actress, respected by my peers, with TV and film credits on my résumé, quality roles at scale or better. I saw myself with a career long enough to qualify for free psychotherapy from the SAG insurance. I could see that! Me with the premium SAG insurance.

How wonderful it would be succumbing to diseases that were covered. "I've got Ebola and I'm loving it . . ." *(Coughs)* "Take me to a specialist. Charge it to SAG." The future looked so bright.

I wasn't The Jaywalker then . . . They called me 215, that was my room number at my hotel in Hollywood. I found it in the yellow pages and was lured by its claim of European-style ambiance. They didn't lie. I felt like I was in Europe, during the war years. Shabby and smelly, but the service was great. Every night housekeeping would turn down my bed and leave a fresh cockroach on my pillow.

I was lucky to get a room there. People say L.A. is transient but nobody ever moves out of hotel rooms. It's the apartment complexes that can't keep anyone. My hotel was never vacant even if most of the hotel guests were. They all seemed to have industry connections. The hotel lobby floor was like the floor of the stock exchange. Messengers were flying in with deal memos. Fed Ex was there twice a day with stacks of scripts for everybody. Even housekeeping was getting scripts (for maid roles) because money can't buy imagination. Incoming faxes were piling up. The phone never stopped ringing. Every message the desk clerk took was urgent. *(Breathing deeply)*

Someday all those messages, faxes and scripts would be for me. But, whenever I asked the desk clerk if anybody called, she would look through all her pink slips and say, "215? . . . No, nothing." Sometimes she'd build me up first, "215? Right . . . let me see. I'm pretty sure we got a fax for . . . 214. But you're 215, right? Wait a minute . . . 315 has an audition on Monday but . . . 215? No. Nothing for you. Nothing," she'd say, always with a smirk.

If she only knew of the career I would've had if it wasn't for Jennifer Lopez. It's all about Jennifer. Everybody loves her.

I bet you wish it was Jennifer Lopez here instead of me. That's cool I'm used to it. Let me tell you something about Miss Lopez. You know how she got where she is? She stole my look. That's how I used to dress. I had the big ass first. She copied me. She stole my moves too. When you watch *Selena* you're watching me. That's not all. I wanted to open a nightclub in town before Jennifer Lopez opened the Conga Room. She upstaged me. Now I can never open the Conjo Room, which would have been a really fresh concept in Latino nightlife. No music, no dancing, just Latino cursing and a full bar. *Conjo! Carajo!*

———

*After The Jaywalker fails to find love.*

Whenever I needed guidance I would make a pilgrimage to John Tesh's Hollywood star. John Tesh is an inspiration to pedestrians everywhere. I didn't just walk to his star I'd walk to it on my knees. It was hard to reach the pedestrian button from that height.  Which made my journey long and lonely.

(*On her knees*) John . . . all those girls at the discotheque tonight, they were kind of stupid but they all had development deals and assistants and babies and their babies had assistants and they drove those sport-utility-starship-trooper vehicles from the future with the 4x4x4x4xInfinity. How do I get that, John?

(*The sound of a UFO/SUV and high beams bear down on The Jaywalker. She hears The Voice of The Industry speak:*)

"*Buenos Dias*, are you looking for acting work today? Here's my card."

(*The Jaywalker stares at the card for a few blissful moments as the UFO/SUV zooms off.*)

He was from TBA. The Big Agency. They represent Matt Damon and New Zealand. He said they were looking for Latinos.

There was a buzz about Latinos. *Variety* had declared it "Week of the Latino." And there was a hot pilot in the works, a Latino spin-off of the hit series *Friends* called *Amigos* and he thought I might be right for the Latina Jennifer Aniston part—Rrrraquel!

I just about floated back to the hotel. Tears were streaming down the face of the desk clerk as she handed me a fax, a script and three dozen long-stemmed roses from The Big Agency. For a glorious week, TBA wined and dined me and left numerous urgent messages for me with the desk clerk. I pitied her. Every morning she was forced to present me with more long-stemmed, American Beauty roses from Equador. Although she was now able to maintain her composure, I could smell the Prozac on her breath.

## Introduction by Alissa Quart

Mike Albo stands on the prop-free stage looking like an Ur-East Village boy, lanky, with a cap of black hair. He's modern dancer-ly, though he's not even trying to have a "physical vocabulary."

"Dear Diary," he reads from his richly unaware, preteen journal. Soon, the diarist has gone, folded into Albo's seething New-Age group leader. Albo's audiences, like San Franciscans at a Steve McQueen festival, laugh with super-ironic glee when Albo morphs from a Goth, fast-food worker searching for the Bloomsbury circle into a morality-free art director. Shape-shifting notwithstanding, Albo and collaborator Virginia Heffernan's writing resembles experimental poetry far more than it does a Tracey Ullman special.

Albo is uneasy listening. His performance style first distances his audience with a wall of words, then absorbs them. Albo and Heffernan concatenate almost-recognizable things—linguistic theory and brand marketing, sophisticated comic books, dystopic fiction, alternative comedy, confessional theatre and John Ruskin. The effect is mildly hypnotic.

Albo's stage persona brings his viewers closer. He widens his eyes with a wizardly intensity and then he's sweet or mad or soigné—the physical con-

371

duit for the double personality of Heffernan/Albo. Though he takes on many characters, it goes a little deeper than trying on roles for size, because these personalities are already parts of Heffernan/Albo. It's both extremely personal and polyvocal. "We see our show as couple's therapy," says Heffernan.

Albo has written poetry most of his life and even has a poetry MFA. from Columbia. Heffernan's personal style is ebullience dusted with erudition. She spent her twenties studying and teaching nineteenth-century literature at Harvard University, and is now a magazine editor. Albo's tastes are a bit more rough. He writes an astrology column for an internet magazine under the pseudonym "Randy Lavender," a spacey, oversexed New-Ager. He listens to elliptical lo-fi music.

One of their shows' major tropes—and source of hilarity—is a rather unfunny thing: the abyss. In sketch after sketch, emptiness threatens to destroy the ornamental surfaces of Heffernan and Albo's characters. "Our shows go from nothingness to everything—rhyming crème fraîche with Anne Heche—to nothingness again," says Heffernan.

For instance, Albo as amoral, manic art director concocts a list of dastardly magazine covers. Suddenly he declares that his job is nothing, that everything is "empty." Then, the art director assimilates this abyssal moment. He turns the nothingness into a style: emptiness, simplicity, rose petals, aromatic oils!

Their sketches resemble Language Poetry, a verse school that emerged in the 1970s. That experimental poetic is organized around the readers' often highly idiosyncratic reception of words in the ear or on the page. If there is a straightforward "meaning" within the poems of this school, the reader has supplied it. Language Poetry's disjunctive phrases, often enumerations of brand-names and technological argot, act as critiques of advertorial language and faulty social structures. The poetry can be gnomically comedic, as in the work of one of Albo's favorite poets, Ron Silliman. As with Silliman, Albo and Heffernan's favorite linguistic units are the sentence and the word, rather than the monologue as a whole. One can sense the duo's faith in the sentence in the excerpts following this introduction.

Albo and Heffernan's shows satirize ad-addled contemporary life, a world where experience has become so mediated that it may not even exist anymore. But Albo and Heffernan also love their junk culture. When Albo recites: "Netscape Yahoo Netanyahu Net HOT Anyahu! Hotbot Not-ham cashmae tastations anorexic orthorexic tanorexic bigarexic literati gliterati digerati castrati noterati notdogs mocktails are all really hot right now," he's really into America's lingo and its hucksterism. The two have got a sweet tooth for our magazine-metaphor self-descriptions, the TV-promo vernacular of our overheard conversation. But they want us to remember that these things are not just amusing, they are also very strange.

**Alissa Quart** is a New York-based poet and freelance writer. She's a regular contributor to the *London Independent* and has written for the *Washington Post*, *New York* magazine, *Publisher's Weekly* and *Kirkus Reviews*.

Written by Mike Albo and Virginia Heffernan; performed by Mike Albo.

## Reeee!

AAAH! Oh My God Hi! Hey! Hi! What's up?

I'm fine. What's up? How are you? I'm fine. What's up with you? How are you? I'm tired. Working . . . nothing . . . I'm tired . . . I can't wait for Friday . . . Wednesday's hump day . . . Thursday's are really fun! Mondays . . . yuck! Tuesday's sort of a blah day.

It's cold. Don't you think it's cold in here? It's so cold. But yesterday I was so hot, phew it was so warm, oh my God it was so humid. It's so weird. It's dry heat.

It's so cold in here!

I am so tired. I just had too much coffee. I have to have some coffee. I love coffee, you know? I am coming off of a total caffeine rush. I am such a coffee addict! Reeee! You Know! Reeee! Reeee! You know?

Really? Actually I don't drink coffee anymore either. Sometimes I do, but most of the time I don't. In a way it makes me more tired. And now I am so much more awake since I stopped drinking it. Sometimes I get too much sleep and that makes me more tired, and sometimes I am so tired I can't sleep because I am overtired.

I don't drink coffee anymore. They say coffee is really bad for you. I drink tea! I don't eat cheese anymore. I cut cheese out of my diet. I eat tofu! I drink a LOT of water. I run about eight miles a day. I think I'm lactose intolerant.

You know I haven't been here in so long. I have been really busy. I haven't been drunk in so long. I'm just busy doing things other than going out, so I can't really waste time drinking. But actually, I don't really drink anymore? So when I get drunk I am a total lightweight. But I never get drunk because I never go out because I am Really, Really, Really busy.

It's really mixed here . . . It's a really mixed bar. Have you been to Cherry Bar? It's pretty mixed. Temple Bar is mixed. Lounge Bar? Mixed. Rebar? Mixed. Mix Bar? Mixed. Big Bar Baby Bar Buddha Bar Beauty Bar The Bar Babar? Mixed, not mixed, mixed, not mixed not mixed not mixed mixed.

It's either going to be really boring or really fun. You know, like one extreme or the other, like really boring or SO FUN.

Oh my God I have so much going on I have something today, something Monday and something Tuesday. I am so busy I never go out. I'm the biggest homebody. I'm like, "What's *Melrose Place*?"

We didn't have a TV when we were kids. My parents were total flower children. My mom and I are like best friends. My mom and I are really different people. I think I am beginning to see my parents as people now. I used to be like, "Hey Mom. Hey Dad" and now I'm like, "Hey." Now it's more like just hey.

Really? Actually my high school didn't have cliques, you know? We all pretty much just hung out with each other without judging each other . . .

I was looking at some old pictures of my grandmother, and she was so beautiful when she was young.

My great-great-grandmother was a squaw so I'm a sixteenth Cherokee Indian.

I tan really easily. I burn really easily, though. I am definitely getting skin cancer because I was in the sun SO MUCH when I was a kid. I am a total beach person. I'm more of a beach person than a mountain person. If I had to choose between the mountains or the beach I would definitely choose the beach.

Wait. Did you get a haircut? It looks different. Something's different. I thought you wore glasses. Maybe that's it. Or your teeth? Your goatee? Pantene? Maybe it's me. I need a haircut. Really? Thanks. Actually, I don't really wash my hair anymore. At first it was greasy but then it became cleaner than if I used shampoo. Shampoo is really bad for your hair because if you think it cleans it it doesn't because it actually cleans it down too low.

Did you see *Faces of Death*? Did you see *Harold and Maude*? Did you see *Wings of Desire*? Have you seen *Clueless*? Have you seen *Kids*?

The thing about Alfred Hitchcock was that he was scarier because of what he didn't show, so that you really had to think. Like when I saw *Pulp Fiction*, which was good . . . but you really didn't have to think, you know what I mean?

My eyes change color with what I wear. I really like to watch people. I take the worst pictures. I don't believe in organized religion. I think I'm agnostic. I am so asexual right now. I am so bisexual right now. I am so celibate right now. I think I was sexually abused when I was little and I can't remember it. I was really depressed last week.

I need to be forced to go to the gym. I love the gym. I hate the gym. Exercise really gets out a lot of stress. I am so stressed out sometimes. It's probably because it's fall. It's probably because it's a full moon. Oh God, I am such a freak. I am such a dork. I am such a slut. I am such a space cadet. I am so out of it today. I don't know what's wrong with me. I don't know what's wrong with me. I'm just so tired! I am just so tired.

Alright, I'll see you later. Good luck with your laundry. Good luck finding your dress, good luck with add/drop form. Good luck getting where you're going. Good luck. Yea, whatever! OK, OK, 'bye, 'bye, see you soon, 'bye. Hahaha. 'Bye!

## Oh My God Remember

Someone is killing off all the models and it's up to Matt Houston to catch the killer. Someone is killing off all the models and it's up to Decker to catch the killer. Someone is killing off all the models and it's up to Slater to catch the killer. Tonight Magnum is stranded on an island of beautiful women. The Fall Guy loses his face when a machine goes haywire on the set. And Jamie Sommers finds more than she bargained for in a deadly piñata. With special guest star, *People* magazine's sexiest man alive, Scott Bakula.

On a *Growing Pains* you'll never forget! On a very special *Webster*. On a very special *Full House*. On a very special *Wonder Years*. On a *Sister Sister* you can't miss! Tonight the Hogan Family says good-bye to five seasons in America's living rooms! Roarke's final fantasy. Lobo's last lockup. Thorpe's last layup. The final *Hulk*. The last *Family*. Good-bye Larry. And America's funniest child stars salute floats with special guest host Joe E. Tata and Anne Jillian!

Tuesday night! Wednesday night! Thursday night! Friday night! That night! That night! That night? That night? Remember? That night we slept together? Remember that night we slept together?

Remember *Happy Days*? Remember the Fonz? Remember how the Fonz was a dropout and then he became cooler and cooler and cooler until he just became purely magic and could turn on lights and had telekinesis? Remember how you tried to get telekinesis for so long by sitting and trying to move the curtains with your mind? Remember how it sort of worked?

Remember *The Love Boat*? Julie the Cruise Director! Remember how on *Love Boat* everyone went into their rooms and had nightcaps? And that's where you first learned the word nightcap? But first you thought that a nightcap was sex because they always had sex when they said they were going to have a nightcap and you never noticed the drink?

Remember before you ever even wanted sex and had no desire to drink nine nightcaps and stick your tongue in someone's mouth?

Remember when we slept together?

Remember having toys? Remember Dumb Dumb Ditties, Hungry Hungry Hippos and Trouble and Sorry and Mousetrap and Hi Ho Cherry O, Micronauts Muppets Hot Wheels Etch-a-Sketch Fuzzy Pumper Barber Shop Nerf Toughskins Tiddleywinks Twister Toss Across Sit and Spin Stay Alive Legos Lester Kerplop and Gnip Gnop? And Merlin and how on Merlin you could play six games, oh what were they, what were they?

Remember being a child, remember kind of being a child, remember not being a child at all? Remember *MacGyver TJ Hooker Dr. Shrinker Mr. Belvedere Bewitched Benson Bloopers*? Remember? Remember we slept together? Remember when we slept together? Remember you were going out with someone else so it was imperative that I get all my clothes on and leave at five in the morning?

Remember me? Remember I met you at that seventies party? That eighties party? That nineties party? The all-four-decades, bonanza, blowout barbeque!? Remember when you called me and you were drunk and I didn't care that it was late? Remember when we went on that lame, shapeless date? Remember we talked on the phone and totally built things up? *Sleepless in Seattle!* Remember you were such a freak that you made me wear five condoms? *Boy in the Plastic Bubble!* Remember when you wore face powder and eyeliner and ruffly sleeves? *Man in the Iron Mask!* Remember when you called me Mr. Weiner the Taffy Man? . . .

OK, I was wearing seventies bell bottoms and a green polyester shirt and I was carrying a *Bionic Woman* lunchbox and you were wearing this Members Only jacket and these Jackie O. sunglasses and had Doug Henning hair and *Grizzly Addams* beard and *90210* sideburns and holding a Fabulous Fred (remember that!) a god's eye (remember those?) a pet rock (remember those?) and a Rubik's Cube (remember those?)

Remember all those crazy clothes? Forenza and Jordache and Swatch and Chams! Flats and Sassoon bags and pegged pants and checkered Jams! Merry Go Round and Up Against the Wall and TJ Maxx! Acid wash and skorts and painter pants! Remember wearing them? Remember wearing them again? Remember buying them for hiked-up prices at vintage stores and they never fit? Remember they smell like baby spit? Remember wearing them and unzipping them off each other and sleeping together? Remember? Remember?

Remember a possible time when we were actually experiencing something?

Remember when I blew you off because the world is so sadly out of balance and no one seems to like each other equally anymore? Or when you blew me off because I talk too much . . . just like *Funny Girl* or *Whose That Girl* or *That Girl* or *Georgie Girl* or *Girl Interrupted* or all five mixed up together! Don't you remember?

I don't wanna grow up, I'm a Toys "R" Us kid! Gimme a Break I sure deserve it Here's a story of a lovely lady Well it's time to change A Temporary Layoff Come and knock on our Door A noun is a person place or thing When you skate a figure eight I'm Mister Heatmiser boy the way Glenn Miller played Wonder Woman it takes Diff'rent Strokes Electrowoman and Dynagirl The Facts of Life A Doll A doll Lolly lolly lolly De Plane! De Plane! Moncheechee Moncheechee Schlameel Schlamozzle Oompa Loompa Nanoo Nanoo Get a little bit softer now get a little bit softer now get a little bit softer now get a little bit louder now get a little bit louder now get a little bit louder now.

Remember me? Remember I was so fucked up? Remember you were so fucked up? Remember that we slept together? Remember that we kissed? Remember that? Remember that? Remember that? Remember? Remember?

I'm sick of remembering! I'm sick of remembering! I'm sick of remembering!

---

## from **Spray**

Written by Mike Albo and Virginia Heffernan; performed by Mike Albo.

### Hot/Not

OK, the gift bag is only for people who came to the Dunkin' Donuts Twisties 2.0 reception at Wipe, I'm going to have to ask you not to take one. You have reached the R.S.V.P. line for Adore the Poor, today's hit-makers respond to poverty hosted by Beck, Brandy and Debbie Matenopoulos—this R.S.V.P. line is full. Happy Easter. Excuse me, Hahaha, I'm sorry the poinsettia mint terrariums are for display only, OK, so let's try not to take them. If you move through here, I can take your coat and you can grab a cushion for Demi's reading.

Hello do I know you? Do you know my husband? I'm sorry but this is a private party, and these are my close, personal friends. I am afraid I will have to ask you to leave.

Look you have several TBIs on the guest list but not—yes you do. It says your name plus twelve, Lizzie Grubman, Russell Simmons, Shoshana Lohnstein, OK, OK, OK, check it, check, check it yourself but I really need for you to tell me at least fifteen minutes before I open the door who you're inviting!

Excuse me. Excuse me, SIR! You cannot take your drink beyond this point, excuse me either stay inside or throw away your container! Excuse me, you can't smoke, touch the walls, laugh, intibate, or peep here—this is an historical landmark and the room is very delicate. Excuse me, the cover is eighteen dollars. Excuse me, there are no reentrances. Excuse me, don't—Excuse me, would—Excuse me, we—Excuse me— *(Long pause, he holds up a finger)* We are filming a movie. You're going to have to be quiet, could you please shut up, we are filming something, we have turned the entire city into a set so could you please not move!

## 3 Secrets

In second grade I had a girlfriend during recess named Michaellyn. She had blond hair and bright pixie pixie blue eyes. We were the hot couple that spring. We would walk out on the blacktop and people would say, "Michael A. and Michaellyn!" We were really in demand and highly visible. We spent the better part of recess walking around holding hands, making appearances in the gravel section, visiting friends at the jungle gym, dropping by the old dodge ball court to see the old dodge ball gang, still single and smackin' the ball around. But I was under such pressure. She wanted to be a horse, and she would trot around and make me call her: "Cloudy! With a chestnut coat, and a white star on my forehead and snout!" When we walked through the playground she would harumph and clomp her feet with purebred pride. She would take me to the part of the playground hidden by hedges and I would have to pretend to feed her sugar cubes and carrot tops and she would lick my hand and then talk about getting lathery. I didn't mind for a while, but I just remember this time near the end of our relationship, we were holding hands and one of the tetherball kids asked if we were going to get married. "Yes! Definitely!" I heard myself say. I just stood there and smiled and inside thought, I am living a lie.

In third grade, my family weirdly moved to Las Vegas for two years. We lived in this *Knots Landing*, stucco house in a cul-de-sac. Everyone around us was divorced. My mother got really into the whole Santa Fe style and decorated every room in this contempo, Southwestern, teepee motif. Our whole house was covered with Native American rugs and horsehair sculptures and cactuses and Katchina Dolls, grasscloth wall-paper in salmon and rust colors, and a cute miniature papoose door-knocker. We didn't have pets because my mom didn't want poo tracked all over the house. I had a hermit crab named Felix. I wanted to pet it really badly, but it always shied away into its shell. One time I opened up the top and tried to pet it and the terrarium smelled like butter and I ran to the bathroom and threw up. I put Windex in its water tray, not to kill it, really, just *because*, and it turned gray and died. I had a gerbil in sixth grade for three days. I really wanted to pet that too. I wanted to pet it all the time. I would get these funny urges in school and yearn to go home and pet that fucking gerbil. On the third day I took it out of the cage and petted and petted it and held it in my hands and looked in its little teeny, tiny, beedy eyes and I wanted to pet and get inside its furry warm fuzziness and its little fur and I wanted to be inside it and love it so much so I squeezed it. I love you so much, little gerbil. I love you so much. I love you so much. I couldn't stop squeezing it so much and then . . . it stopped jerking . . . and went limp. And died. I lightly put the body back in the cage. "I don't know what happened, Mom, it just died. I don't know what happened! It just died!"

Seventh grade summer I spent every single day at the pool until my eyes were two burning, chlorinated balls. All I did all day was play Marco Polo and eat candy from the snack bar. One time I was at the pool and it was a really hot day and I don't think I drank any water. I went to the snack bar and had some Good-N-Plenty, some Pixie sticks and then bought a big bag of Skittles and stood in the grass eating Skittles. I just was crunching so many of them that all the color flavors were intermingling and I just kept eating and eating them and then, uuuuuh! My throat closed and my eyes started watering! And I thought I was going to die and I suddenly peed this sugary Skittles pee, and peed in my Speedo and dove into the pool!

## **Introduction** by Peter Askin

**D**ael Orlandersmith kicks ass. A wonderful poet, a force of nature on the stage, Dael writes and performs with a fearlessness that allows her to cut deeply and make you look at what she unearths. Whether challenging a belligerent drunk outside the rehearsal hall, or challenging an audience with a harrowingly raw monologue, Dael isn't afraid to get in your face.

Her work harnesses the extemporaneous, free associative energies of the jazz musicians her characters so often admire. She composes as they do—writing in a poetic form, she riffs, improvises, experiments, all the while discovering what her story is and who the characters are.

Most often, those characters are loners, losers, outsiders seeking release from spirit-crushing circumstances. Their efforts sometimes bring tragedy, sometimes transcendence, frequently both. The catalyst may be at the bottom of a liquor bottle, a rape, or in the books of a local library. Those not drawn totally down into the mire of despair float away on a river of James Baldwin and Arthur Rimbaud, or on a riptide of Lou Reed and Miles Davis. The power of music and literature frees Dael's heroic outsiders from their families, their neighborhoods, themselves—if only for a moment. Such moments define her characters' purest joys, their most enduring relationships. But in Dael's work, even the exhilaration of escape is shadowed by pain: those who get out invariably do so alone.

Dael grew up in Harlem, started writing at an early age and by her early teens was performing her poetry at the Nuyorican Poets Café with the encouragement of Miguel Piñero. Her work has often been labeled autobiographical because it feels so naked, so honest, so close to the bone, but such conclusions make her bristle. She once said, "I have the right to invade my own privacy," from which one might infer, "and *you* don't." But that's what her monologues feel like: an invasion, an unsparing revelation of dark and personal things; those watching often squirm at the unaccustomed intimacy.

In a recent interview, Dael noted that any time someone does a one-person show people assume it's autobiographical but, "It is not the fact that it's based on somebody's life that interests me," she says, "What interests me is if it comes alive on the page and on the stage. Anybody can get up and tell you their life story—but they have therapists offices for that. I could care less. What interests me is the darker side of human nature—because it gets us to the light. I like it when people are forced to look at themselves."

When I first saw Dael perform her solo piece *Liar, Liar* in 1993 at Manhattan Class Company I was totally intimidated, when I recovered—impressed. I introduced myself and we started working together, fleshing out character monologues and using her poetry as bridges between them. The result was *Beauty's Daughter* which received an OBIE Award.

The dramatic spine of her next show, *Monster*, was the history of the family of black women who owned a house in Harlem, and the abuse that was being passed from generation to generation within it. But as usual, the most compelling aspect of the story was Dael's own voice, and the "poetic narrative" of the character, Theresa.

Once a show begins, Dael's locked in; it's hard to tell how aware of the audience she is. She's in her own world, ready to start cutting. In *Monster*, the back to back description of the rape from Theresa's perspective and then from Winfred's (the rapist) is always a powerful transformation. In all of her pieces, costumes, sets and props are kept to a minimum. The work is about her voice and the power of her presence on the stage. With everything else stripped away, the audience can maintain its focus where it belongs: on Dael Orlandersmith—alone, the soloist in full command of her instrument.

**Peter Askin** is a writer and director in New York City. Among many other shows, he directed Dael Orlandersmith's *Beauty's Daughter* and *Monster*, John Leguizamo's *Mambo Mouth* and *Spic-O-Rama* and the John Cameron Mitchell / Stephen Trask musical *Hedwig and the Angry Inch*.

## from **Beauty's Daughter**

### Thirteen 'n' Bleeding

I am thirteen 'n' Bleeding
'N' there are bloodstains in my
Panties
And the Catholic school
Uniform itches my skin and
I'm
Told that I gotta watch
Myself now
'Cause
I'm a girl now
And
I gotta get my hair
Pressed 'n' curled 'cause I'm
A girl now
And
If I wanna go to Randall's
Island to shoot dice and
Play stickball with a gang
Of boys, I can't
'Cause I'm a girl now
And
If I dream of
Touching boys differently it's
Because I'm becoming
A young woman now and
If I dream of lipstick
Traces, it's because
I'm becoming a young woman
Now . . . but I think
"What about my leather jacket
And how I wanna wear it
With one earring, with the
Bold/cold air of a
Reinvented female?"
And I'm thirteen 'n' bleeding
With blood
Gushing from between
My legs, for the

Next forty years
And
The woman I'm supposed to
Emulate is standing
Before me caught up in
Some inebriated spent
Perception
And
I can't believe I sucked
Milk from those defeated
Breasts or
Whispered childhood secrets
In those withered ears and
I don't want to have babies
Give life from red—gore—
Blood.
I'm thirteen 'n' bleeding
In a Harlem living room
Left to flick switchblades
In the dark.

---

## from **Monster**

THERESA: Marsha—remember the voices / the paper-thin, Harlem wall-dwellers / in / around this house / raging / screaming voices / bitter / beat / angry / voices / around this house / this house Grandmother Sophia owned / then later my mother Beula / who just died / just died / can't believe / she just died / gone / left me this house / this bitter / beat house / and I can still hear the voices / Nana Sophia's raging / snarling / voice, "beat, beat, beat your children" / more voices / my mother Beula's voice / "Make sure that men want you / be pretty for the men / act pretty for the men / for the men" / Then the voices from the tenants / hanging onto every word / they listen / listen to me dream / talking to myself / "She's crazy," they say / "listening to that ole weird shit / who she talking to?" / they're listening to me / laughing at me / they would you know / they would / you knew / felt it / how it could suck / suck / suck / you / me dry / and those voices off the avenue / the voices in Harlem / 122nd Street and Madison Avenue, Harlem / cut / you / me / cut / you / me / cut me down / down to the ground / those voices / that went through you /

Dael Orlandersmith

straight to me / words / voices meant to cut / you / me / down—
"hey, here comes the white girl / actin' like a white girl" / Walter,
Tootie, Brother and Peaches would say / aiming their voices
through you / at me / aiming their voices at me / watching me /
standing on the corner / watching me / standing on the corner /
smoking reefer / wasting time / they had nothing but time / their
voices crashing into this house / Marsha, I want to break down
their voices / Marsha / smash their voices / I would, you know /
but there's Emma / Emma's voice / face / smile / how can I sell the
house / leave Emma's voice / smile / love / behind / I need to go /
sell the house and go / painful here, Marsha / it's painful / I can't
hear mine / my own voice / I got a hole in my heart / I can back
it up / I can kill / I want / need to burn down their voices / 'cause
it's my time / My time . . .

———

. . . I'm walking 122nd Street and Madison Avenue / trying to walk
erect and correct / trying not to get lost / trying to block out my
grandmother's and my mother's machete voices screaming
through at each other / I'm seeking quiet or hard-core riffs from
a sparse guitar / Walter, Tootie and Brother are dancing a Kool 'n'
the Gang / mandrill dance / and Tootie and I / Tootie and I / I look
in Tootie's eyes / a second / her / my eyes lock / a second / I /
she / we remember a conversation about a book we both read
three years ago / we connected three years ago / on my stoop /
two black girls on a Harlem stoop / then somebody / her brother
they say / does her / does her they say / and she cries / goes hard /
street hard / doesn't call my name no more / in a second / I /
she / we / remembered just now / I knew / felt / saw / she remembered / Let's go back to three years ago / she turns her back / keeps
on dancing / they / they don't want to let me pass / but I keep my
hand on my shank / If you're on 122nd Street and Madison
Avenue trying to find your own / and you know it's not there /
where a game of hopscotch means dodging used syringes / you
learn to cut / you better learn to cut someone deep / On 122nd
Street and Madison Avenue in my room / my head / my head-
room / I discover Iggy, Lou Reed, Hendrix / and I wanna James
Baldwin, Kerouac, Jean Genet, John Cocteau / Go Rimbaud / Go
Rimbaud / I better find the longest shank I can / What I listen to,
it bleeds out to the streets / I get called "white girl" and mother
Beula shakes her head / wishes me dead / I brace myself for that
long walk from 122nd Street to the subway contemplating ways
to kill everyone / kill myself / chanting a genocide suicide mantra.

I walk downtown / Kerouac / Baldwin / they said it's down-town, East Village / black / yellow / white / brown / jazz / jazz / more jazz / people / me / I'm lookin' for rock 'n' roll / I'm lookin' for home / lookin' for family / and the people are wearing different kinds of clothes / and the people are walking a walk / different / the same / of / everybody else / I wanna get next to / in / connect / how do I do that? / Get into / next / connect / be part of / Want to know their names / café / bar / rock 'n' roll people / what are your names? / And another black girl / sister / rocker gives me the power sign as we hear the New York Dolls from a car radio / and I think it might be / may be / down here / East Village / might me / may be /

all right
all right
all right

But I'm only fifteen, and soon I gotta get home / Soon I gotta put my hand back on my shank / Soon I gotta prep myself for that subway / bus ride that takes me back to Harlem and Lee, Brother, Walter, Peaches, Tootie / they're still on the corner / 'cause they got nothing but time / "White Girl / Here comes the white girl," they yell / 'cause they say, they figure if you're black / you shouldn't read / they figure I'm black / kick back / stay back / back in the ghetto / "Where you belong" / they say that / They say not to read / or hear / see colors / see / hear / music / different kinds of music / to wanna live elsewhere / somewhere / somehow / good / well 'n' fine / it means to be white / not black 'n' proud / black 'n' proud / in the ghetto / Stay black in the ghetto / stay black 'n' poor / in the ghetto where you once / always / belong / cut / shoot / gun 'n' shank they say means to be black / stay black / stay black / cut / shoot / cut / don't dream of leaving / 'cause you're black / and Kool 'n' the Gang is at full volume screamin' out "Hollywood Swingin'" / Kool 'n' the Gang / is just loin-groin riff / Harlem ghetto riff / a loin-groin, fuck-in-the-alley, ghetto riff / I've seen / heard that / all the time / all my life / against the wall / against the wall / but Jimmy, Iggy 'n' Lou gonna give me more than that / I walk to the house / ease the key in the door / peep down the hall / Marsha, my homegirl, looks out / shakes her head / her mother and my mother are scotch high / scotch high / Johnny Walker Red high again.

———

WINFRED: I'm thinking of my girl Theresa. An' I'm feelin' bad 'cause, you know, she ain't with me, right? I mean, you know what I'm talkin' about? Like when your woman ain't around, man? Dat's some hard shit. *(Beat)* She write poetry and listen to classical rock. You know 'bout that shit, right? Well, my girl, she like it, too. *(Beat)* You should see her, man, she got soft, smooth skin. Yeah, and she got much booty—I likes dat booty, man. In order for me to peep a broad she gotta have some ass. Gots to. *(Beat)* Man, ever since we wuz kids, she wuz writin' poetry and stuff to me, thru the wall. Readin' thru da wall. See, the buildin' I lived in, right, her mother owned. Me, my sister Marsha and my mother live there. And me, Theresa an' Marsha wuz friends. Tight, like family, right? Like I would look after dem, you know, 'cause it's rough. *(Beat)* Like, I protect Theresa. Niggas 'round the way hated her 'cause she listened to rock and all that shit, and dressed different from them. But see, dey ain't know her like I did. Niggas wanted to get next to her, man—see, dat's what it wuz. An' they wuz jealous, 'specially when I tole 'em how she would talk to me through the wall. *(Beat)* See, me and Tee, see das what I call her, "Tee," right? We close. We have our own thing. Ya'll wouldn't understand it. It was like a made-up language, the way she talks to me, an me listenin'. *(Beat)* "I spread my dreams under your feet. Tread softly, for you tread on my dreams." And she got this white gown on? And she ain't wearing nothin' underneath it or nothin'. And she got her hair, right, she got nice, long hair and it's spread all over the pillow. And she sayin' all this, lyin' on the bed. And her legs is open. She's touchin' herself. Puttin' her fingers up there and gettin' wet. She's gettin' real wet. And this classical music is playin', and her eyes is close, and I hear her call my name in our language. She's talkin' through the wall 'cause she want me to come to her. But she scared 'cause she never did it before. *(Beat)* So this one night I'm goin' upstairs, but I sees Theresa's door is open. And I walks down da hall and she cold 'sleep in da bed. Like she waitin' for me? An' I walks over to the bed an' sits down, and she wakes up an' I say, "Hey baby," and she say, "Winfred, whachoo doin' here?" An' I say, "Well you want me here. I'm here." *(Beat)* Den she say, "Winfred, I don' wanchoo here, go!" And I'm lookin' at her like she crazy an' I say, "Well, you tole me so, readin' and talkin' to me through the wall." Then she like, "I never tole you nothin'. Get outta my room. Get the fuck out now." And then I gets mad 'cause all this time the bitch wuz playin' me. Bitch wuz playin' me. So I slaps the bitch an' say, "Put yo' face in dat pillow, bitch, and don't even look at me." And she's breathin' hard and she got on pajamas and got a big ass. Nice, big ass. Always did like dat big ass o' hers. I tell her, "I want me some of dat fat ass of yours, I'm gonna get some." And I'm lookin' at all dese posters of white boys 'cept for dat nigga Jimi Hendrix. An' I goes over to him and pulls his face down, 'cause he ain't nothin' but a white nigga too. And I say to her, "You a white bitch. You a real white bitch. Dat's why nobody like you." And I gits on top of her and she says, "I hope nobody raped Marsha. I hope nobody did to her what you're doin' to me now. I hope your dick rots, faggot." An' I slaps her ass an' say, "Bitch, you talks white, too, huh? You talks like a whitey. Git bad wit me again." Then I slaps her across the head but she don't cry and I say, "Oh, you a hard rock bitch? You hard." An' I pulls down her pajama pants and she says, "Oh my God." And I say, "He ain't gonna help you now." And this white music is playing in the background and I'm sweatin' and I know if somebody catches me I'm gonna go to jail, but I don't care. So I goes to the record player and takes that white rock shit off, 'cause I can't get hard to that shit, and put on some Marvin Gaye and my dick is on the bone. And I says, "You gotta nigga dick in yo' ass now, bitch." And she starts to cry and I say, "You like it bitch. Like it? I ain't no white boy in yo' ass. You got a man's dick in yo' ass. A real nigga dick, bitch. A black, black dick. Ain't no pink or some high yella nigga he'ah either. You ain't so high an' mighty now, bitch." And I rides this bitch. I ride her hard and say, "You gonna 'member me, bitch. Yeah, you and all this white shit. I'm too low for you to talk to, huh, bitch? Yeah, I got me a white bitch wid a nigga ass in Harlem. *(He closes his eyes)* I'm ridin' her, man. I'm in her, man. She's my girl, my girl. An' I say, "Theresa, let's make a baby." I say, "I want you to have my baby. An' I'm a be the man of da house." And she cries real hard and says, "No." And I slap her 'cross da back and ride her harder. *(He smiles)* And she's sayin', "Winfred, why? Why?" She got her head in da pillow. An' I tell her, "See, you like it, right? You do." Then I gets off. Walk 'round da room. TV's too big for me to take. Then I goes back to the dresserette, dere's only five dollars, I take dat and I say, "I got to go now, Honey. But I'm gonna take dis five dollars off da dresserette, okay." Then I piss all over dat white linoleum floor.

*(Patti Smith's "Gloria" plays in the background.)*

THERESA: And Winfred's dick is in my ass / In my ass / He mocks me for liking rock 'n' roll / He doesn't like rock 'n' roll / Doesn't wanna like rock 'n' roll / "White bitch," he calls me / And Patti's in the background chanting, "GLORIA," and I'm thinking / "How could this happen?" / I'm blindfolded / cold, sharp metal and he wants to make a baby / he says, "You and me," he says / and he could be the man of the house, he says / 'Cause he was always the man of the house / and I'm thinking / "I'm only fifteen / I don't want a baby" / I'm thinking how God doesn't like me . . . God doesn't know I'm here / Or if he did, he doesn't care / I left the door open / how could I have done that / his dick is way in my ass / Winfred, he's forcing his dick in / through me / I'm going to shit myself / I can't / won't / cry out / Winfred wants to know if there's any more pussy for the taking / My mother, she's in her room / Can't / won't / let him do it / Get next to her / "Put your shit on me," I say / "Get your shit off on me," I say / He's laughing, calls me a freaky bitch / freaky / white / freaky, nigga / bitch, he says / Winfred, he's forcing his dick in / through me / and I say, "I hope it rots motherfucker / I hope it rots" / He slaps me / I talk to myself / I talk to myself / Maintain myself / Try to maintain some cool by talking to myself / 'Cause that's all I've got right now / Myself / Cold metal / Cold metal / In / through me / He mocks me for liking rock 'n' roll / He's in / out of my ass / He's in / out of my ass / Where is God right now? / Where is God? Why God? There is no God / Take me now, God / Take me now / He gets off / pees on the linoleum / kisses me / kisses me like a sister / like a child / says it's our secret / I'm blindfolded / I fall off the bed / belly crawl / belly crawl / through in his urine / my face wet with his urine / it lands on my tongue / I'm belly crawling / belly crawling / I belly crawl to Beula's door / She screams how she wants to die / she wants to die / "He should have killed us both," she screams / I'm on the floor doing a belly crawl / I can't feel myself / Emma / she holds me close / Mommy Beula swigs from scotch / she reaches for Johnny Walker Red Label / I reach for Emma, "Don't let me go, Emma / please don't let me go" / There are policemen / questions and a hospital room / How'd I get here / I'm on a table, my legs are bound in stirrups / Stirred up legs / A male doctor / Jamaican, demands, yells / screams that I open my legs / "Stop being foolish," he says / I unbind my legs / punch him / punch him, he screams like a punk / like a faggot-hearted, punk-ass bastard / then a nurse, a white nurse / pink lips, uneven pink lips on pasty skin / gonna try and jump and stop me / jump and stop me / I twist her arm back / I'll take you down, bitch / low down bitch / down / Down / I bring her down / down, down to her knees / Security guards come, warn me, "Someone will give you a hypo" / they say, "Be cool," they say / "Better be cool," they say / I adjust myself / check / rearrange myself / I become cool.

**Introduction** by Charles Mee

**D**awn Saito works from within, from material that is deeply personal and at the same time implicitly shaped by the history and culture in which she grew up. Saito is a first generation Japanese-American. Her father is a Buddhist priest and was in the Japanese Imperial Army during the Second World War. So her sense of theatre and of character—of what it is to be human—is not a mode of psychological realism but something more complex. She takes the stuff of her life, often chaotic stuff, often unbearable stuff of pain and ugliness and despair, and casts it in aesthetic form.

Physically, she can't put a foot wrong; she can't put her body into a position that is not completely pleasing and amazing to look at; she can't create a visual cliché or a banality. Each image in her work burns into the memory—vivid, crystal clear, beautiful and deeply moving. In this way, she can deal with material that is too personal, too inchoate, too unedited, too raw, too excruciating to hear, and render it with such eloquence that we can't bear to turn away.

Several years ago Dawn and I worked together on a dance theatre piece called *My House Was Collapsing Toward One Side*. She was not only choreographer and performer, but also wrote much of the text. It was the story of a woman who lived through several centuries, through love affairs and war, under various expectations of the kind of woman she should be. The dramatic tension lay in the juxtaposition of listening to the nightmarish text and seeing, in her movement, sometimes grotesque, but always riveting, the longing for beauty.

She has been greatly influenced by Butoh—which, of course, is pure movement performed without text—in particular by the work of Hijikata and of her own teachers, Mariko Okamoto and Oguri. And she has been influenced by the work of Robert Woodruff, Robert Lepage, Ping Chong, Joanne Akalaitis, Mabou Mines, The Wooster Group and Henry Threadgill. These two strains of influence, from Japan and from some of the cutting-edge artists of North America, combine in her work a deep sense of Asian history and performance with a very keen interest in life in America today. As Robert Woodruff notes, "Saito combines the sensual, the grotesque and the musical into an investigative shout of celebration, grief and awe. Plus she tells a great story."

Her most recent piece, *HA*, was greatly supported by Ruth Maleczech and the Mabou Mines/Suite and was developed in close collaboration with director Maria Mileaf. Mileaf describes *HA* as "a mythical dreamscape unraveled through the adventures of one woman, mute as a child, who must confront her family secrets in order to reclaim her voice." Except for a small stack of various-sized wooden boxes, Dawn performs on a bare stage (black floor, white cyclorama). She enters wearing a long flesh-colored latex dress, spinning and transforming from young girl to animal to old man and then, at last, she speaks as herself, telling the story of her grandfather.

The music of Erik Satie plays, and she moves as if flying; she speaks of her mother, and her elbows seem tied to puppet's strings; she speaks of her grandmother, who used to fan-dance; feathers rain down from the sky and she falls to the ground as if she were a bird shot down. At one point, the cyclorama shifts to a "cool blue" as Dawn puts on a white wig and becomes her grandmother, sledding through the arctic expanse; at another point she is a snake doing an erotic burlesque. The real world is rendered as hallucination.

In the end, she opens a box of red ash, wipes it across her lips, lifts her hands above her head and lets the ash rain down on her face; and at last, as the lights fade, she vanishes in a cloud of red dust.

This is neither Butoh nor Woodruff; it is unique to Saito.

**Charles Mee** is a playwright whose most recent pieces are *Time To Burn* and *Full Circle*.

# from **HA**

*The performer appears in a dim light wearing a long, flesh-colored latex dress resembling snake skin. She spins and transforms into different characters. She struggles to speak to the audience.*

The first time I saw my grandfather, I lost my voice. I was five years old. My grandfather Yuzo had only half a face. When he tried to speak, his one eye bulged as he sputtered and grunted like a rabid beast. I thought he wanted to tear me apart and devour me. I got so scared, I swallowed my cry. I stopped talking. *(Pause)*

My grandparents lived in the Arctic. My grandfather wanted to move there from Nagasaki to live in quiet isolation. They blended in with the peaceful Inuits who at times looked Japanese, and they didn't have to speak much, but just smile and gesture with their hands.

My mother hated her parents. She never adapted to the arctic cold and wanted to leave as soon as it was possible—but you couldn't rush time there—the sun wouldn't set in the summer and would barely come out in the winter. She eventually moved to San Diego and met my father in the zoo.

*(The performer transforms into a monkey and leaps about the stage during the voice-over of the Naturalist. She circles wooden boxes and opens one and pours popcorn over her head. She picks the popcorn off the floor and nibbles.)*

**NATURALIST** *(Voice-over)*: **Bolivian Titi Monkey, Central South America. The Spanish word "titi" means "little monkey." These small primates inhabit tropical forests feeding on leaves and fruit. Titi monkeys are monogamous and pairs defend a fixed territory. The male helps in child rearing and the close bond between the family may be seen when they huddle together with their tails entwined.**

*(She speaks from a squat)* When I was seven, I started to eat white food. I became obsessed with controlling the color of my shit. I would be an experimentalist like my father who was a cage cleaner in the zoo—and would bring home samples of animal excrement for fertilizer. He methodically tested different animal feces and labeled separate plots to see what would bring in the most opulent harvest. My father had this notion that if he could grow the best okra, the slippery juice would lubricate my tongue and throat to initiate the motion of my talking. For a long time he focused on monkey turds, especially the Kikuyu Colobus from Kenya. This inspired me to study my shit every day. And I was only interested in white food—cottage cheese, wonder bread, marshmallows, tofu and coconuts. I wanted to be white so badly, inside and out. *(Begins*

*to rise to a stand)* I figured if I could shit out white, I could achieve spiritual purity like my sister who was twelve years older and dedicated to eliminating dirt.

*(Erik Satie piano solo begins and the performer moves forward as if flying.)*

My sister Tukta lived in a beautiful apartment in Manhattan. After anyone walked on her floor or touched any surfaces, she'd paint it white. Every day, she painted her cabinets, closets and cupboards. Then she stopped eating except for bits of white powder, and she smoked cigarettes incessantly. Tukta talked about her teacher Sai Baba and opened a box and dipped her finger into white ash. She sucked the powder off her finger and said these were the ashes from his body. Baba would wave his hand and ashes would materialize. To eat his body was all that she needed. "Baba loves you," she repeated. Then she poured some ash in a folded piece of paper and said, "When you go home, you eat him too." She wrapped her thin arms around me and kissed me, leaving a taste of Baba on my lips.

*(During the voice-over, the performer descends to the floor and rolls around in awkward contortions.)*

NATURALIST *(Voice-over):* **Did you know . . . they are not picking fleas! Grooming is a social behavior often exhibited by primates . . . Monkeys and apes use fingers to part fur and pick out bits of food, dirt or dead skin. Grooming may also serve to cleanse wounds, stimulate oil production, aid in temperature regulation and demonstrate friendliness toward fellow primates.**

———

When I moved to the Tenderloin District in San Francisco, *(She looks stage left to see if she is being watched, then turns back to the microphone)* I started to eat meat. I still had a hard time ARTICULATING, and thought meat will make me assertive. I could hear my mother preaching, "You need meat, you have no color!" What did she expect from a white diet? My inability to communicate encouraged a kind of . . . isolation. I was lonely. Meat demands attention, just the sizzling aroma alone is aggressive. Unlike my grandfather, I forced myself to live with people and looked in newspapers for shares with meat eaters. I thought I would take a chance, even though meat constipated me.

     My first apartment was a funky railroad with greasy wallpaper that smelled like bacon. I was in the middle of three bedrooms lined next to each other like cages. Jack was on my right. April to my left.

     Jack, to my right, was a cable TV disciple of this Japanese guru by the name of Assahara. Assahara was blind in one eye, like my grandfather, and unattractive in a beefy sort of way. Jack told me that fortunate disciples would get to drink Assahara's bath water or eat a cut of his hair.

Jack also had a penchant for confessions. One night he told me that the biggest sin he committed was when he was working in a medical school hospital. He had to work on his thirtieth birthday. Part of his job was to transport the cadavers from the freezers to the classrooms. On route, he touched a dead woman's clitoris. He told me that was the first time he touched a woman down there. He said, "SHE was CHILLY, and also kind of hard and rubbery and . . . BLUE." He said, "At least I can die and say, 'I touched a woman' . . . I have death hanging all around me on that job, you know . . . I ask a lot of death questions, Father." Father? Did he say Father? I've become a catholic priest? What do I say? I, I try to be supportive. I could say, "Well, that was an unforgettable learning experience . . . son." . . . OR . . . UH . . . "Have you thought about taking a good stretch class? *(She stands up and stretches)* You know, to release all that pent up tension. Personally, I hold it all in my teeth. I've been told I'm a real gnasher when I sleep." Or I could say, "Get some therapy you sick fuck. Who do you think this one-eyed Japanese cat named Assahara is? You say he makes some shit-kicker holy water cut from his own bath water that sends you High on a Skyfari Ride! No wonder you feel fucked-up, that mix will screw you up. And Assahara says we are an endangered species and we've got to save ourselves and multiply and he's making this gas that will sting your nerves and he wants to release it on subways to make you sing out the news of Trans-Global Amnesia. Yeah, right. It's like a non-sectarian-secularized-psilocybin denomination where ANY-THING GOES! And another thing, DON'T CALL ME FATHER! I've never gone to church, and my parents are strict empiricists!" *(She drops the microphone)*

Instead, I just made a noise . . . HA. It's simplistic, yet it covers the spectrum of all that goes in between the ambiguous UH-HUH to MMMM?—it's controlled, yet respectful enough to slip by.

*(She speaks into the microphone again)* Anyway, Jack didn't even eat meat, but April did. I looked forward to sharing a bratwurst with her, but whenever April was home, she locked herself in her room. I took it personally, after all, I know I wasn't a great conversationalist, but I felt a real bond with April. I wanted to tell her that I came from a family of entertainers too. April. April Fresh was her stage name. April danced at Fantasy in the Flesh, where you stick a quarter in a booth that's part of a glassed-in strip floor in the round. April met her boyfriend Andrew off stage. Andrew worked the booths. He had to hose them down and douse them with Lysol, kind of like cleaning out the cages in the zoo.

*(She howls into the microphone like a wolf.)*

———

*(Sound of wild animals. Performer looks stage left to that same ominous place, then walks stage right to a medium-sized box. She opens the lid, unleashing the sound of a tremendous wind blizzard. The cyclorama changes to a cool blue, creating an arctic landscape. As she speaks to the audience, she puts on green latex gloves and pulls out a feather boa. She wraps the boa around her head like a parka.)*

I had just turned ten when my grandfather Yuzo went off on his sled one day with his huskies to go ice fishing. He never came back. The only thing my grandmother could think of was that the ice cracked beneath him and he fell into the sea and could not find the hole above him and was trapped beneath the ice which was at least several feet thick.

*(She carries another large box to center stage and sits on it sideways)* Right after Grandpa died, I visited Grandma. She never cut her hair. It was in a tight long braid. She picked me up on a sled with her new huskies. *(She lifts her legs as if riding a sled)* "HHAAAAAAA!!" she screamed and the huskies took off as if soaring on ice. "HHAAAAA!!" I screamed, the cold stinging my face. I was flying!!

*(She turns toward the audience and unwraps the boa from her head. She props her feet up on the box like a little girl)* That night, the arctic light descended, deepening the bitter cold. It hurt to breathe and I couldn't sleep. Grandma unbraided her hair and wrapped me inside. She took off all my clothes knowing the best way I could get warm was skin next to skin. I was frozen . . . I couldn't feel my fingers or toes. She blanketed me in her hair and nuzzled her nose against mine, her face felt like leather, but the skin on her body was smooth and smelled like olives. Her breasts melted my cheeks and I felt like I was covered in fur, beautiful white, smoked with spices. She squeezed me tight and said, "I wish Grandpa could hear you talk, he felt so bad when you lost your voice . . . he said HE DID IT, that it was all his fault."

When Grandma died, Tukta sent me a box.

*(The performer gets off the box and opens it. She lifts out a long white wig and puts it on as if she's putting on grandma's hair. She takes out a small wooden box and opens the lid, but it frightens her and she quickly shuts it. She takes out another small box and pulls out a calla lily. She stands and starts to exit. She hesitates and turns to look back. She uncoils the calla lily and reads the message inside.)*

". . . when the last individual of a race of living things breathes no more, another heaven and another earth must pass before such a one can be again." William Beebe, Naturalist.

*(She takes a bite out of the lily. Glass harp music begins and the performer drops the lily as if hypnotized, and moves forward as if attached to a low-to-*

*ground, slow, torturous stretch machine. She speaks and at different points, she is pulled from a different part of her body.)*

Several years after my grandmother died, my mother took me on a Skyfari Ride in the zoo and told me the real story about Grandpa Yuzo. As I was hanging on the sky looking down at all the caged animals, she told me that Grandpa was a medical researcher in Unit 731 headed by General Shiro Ishii. The unit operated in the prison of war camps near Harbin in Manchuria, where Japanese specialists experimented with human torture and biological weapons. Grandpa lost half of his face when he was testing balloon bombs to carry plague-infected fleas targeted for San Diego for the summer of 1945. Inside the camps, he witnessed prisoners being drained of all their blood and pumped with pineapple juice or coconut milk. He witnessed torture with electrical currents to see how much voltage a person could stand, or body parts being cut off without anesthesia. Mom said Grandpa would wake up screaming, remembering a Russian soldier in a six foot jar, pickled in formaldehyde, cut in two pieces vertically. There were other jars containing feet, heads, internal organs, all neatly labeled "American," "English," "Frenchmen," "Chinese," "Korean" and "Mongolian."

*(Sound of electrocution. The Naturalist officiously shouts into a megaphone. Then performer freezes into different tortured poses mixed with past characters.)*

**NATURALIST** *(Voice-over)*: **DO NOT ANNOY, TORMENT, PESTER, PLAGUE, MOLEST, WORRY, BADGER, HARRY, HARASS, HECKLE, PERSECUTE, IRK, BULLY RAG, BOTHER, TEASE, NETTLE, TANTALIZE OR RUFFLE THE ANIMALS!!!**

*(Lights illuminate the stage as if broiling in desert heat.)*

I am wandering in the desert to catch a glimpse of the ocotillos in bloom when I get stabbed by cactus needles as big as sea urchin spikes. *(She walks over to another box and pulls out bright yellow CAUTION tape)* I am told if I pull out the needles, venom will be released and I will die instantly and I can't move until an antidote is processed in Sumatra where an indigenous plant possesses the cure. Not to mention the nasty scars I will have after pulling out the needles.

    *(She walks downstage, closer to audience as if confiding a secret)* I had this job interview once where I was filling out the application, when I came upon the question, "Do you have any scars? If so, where?" I'm not going to tell where my scars are. It's like undressing in front of strangers. Whether you like it or not, exposed scars leave you naked with a story everybody wants to know. Why can't scars be emblems of survival or beauty marks instead of marks of ugliness. Why couldn't I see past my grandfather's face?

*(She looks stage left as if confronting that haunting presence, then begins to wrap herself in the CAUTION tape for protection. The cyclorama turns mango)* I stand erect in the burning desert watching the horizon melt into shades of mango when the sky turns into a red snake whipping and slashing around and clamping its fangs into my throat to choke the breath right out of me. Ruby suddenly appears with hands like eagle claws and yanks the snake from my neck just as it's about to release its venom. She puts the head of the snake to her mouth and sucks it slowly inside, the whole of its body down her throat. The snake slithers its way inside her, finding its way down, out of her hole, sliding out creamy from her juices, coiling around her legs, and dropping at her ankles.

Grandma tells me, "The poison of the Red Spitting Cobra can kill you. But not me! I eat the snake and give birth to your mother. Poor Yuzo, no one else ever talked to him, not your mother, not even you. Tukta talks to him now. But it's too late. He's trapped in ice. Why didn't you talk to him. Why didn't you talk to your grandfather?"

*("Harlem Nocturne" begins and the performer transforms into a scary snake doing an erotic, grotesque burlesque. She peels off the CAUTION tape, green latex gloves and feather boa. She is lit in the front, so you see her magnified shadow dancing on the back wall. After the dance, she runs over to the microphone and confesses as if being interrogated.)*

There were no eyes, no nose, not even any lips, but these teeth were thick and heavy like . . . AMBER . . . like they had this ancient history of never being brushed and they had the stains of tobacco and blood that were polished into this translucent gold. I was waiting to hear a voice. I thought maybe these were the teeth of God—maybe I'm finally having some kind of . . . transcendental experience like I'll hear the message of TRUTH, or something like that. The teeth were JUST getting ready to speak . . .

*(Sound of icebergs crashing into a loud heartbeat. Performer speaks while spinning slowly and transforming into the same faces at the top of the play.)*

I float down layers of strata exposing bones embedded in ice. I hear a chorus of huskies barking in an echo chamber. Those teeth belong to Grandpa Yuzo. He's swallowing me up, I'm in his esophagus. I hear his voice for the first time, since I was five years old, but it is clear and effortless. "I'm so sorry. It was my fault."

Of course it was your fault, you rotting beast! You killed all those people! That's why we're all fucked-up!

He laughs. "You speak well. You have no trouble now. That makes me happy. HAHAHAHAAAAAAAAA!" The walls of his esophagus are vibrating.

HHAAAAAAAAA!!! I want to split him open!

I feel a splash of air. I smell the arctic turning into summer, when the ice melts into the ocean. *(Pause)*

If only my grandfather could have survived the winter, where his prison could have melted away, where he could have moved forward and my grandmother could release him in her heart.

The air is getting thicker and hotter and my body is weightless. Slowly I touch the ocean, warm like bath water. I am floating, in the heat of the sun. *(Pause)* I wanted to say something . . . to my grandfather . . . I wanted to tell him . . . something . . . but nothing, nothing came out.

*(An old Japanese folk song plays which reminds her of her grandmother and the box she couldn't face before. She gets down on her knees and opens the box. She pours red ash into her hand and wipes it across her mouth. She stands and continues to lift her hands above her head and rubs her palms together to let the red bleed over her face. She claps her hands to create a red cloud as she smiles and the lights fade to black.)*

# Artist Biographies and Bibliographies

A rtist biographies and bibliographies are presented here in alphabetical order. They are not meant to be comprehensive, but list highlights from the artists' careers. Where possible, a mailing, Web Site or E-mail address has been provided for further information.

**MIKE ALBO** has performed his monologue/rants (co-written with Virginia Heffernan) for close to seven years in various New York City venues. His work has appeared in *Out* magazine, *New York* magazine, *Paper, Details, BOMB, Word.com,* the *Baffler,* the *Village Voice* and the *Washington Post*. His first novel *Hornito: My Lie Life* will be published in June 2000 by HarperCollins; and his two-act play *Sexotheque* is being produced in Austin, Texas and New York City.

**Performance Work:** first short works (1992); *Just Open Your Throat* (1997); *Mike Albo* (1998); *Spray* (1999); *Please Everything Burst* (2000). **Anthologized Work:** *Queer 13* (Rob Weisbach Books/Morrow Publishing, 1998). **Audio Tape/LP/CD:** "Rainbows!" on *Stories at The Moth* (benefit CD, soon to be released). **For Further Information:** virginia@inch.com.

**LUIS ALFARO** is a writer/performer who has been balancing the worlds of poetry, plays, short stories and journalism since 1987. Alfaro has written for several magazines and newspapers and is a resident artist and co-director of the Latino Theatre Initiative at the

Mark Taper Forum in Los Angeles. His current plays include *Mojave Medicine, 52 Mexicans* and *Black Butterfly, Jaguar Girl, Piñata Woman and Other Super Hero Girls Like Me*. He is a recipient of a MacArthur Foundation Fellowship and an NEA/TCG Theatre Residency for Playwrights. He is a member of New Dramatists.

**Performance Work:** first short works (1987); *Downtown* (1993); *Bitter Homes and Gardens* (1994); *Speaking in* Tongues (1995); *Cuerpo Politizado* (1995); *Straight as a Line* (1997); *The Ballad of Ginger Esparza* (co-written with Diane Rodriguez, 1995); *Diva L.A.* (co-written with Diane Rodriguez, 1995); *Spirits Rising* (co-written with Diane Rodriguez, 1996); *Los Vecinos/The Neighbors* (co-written with Diane Rodriguez, 1997). **Anthologized Work:** *Blood Whispers, Volume I* (Silverton Books, 1991); *Men on Men 4* (Nal/Dutton, 1992); *Blood Whispers, Volume II* (Silverton Books, 1994); *Uncontrollable Bodies: Testimonies of Identity and Culture* (Bay Press, 1994); *HIS: Brilliant New Fiction by Gay Writers* (Faber & Faber, 1995); *Out in All Directions: The Almanac of Gay and Lesbian America* (Warner Books, 1995); *The Goddess of the Americas: Writings about la Virgen* (Riverdale Books, 1996); *The United States of Poetry* (Harry Abrams, 1996); *Sundays at Seven: Stories from a Different Light* (Alamo Square, 1996); *Twelve Shades Read* (Graphically Speaking LTD, 1997); *Particular Voices: Portraits of Gay and Lesbian Writers* (MIT Press, 1997); *O Solo Homo* (Grove Press, 1998); *Urban Latino Cultures* (Sage Publications, 1999); *Out of the Fringe* (Theatre Communications Group, 2000). **Audio Tape/LP/CD:** *Downtown* (New Alliance/SST Records, 1994); *Internal Journal* (New Alliance/SST Records, 1994); *LIVE!* (KXLU, 1997). **Film/Video/TV/Laserdisc:** *L.A. Journal, Volume II* (New Alliance/SST Records, 1994); *The United States of Poetry* (Washington Square Films, 1995); *Pocho Novela* (Soy Cabrona Productions, 1995); *Chicanismo* (PBS/KCET, The Works IV, 1996). **For Further Information:** luisalfaro@aol.com.


**LAURIE ANDERSON** is a poet, writer, visual artist, sculptor and social commentator. Her work often utilizes media, film, electronic and acoustic music, slides, costumes and special effects. Anderson holds an MFA in sculpture from Columbia University and has written art reviews for many magazines and taught art history at various colleges in New York and California. Anderson was part of the 1970s downtown New York art scene. She has received grants from the New York State Council on the Arts, the NEA and the Guggenheim Foundation. In 1984, Anderson won a Grammy for *Gravity's Angel*. She is a founding member of the Women's Action Coalition.

**Performance Work:** *Automotive* (1972); *Institutional Dream Series* (1972); *O-range* (1973); *As If: Tales from the Vienna Woods* (1974); *In the Nick of Time* (1974); *Songs and Stories for the Insomniac* (1975); *Out of the Blue* (1975); *For Instants* (1976); *English* (1976); *Americans on the Move* (1979); *United States II* (1980); *It's Cold Outside* (1981); *United States* (1983); *Natural History* (1986); *Empty Places* (1989); *Stories from the Nerve Bible* (1992); *Brighter Red* (1993). **Published Work:** *October* (self-published, 1972); *Handbook* (self-published, 1972); *The Talking Book* (self-published, 1972); *Individuals* (E. P. Dutton & Company, 1977); *Words in Reverse* (self-published, 1979); *United States* (HarperCollins, 1985); *Empty Places* (HarperCollins, 1990); *Stories from the Nerve Bible* (Harper Perennial, 1994). **Audio Tape/LP/CD:** *O Superman* (110 Records, 1981); *Big Science* (Warner Brothers Records, 1982); *Mister Heartbreak* (Warner Brothers Records, 1984); *Strange Angels* (Warner Brothers Records, 1988); *Bright Red* (Warner Brothers Records, 1994). **Film/Video/TV/Laserdisc:** *Dearreader* (with Bob George, 1974); *Fourteen Americans* (by Michael Blackwood, 1980); *Home of the Brave* (Paula Mazur, producer, 1985); *What You Mean We?* (KTCA, 1986); *The Eleventh Hour* (PBS, 1989); *One World, One Voice* (BBC, 1990); *The Human Face* (BBC, 1991). **For Further Information:** Canal Street Communications; 530 Canal Street; New York, NY 10013; www.laurieanderson.com.

**BRENDA WONG AOKI** is a contemporary storyteller. Her one-woman shows synthesize Noh and Kyogen (Japanese classical theatre), original music and Western physical theatre and have been performed throughout the world. Her show, *The Queen's Garden*, won four Dramalogue Awards and a Critics' Circle Award; the CD won an Indie Award. *Mermaid* (a monodrama for symphony) was commissioned by Maestro Kent Nagano and won an ASCAP Innovative Composition Award. Aoki and her partner, composer Mark Izu, are the Artistic Directors of First Voice, a not-for-profit arts organization based in San Francisco dedicated to the music and stories of people caught between cultures speaking in their own voice.

**Performance Work:** *Whisperings* (1985); *Tales of the Pacific Rim* (1990); *Obake: Some Japanese Ghosts* (1991); *The Queen's Soul of the Great Bell* (1992); *Garden* (1992); *Random Acts* (1994); *Mermaid* (1997); *Uncle Gunjiro's Girlfriend* (1998). **Anthologized Work:** *Best Loved Stories* (National Storytelling Press, 1991); *More Best Loved Stories* (National Storytelling Press, 1992); *Contemporary Plays by Women of Color* (Routledge, 1996). **Audio Tape/LP/CD:** *Tales of the Pacific Rim: Dreams and Illusions* (Rounder Records, 1990); *Black Hair: Some Japanese Ghosts* (Pele Productions, 1997); *The Queen's Garden* (Asian Improv Records, 1998). **Film/Video/TV/Laserdisc:** *No Way Out* (RCA, 1984); *Living on Tokyo Time* (Farallones Films, 1987); *Oral Tradition Through Time* (Laserdisc, Houghton Mifflin/McDougal-Littell and Rymel Multimedia, 1996). **For Further Information:** www.firstvoice.org.

**ERIC BOGOSIAN** is the author of three OBIE Award-winning solo works as well as other solo works and three ensemble plays. His work has been staged around the United States and the world. He wrote the screen adaptations of his first two plays, *Talk Radio* and *subUrbia*, receiving the Berlin Film Festival's "Silver Bear" for *Talk Radio*. As an actor, Bogosian has appeared in over a dozen feature films. He is best known for starring as the misanthropic "shock-jock" Barry Champlain in Oliver Stone's film version of his own *Talk Radio*.

**Performance Work:** *Lecture* (1977); *Sheer Heaven* (1979); *That Girl* (1979); *The New World* (1980); *Men Inside* (1981); *The Advocate* (1982); *FunHouse* (1983); *Drinking in America* (1986); *Talk Radio* (1987); *Sex, Drugs, Rock & Roll* (1990); *Pounding Nails in the Floor with My Forehead* (1994); *subUrbia* (1994); *Wake Up and Smell the Coffee* (1995); *31 Ejaculations* (1996); *Griller* (1998); "Bitter Sauce" in *Love's Fire* (1998). **Published Work:** *Sex, Drugs, Rock & Roll* (Theatre Communications Group, 1991); *Notes from Underground* (Theatre Communications Group, 1993); *The Essential Bogosian* (Theatre Communications Group, 1994); *Pounding Nails in the Floor with My Forehead* (Theatre Communications Group, 1994); *subUrbia* (Theatre Communications Group, 1995); *subUrbia* (screenplay, St. Martin's Press, 1997). **Anthologized Work:** *Love's Fire* (Quill, 1998). **Audio Tape/LP/CD:** *Sex, Drugs, Rock & Roll* (SBK Records, 1990); *An Interview with Eric Bogosian and Readings of Selected Monologues* (The American Audio Prose Library, 1996); *Pounding Nails in the Floor with My Forehead* (The Blackbird Recording Company, 1998). **Film/Video/TV/Laserdisc:** *FunHouse* (Ararat Productions, 1988); *Talk Radio* (Universal Pictures, 1989); *Sex, Drugs, Rock & Roll* (Avenue Entertainment, 1991); *Confessions of a Porn Star* (Ararat Productions, 1996); *subUrbia* (Castlerock Entertainment, 1997). **For Further Information:** www.ericbogosian.com.

**LENNY BRUCE** (1925–1966) was born Leonard Alfred Schneider in Long Island, New York. His scene was the night club stage where his career had three phases: "bits" that polarized show-business and launched audience walkouts; free-form improvisation; and finally, his obsession with our legal systems' ambiguities and contradictions. Early on Bruce was roasted by *Variety* for "only trying to make the band laugh," but the span of his work reveals his development from a comic to a satirist "in the tradition of Swift, Rabelais and Twain." Bruce consistently returned to the same themes—religion, sex, politics, Jews, gentiles, blacks, drugs, obscenity, the law and others—but his performances of these "bits" varied from night to night. He never wrote down his texts; all printed versions of his work, except for his autobiography, were transcribed from live performances. With these themes, Bruce violated the cabaret rules against discussing religion, race, sex and foul language and, as a result, was repeatedly arrested on obscenity charges. The first time was in 1961 and the last in 1964 when a court convicted him of being "obscene, indecent, immoral and impure." Bruce died in 1966 of a heroine overdose, but at the time of his death, a friend commented that he died of "an overdose of police."

**Performance Work:** among many others: *The Interview*; *Enchanting Transylvania*; *Interview with Doctor Sholem Stein*; *The March of High Fidelity*; *Father Flotski's Triumph*; *All Broadway Musicals Sound the Same*; *Especially the Baritones*; *The Kid in the Well*; *Adolph Hitler and the M. C. A.*; *Ike, Sherm and Nick*; *Psychopathia Sexualis*; *Religions, Inc.*; *White Collar Drunks*; *The Defiant Ones*; *The Phone Company*; *The Steve Allen Show*; *Esther Costello Show*; *Bronchitis*; *My Trip to Miami*; *The Tribunal*; *The Palladium*; *How to Relax Your Colored Friends at Parties*; *Jewish and Goyish*; *Christ and Moses*; *That's What I Got Busted For*; *The Lone Ranger.* **Published Work:** *The Essential Lenny Bruce* (Ballantine Books, 1967); *The Almost Unpublished Lenny Bruce: From the Private Collection of Kitty Bruce* (Running Press, 1984); *How to Talk Dirty and Influence People: An Autobiography* (A Fireside Book, Simon & Schuster, 1992). **Audio Tape/LP/CD:** *The Sick Humor of Lenny Bruce* (Fantasy Records, 1958); *Lenny Bruce the Berkeley Concert* (Bizarre Records/ Enigma-Retro, 1958); *Lenny Bruce's Interviews of Our Times* (Fantasy Records, 1958); *The Lenny Bruce Originals Volume 1* (Fantasy Records, 1958); *I Am Not a Nut, Elect Me!—* *"Togetherness"* (Fantasy Records, 1959); *The Lenny Bruce Originals Volume 2* (Fantasy Records, 1959); *Lenny Bruce—American* (Fantasy Records, 1960); *Lenny Bruce: The Carnegie Hall Concert* (Capitol/World Pacific, 1961); *Lenny Bruce Live 1962—"Busted"* (Viper's Nest, 1962); *Lenny Bruce—"Thank You Masked Man"* (Fantasy Records, 1963); *The Beat Generation* (Rhino Records, 1992); *Howls, Raps and Roars—Recordings from the San Francisco Poetry Renaissance* (Fantasy Records, 1999). **Film/Video/TV/Laserdisc:** *Dance Hall Racket* (1958); *Lenny Bruce Performance Film* (Grove Press, 1968); *Lenny Bruce: Berkeley Concert* (Baker & Taylor Video, 1991); *Lenny Bruce: Without Tears* (Atlantic, 1992). **Related Material:** *Lenny: A Play, Based on the Life and Words of Lenny Bruce* (Grove Press, 1971); *Lenny* (film, United Artists, 1971); *Dirtymouth* (film, 1971); *Lenny Bruce: The Comedian as Social Critic and Secular Moralist* (Pathfinder Press, 1974); *Bruce: The Making of a Prophet* (Archon Books, 1989); *Ladies and Gentlemen: Lenny Bruce!* (Penguin Books, 1991); *Lenny Bruce Documentary* (COURT TV, 1999); *Lenny Bruce: Swear to Tell the Truth* (film, Whyaduck Productions and HBO Documentary Films, 1999). **For Further Information:** Fantasy Inc.; Tenth and Parker; Berkeley, CA 94710; members.aol.com/dcspohr/lenny/lenny1.htm.

**LORD BUCKLEY** (1906–1960) was born Richard Myrle Buckley, the youngest of seven, in the coal mining town of Toulumne, California. As a teenager, Buckley worked for a short time as a lumberjack and then left to tour with a vaudeville act. In 1928 he performed at the World's Fair in Chicago. In the thirties, he was an emcee for dance marathons, walkathons and speakesies with Milton Berle and Red Skelton and later worked as a radio deejay in Kansas City. During World War II, Buckley performed in Ed Sullivan's USO shows in hospitals and military bases. In 1949, he appeared on the first of eleven episodes of the *Ed Sullivan Show*. Buckley made an appearance on *The Tonight Show* in 1955 and in 1956 on Groucho Marx's show *You Bet Your Life* where he won the money. Buckley and his wife were later hired by the Ziegfeld Follies in 1957, but by 1958, he and his family had moved to Las Vegas. Buckley was holding court with other hipsters, including Sammy Davis, Jr., Jonathan Winters, Sheky Green, Louis Prima, Frank Sinatra, Count Basie and Louis Armstrong, at the El Rancho until it burned down. In 1959 Buckley was playing in San Francisco at The Hungry Eye with the likes of Lenny Bruce and Mort Sahl. Lord Buckley died in 1960 after turmoil over a cabaret card.

**Audio Tape/LP/CD:** *Euphoria* (Vaya Records, 1952); *Miracles in Hip* (RCA Records, 1955); *James Dean* (Hip Records, 1956); *His Lordship Live in Hollywood at the Ivar Theatre* (World Pacific, 1958); *His Royal Hipness* (Discovery/WEA, 1983); *Lord Buckley Live/The Tales of Lord Buckley* (Richard Buckley, Jr. and Shambhala Records, Lion Editions, 1991); *The Beat Generation* (Rhino Records, 1992); *Bad Rapping of the Marquis de Sade* (Blue Note Records, 1996). **For Further Information:** lordbjr@aol.com.

**DAVID CALE** is an author and performer who has presented his work throughout the U.S. including at several Off-Broadway theatres. *Lillian* received an OBIE Award, *The Redthroats* and *Deep in a Dream of You* both received Bessie Awards and *The Redthroats* also received an L.A. Dramalogue Award. His monologue *Welcome to America* was filmed for the HBO Special *Bette Midler's Mondo Beyondo*. He wrote and performed the text for the dance *Chickens*, choreographed by Charles Moulton for Mikhail Baryshnikov's White Oak Dance Project. As a lyricist for The Jazz Passengers, his songs have been performed by artists including Deborah Harry, Elvis Costello, Jimmy Scott and Freedy Johnston. As an actor he has appeared on Broadway and Off-Broadway, and in feature films. Cale is the recipient of a Sundance Institute Writing Fellowship, an NEA Solo Performance Fellowship, a New York Foundation for the Arts Fellowship and grants from the New York State Council on the Arts.

**Performance Work:** first short works (1982); *The Redthroats* (1986); *Smooch Music* (with composer Roy Nathanson, 1987); *The Nature of Things* (with Roy Nathanson and Marc Ribot, 1990); *Deep in a Dream of You* (with Roy Nathanson, 1991); *Somebody Else's House* (1994); *Nightwear* (1994); *Lillian* (1997). **Published Work:** *The Redthroats* (Vintage Books, 1988). **Anthologized Work:** *Out of Character* (Bantam Books, 1997); *The Sex Life* (Harper's, 1989). **Audio Tape/LP/CD:** *The Uproar Tapes* (Island Records, 1986). **For Further Information:** davcale@aol.com.

**RUTH DRAPER** (1884–1956) began performing in her early childhood, mimicking her family's tailor and seamstress. Her fame as a gifted amateur from New York society took her to state dinners at the White House and many royal occasions in Europe. Prior to her first professional stage performance in London in 1920, Draper performed for King George and Queen Mary in 1913, on stage at the neighborhood Playhouse in New York in 1915 and for the American troops in Europe in 1919. She began extensive tours soon after which from the early 1920s to the 1950s took her throughout the United States, Europe, Asia, South America, South Africa, Russia and Cuba. In 1929 she performed for eighteen weeks at The Comedy Theatre in New York. She only performed in plays she wrote herself, developing a repertory of more than sixty pieces in which she appeared on stage alone. From 1941–1945 she entertained the troops in America and Canada. She received honorary degrees from Hamilton and Smith Colleges and from Cambridge and Edinburgh Universities, and in 1951 King George VI awarded her the Order of the British Empire, Honorary Commander (CBE). Draper never wrote out scripts for her monologues, but in 1954 her managers, Charles Bowden and Richard Barr, convinced her to record her work for RCA Victor, thus preserving it just prior to her death in 1956. Draper died in her sleep after a matinee and evening performance on Broadway.

**Performance Work:** Before 1913: *On a Porch in a Maine Coast Village*; *A Scottish Immigrant at Ellis Island*; *A Class in Greek Poise*; *Three Breakfasts*. Before 1920: *At an English House Party*; *Vive la France! 1916*; *The Actress*; *Three Generations in a Court of Domestic*

*Relations; Showing the Garden.* 1920 and after: *In County Kerry* (1920); *In the Court of Philip IV* (1921); *Love in the Balkans* (1922); *In a Church in Italy* (1925); *Doctor and Diets* (1925); *Five Imaginary Folksongs* (1925); *The Italian Lesson* (1926); *Three Women and Mr. Clifford* (1929); *Opening a Bazaar* (1929); *Vive la France!* 1940 (1941); *The Return* (1943); *A Cocktail Party* (1950). **Audio Tape/LP/CD:** *Art of Ruth Draper* (five albums, Spoken Arts, 1958). **Related Material:** *The Art of Ruth Draper* (Doubleday, 1960); *The Letters of Ruth Draper: Self-Portrait of an Actress 1920–1956* (Southern Illinois University Press, 1999; originally published by Charles Scribner's Sons, 1979); *The World of Ruth Draper: A Portrait of an Actress* (Southern Illinois University Press, 1999). *The World of Ruth Draper, Performed by Patricia Norcia* (CD, Original Cast Records, 1999). **For Further Information:** The Draper Company at www.ruthdraper.com.

**ETHYL EICHELBERGER** (1945–1990) was a key player on the explosive East Village avant-garde theatre scene of the 1980s and is primarily remembered as a drag performer. He wrote and performed over two dozen solo plays based on the lives of great women of history, literature and myth. He also acted with Charles Ludlam's Ridiculous Theatrical Company and on Broadway. In 1989, Eichelberger performed in the twenty-six episode educational children's series *Encyclopedia*, produced by HBO. He was awarded a 1981 Villager Award for *Minnie the Maid* and a 1982 OBIE Award for *Lucrezia Borgia.*

**Performance Work:** *Phèdre* (1972); *Nefert-iti* (1976); *Auntie Belle Emme* (1979); *Medea* (1980); *Carlotta, Empress of Mexico* (1980); *Minnie the Maid* (1981); *Shi Liu* (1981); *Jocasta or Boy Crazy* (1982); *Catherine was Great* (1982); *A Virgin and a Queen* (1982); *Lucrezia Borgia* (1982); *Marie Antoinette* (1983); *Lola Montez* (1982); *Toulouse Women or Moulin Rage* (1984); *Ruth Ruth* (1984); *Souled Out or Dr. Mary Faustus* (1984); *Klytemnestra or The Nightingale of Argos* (1985); *Mrs. Wiggs in the Cabbage Patch* (1985); *Hamlette* (1985); *Medusa* (1985); *Leer* (1985); *Fowl Ball* (1985); *Casanova* (1985); *Rip Van Winkle* (1986); *Saint Joan* (1987); *The Tempest of Chim-Lee* (1987); *The Lincolns* (1988); *Ariadne Obnoxious* (1988); *Herd of Buffalo* (1989); *Dilbert Dingle Dong, the Doomed or a Nest Full of Ninnies* (1989); *Das Vedayna Mama* (1990). **Anthologized Work:** *Grove New American Theatre* (Grove, 1993); *Out of Character* (Bantam Books, 1997); *Shattered Anatomies: Traces of the Body in Performance,* (Arnolfini Live, 1997). **Audio Tape/LP/CD:** *The Uproar Tapes,* (Vol. 1, Antilles AN-7084). **Film/Video/TV/Laserdisc:** *Live from Lincoln Center: The Comedy of Errors,* (PBS, 1987). **Related Material:** *Theatre History Studies* (Vol. XIV, 1994); *Theater* (Vol. 21, #3, 1990); *Theatre Crafts* (January 1989).

**JOHN FLECK** works frequently in theatre, film and television. He has won numerous grants and awards, most recently a 1996 Getty Fellowship. His work received national attention in 1990, when, along with three other performance artists, he became part of the "NEA Four." Labeled by some political pundits as too dirty to be funded, the NEA Four spearheaded a national campaign against artistic repression. They won a court case against the NEA, but the decision was later overturned on appeal. Fleck appeared on TV as Louis Heinsbergen, a series regular, on *Murder One*, and has made other appearances on *Ally McBeal, NYPD Blue, Chicago Hope, Family Law, Seinfeld,* PBS's *Tales of the City* and *Sweet Bird of Youth.*

**Performance Work:** *Pagan Holiday* (1984); *I got the He-Be-She-Be's* (1986); *Psycho Opera* (1987); *Blessed Are All the Little Fishes* (1989); *A Snowball's Chance in Hell* (1992); *Me* (1995); *DiRT* (1999). **Anthologized Work:** *Out of Character* (Bantam Books, 1997); *Outside the Frame: Performance and the Object* (Cleveland Center for Contemporary Art); the *Drama Review* (Vol. 35, #3, Fall 1991); *TheaterWeek* (July 16, 1990). **Film/Video/TV/Laserdisc:** *Sweet Bird of Youth* (Triboro Entertainment, 1989); *Indecency* (TriStar, 1992); *Falling Down*

(Warner Brothers, 1994); *Grief* (Strand Releasing, 1994); *Me* (Museum of Contemporary Art, Los Angeles, California, 1995); *Waterworld* (Universal, 1995); *Box* (1999); *Crazy in Alabama* (Columbia Pictures, 1999); *The Art of Controversy* (Media Vision Arts, 1999).

**DIAMANDA GALÁS** is a singer, writer and performer with a four-octave vocal range. She has an urgent need to wake the morally dead or sleeping with her work, which draws upon religious texts, poetry, gospel spirituals, social and political themes, cultural traditions and foreign languages. She first rose to international prominence with her three-album set *Plague Mass*, a requiem for those dead and dying of AIDS, but her first live performance was at the Festival d'Avignon in France in 1979. Galás's first recorded work was *The Litanies of Satan* in 1982. Galás has been awarded Ford Foundation and Meet the Composer grants.

**Performance Work:** Festival d'Avignon performance (1979); *Wild Women with Steak Knives* (1981); *Tragouthia apo to Aima Exon Fonos (Song from the Blood of those Murdered)* (1981); *Masque of the Red Death* (1984–1989); *You Must Be Certain of the Devil* (1988); *The Litanies of Satan* (1989); *There Are No More Tickets to the Funeral* (1990); *Vena Cava* (1992); *The Singer* (1992); *Insekta* (1993); *The Sporting Life* (with John Paul Jones and Pete Thomas, 1994); *The Divine Punishment* (1996); *Saint of the Pit* (1996); *Schrei X Live/Schrei 27* (1996); *Malediction and Prayer* (1996); *Defixiones, Will and Testament* (1999). **Published Work:** *The Shit of God* (Serpent's Tail/High Risk, 1996). **Anthologized Work:** *Theater* (Vol 26, #1&2, 1995). **Audio Tape/LP/CD:** *The Litanies of Satan* (Mute, 1989); *Plague Mass* (Mute, 1991); *Vena Cava* (Mute, 1993); *The Sporting Life* (Mute, 1994); *The Divine Punishment* (Mute, 1996); *Schrei X Live/Schrei 27* (Mute, 1996); *Malediction and Prayer* (Mute, 1998). **Film/Video/TV/Laserdisc:** *Judgement Day* (Mute, 1993). **Related Material:** *Feminine Endings: Music, Gender and Sexuality* (University of Minnesota Press, 1991); *On Edge: Performance at the End of the Twentieth Century* (Wesleyan University Press, 1993); *Queer Notes: Male and Female Homosexuality in Twentieth Century Music* (Cassel Press, 1995); *The Sex Revolts* (Harvard University Press, 1995). **For Further Information:** www.diamandagalas.com; www.brainwashed.com/diamanda.

**ANNE GALJOUR** began her solo performance career in 1990 at Climate Theatre in San Francisco where she first presented her collection of four dramatic short stories entitled *Alligator Tales*. In 1993, *Hurricane* was listed by The American Theatre Critics Association as one of the three outstanding plays produced outside New York City. That same year Galjour also received the first annual Osborn Award for Emerging Playwrights. *Mauvais Temps* received the Bay Area Theatre Critics Circle Award for Best Original Script in 1996, and in 1997 *Hurricane* and *Mauvais Temps* were combined and retitled *Alligator Tales*. Her first multi-character play, *The Queen of the Sea* premiered in 1999 for Berkeley Repertory Theatre's school tour. Galjour teaches creative writing and solo performance classes at Writers Who Act Workshop through Climate Theatre. Galjour gets her inspiration from her Cajun heritage growing up in Cut Off, Louisiana. It is said that she introduces her audiences to a culture they know precious little about.

**Performance Work:** *Alligator Tales (Four Dramatic Short Stories)* (1990); *The Krewe of Neptune* (1991); *Hurricane* (1993); *Mauvais Temps* (1996); *Alligator Tales* (1997); *The Queen of the Sea* (1999). **Anthologized Work:** *Mantle Theatre Yearbook of Best Plays* (Otis Guernsey/Burns, 1993). **Audio Tape/LP/CD:** *Hurricane* (1995, available from the artist). **Film/Video/TV/Laserdisc:** *Alligator Tales, Hurricane, The Krewe of Neptune and Alligator Tales (A Collection of Four Dramatic Short Stories)* (1994, available at the Performing Arts Library at Lincoln Center). **For Further Information:** Wendy Streeter; The Joyce Ketay Agency; 1501 Broadway, Suite 1908; New York, NY 10036; galjrmayn@aol.com.

**WHOOPI GOLDBERG** began performing at age eight in New York with the Children's Program at the Hudson Guild and the Helena Rubinstein Children's Theatre. In 1975 she moved to California and appeared in productions with the San Diego Repertory Theatre and the Blake Street Hawkeyes. Her first solo show, *The Spook Show*, caught the attention of Mike Nichols, who later produced her first Broadway show in 1984 which was then taped for an HBO special, *Whoopi Goldberg: Direct from Broadway*. The album of the show won a Grammy Award in 1985. Goldberg's first major film was *The Color Purple*, for which she received a Golden Globe and an NAACP Image Award. Since then, she has appeared steadily in feature films and won many awards including five Nickelodeon Kid's Choice Awards and an Academy Award for Best Supporting Actress. Goldberg's regular television appearances have included *Bagdad Café* and *Star Trek: The Next Generation*. She is also the author of the children's book *Alice*.

**Performance Work:** *The Spook Show* (1982–83); *Whoopi Goldberg Live* (1984); *Moms* (1984); *Living on the Edge of Chaos* (1988). **Published Work:** *Alice* (Bantam Books, 1992); *Book* (Rob Weisbach Books, 1997). **Audio Tape/LP/CD:** *Whoopi Goldberg Live* (taped live, 1984); *Whoopi Goldberg: Original Broadway Show Recording* (Geffen Goldline Records, 1985); *Fontaine: Why Am I Straight?* (MCA Records, 1988); *The Best of Comic Relief '90* (Rhino Records, 1990); *Comic Relief V* (WEA/Atlantic/Rhino Records, 1992). **Film/Video/TV/Laserdisc:** *Whoopi Goldberg Direct from Broadway* (taped live, HBO, 1984); *The Color Purple* (Warner Brothers, 1985); *Jumpin' Jack Flash* (Fox, 1986); *Clara's Heart* (Warner Brothers, 1988); *Whoopi Goldberg's Fontaine: Why Am I Straight?* (HBO, 1988); *Star Trek: The Next Generation* (Fox, 1988–1992); *The Long Walk Home* (Miramax, 1990); *Ghost* (Paramount, 1990); *Bagdad Café* (CBS, 1990–1991); *Whoopi Goldberg: Chez Whoopi* (HBO, 1991); *The Player* (Fine Line, 1992); *Sister Act* (Buena Vista, 1992); *Sarafina!* (Buena Vista, 1992); *Sister Act 2: Back in the Habit* (Buena Vista, 1993); *Star Trek: Generations* (Paramount, 1994); *Ghosts of Mississippi* (Columbia Pictures, 1996); *Hollywood Squares* (Fox, 1998–present); *Girl, Interrupted* (Columbia Pictures, 1999). **Related Material:** *Whoopi Goldberg: From Street to Stardom* (Dillon Press, 1993); *Whoopi Goldberg: Entertainer* (Chelsea House, 1994); *Whoopi Goldberg: Her Journey from Poverty to Mega-Stardom* (Birch Lane Press, 1997). **For Further Information:** Bragman, Nyman, Cafarelli; 9171 Wilshire Boulevard, Suite 300; Beverly Hills, CA 90210-5515.

**MARGA GOMEZ** is a writer and performer. She was born and raised in Manhattan but moved to San Francisco in the 1980s where she established herself as a comedic performer in theatre and cabaret. She has performed all over the country and at international theatre festivals. Gomez is the recipient of San Francisco's Solo Mio Award and Theater L.A.'s Ovation Award for her collaboration with Culture Clash. Her film and television appearances include *Sphere*, *Batman Forever* and *Tracey Takes On . . . The Supernatural*. As a stand-up comedian, Gomez has been featured on Showtime's *Latino Laugh Festival* and HBO's *Comic Relief VI*.

**Performance Work:** *Memory Tricks* (1991); *Marga Gomez is Pretty, Witty & Gay* (1992); *A Line Around the Block* (1994); *jaywalker* (1998). **Anthologized Work:** *Out, Loud & Laughing* (Anchor Books, 1995); *Contemporary Plays by Women of Color* (Routledge, 1996); *Out of Character* (Bantam Books, 1997). **Audio Tape/LP/CD:** *Hung Like a Fly* (Uproar Entertainment, 1998). **Film/Video/TV/Laserdisc:** *Out There* (Comedy Central, 1995); *Batman Forever* (Warner Brothers, 1995); *In the Life* (PBS, 1996); *The Best of Comic Relief VI* (HBO, 1996); *Sphere* (Warner Brothers, 1997). **Related Material:** *Women and Performance* (NYU School of Performing Arts, 1996); *Latino Performance and Identity* (Aztlan, fall 1997); *Disidentifications: Performance and Queers of Color* (University of Minnesota Press, 1999). **For Further Information:** LaMarga@aol.com.

**GUILLERMO GÓMEZ-PEÑA** was born and raised in Mexico City and came to the United States in 1978. In his work, which includes performance art, video, audio, installations, poetry, journalism, critical writings and cultural theory, Gómez-Peña explores cross-cultural issues and North/South relations. He uses his art and writing to reveal the labyrinths of identity and the precipices of nationality. Gómez-Peña was a founding member of the bi-national arts collective Border Arts Workshop/Taller de Arte Fronterizo, a contributor to the national radio program *Crossroads* and editor of the experimental arts magazine *The Broken Line/La Linea Quebrada*. He is a regular contributor to National Public Radio's *All Things Considered*, a writer for newspapers and magazines in the U.S. and Mexico and a contributing editor to the *Drama Review* and *Performance Research* magazine (Wales). He has received numerous awards and fellowships, and in 1991, Gómez-Peña became the first Chicano/Mexicano artist to receive a MacArthur Fellowship.

**Performance Work:** *The End of the Line* (1986); *1991: A Performance Chronicle (The Rediscovery of America by the Warrior for Gringostroika)* (1991); *The Year of the White Bear* (with Coco Fusco, 1992); *The Temple of Confusion* (with Roberto Sifuentes, 1994); *Borderama* (1995); *The Dangerous Border Game* (1995); *The Mexterminator Project* (with Roberto Sifuentes, 1997); *Border Brujo* (1998); *Borderstasis* (1998); *La Indian Queen* (1998); *El Naftazteca: Cyber-Aztec TV for 2000* A.D. (with Roberto Sifuentes, 1999); *Borderscape 2000* (1999); *The New World Border* (1999). **Published Work:** *Warrior for Gringostroika* (Graywolf Press, 1993); *New World Border* (City Lights, 1997); *The Temple of Confessions: Mexican Beasts and Living Santos* (Powerhouse Books, 1997). **Film/Video/TV/Laserdisc:** *Border Brujo* (Video Data Bank and Third World Newsreel, 1988); *The Son of Border Crises* (Video Data Bank, 1989); *Borderstasis* (Video Data Bank, 1990); *El Naftazteca* (Video Data Bank, 1994); *Temple of Confessions* (The Annenberg/CPB Collection, 1997); *The Great Mojado Invasion* (Video Data Bank, 1999). **For Further Information:** www.mexterminator.com; pochnostra@aol.com.

**SPALDING GRAY**, a writer, actor and performer, has created a series of sixteen monologues which he has performed throughout the world. He has received a Guggenheim Fellowship and grants from the National Endowment for the Arts and the Rockefeller Foundation. In 1977, he co-founded The Wooster Group and with its members wrote and performed the autobiographical trilogy, *Three Places in Rhode Island*. Appearances on and Off-Broadway include as the Stage Manager in a revival of Thornton Wilder's *Our Town* and as Hoss in Sam Shephard's *Tooth of Crime*.

**Performance Work:** *Sex and Death to the Age 14* (1979); *Booze, Cars and College Girls* (1980); *India and After (America)* (1980); *A Personal History of the American Theatre* (1980); *Interviewing the Audience* (1980); *The Great Crossing* (1980); *Nobody Wanted to Sit Behind a Desk* (1981); *In Search of the Monkey Girl* (1981); *47 Beds* (1982); *A Personal History of My Loft* (1983); *Swimming to Cambodia* (1986); *Terrors of Pleasure* (1989); *Monster in a Box* (1991); *Gray's Anatomy* (1992); *It's a Slippery Slope* (1995); *Morning, Noon and Night* (1998). **Published Work:** *In Search of the Monkey Girl* (Aperture Press, 1982); *Sex and Death to the Age 14* (Random House, 1986); *Swimming to Cambodia* (Theatre Communications Group, 1988); *Monster in a Box* (Vintage Books, 1992); *Gray's Anatomy* (Vintage Books, 1994); *Impossible Vacation* (Vintage Books, 1997); *It's a Slippery Slope* (The Noonday Press, 1997); *Morning, Noon and Night* (Farrar, Strauss & Giroux, 1999). **Audio Tape/LP/CD:** *First Words* (Ten Speed PR Audio); *Monster in a Box* (Ten Speed PR Audio); *Terrors of Pleasure* (Ten Speed PR Audio, 1996); *It's a Slippery Slope* (Mercury Records, 1999). **Film/Video/TV/Laserdisc:** *Swimming to Cambodia* (Cinecom, 1987); *Terrors of Pleasures* (HBO, 1988); *Monster in a Box* (Fine Line/New Line, 1991); *Gray's Anatomy* (BBC, 1996). **For Further Information:** Washington Square Arts; 12 E. 10th Street; New York, NY 10003; mshimkin@washingtonsquarearts.com.

**JESSICA HAGEDORN** is a poet, novelist, playwright and performer. She was born and raised in the Philippines and moved to the United States in her teens. She studied theatre at the American Conservatory Theater in San Francisco. She is a recipient of numerous fellowships and her work has been widely anthologized. She is the author of the text for *Burning Heart: A Portrait of the Philippines,* a collaboration with photojournalist Marissa Roth, which Rizzoli Books International published in 1999. Her recent theatrical adaptation of *Dogeaters* premiered at La Jolla Playhouse in 1998 and will be presented at The Joseph Papp Public Theater/New York Shakespeare Festival in the 2000–2001 season.

**Performance Work:** *Mango Tango* (1978); *Tenement Lover* (1981); *TeentyTown* (with Laurie Carlos and Robbie McCauley, 1988); *Black: Her Story* (1993); *Airport Music* (with Han Ong, 1994). **Published Work:** *Dogeaters* (Pantheon, 1990); *Danger and Beauty* (Penguin, 1993); *Charlie Chan Is Dead: An Anthology of Contemporary Asian-American Fiction* (Penguin, 1993); *The Gangster of Love* (Houghton Mifflin, 1996); *Burning Heart: A Portrait of the Philippines* (Rizzoli Books International, 1999). **Anthologized Work:** *Out from Under* (Theatre Communications Group, 1990); *Between Worlds: Contemporary Asian-American Plays* (Theatre Communications Group, 1990); *Critical Fictions* (Bay Press, 1991); *The Open Boat: Poems from Asian America* (Anchor/Doubleday, 1993); *Brown River, White Ocean: Philippine Writing in English* (Rutgers University Press, 1993); *Race: An Anthology in the First Person* (Crown, 1997). **For Further Information:** The Harold Schmidt Literary Agency; 343 W. 12th Street, Suite 1B; New York, NY 10014.

**VIRGINIA HEFFERNAN** is an editor at *Talk* magazine and a Ph.D. candidate in English at Harvard University, where her dissertation is on finance and fiction. Her work has appeared in *Lingua Franca, New York* magazine, *Salon, Glamour, Metropolis* and *Nerve.* Her essay "A Delicious Placebo" appears in *Unholy Ghost* (edited by Nell Casey, William Morrow, 2000). In 1998, she wrote the Emmy Award-nominated documentary *Matthew's Murder* for MTV. With Mike Albo, she co-wrote *Just Open Your Throat* (1997), *Mike Albo* (1998), *Spray* (1999) and *Please Everything Burst* (2000).

**BEATRICE HERFORD** (1868–1952) was born in Manchester, England and immigrated to Chicago with her family in 1874. After a brief return to England, Herford settled permanently in Wayland, Massachusetts with her American husband. She gave her first public performance in London in 1895 and her American debut in 1896 at Association Hall in Boston. She authored and performed her own one-woman shows regularly in Boston from 1896 to 1943, appearing many times at Steinert Hall, Chickerling Hall, Brattle Hall, Jordan Hall and the Repertory Theatre. Her first New York appearance was at the Waldorf Hotel in 1897 and thereafter, she performed at various theatres including the Lyceum, the Palace, the Madison Square, the Klaw and the Booth. After her 1915 vaudeville debut, she performed in both the mainstream, legitimate theatres and on the vaudeville circuit as a headliner. She appeared in several Broadway plays including *Two by Two, See Naples and Die* and *Run Sheep, Run.* In 1904, Herford had a theatre built on her estate and started her own company, The Vokes Players, which is still in operation today. According to the 1938 program for *Run Sheep, Run,* Herford "is considered to have been the originator of the form of entertainment of which Ruth Draper, Cornelia Otis Skinner and Cecilia Loftus are now leading exponents." In 1943, Herford gave her final performance at the Copley Theatre in Boston as a benefit for the Stage Door Canteen. The event celebrated her fiftieth anniversary in the theatre.

**Performance Work:** *In the Art Museum; Choosing the Wallpapers; At the Hairdresser's; Marketing; The Tale of the Train; The Man with a Cold; The Height of Bliss; The Tea; At the Optician's; Telephoning the Doctor; In the Flower Shop; In the Hat Department; The Young Reciter; The Book Agent; Radio Pudding; The Mix Up.* **Published Work:** *Monologues*

(C. Scribner & Sons, 1908); *Beatrice Herford's Monologues* (Samuel French, Inc., 1937). **Related Material:** *Our American Humorists* (Moffat, Yard and Co., 1922); "Miss Herford's Monologues" Clipping File, Harvard Theatre Collection, Houghton Library; "Beatrice Herford" Clipping File, the Billy Rose Theatre Collection, The New York Public Library for the Performing Arts; "Beatrice Herford, Cissie Loftus and Dorothy Sands within the Tradition of the Solo Performance" by Linda Sue Long (dissertation, University of Texas at Austin, School of Communications, 1982).

**DANNY HOCH** spent four years bringing conflict-resolution-through-drama to adolescents in New York City's jails and alternative high schools with New York University's Creative Arts Team. His show *Some People* won an OBIE and a Fringe First Award at the Edinburgh Festival. His *Jails, Hospitals & Hip-Hop* received a Bay Area Theatre Critics Circle Award and a New York Press Best of Manhattan Award. Hoch has written and acted for television and film and his writing has appeared in magazines such as *Harper's, New Theatre Review, American Theatre, Village Voice* and the *New York Times.* Hoch has received an NEA Solo Theatre Fellowship, a Sundance Writers Fellowship, a Tennessee Williams Fellowship and a CalArts/Alpert Award.

**Performance Work:** *Pot Melting* (1991); *Some People* (1994); *Goin' for Dolo,* (with Dael Orlandersmith, 1996); "Clinic Con Class" (for *Pieces of the Quilt AIDS Theatre Project,* 1996); *Jails, Hospitals & Hip-Hop* (1997). **Published Work:** *Jails, Hospitals & Hip-Hop and Some People* (Villard/Random House, 1998). **Anthologized Work:** *Out of Character* (Bantam Books, 1997); *Laughing in the Dark* (Ecco Press, 1997); *Creating Your Own Monologue* (Allworth Press, 1999). **Film/Video/TV/Laserdisc:** *Some People* (HBO, 1996); *Jails, Hospitals & Hip-Hop* (Stratosphere Films, 2000). **For Further Information:** www.dannyhoch.com.

**HOLLY HUGHES** began her thespian career at the WOW Cafe during the dawn of the Reagan era. Hughes has since performed at other venues in New York City as well as throughout the United States, Canada, Great Britain and Australia. She has received several NEA grants and funding from the Rockefeller, Ford and Aestrea foundations. Her collection of plays and essays, *Clit Notes: A Sapphic Sampler,* was published by Grove Press in 1996. Hughes co-edited, with David Román, *O Solo Homo: The New Queer Performance,* which won a Lambda book award. She has also taught workshops at several colleges and universities and will be teaching at Harvard University in the spring of 2000. Her most recent solo piece is *Preaching to the Perverted,* directed by Lois Weaver, which premiered in 1999 and concerns the Supreme Court hearing of a case she filed, with other artists, against the National Endowment for the Arts. In 1990, Hughes was part of the so-called "NEA Four" and more information on that court case (*Finley et al vs. the National Endowment*) can be found on the Internet at www.csulb.edu/~jvancamp/intro.html.

**Performance Work:** *The Well of Horniness* (1984); *The Lady Dick* (1985); *Dress Suits to Hire* (1987); *Into Temptation* (1988); *World without End* (1989); *No Trace of the Blonde* (1993); *Clit Notes* (1994); *Cat O Nine Tales* (1996); *Mystery Spot* (1997); *Turkey! The New Musical* (with Bud Coleman, 1998); *Preaching to the Perverted* (1999). **Published Work:** *Clit Notes: A Sapphic Sampler* (Grove Press, 1996); *O Solo Homo* (Grove Press, 1998). **Anthologized Work:** *Out Front* (Grove Press, 1989); *Out from Under* (Theatre Communications Group, 1990); *The New Fuck You* (Semiotexte, 1996); *Out of Character* (Bantam Books, 1997). **For Further Information:** HHughes334@aol.com.

**RHODESSA JONES** is an actress, dancer, singer, writer and teacher, as well as the Co-artistic Director of the San Francisco-based performance company Cultural Odyssey. She is also the Founder and Artistic Director of the Medea Project: Theater for Incarcerated

Women. This program helps to increase self-awareness and self-esteem in the incarcerated women's population through the creation and production of theatre pieces based on their personal histories. Jones was awarded a 1993 Bessie Award for her one-woman show *Big Butt Girls, Hard Headed Women*. She is currently Adjunct Associate Professor at University of California at Berkeley, where she lectures and teaches a seminar titled "Creative Performance, Creative Survival—Theatre for the Twenty-first Century." Jones is a member of the National Cultural Task Force for the Smithsonian Institute's African-American Museum of Arts and Letters. She was also a resident scholar at the Getty Institute for the Arts and Humanities in 1998 where she participated in a three-month seminar called "The Role of the Humanities in Public Culture."

**Performance Work:** *The Legend of Lily Overstreet* (1979); *I Think Its Gonna Work Out Fine* (with Ed Bullins and Idris Ackamoor, 1989); *Perfect Courage* (with Bill T. Jones and Idris Ackamoor, 1990); *Raining Down Stars* (with Don Moye, Idris Ackamoor and Ed Bullins, 1990); *Big Butt Girls, Hard Headed Women* (1992); The Medea Project: *Reality is Just Outside the Window* (1992); The Medea Project: *Food Taboos in the Land of the Dead* (1993); *The Blue Stories: Black Erotica on Letting Go* (1994) The Medea Project: *A Taste of Someplace Else: A Place at the Table* (1994); The Medea Project: *Buried Fire* (1996); *Deep in the Night* (1998); The Medea Project: *Requiem for a Dead Love* (1998); The Medea Project: *Slouching Towards Armageddon: A Captive's Conversation/ Observation on Race* (1999); *Hot Flashes, Power Surges and Private Summers* (1999). **Anthologized Work:** *Let's Get It on: The Politics of Black Performance* (Bay Press, 1995); *Colored Contradictions: An Anthology of Contemporary African-American Plays* (Penguin, 1996); *Multi-culture* (*Third Force Magazine*, Vol. 4, #1, March/April, 1996); *Raining Down Stars* (*Callboard* magazine, January 1999). **Audio Tape/LP/CD:** *Portrait* (The Idris Ackamoor Ensemble, Cultural Odyssey Records, 1997). **Film/Video/TV/Laserdisc:** *Open the Gate* (PBS-KQED, 1992); *Conversations with Amazing Women* (PBS-KQED, 1999). **For Further Information:** rhodessa@culturalodyssey.org

**ANDY KAUFMAN** (1949–1984) called himself a variety actor, an entertainer and a song-and-dance man—he once remarked, "I'm not a comedian, I never told a joke in my life." He reveled in pushing the limits of comedy and forcing his audiences to take part in unexpected and unfamiliar situations. In college, Kaufman produced and starred in his own campus TV series *Uncle Andy's Funhouse*, and he started working the nightclub scene of New York City. By the mid-1970s, Kaufman had become a regular performer at New York's The Improv and Catch a Rising Star. When he later moved to Los Angeles, he performed regularly at the West Coast Improv and The Comedy Store. His signature characters "Foreign Man," "Elvis" and "Tony Clifton" brought him his fame, but his audience-bating antics which included lengthy, verbatim readings from *The Great Gatsby*, wrestling matches with female audience members, doing laundry on stage and what might best be called elaborate practical jokes earned him his notoriety. Kaufman's work extended beyond the stage and he would often stage mock fights in public spaces and on TV. Although he performed often for TV (he was a frequent guest on *Saturday Night Live* and *Fridays*), his work developed out of the live performances he gave in the comedy clubs, on the college circuit and in larger venues like Carnegie Hall and Town Hall in New York. In 1978, a variation of his "Foreign Man" became the character of Latka Gravas on the TV series, *Taxi*, which lasted five years. In 1983 he tried his hand at Broadway and appeared in *Teaneck Tanzi: The Venus Flytrap* with Debbie Harry which closed after two nights of performances. He was called by one critic, "The Picasso of put-on artists." Kaufman died in 1984 of a rare form of lung cancer despite being a confirmed non-smoker and vegetarian.

**Performance Work:** performed at The Improv, Catch a Rising Star, Bitter End, Playboy Club Resort, The Comedy Store, the West Coast Improv (1970s–1980s); opened for The

Temptations in Northampton, Mass. (1972); the Bijou, Philadelphia (1974); the Hunting-ton Hartford, Hollywood (1978); Town Hall, New York (1978); *Andy Kaufman at Carnegie Hall* (1979); *Teaneck Tanzi: The Venus Flytrap* (Broadway, 1983). **Film/Video/TV/ Laserdisc:** *Saturday Night Live* (NBC, 1975–1982); *Demon* or *God Told Me To* (Larco Productions, 1976); *Comedy Tonight* (Vestron Vid, 1977); *Fridays* (ABC, 1980s); *Taxi* (ABC, 1978–1983); *Andy's Funhouse* (ABC, 1979); *Andy Kaufman at Carnegie Hall* (taped live, ABC, 1979); *In God We Tru$t* (Howard West/George Shapiro, 1980); *Heartbeeps* (Universal, 1981); *Andy Kaufman: Sound Stage* (Lightning Vid, 1983); *My Breakfast with Blassie* (Artist Endeavors, 1984) *Andy Kaufman Special* (Media Home, 1985). **Related Material:** *Andy Kaufman Revealed!* (Little, Brown & Company, 1999); *Lost in the Funhouse: The Life and Mind of Andy Kaufman* (Delacorte Press, 1999); *Man on the Moon* (film, Universal, 1999).

**JOSH KORNBLUTH** worked for several years as a journalist in Chicago and then in Boston where he created and hosted a radio variety show called *The Urban Happiness Radio Hour*. From there he moved to stage performing, joining a political comedy revue in Boston called The Gramm-Rudman Act. After moving to San Francisco, he performed his first monologue, *Josh Kornbluth's Daily World*, in 1989. In 1992 he made his Off-Broadway debut with *Red Diaper Baby* (a piece combining elements of previous work with new material), and was nominated for a Drama Desk Award. In 1993, he premiered *The Mathematics of Change* in San Francisco, and at the same time, the back of his head was making its feature-film debut in *Searching for Bobby Fischer*. Josh went on to par-ticipate in the Sundance Screenwriters' Lab and play the small but pivotal role of "Cigarette Pack Man" in the movie *Jack*.

**Performance Work:** *Josh Kornbluth's Daily World* (1989); *Haiku Tunnel* (1990); *The Moisture Seekers* (1991); *Red Diaper Baby* (1992); *The Mathematics of Change* (1993); *Ben Franklin: Unplugged* (1998). **Published Work:** *Red Diaper Baby* (Mercury House, 1996). **Anthologized Work:** *Best American Plays* (Applause, 1992). **For Further Information:** home.earthlink.net/~jkornbluth/.

**LISA KRON** began writing and performing solo work fourteen years ago at the WOW Cafe in New York City. Since then, her work has been presented at such spaces as New York Theatre Workshop, La Jolla Playhouse, Actors Theatre of Louisville, The Joseph Papp Public Theater/New York Shakespeare Festival and the Barbican Theatre Centre in London. *101 Humiliating Stories* and *2.5 Minute Ride* were both nominated for Drama Desk Awards and *2.5 Minute Ride* was also nominated for an Outer Critics Circle Award and received OBIE and Dramalogue awards. Kron has also received a CalArts/Alpert Award, a New York Foundation for the Arts Fellowship and the Robert Chesley Gay and Lesbian Playwriting Award. She is a founding member of the OBIE and Bessie Award-winning the-atre company, The Five Lesbian Brothers. As an actress, Kron has appeared in Paul Rudnick's *The Most Fabulous Story Ever Told* and in workshops of Paula Vogel's *The Mineola Twins*, among others. Her work has been widely anthologized.

**Performance Work:** *101 Humiliating Stories* (1994); *2.5 Minute Ride* (1999); With The Five Lesbian Brothers: *Voyage to Lesbos* (1990); *Brave Smiles* (1993); *The Secretaries* (1994); *Brides of the Moon* (1998). **Published Work:** *The Five Lesbian Brothers' Guide to Life* (Simon & Schuster, 1997); *The Five Lesbian Brothers/Four Plays* (Theatre Communica-tions Group, 2000). **Anthologized Work:** *The Actor's Book of Gay and Lesbian Plays* (Penguin, 1995); *The New Fuck You* (Semiotexte, 1996); *The Wild Good* (Anchor Books, 1996); *Out of Character* (Bantam Books, 1997).

**JOHN LEGUIZAMO** is an actor, comedian, writer and producer. He runs his own production company, Lower East Side Films, and has appeared in several feature films and television shows. In 1991, Leguizamo received OBIE, Outer Critics Circle and Vanguardia awards for his first one-man show *Mambo Mouth*. The show later aired on HBO and led to his first television special on Comedy Central called *The Talent Pool*, for which he received a Cable ACE Award. *Spic-O-Rama* was awarded a Dramatists' Guild Hull-Warriner Award, a Lucille Lortel Outstanding Achievement Award, a Theatre World Award and a Drama Desk Award. *Spic-O-Rama* also aired on HBO and received four Cable ACE Awards. Leguizamo's *Freak* was nominated for two Tony Awards, and the subsequent HBO special won Leguizamo an Emmy for his performance. In 1995, Leguizamo created and stared in the Latin comedy/variety show, *House of Buggin'* for FOX and received an Emmy Award.

**Performance Work:** *The Bible According to Latinus Spicticus* (1987); *Mambo Mouth* (1991); *Spic-O-Rama* (1992); *Freak* (1997). **Published Work:** *Mambo Mouth: A Savage Comedy* (Bantam Books, 1993); *Spic-O-Rama* (Bantam Books, 1994); *Freak: A Semi-Demi-Quasi-Pseudo Autobiography* (Penguin Putnam, Inc., 1997). **Film/Video/TV/Laserdisc:** *Spawn* (New Line Cinema, 1997); *William Shakespeare's Romeo + Juliet* (Twentieth-Century Fox, 1996); *Too Wong Foo: Thanks for Everything, Julie Newmar* (Universal, 1995); *Miami Vice* (NBC, 1986); *Arabian Nights* (ABC, 1999); *Mambo Mouth* (HBO, 1992); *Spic-O-Rama* (HBO, 1993); *Freak* (HBO, 1998); *The Talent Pool* (Comedy Central); *Summer of Sam* (Touchstone Films, 1999). **For Further Information:** ID Public Relations; 3859 Cardiff Avenue; Culver City, CA 90232; us@id-pr.com.

**JACKIE "MOMS" MABLEY** (1897–1975) was born Loretta Mary Aiken in Bravard, North Carolina. At thirteen she joined a minstrel show and started performing on the Theatre Owners Booking Association circuit. She later performed in the many black-owned and managed clubs in the East, appearing at the Apollo in Harlem more often than any other performer in its history. During the Harlem Renaissance in the 1920s, Mabley often shared billing with Duke Ellington, Louis Armstrong, Benny Goodman, Count Basie and Cab Calloway (in nightclubs such as The Cotton Club and the Savoy Ballroom) and created comedy routines from her encounters and supposed love affairs with these men. During the Depression, she performed in many black theatre revues, and sometimes in blackface. In 1931, she collaborated on a Broadway play with author Zora Neale Hurston called *Fast and Furious: A Colored Revue in 37 Scenes*. The name "Moms" was given to her by her fellow actors, but the character of "Moms" became her signature. In the 1960s, "Moms" appeared on several television variety and talk shows hosted by, among others, the Smothers Brothers, Ed Sullivan, Flip Wilson and Merv Griffin. During her career, Mabley performed at Carnegie Hall, the Playboy clubs, the Copacabana, the Kennedy Center and the White House, while John F. Kennedy was President.

**Audio Tape/LP/CD:** *Now Hear This* (Mercury Records, 1965); *Moms Mabley at the White House Conference* (Mercury, 1966); *Moms the Word* (Mercury Records, 1970); *Live at Sing Sing* (Mercury Records, 1970); *Live at the Greek Theatre* (Mercury Records, 1971); *Moms Mabley on Stage* (Chess, 1984). **Film/Video/TV/Laserdisc:** *The Emperor Jones* (United Artists, 1933); *Boarding House Blues* (All American News, 1948); *Killer Diller* (All American News, 1948); *A Time for Laughter* (ABC, 1967); *Amazing Grace* (United Artists, 1974); *The Howard Theatre: A Class Act* (D.C. Humanities Council, June 26, 1985); *A Laugh! A Tear!* (Fox, 1999); *Mo' Funny: Black Comedy in America* (HBO, 1993). **Related Material:** *The Best Plays of 1932* (Dodd, 1932); *Black Culture and Black Consciousness: Afro-American Folk Thought from Slavery to Freedom* (Oxford University Press, 1977); *Brown Sugar: Eighty Years of America's Black Female Superstars* (Harmony, 1980); *Bowman's Cotton Blossoms, 1919 Blacks in Blackface* (Scarecrow, 1980); *Harlem Heydey* (Prometheus, 1984); *Women's Comic Visions* (Wayne State University, 1991); *Black Women* *in America: An Historical Encyclopedia, Vol. II* (Carlson, 1993); *The Humor of Jackie Moms Mabley: An African Comedic Tradition* (Garland Publishing, 1995).

**ANN MAGNUSON** is an actress, singer, writer and performance artist. She was co-founder and manager of the neo-Dada Club 57 (1979–1981) in New York. As a prominent figure in the 1980s New York performance art scene, Magnuson developed and performed in solo pieces, duets and bands. She performed in the heavy metal outfit Vulcan Death Grip, the sardonic folk band Bleaker Street Incident, and released five albums with the psycho-psychedelic cult band, Bongwater. *You Could Be Home Now*, was developed with director David Schweizer for Lincoln Center's Serious Fun Festival in 1990. It was later produced at Los Angeles Contemporary Exhibitions and The Joseph Papp Public Theater/New York Shakespeare Festival in 1992 before touring the United States throughout 1993. Ann has written for a variety of magazines and has appeared Off-Broadway and in several films.

**Performance Work:** first Club 57 performance (1979); *You Could Be Home Now* (1990); *The Luv Show* (1995); *Pretty Songs* (1997); *Daughter of Horror: An Evening of Appalachian Goth Lounge* (1998). **Audio Tape/LP/CD:** *The Luv Show* (Geffen Records, 1995). **Film/Video/TV/Laserdisc:** *The Hunger* (MGM, 1983); *Made for TV* (with Tom Rubnitz, PBS, 1984); *Vandemonium* (Cinemax, 1987); *Making Mr. Right* (Orion, 1987); *Anything But Love* (ABC, early 1990s); *Clear and Present Danger* (Paramount, 1994); *From the Earth to the Moon* (HBO, 1998). **For Further Information:** www.annmagnuson.com.

**DEB MARGOLIN** is a founding member of the Split Britches Theater Company. She is also a playwright and performance artist with six full-length solo pieces in repertory as well as several plays. Her most recent play, *Bringing the Fishermen Home*, had its world premiere at the Cleveland Public Theater in the spring of 1999. Currently on the faculties of Yale and New York Universities, Ms. Margolin is the author of a book of collected works entitled *Of All the Nerve: Deb Margolin SOLO*, edited and with commentaries by Lynda Hart. She was Zale Writer-in-Residence at Tulane University in the fall of 1997 and has toured the United States extensively, performing selections from her solo work and serving as an artist-in-residence and visiting lecturer at numerous colleges and universities.

**Performance Work:** *Of All the Nerve* (1989); *970-DEBB* (1990); *Gestation* (1991); *Of Mice, Bugs and Women* (1993); *Carthieves! Joyrides!* (1995); *O Wholly Night and Other Jewish Solecisms* (1996); *Critical Mass* (1997); *Bill Me Later* (1998); *Bringing the Fishermen Home* (1999). **Published Work:** *Split Britches: Lesbian Practice/Feminist Performance* (Routledge, 1996); *Of All the Nerve: Deb Margolin SOLO* (Cassell/Continuum Press, 1999). **Anthologized Work:** *More Monologues for Women by Women* (Heinemann, 1996); *Out of Character* (Bantam Books, 1997); *The Ends of Performance* (New York University, 1998). **For Further Information:** debm@juno.com.

**ROBBIE McCAULEY**'s serial performance works are about the history of her family from the nineteenth century—a metaphor for an African-American family surviving against racism. McCauley is one of four women featured in Demetria Royals' PBS documentary, *Conjure Women*. She received a 1991 Bessie Award and a 1992 OBIE Award for *Sally's Rape*. An adaptation of *Turf: A Conversational Concert in Black and White*, one of her local history projects received the 1996 Achievement in Radio (AIR) Award for best cultural program in radio for WGBH in Boston. McCauley held the position of visiting lecturer at Mount Holyoke College in Massachusetts for several years and is now teaching at Trinity College in Connecticut.

**Performance Work:** *My Father And The Wars* (1985); *Indian Blood* (1987); *Sally's Rape* (1991); *Turf: A Conversational Concert in Black and White* (1994); *Poor White People* (1997); *Surviving Virginia* (1997); *Quabbin Dance* (1998-99). **Anthologized Work:** *Mixed Blessings: New Art in a Multicultural America* (Pantheon Books, 1990); *Out from Under* (Theatre Communications Group, 1990); *Moon Marked and Touched by Sun* (Theatre Communications Group, 1994); *Black Theatre U.S.A. Volume 2* (Simon & Schuster, 1996); *Out of Character* (Bantam Books, 1997). **Audio Tape/LP/CD:** *Regeneration Report* (Context Music, 1983); *Turf* (WGBH Radio, 1996). **Film/Video/TV/Laserdisc:** *Color Schemes* (by Shulea Chang, PBS, 1988); *Sphinxes without Secrets/Women in Performance* (a Maria Beatty production, 1989); *Sally's Rape* (Robbie McCauley & Co./Context Studios, 1995); *Conjure Women* (Diamond/Royals Productions, PBS, 1997). **Related Material:** *Performance and Cultural Politics* (Routledge, 1996). **For Further Information:** The Harold Schmidt Literary Agency; 343 W. 12th Street, Suite 1B; New York, NY 10014.

**TIM MILLER** is a writer and performance artist. He is perhaps best known for being one of the notorious "NEA Four" which resulted when the National Endowment for the Arts revoked his grant because of the content of his performances. In his work, Miller strives to find an artistic, spiritual and political exploration of his identity as a gay man. Miller's performances have been presented all over North America, Australia and Europe. He has taught performance at UCLA, Cal State, New York University, and was an adjunct professor in religion and theatre at the Claremont School of Theology. He co-founded P. S. 122 in New York City and Highways Performance Space in Santa Monica where he is currently Artistic Director.

**Performance Work:** *Paint Yrself Red/Me & Mayakovsky* (1980); *Postwar* (1982); *Cost of Living* (1983); *Democracy in America* (1984); *Buddy Systems* (1985); *Some Golden States* (1987); *Stretch Marks* (1989); *Sex/Love/Stories* (1991); *My Queer Body* (1992); *Naked Breath* (1994); *Fruit Cocktail* (1996); *Spilt Milk* (1997); *Shirts & Skin* (1997). **Published Work:** *Shirts & Skin* (Alyson Publications, 1997). **Anthologized Work:** *Amazing Grace: Stories of Lesbian and Gay Faith* (The Crossing Press, 1991); *Sharing the Delirium: Second Generation AIDS Plays and Performances* (Heinemann/Methuen Press, 1993); *HIS: Brilliant New Fiction by Gay Writers* (Faber & Faber, 1995); *Out of Character* (Bantam Books, 1997); *Boys Like Us: Writers Tell Their Coming-Out Stories* (Avon Books, 1996); *Sundays at Seven* (Alamo Square Press, 1996); *O Solo Homo* (Grove Press, 1998). **For Further Information:** MillerTale@aol.com.

**JOHN O'KEEFE** is a writer and performer who was raised in several Catholic orphanages and state juvenile homes throughout America's Midwest. He has worked with the Center for New Performing Arts, the Iowa Theatre Lab and was co-founder of the Blake Street Hawkeyes in Berkeley, California. He was a screenwriter at the Sundance Film Institute and represented Sundance at the Equinox Film Institute in France. O'Keefe has written over twenty full-length plays and his one-man shows have been presented all over the United States and abroad. He is a recipient of a National Theatre Artist Residency grant from The Pew Charitable Trusts and has received many other awards including a Bessie Award for *Shimmer*, a Shubert Grant for Playwrighting, several Bay Area Theatre Critics Circle Awards (one for *The Saints of Father Lyons*) and a Rockefeller grant.

**Performance Work:** *The Sunshine's a Glorious Bird* (1978); *The Saints of Father Lyons* (1980); *The Man in the Moon* (1983); *Don't You Ever Call Me Anything but Mother* (1983); *Aztec* (1984); *The Magician* (1986); *Shimmer* (1988); *The Promotion* (1989); *Vid* (1990); *Palace of Death* (1992); *Sisters of the Wind* (1993); *The Deatherians* (1996); *The Seduction of Charlotte Brontë* (1997); *Brontë* (1999). **Published Work:** *Shimmer and Other Texts* (Theatre Communications Group, 1989); *The Deatherians* (Sun & Moon Press,

1998). **Anthologized Work:** *Playwrights for Tomorrow* (University of Minnesota Press, 1973); *Word Plays 2: New American Drama* (Performing Arts Journal Publications, 1982); *Plays from Padua Hills 1982*, (Pomona College Theatre Department, 1983); *West Coast Plays 19/20* (California Theatre Council, 1986); *Out of Character* (Bantam Books, 1997); *Best Monologues For Women* (Theatre Communications Group, 1998); *Best Monologues for Men* (Theatre Communications Group, 1998); *All Night Long* (American Theater in Literature Series, 1998). **Film/Video/TV/Laserdisc:** *Women in Prison* (HBO, 1989); *Back to the '60s* (HBO, 1990); *Shimmer* (American Playhouse/WMG/Kinowelt, 1994); *The Brontë's* (Sundance Film Institute, 1995). **For Further Information:** bekin@aol.com.

**DAEL ORLANDERSMITH** is a playwright, poet and actor. She grew up in East Harlem and the South Bronx. She has appeared in productions of *Macbeth, Romeo and Juliet, Raisin in the Sun, Goin' for Dolo* (with Danny Hoch) and has toured extensively with the Nuyorican Poets Café throughout the U.S., Europe and Australia. In 1994 Orlandersmith won an OBIE Award for her play, *Beauty's Daughter*. *The Gimmick* was developed at the Sundance Theatre Lab in 1997 before it had productions at the McCarter Theatre Center and New York Theatre Workshop. She is currently working on a book of fiction entitled *Lone Dancer Underground* and a newly commissioned play entitled *Yellowman*. She is the recipient of a National Theatre Artist Residency grant from the Pew Charitable Trusts. An anthology of her solo works, *Monster, Beauty's Daughter* and *The Gimmick* is being published by Vintage Books.

**Performance Work:** *Liar Liar* (1993); *Beauty's Daughter* (1994); *Monster* (1996); *Goin' for Dolo* (with Danny Hoch, 1996); *The Gimmick* (1997). **Anthologized Work:** *Aloud: Voices from the Nuyorican Poets Café* (Henry Holt, 1994); *Out of Character* (Bantam Books, 1997); *American Theatre* (July/August, 1999). **For Further Information:** Judy Boals; Berman, Boals & Flynn; 208 West 30th Street, Suite 401; New York, NY 10001.

**RENO** is a stream-of-consciousness-style, comedic, solo performer. Her work has had several Off-Broadway productions in both commercial and not-for-profit venues and she tours regularly on what might be called the "museum circuit." She began performing her solo work in 1983 at the WOW Cafe, Limbo Lounge and other funky dives, and a few years later, accelerated her performance schedule in such spaces as Dixon Place, the Wah Wah Hut and St. Mark's Poetry Project. She performed in Tony Kushner's *A Bright Room Called Day* at The Joseph Papp Public Theater/New York Shakespeare Festival in 1991. Her HBO presentation of *Reno in Rage and Rehab* was nominated for a Cable ACE Award. Reno has made other, short-form, tragi-comic "essays" for various outlets such as PBS, VH-1 and Comedy Central. Her first feature film, *Reno Finds Her Mom* was made for HBO and she is now in pre-production for her second film, *Reno Finds Her Mind*. Reno was included in Showtime's original documentary *History of Comedy*.

**Performance Work:** various short works (1984–1987); *Reno in Rage and Rehab* (1987–1988); *Reno Once Removed* (1992); *Citizen Reno* (1993–1996); *Reno Finds Her Mind* (1999). **Film/Video/TV/Laserdisc:** *Reno in Rage and Rehab* (HBO, 1990); *Edith Ann* (ABC, 1995–1996); *Hollywood PD* (CBS, 1995); *Kids Are Punny* (HBO, 1999); *Quiz Show* (Disney, 1995); *Reno Finds Her Mom* (HBO, 1998); *Twenty-four Women* (The Shooting Gallery, 1999); *Fear of Fiction* (Pow Wow Productions, 2000); *Harlem Aria* (Bent Nail Productions, 2000). **For Further Information:** Adam Leibner; N.S. Beinstock; 1740 Broadway, 29th Floor; New York, NY 10019; www.CitizenReno.com; renoren@idt.net.

**RACHEL ROSENTHAL** is an interdisciplinary performer whose technique integrates text, movement, voice, choreography, improvisation, inventive costuming, dramatic lighting and imaginative sets. In 1955, she created the Instant Theatre in California which she performed in for ten years. She was a leading figure in the L.A. Women's Art Movement in the 1970s, co-founding Womanspace. She is the Artistic Director of The Rachel Rosenthal Company which she formed in 1989 and in the last twenty years has presented thirty-five full-scale pieces. She has received many grants from various foundations and arts councils, and numerous awards including a Genesis Award for spotlighting animal rights issues in her work.

**Performance Work:** first work with Instant Theatre (1956–1966); *Replays* (1975); *Charm* (1977); *Grand Canyon* (1978); *The Death Show* (1978); *My Brazil* (1979); *Bonsoir, Dr.Schön!* (1980); *Soldier of Fortune* (1981); *Traps* (1982); *Gaia, Mon Amour* (1983); *KabbaLAmobile* (1984); *The Others* (1984); *Foodchain* (1985); *Shamanic Ritual* (1985); *L.O.W. in Gaia* (1986); *Death Valley* (1987); *Rachel's Brain* (1987); *Zatoichi* (1990); *Amazonia* (1990); *Pangaean Dreams* (1990); *filename: FUTURFAX* (1992); *Zone* (1994); *Tohubohu!* (1995); *Timepiece* (1996); *The Unexpurgated Virgin* (1997); *UR-BOOR* (2000). **Published Work:** *Gaia, Mon Amour* (Hallwalls, 1983); *Rachel's Brain* (Johns Hopkins University Press, 1997); *Tatti Wattles: A Love Story* (Smart Art Press, 1997). **Anthologized Work:** *Out from Under* (Theatre Communications Group, 1990); *War After War* (City Lights Review, 1992); *Plays for the End of the Century* (John Hopkins University Press, 1997). **Film/Video/TV/Laserdisc:** *Putting Our Hands to Other Labor/Women's Art Movements in Southern California* (Group W. Cable, 1986); *The Performance World of Rachel Rosenthal* (KCET, 1987); *L.O.W. in Gaia* (KCET, Artworks/Earthworks, 1990); *Art News Report* (Motion by Design Productions, 1992). **Related Material:** *Exposures: Women & Their Art* (New Stage Press, 1989); *The Passion of Rachel Rosenthal* (Parachute, 1994); *Rachel Rosenthal: A Monograph* (Johns Hopkins University Press, 1997); *Performance: Live Art Since the Sixties* (Thames & Hudson, 1998); *Redressing the Canon: Essays on Theater and Gender* (Routledge, 1998). **For Further Information:** www.rachelrosenthal.org.

**DAWN AKEMI SAITO** is a performance artist, actress, writer and butoh dancer/chore-ographer. In addition to creating her own solo pieces, Saito has collaborated on Charles Mee's *My House is Collapsing Toward One Side* and Robert Woodruff's *Women of Trachis*, and has worked with JoAnne Akalaitis, Larry Sacharow, Wyn Handman, Maria Mileaf and Christine Sang, among others. She has also performed in Bill T. Jones's *Last Supper at Uncle Tom's Cabin*; Ping Chong's *Deshima* and *Elephant Memories*; Roman Paska's *Moby Dick in Venice*; Erik Ehn's *Maid*; Victoria Mark's *Father and Daughter Dance*; Catherine Filloux's *Photographs at S21*; Chiori Miyagawa's *Nothing Forever*; *Hedda Gabbler* at The Old Globe; *Suddenly Last Summer* and *The Poet* at Hartford Stage Company; National Asian-American Theater Company's *Midsummer Night's Dream* and many other produc-tions. She has taught workshops at Columbia, Fordham and New York Universities, and also teaches at Cal Arts.

**Performance Work:** *DreamCatcher* (1994); *Shinjin* (1995); *Pastime* (1996); *Ha* (1996); *Red Eye* (1997); *Halo* (1997); *Leaves, Water Sun* (1999). **Related Material:** *Attitude* (Vol. 11, #2, Summer 1995); *The Independent* (January 22, 1998). **For Further Information:** Akemi33@aol.com.

**ANNA DEAVERE SMITH** is an actor, playwright and teacher. Over the past eigh-teen years, Smith has created a body of theatrical work which she calls *On the Road: A Search for American Character*. She received an OBIE Award for *Fires in the Mirror: Crown Heights, Brooklyn and Other Identities* and two Tony nominations, an OBIE Award, a Drama Desk Award and two NAACP Theatre Awards for *Twilight: Los Angeles, 1992*. In 1996 she received a MacArthur Foundation "Genius" fellowship. In association with the

Ford Foundation, Smith founded the Institute on the Arts & Civic Dialogue, which is hosted by the W. E. B. Du Bois Institute and American Repertory Theatre at Harvard University. She is Ann O'Day Maples Professor of the Arts at Stanford University.

**Performance Work:** *Fires in the Mirror: Crown Heights, Brooklyn and Other Identities* (1992); *Twilight: Los Angeles, 1992* (1993); *House Arrest* (ensemble, 1995-1999); *House Arrest* (solo, 2000). **Film/Video/TV/Laserdisc:** *Fires in the Mirror: Crown Heights, Brooklyn and Other Identities* (PBS, 1993); *Dave* (Warner Brothers, 1993); *Philadelphia* (Columbia TriStar, 1993); *The American President* (Columbia TriStar, 1995). **For Further Information:** Stephen Rivers & Associates; 1460 Fourth Street; Santa Monica, CA 90401-2329; stephen@riverspr.com.

**ROGER GUENVEUR SMITH**'s solo work, *A Huey P. Newton Story*, received OBIE, Audelco, Helen Hayes and NAACP Image awards. His work has been presented at The Joseph Papp Public Theater/New York Shakespeare Festival, the Mark Taper Forum, the Actors' Theatre of Louisville and the Barbican Theatre Centre in London. He has also played seasons with the Guthrie Theatre and Mabou Mines and directed the Bessie Award-winning *Radio Mambo* with Culture Clash. Smith's many screen credits include six collaborations with director Spike Lee.

**Performance Work:** *Frederick Douglass Now* (1990); *Inside the Creole Mafia* (1991); *Christopher Columbus 1992* (1992); *A Huey P. Newton Story* (1995); *Blood and Brains* (1999). **Film/Video/TV/Laserdisc:** *School Daze* (Columbia Pictures, 1988); *Do the Right Thing* (Universal, 1989); *King of New York* (1990); *Flight 180* (New Line, 1990); *Deep Cover* (New Line, 1992); *Malcolm X* (Warner Brothers, 1992); *Get on the Bus* (Columbia Pictures, 1996); *Eve's Bayou* (Columbia Pictures, 1997); *He Got Game* (Touchstone Pictures, 1998); *Summer of Sam* (Touchstone Pictures, 1999); *The Color of Courage* (USA, 1999).

**BROTHER THEODORE** was born in Vienna in 1906. His family was extremely wealthy while living in Germany, but when the Nazis came to power they were forced to give up their fortune and then perished in the concentration camps; Theodore was the only survivor. With the help of Albert Einstein, a family friend, Theodore immigrated to the United States in 1941 and worked odd jobs to get by. He embarked on his performing career in the mid-1940s. He moved to New York in 1947 and began performing his serious grand guignol monologues in small venues. In the course of his career he sold out Town Hall six times, performed at Carnegie Recital Hall and had a sixteen-year run at the 13th Street Theatre in New York. He made numerous appearances on the *Merv Griffin Show* (it was Griffin who dubbed him "Brother" because of his priest-like, all-black outfit and wild, white tuft of hair) and in the 1980s was a frequent guest on *Late Night with David Letterman*. He has made several radio and film appearances as well.

**Published Work:** *Chamber of Horrors* (1975). **Audio Tape/LP/CD:** *An Entertainment of Sinister and Discerning Humor, or Tears from a Glass Eye . . . with a Tongue of Madness* (Proscenium, 1955); *Coral Records Presents Theodore* (Coral, early 1960s); *Scary Stories* (Rhino Records). **Film/Video/TV/Laserdisc:** *The Stranger* (1946); *So Dark the Night* (Columbia Pictures, 1946); *The Black Widow* (Republic Pictures, 1947); *Fall Guy* (Monogram, 1947); *The Lone Wolf in Mexico* (Columbia, 1947); *Midnight Café* (1956); *Sombra the Spider Woman* (1966); *Horror of the Blood Monsters* (Independent International, 1970); *Gums* (Masada, 1976); *The Hobbit* (Rankin/Bass, 1977); *Nocturna* (Compass International, 1979); *The Last Unicorn* (Rankin/Bass, 1982); *Billy Crystal: Don't Get Me Started* (Vestron Vid, 1986); *The Invisible Kid* (Elysian Pictures, 1988); *The 'burbs* (Universal, 1989); *That's Adequate* (South Gate Entertainment, 1990). **For Further Information:** www.netsync.net/users/moonfan/; www.jcn18.com/newstand/kalish.

**LILY TOMLIN** has performed on stage, in film and on television. Though she entered college as a pre-med student, she became active in the theatre scene on campus. In a student variety show she improvised her first character, "The Tasteful Lady" whom she has continued to perform since. She left college after her junior year and moved to New York in 1962. She came to prominence in the 1970s with such characters as "Trudy the Bag Lady"; "Lucille," a woman addicted to eating rubber objects; "Sister Boogie-Woman"; "Lupe," the world's oldest living beauty expert; "Crystal," a quadriplegic; "Bobbi-Jeanine," a cocktail-lounge organist extraordinaire; and "Rick," a singles-bar cruiser. Tomlin became a regular on the NBC series *Laugh-In* in 1969 and made frequent appearances on *The Smothers Brothers Comedy Hour*. Most recently, she was a series regular on the sit-com *Murphy Brown*. Tomlin is the recipient of numerous awards, including several Emmy's. She won a Grammy Award in 1971 for her album, *This is a Recording*. In 1977 Tomlin won a Tony Award for her one-woman Broadway show, *Appearing Nitely*. For her performance in Jane Wagner's *The Search for Signs of Intelligent Life in the Universe*, Tomlin won a Tony Award, a Drama Desk Award and an Outer Circle Critic's Award.

**Performance Work:** *The Real Live Lily Tomlin TV Show* (1975); *Appearing Nitely* (1977); *The Search for Signs of Intelligent Life in the Universe* (1985). **Audio Tape/LP/CD:** *This Is a Recording* (Polydor, 1971); *And That's the Truth* (Polydor, 1972); *Modern Scream* (Polydor, 1975); *On Stage* (Arista, 1977). **Film/Video/TV/Laserdisc:** *Rowan & Martin's Laugh-In* (NBC, 1969–1973); *Nashville* (Paramount, 1975); *The Late Show* (Warner Brothers, 1976); *9 to 5* (Twentieth-Century Fox, 1980); *The Incredible Shrinking Woman* (Universal, 1981); *All of Me* (Universal, 1984); *Big Business* (Buena Vista, 1987); *The Lily Tomlin Video Collection: Lily Tomlin: Ernestine: Peak Experiences* (Wolfe Video, 1992); *Lily Tomlin: Lily for President?* (Wolfe Video, 1992); *Lily Tomlin: Appearing Nitely* (Wolfe Video, 1992); *Lily Tomlin: Lily Sold Out!* (Wolfe Video, 1992); *Lily Tomlin: The Search for Signs of Intelligent Life in the Universe* (Wolfe Video, 1992); *In the Life: The Funny Tape* (Wolfe Video and PBS, 1993); *And the Band Played On* (HBO, 1993); *Short Cuts* (New Line, 1993); *Flirting with Disaster* (Buena Vista, 1996); *Getting Away with Murder* (Savoy, 1996); *The Magic School Bus* (PBS series, Scholastic Entertainment, 1994–1997); *Reno Finds Her Mom* (HBO, 1998); *Tea With Mussolini* (MGM, 1999). **Related Material:** *Funny People* (Stein & Day, 1981); *Woman of a Thousand Faces* (St. Martin's Press, 1989); *Women's Comic Visions* (Wayne State University, 1991).

**DANITRA VANCE** (1959–1994) was a graduate of Roosevelt University in Chicago and the Weber-Douglas Academy of Dramatic Art in London. After graduation, she performed in clubs in Chicago and at the American Folk Theatre and other venues in New York City, where she formed her own company, Women in Comedy Lab, with Bronwyn Rucker. Her "performance-art" career, as it was then called, was launched at La MaMa E.T.C., which presented her with the Mell-O White Boys. Later, her show *D'Vance & D'Boys* was premiered on the West Coast at Life on the Water in San Francisco and led to Producer Lorne Michaels recruiting her for the eleventh season of NBC's *Saturday Night Live*. Vance received an NAACP Image Award and a Dramalogue Award for her performance in *The Colored Museum*, and OBIE and Dramalogue awards for *Spunk* (both by George C. Wolfe). In 1993 she won an Independent Spirit nomination for best supporting actress in *Jumpin' at the Boneyard*. *Live and In Color!*, a one-woman show, was presented as part of Crossroads Theatre Company's 1991 Genesis Festival of New Plays. Portions of *Live and In Color!* were also presented at La MaMa E.T.C., The Joseph Papp Public Theater/New York Shakespeare Festival and other East and West Coast venues. Vance died of breast cancer at the age of thirty-five, but before her death, she confronted the stigma of cancer and made it a prominent part of her work.

**Performance Work:** *D'Vance & D'Boys*; *Danitra Vance and the Mell-O White Boys Revisted* (1991); *Live and In Color!* (1991). **Anthologized Work:** *Moon Marked and Touched by Sun* (Theatre Communications Group, 1994). **Film/Video/TV/Laserdisc:** *Saturday Night Live* (NBC, November 9 and 23, 1985; February 8, 1986; April 19, 1986); *Miami Vice* (NBC, October 3, 1987); *The Colored Museum* performed at the Mark Taper Forum (The New York Public Library for the Performing Arts, June 16, 1988); *Sticky Fingers* (High Top Films, 1988); *Limit Up* (MCEG, 1989); *The War of the Roses* (Twentieth-Century Fox, 1989); *The Cover Girl and the Cop* (Barry & Enright Films, 1989); *Spunk* performed at The Joseph Papp Public Theater/New York Shakespeare Festival (The New York Public Library for the Performing Arts, June 28, 1990); *The Colored Museum* (PBS, February 1, 1991); *Little Man Tate* (Orion, 1991); *Hangin' with the Homeboys* (New Line, 1991); *Jumpin' at the Boneyard* (Twentieth-Century Fox, 1992).

**JANE WAGNER** is the author of several books and works written for Lily Tomlin to perform. Among them are *The Search for Signs of Intelligent Life in the Universe* (Harper & Row, 1986) and *Edith Ann: My Life, So Far* (Hyperion, 1994). She is the recipient of two Peabody Awards for *J.T.,* a teleplay for CBS (1969); and "Edith Ann's Christmas: Just Say Noel" (1996). Among other works, Wagner is also the author of *The Incredible Shrinking Woman* screenplay for Universal (1981). Wagner has received five Emmy Awards and a Writers Guild of America Award for her work in writing and producing television specials in which Tomlin starred.

**HEATHER WOODBURY** is a writer and performer. She became involved in the East Village performance-art scene in the early eighties, creating solo pieces at such venues as The Knitting Factory and The Gas Station and founding her own venue in 1986, Café Bustelo. Subsequently she expanded her performances into larger venues like Dixon Place and Franklin Furnace. Between 1984–94 she created sixteen solo pieces, two plays and one screenplay. Her trans-American "performance novel" *What Ever* was originated in weekly half-hour installments performed over thirty-seven consecutive Wednesdays in the back of an East Village bar. It was inspired by her experiences living in several New York City neighborhoods; working as a go-go dancer, barmaid and "cater-waiter"; and criss-crossing the country several times by car, train, bus and thumb.

**Performance Work:** *Hollow Venus: Diary of a Go-Go Dancer* (1984); *Rogue's Gallery* (1987); *Rejuvenilation* (1988); *Delugians of Grandeur* (1989); *Protestitution* (1989); *Virtuesincorruption* (1990); *Introducing Gory Priestess* (1990); *Through the Looking Glass: Diary of an Ex-Ex-Go-Go Dancer* (1990); *Why We Hate Western Civilization* (with Bina Sharif and Jennifer Neff, 1991); *I Want a Man* (1992); *Antagony* (1992); *White Gilt* (1993–94); *Soon-To-Be Famous Suicide of an Obscure Performance Artist* (1994); *The Heather Woodbury Report* (1994–1995); *What Ever* (1995); *X-Static Woman* (1995). **Audio Tape/LP/CD:** "Radio-play" (the complete *What Ever*; The Cavanagh Fund, Austin, TX, 1996; contact the artist for copies); *Haunted by Ghosts* (*This American Life*, Chicago, IL; October 31, 1997; contact: www.thislife.org). **Film/Video/TV/Laserdisc:** *Hollow Venus: Diary of a Go-Go Dancer* (Glass Eye Pix, 1989; contact: www.glasseyepix.com); *Habit* (Glass Eye Pix, 1995); videos of performances are stored by the artist and at Franklin Furnace Archives. **Related Material:** "From Theatre to Soap Opera: Serious Fun in the Work of Rose English and Heather Woodbury" (master's thesis, The Slade School of Fine Art, University College, London, 1999). **For Further Information:** Box 26549, Los Angeles, CA 90026; www.heatherwoodbury.com.

# Photographic Credits

# Citation Credits

The following sources are credited with providing material for this anthology. All work is reprinted by permission. Unless otherwise noted, all material is published here for the first time. Citation credits are in alphabetical order.

**Mike Albo/Virginia Heffernan:** *Mike Albo* is copyright © 1998 by Mike Albo and Virginia Heffernan. *Spray* is copyright © 1999 by Mike Albo and Virginia Heffernan.

**Luis Alfaro:** *Cuerpo Politizado* is copyright © 1995 by Luis Alfaro. *Abuelita* and *A Mu-Mu Approaches* were published in *O Solo Homo: The New Queer Performance* edited by Holly Hughes and David Román, Grove Press, 1998.

**Laurie Anderson:** *New York Social Life* is copyright © 1977; *On the Road* is copyright © 1978; *After Science, Dinner* is copyright © 1979; *Difficult Listening Hour* is copyright © 1980; *Big Science* is copyright © 1982; *Talk Normal* is copyright © 1989; *False Documents* is copyright © 1979; *Camelot* is copyright © 1989; *Wild White Horses* is copyright © 1989. All copyright by Laurie Anderson and published in *Stories from the Nerve Bible*, HarperPerennial, 1994. *New York Social Life* was also published in *United States*, Harper & Row, 1984.

**Brenda Wong Aoki:** *Random Acts* is copyright © 1994 by Brenda Wong Aoki. *Mermaid Meat* is copyright © 1997 by Brenda Wong Aoki.

**Eric Bogosian:** *Sex, Drugs, Rock & Roll* is copyright © 1990, 1991 by Ararat Productions, Inc.; published by Theatre Communications Group, New York, 1996. *Pounding Nails in*

*Herford's Monologues* is copyright © 1937 by Samuel French, Inc., and copyright © 1965 by Helen Brooke Herford. Inquiries regarding performance rights or the purchase of the authorized acting edition must be directed to Samuel French, Inc., 45 West 25th Street, New York, NY 10010 with other locations in Hollywood, Toronto and Canada.

**Danny Hoch:** *Some People* is copyright © 1993, 1998 by Danny Hoch. *Jails, Hospitals & Hip-Hop* is copyright © 1998 by Danny Hoch. Both published in *Jails, Hospitals & Hip-Hop and Some People* by Villard Books, a division of Random House, Inc., New York, 1998. Permission for use must be secured from the author's agents: Peter Hagan, The Gersh Agency, 130 West 42nd Street, Suite 2400, New York, NY 10036, (212) 997-1818; Kathleen Russo, Washington Square Arts, 12 East 10th Street, New York, NY 10003, (212) 253-0333.

**Holly Hughes:** *World without End* is copyright © 1989, 1990 by Holly Hughes; published in *Out from Under: Texts by Women Performance Artists* edited by Lenora Champagne, Theatre Communications Group, New York.

**Rhodessa Jones:** *Big Butt Girls, Hard Headed Women* is copyright © 1992 by Rhodessa Jones.

**Andy Kaufman:** *Andy Kaufman Plays Carnegie Hall* is copyright © 1979 by Andy Kaufman, reprinted here by permission of Stanley Kaufman. "Carolina in the Morning" is copyright © 1922 by Donaldson Publishing Company and Gilbert Keyes Music Company, lyrics are by Gus Kahn, music is by Walter Donaldson.

**Josh Kornbluth:** *Red Diaper Baby* is copyright © 1996 by Josh Kornbluth; published by Mercury House, San Francisco, CA.

**Lisa Kron:** *2.5 Minute Ride* is copyright © 1999 by Lisa Kron.

**John Leguizamo:** *Freak* is copyright © 1997 by John Leguizamo and David Bar Katz; published and reprinted here by permission of Putnam Berkley, a division of Penguin Putnam, Inc., New York.

**Jackie "Moms" Mabley:** *Live at the Greek Theatre, Moms Mabley on Stage* and *Live at Sing Sing* are copyright © 1995 by Garland Publishing, New York; published in *The Humor of Jackie Moms Mabley: An African Comedic Tradition* by Elsie A. Williams.

**Ann Magnuson:** *You Could Be Home Now* is copyright © 1990 by Ann Magnuson. *Pretty Songs* is copyright © 1997 by Ann Magnuson.

**Deb Margolin:** *Bill Me Later* is copyright © 1998 by Deb Margolin.

**Robbie McCauley:** *Surviving Virginia* is copyright © 1999, 2000 by Robbie McCauley.

**Tim Miller:** *Spilt Milk* is copyright © 1997 by Tim Miller.

**John O'Keefe:** *Shimmer* is copyright © 1989 by John O'Keefe; published in *Shimmer and Other Texts*, Theatre Communications Group, New York.

**Dael Orlandersmith:** Introduction quotation from "On Beating the Odds" by Chris Coleman published in *American Theatre,* December 1999, by Theatre Communications Group. *Beauty's Daughter* is copyright © 1994 by Dael Orlandersmith. *Thirteen 'n' Bleeding* was published in *Out of Character: Rants, Raves and Monologues from Today's Top Performance Artists* edited by Mark Russell, Bantam Books, New York, 1997. *Monster* is copyright © 1996 by Dael Orlandersmith.

**Reno:** *Reno Once Removed* is copyright © 1992 by Reno. *Reno Finds Her Mind* is copyright © 1999 by Reno.

**Rachel Rosenthal:** Introduction quotation from "Worm's Eye View," by Alisa Solomon published in *Village Voice,* August 18, 1987. *filename: FUTURFAX* is copyright © 1992 by Rachel Rosenthal. *Rosencrantz and Gildenstern Are Dead*, screenplay, is copyright © 1991 by Tom Stoppard, published by Faber & Faber.

 **JO BONNEY** has been directing solo performance since the early eighties for Eric Bogosian (*Funhouse*; *Sex, Drugs, Rock & Roll*; *Pounding Nails in the Floor with My Forehead* and *Wake Up and Smell the Coffee*), Danny Hoch (*Some People* and *Jails, Hospitals & Hip-Hop*) and currently Anna Deavere Smith (*House Arrest*). She has directed numerous ensemble pieces including the premieres of Diana Son's *Stop Kiss* at The Joseph Papp Public Theater/New York Shakespeare Festival and Seth Zvi Rosenfeld's *The Flatted Fifth* with The New Group (New York). She has directed shows at, among others, P. S. 122 (New York), The Joseph Papp Public Theater/New York Shakespeare Festival, Classic Stage Company (New York), ICA (Boston), American Repertory Theatre (Boston), Berkeley Repertory Theatre, Mark Taper Forum (Los Angeles), Edinburgh Fringe Festival and the Almeida Theatre (London). She is the recipient of a 1998 OBIE Award for Sustained Excellence of Directing.